Incorporating
spirituality
in Counseling
and Psychotherapy

Incorporating
spirituality
in Counseling
and Psychotherapy

Theory and Technique

Geri Miller

JOHN WILEY & SONS, INC.

Library of Congress Cataloging-in-Publication Data:

Miller, Geraldine A., 1955–
    Incorporating spirituality in counseling and psychotherapy : theory and technique : Geri Miller.
      p.   cm.
   Includes bibliographical references and index.
   ISBN 0-471-41545-6 (alk. paper)
   1. Counseling—Religious aspects. 2. Psychotherapy—Religious aspects. 3. Psychology
and religion. 4. Spirituality.   I. Title.
   BF637.C6 M5245   2002
   158'.3 dc21

                                                    2002069140

Printed in the United States of America.

10 9 8 7 6 5 4 3 2

This book is dedicated to Ron Hood, my husband and best friend,
who stayed with me on the remarkable journey of this book
in the midst of American Red Cross disaster mental health work
in response to the September 11, 2001, World Trade Center disaster,
the attack on the Pentagon, and the downed plane in Somerset, PA;
my family, Gale, Abby, and Jason Miller and Tom, Laura, and
Natalie Prow; the clients I had the privilege of counseling at
Pier 94 in New York; and the American Red Cross volunteers
at Pier 94 with whom I had the privilege of working.

This book, *Incorporating Spirituality in Counseling,* is designed for prospective and practicing counselors to provide a knowledge base of the process of integrating spirituality in the counseling process. It emerged from a personal and professional interest in the area of spirituality and religion as a way to help us live as human beings. My interest in this area began as a social worker over 20 years ago when I watched the elderly use their spiritual and religious beliefs as a way of coping with life stresses. It has grown and developed over time as I have worked as a counselor with people in a variety of settings. At times, writing this book felt like jumping off a cliff because I needed to combine unique areas in ways that were different than other authors: I wanted to blend counseling issues with the spiritual or religious realms.

The book provides specific guidelines and suggestions for this integration as well as addressing issues that arise in this process. To assist you, the book includes suggested readings at the end of each chapter, and case examples and exercises that can be used within as well as outside of the classroom setting. You may use these experiential activities individually, in dyads—such as supervision, or in groups—such as staff meetings or staff retreats. You are encouraged to discuss the case examples and exercises with others to enhance the application of the material to your own counseling practice. Use of the case examples and exercises may assist you in learning more about yourself, your spiritual views, and your approach to this integration in the counseling practice.

The chapters highlight pertinent areas in the process of integrating spirituality and counseling. Chapter 1 provides an overview of spirituality and its incorporation into counseling, examining the need for counseling to address spiritual issues and the commitment of the mental health professions to examine this area. Recommendations are made to assist both educators and counselors in addressing this dimension. A definition of spirituality is introduced. The remaining elements of this chapter discuss facilitating the discussion of spirituality by creating a sacred place, encouraging self-care, and encouraging a spiritual practice.

Chapter 2 reviews the history between spirituality and mental health including a discussion of the barriers and the bridges between them. Historical and common barriers are discussed, such as internal bias and countertransference. The bridges between both areas are also presented in historical and common contexts. The common bridges examined include the human experience and the need to make sense of our experience.

Chapter 3 focuses on the five Western or Monotheistic religions of Judaism, Christianity, Islam, Zorastrianism, and Sikhism, as well as Native American religions. Chapter 4 addresses the six Eastern religions of Hinduism, Shintoism, Jainism, Buddhism, Confucianism, and Taoism. Both chapters provide a summary of the basic concepts of the different religions, including how these concepts may influence the client's worldview. Suggestions are made to counselors on how to work across potentially different perspectives between counselor and client.

Chapter 5 continues to focus on cultural implications by discussing the theoretical integration of the counselor and its impact on counseling. The chapter begins by discussing the importance of integrating spirituality in counseling and then the impact of this integration on transference and countertransference. Specific issues related to transference and countertransference are explored. Finally, the cultural implications of such integration are discussed.

Chapter 6 also addresses the integration of spirituality in counseling. The primary focus in this chapter is on how the counselor can help the client develop a spiritual identity. The areas of supervision, assessment, and treatment are explored as avenues to assist the client in this development.

Chapter 7 examines the ethics of integrating counseling and spirituality. General ethical concerns are presented, such as informed consent, spiritual identity development, dual relationships, collaboration with religious leaders, respect of clients' religious or spiritual values, boundaries of the counselor's work setting, and counselor's area of competence. Suggestions for resolution of such conflicts are explored.

Chapter 8 explores specific techniques counselors can use for incorporating spirituality in counseling clients, including religious practices such as prayer, sacred writings, and religious community. General techniques used in counseling practice such as bibliotherapy and journal writing are discussed. Finally, practices that overlap both religiously oriented counseling and general counseling practice are presented (meditation/relaxation/imagery, and rituals).

Integrating the spiritual dimension in your counseling practice is critical, yet it needs to be done in a manner that is respectful to both the counselor and the client. Although there are no absolute rules about how to proceed with this dimension, this book offers guidelines to counselors who are open to including this dimension in their work. The word *counselor* refers to the mental health practitioner or student who is reading this book. Although we may practice in different fields and under different titles (psychologist, counselor, social worker, etc.), we have in common that we strive for the betterment of the client. The counselor as well as the client may want to use the spiritual dimension as a resource for healing the client.

This book was being written at the time of the terrorists attacks on September 11, 2001. Although this acknowledgment will date this book, I want to include something I wrote on September 27, 2001:

I am in an office away from my home and work, two days and two weeks after September 11, 2001, just having left the office of my local American Red Cross chapter. I am going to try to pick up the work on this book again as I attempt to complete one of the final drafts, but it is so hard to resume the work. I will be sitting somewhere and out of nowhere will be a picture in my brain of the plane flying into the second tower—or I will hear another story that will bring me to tears—stories all of us in America, maybe in most of the world, have been hearing the last few weeks; stories that touch our hearts.

Like the one of the four-year-old niece of one of my students who told her mother on the way to preschool, "Mommy, I want you to know if my building burns down, know that I love you and I am with Jesus." Or the person with a limited income who put a donation in the American Red Cross can I was carrying to my local chapter after asking me, "Is that for the people in New York?" So how do I move to the cognitive realm and complete this book on spirituality in counseling; move out of my grief, while I am in my own limbo of being on call as a Disaster Mental Health Service worker for the American Red Cross, wondering if I will be called up for my first disaster work?

Have I caught my breath enough to go on? Where have I taken refuge spiritually in the last few weeks? I have gone back to basics: old friends, family, my husband, my dog and cat, the outdoors, running, meditating, massage, art work. Simple, basic connections reassuring me that the world is still a good place with many good people in it. People and activities that keep my spirit alive. As I told my graduate students this week, "There are many ways to be brave right now. We are being brave by showing up for our normal responsibilities and caring about each other."

So I too need to be brave by completing a book on spirituality and counseling during a war that is housed in spiritual differences. It is a book that I hope supports the care we need to give one another in the world and the need we have for a force to feed our spirits when facing that world's horrors.

Since that writing, I have been to New York twice as a disaster mental health service worker for the American Red Cross for two-week stints—once over Thanksgiving and once over Christmas. My first trip was with my husband, Ron Hood, and my second trip was alone. I consider it an honor to have twice served my country and the American Red Cross in response to this disaster. Why mention such work in the acknowledgment section of a book? Because my own spiritual views and resources were tested in this experience and, repeatedly, I heard from disaster victims how they were drawing on their spiritual and religious views to cope with what had happened to them. These clients came from many different faiths and traditions, but repeatedly I heard, "If it were not for my beliefs, I would not be able to go on."

I had a colleague approach me after my first time to New York and say, "I do not know if I am strong enough to do counseling like that." I was strong because I was a part of a strong "we." I did not rely on myself alone. I was a part of a team. Many others supported me. I worked on teams at the disaster site. I used spiritual activities that helped keep my spirit alive in order to be of assistance to individuals who had experienced the tragedy.

There were many people who helped me get to New York as a volunteer. I thank each of you for helping me. In terms of this book, I especially want to thank Tracey Belmont, my editor, who worked with me on deadline extensions; Amy Hudnall, my local editor, helped me with rewrites with a great amount of patience and dedication; Jen Anthony, my graduate assistant who worked so hard and carefully with me on the book; and my friends at Sweet Aromas, the best bakery in the world located in West Jefferson, North Carolina; and particularly Ken Schmidt and Jacky Brown, whose philosophy of "Just do it" helped me on the days I was stuck in the writing process. Finally, to my husband, my best friend Ron, who encouraged me both to go to New York—"We have a chance to do something decent, let's do it"—and complete the book—"It is an important topic."

Chapter 1

Introduction — 1

Chapter Objectives — 1
Spirituality in the Context of Counseling — 1
Creation of a Sacred Place — 6
Encouragement of Self-Care — 9
Encouragement of Spiritual Practice — 11
Case Studies — 17
Exercises — 18
Suggested Readings — 19

Chapter 2

Historical Development — 21

Chapter Objectives — 21
Separateness and Integration — 21
Barriers between Spirituality/Religion and Therapy — 23
Bridges between Spirituality/Religion and Therapy — 30
Case Studies — 39
Exercises — 41
Suggested Readings — 43

Chapter 3

Western or Monotheistic Religions — 45

Chapter Objectives — 45
Overview — 45
Working across Differences — 55
Judaism — 58
Christianity — 62
Islam — 74
Zoroastrianism — 77
Sikhism — 81
Native American Religions — 83
Case Studies — 86

Exercises   87
Suggested Readings and Web Sites   89

Chapter 4

Eastern Religions   93

Chapter Objectives   93
Overview   93
Hinduism   94
Shintoism   99
Jainism   102
Buddhism   105
Confucianism   108
Taoism   111
Case Studies   114
Exercises   116
Suggested Readings and Web Sites   117

Chapter 5

Theoretical Integration with Cultural Implications   121

Chapter Objectives   121
Therapy Integration   121
Transference Issues   126
Countertransference Issues   128
Types of Integration   131
Cultural Implications   133
Case Studies   136
Exercises   138
Suggested Readings   140

Chapter 6

Counseling Focus Integration   141

Chapter Objectives   141
Helping Clients Develop a Spiritual Identity   141

Case Application 151
Counseling Avenues 153
Case Studies 158
Exercises 160
Suggested Readings 162

Chapter 7

Ethical Issues 163

Chapter Objectives 163
Overview 163
Informed Consent 164
Determination of Secular or Religious Counseling 171
Development of a Spiritual Identity 172
Avoidance or Minimization of Dual or Multiple Relationships with Clients 175
Collaboration with Clients' Religious Leaders 177
Respect for Clients' Religious or Spiritual Values 178
Boundaries of the Counselor's Work Settings 181
Counselor's Area of Competence 182
Case Studies 184
Exercises 186
Suggested Readings 188

Chapter 8

Specific Treatment Techniques 189

Chapter Objectives 189
Overview 189
Religious Practices 191
General Practices 199
Religious and General Practices 204
Case Studies 211
Exercises 212
Suggested Readings 214

Appendix A
**American Association for Marriage and Family
Therapy (AAMFT) Code of Ethics**   **215**

Appendix B
**American Counseling Association (ACA) Code of
Ethics and Standards of Practice**   **225**

Appendix C
**American Psychological Association (APA)
Ethical Principles of Psychologists and Code of Conduct**   **251**

Appendix D
National Association of Social Workers (NASW) Code of Ethics   **275**

References   297

Author Index   309

Subject Index   313

Introduction

Chapter Objectives

1. What are three questions that need to be addressed before a counselor incorporates the spiritual dimension in counseling?
2. What is a working definition of spirituality?
3. What are some of the elements of creating a sacred place in counseling?
4. What can a counselor do to encourage a spiritual practice?

1

Chapter

Spirituality in the Context of Counseling

It is legitimate for you to ask a question such as, "Why is it important or even necessary to include the spiritual or religious dimension in counseling?" In this chapter overview, some specific areas are explored in answer to this "why" question: the widespread interest in this area nationally and internationally, the impact of this dimension on the health of our clients, and the focus on this arena by professional organizations.

American culture has become increasingly interested in spirituality and religion. Baker (1997) found that 95% of Americans believe in God and 85% believe in personal prayer having healing powers (Wallis, 1996). Also, the majority of Americans belong to religious organizations (62%), believe religion is "very important" as a part of their lives (60%), and a large percentage worship weekly or close to weekly (*The Harvard Mental Health Letter*, 2001). These statistics indicate that Americans tend to think about the spiritual and religious aspects of their lives. Although this book primarily discusses spirituality and religion within the context of American culture, it is important to note here that the concern about spiritual and religious beliefs is not limited to America. Organizations such as Amnesty International Interfaith Network for Human Rights indicate that concerns about spiritual and religious beliefs are international.

Given this widespread interest in the spiritual and religious realm, counselors need to prepare for clients who come for counseling who have spiritual or religious concerns that impact the mental health struggle that

---

**AMNESTY INTERNATIONAL INTERFAITH
NETWORK FOR HUMAN RIGHTS**

Amnesty International United States' (AIUSA) Interfaith Network for Human Rights assists people internationally in the protection of human rights. They have three main purposes:

1. To stop human rights abuses by involving communities of faith.
2. To assist people of faith in their attempts to stop the abuses of human rights.
3. To facilitate awareness of violations of human rights focused on religious beliefs.

The group can be contacted by:

> AIUSA Interfaith Network for Human Rights
> 53 West Jackson Boulevard, Suite 731
> Chicago, IL 60604
> (312) 427-2060
> interfaith@aiusa.org (e-mail)
> www.amnestyusa.org/interfaith (Web)

---

has brought them to counseling. Also, counselors need to be prepared to assist clients in applying comforting spiritual or religious perspectives as a healing resource in their lives.

The importance of examining spiritual issues in counseling is supported by Propst (1980) who reported that ignoring clients' religious beliefs can reduce counseling efficacy and increase premature termination. Recent research underscores the importance of an examination of the impact of spirituality on client health. While there are various definitions of health, W. R. Miller and Thoresen (1999) define health as consisting of suffering, functional ability, and coherence (inner peace, a sense of predictability, and optimism) which operate on a continuum. The National Institute for Health Care Research conducted an examination of research involving spirituality and religion (Larson, Swyers, & McCullough, 1997). Three of the expert panels that looked at spirituality and health (physical, mental, alcohol, and drug) found a positive relationship between spirituality and religion with health and a negative relationship between spirituality and religion with disorders. One example of research that supports the positive relationship is Simmons' (2001) summary of a two-year study by Pargament and Koenig of hospitalized elderly patients. The researchers found that patients who reported spiritual struggles, such as not feeling connected with God, showed a higher risk of dying (up to 28%). There are two thorough reviews of the literature on the relationship between spirituality and religion and health: Gartner's (1996) review on the relationship between religious commitment, mental health, and prosocial behavior, and Richards and Bergin's (1997) review of the influence of spiritual and religious factors on mental and physical health.

W. R. Miller and Thoresen (1999) state that clients are frequently involved in the spiritual and religious realms in a manner that is important to the clients and related to their health. They argue that understanding clients' spiritual and religious views may assist the counselor in understanding the client's problem(s) and positively impact treatment. Therefore, to positively impact the mental and physical health of clients, counselors need to be prepared to address these spiritual and religious concerns in counseling.

Professional organizations such as the American Psychological Association (APA) and the American Counseling Association (ACA) have increasingly focused on the importance of the spiritual dimension in counseling. Both organizations feature professional divisions related to spirituality and religion. According to their 2000 membership directory, the APA's Division 36, the Psychology of Religion, has approximately 1,197 members, and as of December 2000, the ACA's Association for Spiritual, Ethical, and Religious Values in Counseling (ASERVIC), has approximately 2,705 members. The ACA's educational training body also has specific training requirements in spirituality. In 2001, the ACA expanded its multicultural training requirements to include spirituality in the revised Council for Accreditation of Counseling and Related Educational Programs (CACREP) standards. Programs that have CACREP accreditation or are seeking accreditation need to have this component included in their curriculum. This spirituality requirement speaks to both the importance of the spiritual dimension in counseling and the commitment professional counseling organizations are making to its inclusion in the curriculum. Mental health counselors need to learn to work effectively with this dimension of clients' lives and professional organizations are beginning to encourage such involvement.

The widespread interest in spirituality, the impact of this arena on clients' health, and the increasing professional focus on this area highlight the need for the inclusion of the spiritual and religious dimension in counseling. This book is biased toward the benefits of the inclusion of this dimension in counseling. If counseling is meant to assist clients in healing from their difficult life experiences, then *all* possible healing resources need to be explored, including the spiritual and religious dimension. Possible pathology related to spiritual or religious beliefs is explored in Chapters 5 and 6.

Although the inclusion of spirituality in counseling is important, there is a history of conflict between the spiritual and the counseling realms that inhibits such an inclusion. Although this history is explored more in depth in Chapter 2, a brief overview places the development of this integration into context. Historically, the discipline of psychology broke away from the spiritual dimension to establish itself as a field separate from philosophy. Likewise, the mental health counseling field in America has supported a more secular approach to people's problems until treatment programs for wellness and for problems such as addiction began to include the spiritual dimension as a component of counseling.

Even with a shift toward the inclusion of the spiritual dimension in counseling, spirituality and religion are not always included in counselor training. Kelly (1995) surveyed 341 counselor education programs and found that only 25% had the spiritual/religious dimension as a course component. In another survey (Pate & High, 1995), 60% of the 60 CACREP accredited programs considered the impact of client's religious beliefs and practices on counseling. Now that CACREP requires accredited programs to include the spiritual dimension in training, counselor education programs are in need of textbooks that encourage the inclusion of spirituality within their curriculum. Educators need to work at creating places to discuss the spiritual dimension within their training programs. These places need to be ones in which: (a) both educators and students feel comfortable exploring their spiritual views without judgment, (b) spirituality is included as a part of culturally diverse discussions, and (c) counselor bias about spiritual beliefs and their relationship to mental health is discussed (G. Miller, Fleming,

---

ALCOHOLICS ANONYMOUS

The self-help recovery group of Alcoholics Anonymous (AA) began on June 10, 1935. In the following four years, it grew to 100 members and received its name in 1939 based on the book *Alcoholics Anonymous* (Alcoholics Anonymous World Services, 1976). The AA program has been viewed by some as based in Christianity because it has roots in the Oxford Group that consisted of nondenominational Christians (Judge, 1994). The spiritual dimension of recovery is evident in the wording of some of its 12 steps ("a Power greater than ourselves" "God as we understood Him"). This 12-step, self-help group philosophy has been used in addiction treatment (Le, Ingvarson, & Page, 1995). Counselors have used it to help clients receive support (Flores, 1988), feel less isolated (Talbott, 1990), and improve self-regulation (Khantzian & Mack, 1994). Others have found that it can augment the support of therapy for recovering clients (Bristow-Braitman, 1995; P. N. Johnson & Phelps, 1991; Riordan & Walsh, 1994).

et al., 1998). Educators entering into this arena need to dialogue with other educators regarding their difficulties and successes in incorporating this perspective into the classroom, as well as share resources and classroom exercises with one another (G. Miller, Arena, et al., 1999). Educators who choose to incorporate this dimension in their training need to be aware that they run the risk of being stereotyped or ostracized for their spiritual perspective by students, colleagues, or both. To work effectively with spiritual issues, counselors need knowledge of all aspects of spirituality. In addition, they need guidelines and suggestions on how to include this dimension in their counseling practice in an ethical and skilled manner. G. Miller (1999a) identified three questions that need to be addressed as a counselor moves toward the incorporation of this dimension in counseling:

1. How do we help people develop a spiritual identity?
2. Do we have a right and/or an obligation to help people develop a spiritual identity?
3. How does context impact application? (p. 501)

G. Miller (1999a) introduced some answers to these questions. Although Chapter 8 provides techniques counselors can use to incorporate spirituality in counseling, these techniques need to be shaped to the client's needs. In addition, the mental health field needs to continue to work to develop techniques that can effectively assist clients in developing a spiritual identity. When determining when to incorporate a spiritual dimension in counseling, counselors need to examine their own motivation and possible bias to avoid attempting to convert their clients to their own spiritual views or ignoring a client's spirituality altogether. With regard to context, counselors need to look at the setting in which they work as well as their own spiritual development and views because both can influence the inclusion of spirituality in counseling.

Finally, counselors need to be sensitive to how spiritual and religious beliefs are imbedded within a cultural context. While this area is explored in depth in Chapter 5, a few notations need to be made here. Even when a client self-identifies as being of a particular spiritual or religious group, the counselor needs to explore that identification for that particular client. Where a client lives in a country, in combination with his or her religious community's culture, can have a great impact on that client's beliefs, values, and the application of those beliefs and values. The counselor needs to be very careful about making assumptions regarding the spiritual or religious dimension of a client's life. Understanding the many facets of a client's culture (gender, age, ethnicity, locale, and so on) can assist the counselor in understanding this dimension of a client's life and thereby increase the chances for effective counseling.

Definition

West (2000) stated that spirituality is an important concept that is difficult to define. Cornett (1998) said that it is difficult to define spirituality in part, due to its being equated with religion. Kelly (1995) pointed out that although spirituality and religion can be difficult to define, both share a sense of transcendence, of *other*. They differ in that spirituality is a personal connection with the universe and religion involves a creed, institution, and rituals connected with a world religion. Richards and Bergin considered religion to be a "subset of the spiritual" (1997, p. 13), yet, it is possible to be one without the other. W. R. Miller and Thoresen (1999) define spirituality as an attribute that does not necessarily incorporate religion. It consists of three areas: practice (prayer, meditation, etc.), belief (morals, values, deity, transcendence), and experience (of the individual). They define religion as organized and societal in nature. The word *spirituality* comes from the Latin word *spiritus* that means *breath of life*. The definition of spirituality used in this text is one that evolved from the 1996 Summit on Spirituality sponsored by ASERVIC:

> *Spirit may be defined as the animating life force, represented by such images as breath, wind, vigor, and courage. Spirituality is the drawing out and infusion of spirit in one's life. It is experienced as an active and passive process. Spirituality is also defined as a capacity and tendency that is innate and unique to all persons. This spiritual tendency moves the individual toward knowledge, love, meaning, peace, hope, transcendence, connectedness, compassion, wellness, and wholeness. Spirituality includes one's capacity for creativity, growth, and the development of a value system. Spirituality encompasses a variety of phenomena, including experiences, beliefs, and practices. Spirituality is approached from a variety of perspectives, including psychospiritual, religious, and transpersonal. While spirituality is usually expressed through culture, it both precedes and transcends culture.* (Position Paper, n.d., para. 3)

Although this definition is not absolute, it can be used as a common thread in counselor and client dialogue when examining spiritual views that may involve religious views for either the counselor or the client. The remainder of this chapter examines how the counselor can assist clients in developing the spiritual dimension of their lives.

Creation of a Sacred Place

> *When one listens to a barking dog, one might imagine emotion, pain, reaction, anxiety, and self-identification, but actually there is nothing there—just sound from a long and deep corridor, channeled out of nothingness and fading into nothingness*

again. Like that dog, we may all strive, but there is truly nothing to be done. If we look deeply into our lives, there is only a thin veneer of self-generated meaning over an immense ocean of nothingness. What we do only has meaning in the here and now. It will not remain in the next instant. Just do what you can for the present, and leave everything else to happen naturally. Work. Wash. Meditate. Eat. Study. Urinate. Sleep. Exercise. Talk. Listen. Touch. Die each night. Be born again each morning. (Ming-Dao, 1992, p. 151)

This quote captures the issues that many clients bring with them to counseling when the thin veneer of meaning has been stripped from their lives. The resulting anxiety, fear, anger, and other intense, uncomfortable emotions in combination with negative, self-defeating thoughts cause them to seek therapy. When a client's life perspective, the illusions about who he or she is, who others are, and how the world operates, is pierced or shattered, this sense of meaninglessness can be overwhelming and, to varying degrees, devastating.

The problem a client brings to a therapist is a metaphor for the issues related to experiencing *nothing* or *meaninglessness*. The therapist needs to create a sacred space so that the metaphor can emerge and be explored in layers. In sacred places, there is often space that allows the individual to simply *be*. Physical space such as gardens and parks, and emotional and cognitive space such as massage and wordless music, are examples of sacred places where we have the opportunity to catch our breath, to experience silence, and thereby experience ourselves. The therapist creates a sacred place, a space where nothingness can exist, by setting up a time and space for clients to discuss the metaphor or the life story. This commitment to sacredness is evident in the typical therapy stance of no interruptions or contact with the outside world during the therapy session. This creation of space allows for a focus on the metaphorical struggle of the client and stresses the necessity of honoring the client's story by making the therapy a sacred space, a place of refuge. As an experienced clinician once stated, "If we create the space, the stories will come."

Safety

Involving the spiritual dimension in counseling requires a deep trust and respect between counselor and client. Spiritual beliefs are very personal and clients may pick up cues from their counselors that discourage them from sharing their views or concerns in session (West, 2000). Counselors need to be aware of sending verbal and nonverbal messages that communicate openness to hearing about such issues or beliefs in the session.

Asking questions about spirituality as a normal part of the counseling process communicates an openness to this realm. These questions may focus on spiritual views, experiences, or resources. The counselor's responses to the client's answers to these questions send a deeper message about openness to discussing this realm in session. Also, *how* the client answers such questions directs the counselor if and how to pursue an exploration of this area. By monitoring a client's nonverbal and verbal responses to questions, a counselor can be assured of exploring this dimension with a client rather than forcing a client into a discussion. A respectful dialogue between counselor and client sets the stage for the inclusion of the spiritual dimension of the client's life in counseling. Even if the counselor does not ask specific questions about spirituality, the client may *test the waters* by presenting some relatively low-level risk-taking disclosure with the counselor or the client may boldly state his or her views or experiences to the counselor. The counselor's ability to *pass the test* depends on the genuineness and honesty of the counselor as well as the match between the counselor's and client's perspectives in terms of mutual respect. The client may carefully listen to the counselor's comments made during the dialogue regarding the client's spiritual views. If the client experiences a nonjudgmental acceptance of and genuine interest in his or her views, a trusting atmosphere has begun. If the counselor can set up a trusting atmosphere where the client feels safe in session to discuss this area of his or her life, the spiritual dimension can readily be introduced as a part of the counseling agenda.

Counselors also need to be sensitive to nonverbal messages sent to the client that may impact a trusting atmosphere. For example, what types of religious or spiritual symbols or pictures are displayed in the counselor's office or as a part of his or her attire? Is there a symbol such as a cross or a statue or picture of a religious figure? In some settings, a counselor will be limited as to how publicly such items can be displayed, but in settings without such restrictions, a counselor needs to examine such nonverbal statements to determine if this is the type of message he or she wants to send to clients. A thoughtful awareness and choice of such nonverbal statements by the counselor can again determine the comfort level and trust of the client in involving the spiritual dimension as an aspect of counseling.

Honoring the Client's Story

In the beginning of counseling, the counselor primarily focuses on listening to the client and his or her story without trying to effect change. This listening process shows respect and concern but also allows the client to tell his or her metaphorical stories of suffering and struggle in the session. The counselor hears the client's metaphor or story as it unfolds and may ask clarifying questions to better understand the story. While listening, the therapist listens for the client's suffering or anguish because it is in the causes of pain that the relief of the suffering lies.

In the midst of their suffering, the client tends to view reality as fixed, rather than fluctuating, resulting in a tendency to grasp at the desired objects. Thus, client mental suffering is based on his or her misperception of essential reality. Honoring the client's story requires the counselor to listen without judgment, listen with an awareness that the story is a metaphor for the client's struggle, and listen for the points in the story where the client holds fast to a fixed reality that does not exist. For example, a counselor may listen to a stepmother describe her struggles with her stepdaughter who is an adolescent. Rather than focus on the *truth* of the story, the counselor listens to the stepmother's struggle allowing her to express her thoughts and feelings freely which she may not be able to do in any other area of her life without substantial consequence. In hearing the story, the counselor can look for spiritual themes related to the struggle, such as not being allowed to nurture a child because of the child's view of the role of a stepmother. The counselor can help the stepmother make choices about when this reality does not exist and ways she can respond differently to the ongoing, hurtful behavior of her stepdaughter to her. This case indicates how simply the honoring of a client's story can assist in the healing process.

Encouragement of Self-Care

The counselor needs to work with clients on finding ways to anchor themselves in the process of self-exploration because of the discomfort and fear experienced in facing the lack of a fixed reality. As stated previously, the lack of this fixed reality is what the client confronts when the meaning, the structure of his or her life, is stripped away. The client may be afraid, overwhelmed, confused, or angry—basically suffering because what was *known* and trusted about the world is gone, leaving the client to face and experience a void. For example, a married client may believe that his spouse is faithful sexually to him and operates out of that worldview. The client then finds out that his partner has been unfaithful thereby altering his perception of the reality of his marriage. This change in perception may cause intense affect because his trust of fidelity has been shattered. The client's uncertainty about his partner and his marriage may cause further suffering because he may wonder about what he knows about others and the world. He comes to therapy, then, with a desire to find a new meaning that can assist him in understanding and coping in the world. To assist in this self-exploration, the counselor needs to help the client find ways to reassure himself so during unsettling moments in and out of the therapy sessions, the client can learn how to ground or comfort himself as his or her perception of the world is altered in the counseling process.

Using Self-Care for Reassurance

Initially asking clients how they care for themselves can provide the counselor with important information about self-care options available to them when feeling overwhelmed and vulnerable. Sometimes this can be framed as "How do you reassure yourself when you awake from a nightmare?" This question can also indicate the need for clients to learn some healthy self-care behaviors. In the face of nothingness, the uncontrollable mystery of life, some possibilities for clients to anchor themselves include practicing spiritual beliefs and rituals, meditation, exercise, readings/videos, and massage. These options can provide clients with a sense of calm and comfort without the risk of denial or repression of the anguish. To avoid or minimize acting on countertransference issues, the counselor also needs to examine his or her own comfort level with the lack of a fixed reality and find ways to anchor himself or herself while facing it. A counselor who experiences difficulty living with his or her own uncertainties about the world may rush to rescue a client who is unsure or unsettled with regard to action to take about a problem. The well-intentioned counselor who is uncomfortable with the client being unsure, may offer advice or suggestions that may essentially prevent the client from experiencing the underlying struggle of his or her problem and instead provide only momentary symptom relief. Each counselor must find and use ways to ground and comfort self both within and outside of sessions to allow the client to experience the nothingness, the void of his or her life as a part of the counseling process.

Using Self-Care for Healing

Once the counselor obtains a greater understanding of the client's anguish inherent in his or her metaphorical story, the counselor listens for teachable moments. These are moments in story telling and processing where the client's anguish can be emphasized and understood, and where the suffering can be honored, respected, and explored in terms of how it can be diminished or eliminated. The counselor operates both as a witness to the anguish and as a mirror of the suffering.

Although witnessing and mirroring facilitate the expression of the story and client trust, the counselor can also help clarify other options or perspectives for the client. For example, the counselor may simply ask the question, "If we have a problem in our lives, we need to look at what we are doing to feed that problem." This encourages the client to look at any thoughts, feelings, or behaviors he or she has that encourages the existence of the problem.

To facilitate healing, the therapist must avoid becoming caught in the client's dichotomies and assist the client in seeing all things as interdependent. Questions and comments that encourage an exploration of the client's fixed reality can assist the client in becoming free of the suffering: "What would it be like if you did not have this suffering?" "Being (depressed) is important because . . ." "Feeling as though you have accomplished something is important because . . ." These questions and comments in turn encourage mindfulness. For example, in Tibetan Buddhism, the mind is defined as individual moments of knowing (Rinbochay, 1986). Therapy, then, is based in assisting the client in becoming more mindful. It is important to know the mind, shape the mind, and free the mind (Nyanaponika, 1996). The counselor can work with the client's story with the intent of knowing, shaping, and freeing the mind. Clients can use this increased mindfulness of self, life, and others to become free of their suffering (Sopa, 1985; Wilson, 1980). Through enhanced awareness, clients can learn from life experiences and be more comfortable with the lack of a fixed reality. For example, one writer in describing a man's grief reaction to his father's death writes: "After his father died, he carried his life more gently & left an empty space for the birds & other creatures" (Andreas, 1999, p. 1).

Spirituality is one option for addressing these issues of anguish. Lucia Rijker, a female boxer, states, "I practice spirituality so I can be alone without being lonely" (Wright, 1999, p. 103). The spiritual views and practices of clients can provide them with rituals and safe places where they can both anchor and restore themselves as they process their issues. In addition, the spiritual views of the counselor can clarify the therapeutic approach and technique used with the client.

Encouragement of Spiritual Practice

Richards and Bergin (1997) considered human personality as having a spiritual core; therefore, they believed that people live better lives when they live according to universal principles that encourage their spiritual growth and development. The spiritual realm may also assist people in coping with life stress that brings them to counseling; a desire to find significance in stressful times (Pargament, 1996). Pargament described *coping* as an attempt to find significance in stressful times. He identified two types of coping mechanisms that are separate yet complementary: conservational and transformational. Conservational coping occurs when a client tries to protect what he or she values and transformational coping occurs when a client cannot protect what he or she values, but instead needs to replace what is lost or incomplete. Counseling may assist people in both types of coping by helping them find a type of coping that is most functional for them in their circumstances. Assisting a client in finding a functional coping style may require the exploration of the spiritual dimension of the client during the counseling process. It seems very appropriate then for counselors to address spiritual issues in counseling.

Refuge

West (2000) defined *psychotherapist* by examining its Greek origin (*"psyche* meaning soul or breath of life, and *therapeia* denoting attendant or servant,"* p. 23) resulting in Tick's (1992) definition of a therapist as a tender of the soul. West stated that counselors need to raise the topic of spirituality to encourage the client to speak about it in session, thereby avoiding the danger that the topic is not brought up at all. By asking about spirituality in a session, the client and counselor can examine this area together to determine if it is a source of refuge for the client as he or she sorts out personal struggles and issues in session. If the spiritual realm is a refuge or a potential refuge for a client, this arena can assist the client as he or she sorts through the personal issues needing to be addressed in counseling.

A counselor can assist clients by examining the sources of support in their lives that provide a spiritual refuge. A spiritual refuge is a place that gives individuals hope and meaning for their lives. These are places that can "heal the great chasms that seem to have developed between self and other; being and doing; body, mind, and spirit; people, animals, and earth" (Ross, 1990, p. 25). A counselor needs to examine with the client where these places of refuge for spirit occur for the individual. The following are some suggestions for a counselor to use in a session with a client:

1. Where do you go to "catch your breath" in the stress of living?
2. Do you consider these places spiritual? If so, what about them makes them that way?
3. What prevents you from experiencing these places as much as you would like to?

The counselor needs to be aware that the client may not be able to readily answer these questions or may have "pat answers" that do not really examine if and why such a place is a refuge. The counselor needs to assist clients in slowly examining their lives for the sources of refuge that exist for them. Question number 3 assists clients in predicting the barriers in their lives that inhibit the opportunity for refuge. The capacity to anticipate such barriers can reduce the likelihood that they will prevent the client from seeking refuge.

In some cases, a client may not have any sources of refuge. In this situation, the counselor needs to help the client examine how to create places of refuge. To determine these sources, the counselor may need to step back with the client to examine what he or she values and enjoys in order to determine places in life that encourage growth and development. For those clients who may not be aware of their values or sources of enjoyment, the counselor may need to start simply and experientially by suggesting that they try new arenas and experience their responses. For example, a client may want to join a Bible study group or a yoga class. The counselor can encourage such interests and then offer the client the opportunity to process his or her reactions to the possible source of refuge in counseling. Such processing affords the client the opportunity to learn about his or her values while determining what provides a sense of refuge for the client.

Ritual

One way spiritual life can be life-enhancing is in terms of rituals. Rituals can be healing both psychologically and physically (Richards & Bergin, 1997). They can comfort during a stressful time by providing a soothing or familiar activity, a distraction from the stress of the current life situation. Those rituals that are growth and development enhancing need also to be explored with the client. Questions that can be asked of the client in this area are:

1. What activities revive you with hope and a desire to live?
2. What activities cause you to become excited about being alive when you wake up in the morning and realize you will have the opportunity to do them that day?
3. How do these activities help you spiritually?
4. What keeps you from doing these activities?

The first three questions are meant to help the client determine activities and rituals that are already occurring possibly without recognition for their life-sustaining abilities. As Morgan stated: "what passion, irony, and wit, what love, what courage are disguised in all her daily movements" (1991, p. 195)? The recognition of their spiritual enhancement can encourage the client to perform them more frequently. This recognition in combination with barriers to their access in question 4 can help the client perform these activities with an important intentionality. Counselors need to be aware that some clients may perform some rituals (e.g., getting drunk) that are a manifestation of the problems that need to be addressed. Thus, counselors should encourage clients to perform rituals that are life enhancing. Also, the counselor needs to be aware that a client may be performing a ritual because at one time it was fulfilling, but no longer is. Questions 1 and 2 can also assist the counselor and client in determining those activities that are spiritually encouraging.

As stated in the section on refuge, the client may not have any soothing rituals. As one traumatized client said to me, "I have no idea how to comfort myself." This individual had coped with his childhood trauma by "freezing up" his emotions and needs to the point that they were unrecognizable. In counseling this individual, I used the metaphor of thawing out emotionally. Like body parts that are frozen, his emotional parts needed to be carefully wrapped to protect them in the thawing out process. The way we "wrapped" his emotional parts was by introducing rituals of comfort. Because he had no idea how to comfort himself, we began to look at any activities that he could introduce through his senses to bring him comfort. What did he see, hear, feel, smell, or taste that reassured him? With that question as a rudder, we began to introduce ritual into his life that rejuvenated his spirit.

Spiritual rituals are related to self-care. As G. Miller (1999a) discussed, leisure activities where you participate in a sense of play and suspension of time are critical. Such activities encourage us to forget about our worries and allow for the creative expression of self in some activity where there may be a source of pride or accomplishment or at the very least a chance to be in the present without concern for the future. These activities do not need to take a long period of time. They may be a brief break that offers a shift in perspective allowing our spirits to rejuvenate.

A client's religion may contain specific rituals that provide meaning and healing especially during difficult transitions (Richards & Bergin, 1997). Some of these rituals may relate to purification, which can assist people in recovering from life mistakes. For example, reconciliation and confession are two examples of purification rituals that clients may find beneficial. Also, rituals related to rites of passage such as funerals help clients confront the reality of their situation and provide them with support for coping with it (Shafranske, 1996). Sensitive questioning about both the individual and his or her situation within the context of religious beliefs can help the counselor guide the client toward religious rituals that may be personally beneficial.

Safe Places

Safety is an important concept with regard to counseling and spirituality. Although it has been implied in the two previous sections about refuge and ritual, counselors need to be aware of how their own countertransference can operate in helping clients find beneficial resources. Counselors, depending on their own spiritual views and personal needs, may project what they would anticipate needing if they were in the client's situation. This projection can distort their effectiveness in assisting their clients. A refuge for the counselor, for example, might be a church, while for the client the local church may represent a source of harm done to him or her. The well-intentioned counselor may encourage church attendance, though the client may not even view it as an option given his or her experiences. The same is true of rituals. A counselor may find confession to be healing while for a client it is a meaningless activity. Who is involved in these refuges and rituals is also important for the client. The counselor may have individuals with whom he or she feels safe connected to these refuges and rituals and may mistakenly assume that the same situation is true for the client.

A guiding principle in this process of determining spiritual refuges and rituals that are helpful for the client is one of *safety*. A friend said to me once, "Be in touch with your heart, but don't expose it to the entire world." This underscores the importance of our clients having people and places in their lives where they can take their hurts and mistakes and not have them used against them. The counselor can assist the client in clarifying who those people are and where those places are. To guard against countertransference in this process, it may be beneficial for the counselor to ask the client specific questions regarding safety, such as:

1. Where do you feel most safe spiritually?
2. What rituals help you feel safe in the world?
3. Who are people with whom you feel most comfortable discussing your spiritual beliefs?
4. Who are people from whom you feel the most acceptance of all parts of you?
5. Who do you tell about your most shameful mistakes?
6. How have you experienced forgiveness from yourself and others?

Sense of Community

Having an oasis of support outside of the counseling session is important for clients. Simply in terms of practical reality, a counselor is unable to meet the needs of his or her clients 24 hours a day. Therefore, it is important that clients have a community of support to whom they can turn outside of therapy. Even when they do not need a support community to sustain them through a crisis, research evidence supports the finding that close relationships help people have good health, and that a lack of meaningful relationships can be harmful to the individual (D. G. Myers, 2000).

In terms of spiritual well-being, people who have religious faith appear to handle crisis better (D. G. Myers, 2000). This may be in part because their religion provides them with a framework that allows them to look at their lives as making a difference, gives them hope as they face existential questions of death and suffering, and provides them with social support (Myers, 2000).

Having a supportive spiritual community, then, can provide clients with an oasis that reminds them of their values and encourages them to continue with their lives. A supportive spiritual community may be formal or informal.

Some spiritual communities are religious ones. In this context, clients may derive support from the clergy, other members, or activities connected with the community (Shafranske, 1996). The formal community may provide clients with a chance to interact with others in a healthy manner and with an altruistic intent. The formal community may also be beneficial to clients who are isolated from others or who struggle with the meaning of their existence. Counselors can assist clients by exploring the following questions:

1. Do you belong to a formal spiritual community?
2. What aspects of that community are uplifting to you?
3. Who are people in that community that are accepting and supportive of you?
4. What activities have you been involved with in that group that have caused you to feel as though you make a difference in the world?
5. Do you want to be more involved in your spiritual community at this time in your life?

Some clients may be involved in a spiritual community that is more informal and focused around a network of friends or has a nonreligious value focus. For example, a client may be involved in a group with an environmental focus, and the client derives meaning and hope from service work connected with that group. Questions 2, 3, and 4 may be useful in assisting a client in determining the healing nature of this community. Questions 1 and 5 may also be helpful to assist clients in determining if they should formalize and expand their spiritual community. Such an assessment requires counselors to be sensitive to the needs and values of their clients as well as being aware of community resources available to them. The counselor may need to view such a formalization and expansion as a process in which clients "search out" a spiritual community and use the counseling sessions in part as a safe place to assess the value of such a community.

For clients who have or who have had a spiritual community, it may be helpful to assist them during counseling in determining how well that community currently serves them as a support or the specific aspects of that community that they find helpful. If clients have had a spiritual community that meant a lot to them, a series of thoughtful questions by the counselor may help the client determine the aspects of the community that they would like to include in their current life and how they may be able to create such a community even though their past one no longer exists.

The creation of a sacred place and the encouragement of self-care and a spiritual practice by a counselor can assist a client immeasurably in the counseling process. A sacred place of counseling provides the client with the space to safely discuss concerns in an arena where the client can count on being heard and respected. The encouragement of self-care can assist the client in learning or practicing skills for living that facilitate a more balanced and aware life, thereby, increasing a sense of control. The encouragement of a spiritual practice can help the client find and use avenues of support as he or she addresses concerns in counseling that can be used in the future by the client. These related aspects of counseling can provide a client with the strength to examine and address profound issues of anguish both within and outside of the counseling session as well as teaching living skills to the client. This approach to counseling involves the integration of the spiritual dimension in counseling that can facilitate the healing process of the client.

Case Studies

CASE STUDY 1

Imagine yourself in a counseling setting. You are the counselor. Your client is a 55-year-old woman who enters the session and tells you that her religion is very important to her, but before she talks with you about her concerns, she wants to know if you are a Christian as she is. She asks you to tell her your religious views and how they impact your life and your work as a counselor. She says she does not believe that she can work with someone on her personal issues if that person does not share the same values as she—and those values are anchored for her in her spiritual views. Ask yourself the following questions:

1. What aspects of her comments might throw you off balance?
2. Assuming that her statements throw you off balance mentally and emotionally, how would you regain your balance before you responded to her request?
3. In general, what kinds of introductory comments would you give her with regard to your professional orientation as a counselor?
4. Specifically, which parts of your spiritual views and how much of these views would you share with her?
5. What are the pros and cons of your approach in question 4?

CASE STUDY 2

A local religious leader contacts you with a referral for counseling because he has heard of your good reputation as a counselor. He has been working with a couple on their marital issues for the past year, but believes that more counseling expertise is needed in addition to the exploration of the spiritual and religious concerns. He wants you to work with them on their marriage while he continues working with them on their spiritual and religious concerns. Ask yourself the following questions:

1. Would you be willing to work with this religious leader's request?
2. What additional information would you need about him, the couple, the work they have done together, the issues that have been addressed, before you could determine if you were willing or able to do the work?
3. What boundaries and agreements would you need to set to work with this religious leader and the couple in terms of contact with the religious leader and counseling focus?

Exercises

Exercise 1

1. Write down your own definition of spirituality.
2. Note the sources of origin of this definition. For example, which aspects come from your family, your religious experiences, your life experiences, your ethnicity, gender, or sexual orientation?
3. How does this view of spirituality influence your work as a counselor?
4. Note the pros and cons that you believe may exist when you attempt to integrate spirituality into counseling.

Exercise 2

For at least 20 minutes, share your responses to items 1 through 4 in the self-awareness exercise with someone else who is in training to be a counselor or who is a counselor. Ask clarifying questions of the other person and assist that person in clarifying the presentation of his or her views, especially with regard to the pros and cons of the inclusion of spirituality in counseling.

Exercise 3

Interview a counselor whose work you respect. Ask this counselor how he or she incorporates the spiritual and religious realm in counseling clients. The following questions may be helpful:

1. Are there any guidelines you have developed in your work with clients around spiritual or religious issues?

2. Do the guidelines you use vary in terms of the presenting issues of clients?

3. Are there any specific issues you struggle with as a counselor when helping clients address their unique spiritual or religious issues or address these issues as a part of their presenting problems?

4. What are your overall views of both encouragement and caution as a counselor enters into this realm with a client?

Exercise 4

Now interview a religious leader in your community whose religious views you respect. Ask this person about his or her views on a counselor incorporating the spiritual or religious realm in counseling clients. Again, some suggested questions are:

1. As you have worked in our community, how have you seen counselors be helpful to clients with regard to spiritual or religious concerns? Can you provide any specific examples?

2. How have you seen counselors be hurtful to clients with regard to spiritual or religious concerns? Can you provide any specific examples?

3. What encouragement and caution would you give a counselor who wants to work with clients in the spiritual or religious realm?

Suggested Readings

Kelly, E. W. (1995). *Spirituality and religion in counseling and psychotherapy.* Alexandria, VA: American Counseling Association.

Richards, P. S., & Bergin, A. E. (1997). *A spiritual strategy for counseling and psychotherapy.* Washington, DC: American Psychological Association.

Shafranske, E. P. (Ed.). (1996). *Religion and the clinical practice of psychology.* Washington, DC: American Psychological Association.

West, W. (2000). *Psychotherapy & spirituality.* Thousand Oaks, CA: Sage.

Historical Development

Chapter Objectives

1. What are some of the barriers between spirituality/religion and therapy?

2. What are countertransference issues a counselor needs to be aware of?

3. What are some factors counselors can use to build bridges to facilitate discussion of spiritual issues in counseling?

Separateness and Integration

There was a god who knew how men and women love to believe things to be true and make clubs and religions and political systems with the people who agree with them. They just love to make something out of nothing and then write its name on a big banner and march down the street waving it and yelling and screaming, only to have people who believe the opposite come toward them with their banner, yelling and screaming. This god decided to try to prove a point about the human condition so that people might, in seeing the absurdity of it, have a good laugh. (A good laugh is the best way to kill the Buddha.) He constructed a big hat divided right down the middle, the left side of which was brilliant blue and the right side flaming red. Then he went to a place where many people were working in the fields on the left side of a road and many other people were working in the fields on the right side of the road. There the god manifested in all his glory; no one could miss him. Big and radiant, wearing his hat, he walked straight down the road. All the people on the right side of the road dropped their hoes and looked up at this god; all the people on the left side of the road did the same. Everybody was amazed. Then he disappeared. Everyone shouted, "We saw God! We saw God!" They were all full of joy, until someone on the left said, "There he was in all his radiance and in his red hat." And the people on the right said, "No, he had on a blue hat." This disagreement escalated until the people built walls and began to throw stones at each other. Then the god appeared again. This time he walked in the other direction and then disappeared. Now all the people looked at each other and the ones on the right said, "Ah, you were right, he did have on a red hat. We're so sorry, we just saw incorrectly. You were right and we were wrong." The ones on the other side said, "No, no. You were right. We were wrong." At this point they didn't know whether to fight or to make friends. Most of them were completely puzzled by the situation. Then the god appeared again. This time he stood in the middle and he turned to the left and then he turned around to the right, and everyone started to laugh. (Chodron, 1996, pp. 74–77)

This passage captures both the separateness and integration that are possible regarding spiritual views because the history of the relationship between these two fields shows both antagonism and cooperation. The fields of psychology and religion can easily be viewed as the two groups described in the scenario who disagreed so vehemently on spiritual and religious topics. However, these two groups have the chance of seeing beyond the parameters of their own perspective and valuing the other group's perspective.

We noted that *psychotherapist* is a word made up of two Greek words, *psyche,* which means soul/breath of life, and *therapeia,* which means attendant/servant (West, 2000). Tick (1992) stated that the literal meaning of the word psychotherapist means servant/attendant of the soul. Therapists, or counselors as the term is being used in this book, who are working with spiritual issues with clients, are working within the historical parameters of their profession based on the meaning of the word *psychotherapist.* Yet, there is a history of controversy within this domain that needs to be reviewed to understand the current frictions and the hope for collaborative work between counseling and spirituality.

Zeiger and Lewis (1998) described two typical approaches that psychology has used to address spiritual and religious issues. The first approach they describe as *explanatory,* which was practiced by individuals such as Freud and Skinner. In this approach, religion is seen as the result of external influences impacting the client. The environment determines the reactions of the client resulting in beliefs/behaviors that are not rational. Religion, then, was not seen as credible. This approach encouraged controversy and mistrust between the fields of religion and psychology. Wulff (1996) described this approach as more critical because it considered religion from an outside perspective. This approach continues in the present day and is explored in this chapter under "Barriers between Spirituality/Religion and Therapy."

The second approach is *descriptive,* and was practiced by individuals such as James, Jung, Allport, and Fromm (Wulff, 1996). The focus in this approach is on the benefits that religion brings to the individual and the belief that what happens for the individual inside helps him or her change and develop. There is not a concern with what causes the person to believe in something. This approach lends itself to a more cooperative relationship between psychology and religion. Because the focus is on what is helpful to the individual, the spiritual and religious realm can be viewed as a potential resource for clients as they change and grow in therapy. Wulff described this approach as being more sympathetic and inner-focused in terms of how it views religion.

The use of the spiritual realm as a coping resource for clients is one that needs to be explored. Christian's (1994) quote emphasizes this aspect:

> *Can we be like drops of water falling on the stone? Splashing, breaking, dispersing in the air. Weaker than the stone by far, but be aware that as time goes by the rock will wear away. And the water comes again. (p. 162)*

The spiritual realm can be like a never-ending resource of water for our clients that can assist them in wearing down the stones in their lives.

Counselors need to be open to the helpfulness of spiritual values in their clients' lives as well as viewing these values as a part of their clients' cultural make-up (Bishop, 1992). The counselor can help clients clarify how to use this area to assist with coping or can support their use of this resource if spiritual supports are already in place. For clients who do not have supports developed in this dimension, the counselor can also assist them in exploring this dimension, thereby creating another resource that can be beneficial for them. Chapter 1 discussed how the spiritual realm can be a refuge for clients as they address their issues in counseling. The importance of such a refuge cannot be minimized. When clients are experiencing anguish in the absence of the counselor, the spiritual realm can provide them with hope, meaning, and encouragement to continue on with their therapeutic work. It can also provide them with direction in their therapeutic work and help them understand the meaning of their counseling in the larger framework of their lives.

The spiritual realm, then, can be a resource that assists clients in coping with the stresses of day-to-day meaning and making sense out of their lives. Counselors who use this resource, while keeping in mind the welfare of their clients, have done their clients a great service. The remaining section of this chapter examines both the barriers, past and present, and bridges, past and present, to the use of the spiritual realm as a resource in counseling.

Barriers between Spirituality/Religion and Therapy

Richards and Bergin (1997) posited that theory, research, and training in psychology have not sufficiently addressed issues of a religious or spiritual nature. This lack has resulted in barriers between the two fields. When this area is not emphasized in theory, research, and training, counselors may miss these concerns with their clients or address them inadequately or inappropriately. Even when counselors are aware of this area, they may avoid it because they do not believe they are knowledgeable, have no religion or a different one from their client, or have a bias against religion (Theodore, 1992).

Examination of the views of psychotherapists with regard to the spiritual realm in counseling indicates an overall acknowledgment of the importance of the spiritual realm in counseling. In a survey of 147 licensed professional counselors in two southeastern states, counselors (a) believed it was important to be aware of their own spiritual views and (b) saw spirituality as an important change agent (Hickson, Housley, & Wages, 2000). Psychologists as a group appear to see religion as important, have religious beliefs, are involved to some degree with religious institutions, and examine this dimension in their work with clients to an extent related to their personal views more so than any exposure they had in this area in their training (Shafranske, 1996). Yet, despite the general interest of psychotherapists with the spiritual/religious realm, there has been, and continues to be, a tension between these two disciplines.

Another example of this cooperation and tension is with the American Psychiatric Association (APA). In terms of cooperation, APA has had a religion and psychiatry committee (Committee on Religion and Psychiatry) since the 1950s (Thurrell, 2000), and has included a *DSM-IV* V-Code, Religious or Spiritual Problem (Mountain & Muir, 2000). In terms of conflict, APA and the Committee on Religion and Psychiatry received complaints in the 1970s and 1980s that certain hospitals and health care agencies were imposing specific religious perspectives on clients, providing biased treatment that was less than adequate for those of the religion not related to the service provider. This resulted in the Committee on Religion and Psychiatry issuing a controversial statement within APA that described the necessary interaction between treatment and the psychiatrist's religious beliefs (Thurrell, 2000).

Historically, psychology evolved at the end of the nineteenth century at a time when religion was challenged as the holder of truth. In an attempt to establish psychology as a separate discipline, Freud and other behavioral psychologists leaned toward scientific theoretical constructs and painted religion in a negative perspective. In their explanatory approach to behavior (Zeiger & Lewis, 1998), they believed that they could explain behavior naturally rather than spiritually. They also believed that people were motivated by rewards (e.g., ethical relativism and hedonism). The negative views of religion espoused by some of these early leaders could have been a result of their own views in combination with a context where religion was being challenged by science. The views of some of these leaders are explored here because of their relationship with the barriers set up between the two fields.

Freud proposed that early childhood experiences and forces within the individual explained and controlled motivation and behavior (i.e., determinism, reductionism, atomism, mechanism).

Freud (1927) viewed religion as an illusion or an expression of neurosis. Kelly (1995) described Freud's views as imbedded within his human behavior theory in terms of development, behavior that is unconscious, and the use of defense mechanisms. From Freud's perspective, the need for religion resulted from infantile, neurotic impulses of the client (Wulff, 1997). To that end, Freud viewed the mature person and civilization as needing to abandon religion (Wulff, 1996). Because of the prevailing atmosphere (i.e., science versus religion) during which he was attempting to establish psychoanalysis as a science, Freud may have needed to take an opposing view of religion (West, 2000).

Corveleyn (2000) presents an alternative perspective on these views by looking at the contrast between North American and European perspectives on incorporating spirituality in counseling. Speaking from a European, psychoanalytic perspective, he suggests that Freud was advocating a neutrality toward religious views of clients. He describes the neutrality as not a "cold indifference or detached condescension" (p. 349), but rather one that is more benevolent where the client is given as much freedom as possible in the process of self-exploration because the counselor does not take a stance on the religious beliefs of the client.

DEFINITIONS

Atomism: In this area of psychology, complex ideas are perceived as open to analysis because they are made up of simpler ideas or sensations that have been associated. Atomists believe in materialism, reductionism, and determinism. Materialism denies God and soul and supports the view that in life people attempt to pursue pleasure and avoid pain.

Determinism: All behavior is determined; freedom of choice does not exist. Behavior is therefore controlled through positive reinforcement.

Mechanism: In this view, human beings are like machines. Psychology looks at how people process information.

Reductionism: This is a cognitive science that believed even complex behaviors could be reduced to simpler behaviors that together make up the complex behavior. Also, it believed that the thinking of humans could be reduced to neurophysiological factors (Leahey, 1987).

Behaviorist psychology, which is deterministic and mechanistic, began to dominate psychology in the 1920s (Wulff, 1997). Watson, one of the leaders of the movement, believed that the environment controlled behavior through a stimulus-response exchange (i.e., reductionism, atomism, materialism, mechanism). This environmental-causality view of behavior did not have room for the inner world of the individual or such concepts such as the "soul." People were machines controlled by their environments (Krasner, 1962). In general, Watson saw religion as holding psychology back in its development as a science. Skinner (1953) followed up on these views by seeing religion as the result of reinforcing stimuli. He criticized religion in part because of the use of negative reinforcement/punishment threats, yet, he acknowledged that religion might be necessary for some people (Wulff, 1996).

Overall, the attempt was for psychology to distinguish itself from religion and philosophy by positioning itself as a science based on universal laws that explained humans and human behavior. Along the way, this attempt resulted in an antagonistic role with regard to religion. Spiritual concepts such as the existence of a Higher Power that influences human behavior, that not everything real can be seen or touched, and the belief that people should be viewed as more complex in terms of their motivation and behavior, did not mesh with the scientific view of psychology.

Common Barriers

The roots of the barriers between psychology and religion may stem from the history of the conflict between these disciplines. Theories of personality development, when examined from a religious perspective, may continue to be taught to and espoused by counselors from a negative view of religion. Information provided to counselors and counselors-to-be, inherently can include some of the historical biases of the profession of psychology. As a result of their training (perhaps in combination with their own personal experiences), counselors may view religious behavior as neurotic behavior based on an illusion necessary to the functioning of an immature person (Psychoanalysis). Counselors may also view religious behavior as the result of stimulus-response reactions of the client: They have been reinforced to participate in specific behaviors and to believe certain ideas (Behaviorism). Finally, counselors may not view the inner spiritual life of the individual as existing or of any import (Behaviorism). These theoretical biases may inhibit the sensitivity of the individual counselor by inherently introducing negative biases toward spirituality and religion. Even though the historical conflict has been primarily with religion, it is also possible that counselors may have biases in general toward the broader spiritual realm and not simply focused on religious practice. The following section examines some of the possible bias and countertransference

COUNTERTRANSFERENCE

Countertransference Issues

- Significant previous professional or personal experiences with religion that are extreme in terms of being positive or negative.
- Different or similar religious backgrounds from clients.
- Personal projections on existential issues.

THE IMPACT OF THESE ISSUES ON COUNSELING

- Assessment: Extreme in focus (too much or too little) on religious issues.
- Treatment:

  Avoid addressing religious concerns.

  Negative reactions to topic of religion.

  Positive reactions leading to an urge to "convert" clients.

  Inappropriate disclosure or intervention.

barriers experienced by the individual counselor with regard to religious or spiritual views of the client.

Internal Bias and Countertransference. Counselors are no different in the spiritual area than in any other aspect of their lives, bringing their own biases and views on spirituality and religion. These biases, as stated in the previous paragraph, may evolve from professional experiences, such as education, training, supervision; they may evolve from personal experiences; or they may evolve from a combination of both. These experiences may have left a general impression or scars that impact the counselor's personal and professional life and result in biases toward the spiritual realm that range from positive to negative. Abernathy and Lancia (1998) indicated that a lack of training or personal religious experiences may cause counselors to avoid addressing spiritual concerns as well as cause the counselor to go to the other extreme of being preoccupied with this area. Even the mention of a specific religion or spiritual practice may give rise to an intense emotional reaction (positive or negative) on the counselor's part or cause the counselor to be drawn to or repulsed from a spiritual or religious area of concern. Therefore, it is important for mental health practitioners to be aware of their own personal perspectives within the spiritual realm.

For example, Thurrell (2000) advocates such awareness in psychiatrists to meet client needs.

To facilitate the counselor's awareness of countertransference, Abernathy and Lancia (1998) described two types of countertransference that can affect a counselor: interreligious and intrareligious. *Interreligious* countertransference may occur when counselors perceive that they have different religious backgrounds from their clients. They provided a case example where a counselor pulled away from these concerns because of a perception of being unable to fully understand the client's perspective and acknowledged that the client may have encouraged these feelings of the counselor by openly challenging the counselor's spiritual orientation. In another case example, they stated that a counselor had different views from the client of a Higher Power and struggled with urges to convince the client to view his or her Higher Power from a different perspective.

Intrareligious countertransference may happen when counselors perceive that they possess similar religious backgrounds with their clients. In this case example, a counselor was concerned about emphasizing religious or spiritual views too much. Both types of countertransference show the danger of extreme reactions of the counselor with regard to the client's spiritual welfare.

In terms of countertransference, the counselor needs to be aware of specific issues. The first of these is with regard to personal projections on existential questions facing the client. Particularly those questions that involve themes of mortality, suffering, or meaninglessness may bring up the counselor's own struggles because they inherently involve the unknown mysteries of life (Lannert, 1991). For example, helping a client face issues regarding death and grief may cause the counselor to reflect on these issues in his or her own life. That common human connection between the counselor and the client can lead to intense countertransference in which the counselor places his or her reactions to these concerns within a specific spiritual context that is comfortable for him or her. Again in terms of a continuum, the counselor may too readily turn to the spiritual realm for a pat answer or may too readily turn away from the discussion of such issues as a whole.

Other countertransference dangers may impact the assessment and treatment process with clients. In the assessment process, the danger for counselors is in terms of extremes. Counselors may not pick up on spiritual concerns of their clients due to their own bias, or they may pick up on these themes too readily at the exclusion of other issues. They may also make an inappropriate diagnosis that misses the spiritual concerns (Kahoe & Meadow, 1984). Thurrell (2000) states that the religious or spiritual arena of clients is most likely not to be addressed in a biopsychosocial assessment in a "near-phobic manner" (p. 557) or a belief that it is not relevant to the mental health problems. However, the author states that it is important to address this arena because it may be directly involved in symptoms or indirectly involved as expressed in their language, family problems, or referrals. An excellent example of a case study of the biopsychosocial realm involving a religious or spiritual dimension is provided by Stotland (1999). In this case study, a psychiatric consult was requested for dealing with the aftermath of a medical situation involving a Jehovah's Witness, female patient, who in a life-and-death situation, gave consent for medical assistance except for blood administration because of her religious beliefs. This case underscores the complications that can arise when working with an individual's religious or spiritual beliefs with regards to their physical and mental well-being.

Your setting as a counselor may also facilitate or inhibit the integration of these areas. For example, religious counselors working in secular agencies may have difficulty incorporating their religious views into their practice (Guinee, 1999). At the same time, a counselor who has a good match with his or her agency in terms of the degree of incorporating spiritual or religious views in counseling will have few issues in this application.

In the treatment area, countertransference issues include (a) not addressing concerns due to a lack of knowledge or lack of confidence and (b) being drawn into a topic of a spiritual nature that is at best tangentially related to the concerns of the client. Negative personal experiences with religion or being aware of others' negative personal experiences may cause counselors to experience a negative reaction when religion is mentioned generally by clients or when a specific religion is mentioned (R. J. Lovinger, 1984). These personal barriers can impede the therapeutic process (Lovinger, 1984) or be destructive to it in terms of unresolved religious issues (Humphries, 1982). At the other extreme, the motivation of a counselor who has had positive spiritual experiences to *convert* clients to his or her way of believing, to *feel good* by talking about uplifting spiritual matters, or to discuss religious or spiritual issues because they are more comfortable than the confusing issues clients have raised can be dangerous to the welfare of the client.

Also, a countertransference reaction may cause the counselor to make an inappropriate disclosure or introduce an inappropriate intervention. The counselor who has a negative countertransference reaction may too strongly avoid disclosure of spiritual views or interventions regarding spiritual concerns. The counselor with positive countertransference may discuss, unnecessarily, his or her spiritual beliefs as a way to calm him- or herself and the client or feel compelled to suggest an inappropriate therapeutic intervention such as praying in a session with a client.

Some areas of counseling may require counselors to closely examine their potential countertransference to an even greater depth. For example, Brady, Guy, Poelstra, and Brokaw (1999) stress that counselors working with trauma survivors may need to examine the relationship between spirituality and trauma because of the confrontation with existential issues (suffering, life meaning) that may arise for the counselor as they work on the trauma. In their study of 1,000 female counselors, they found those treating abuse survivors had a more satisfied life spiritually. The authors explained this finding as a possible result of (a) trauma clients encouraging counselors to grow and change as a result of the therapeutic work, and (b) counselors who have greater spiritual well-being may be more drawn to trauma work. The authors encourage counselors to look at the aspect of spirituality in both their personal and their professional lives. Such examination may facilitate the process of counseling and reduce countertransference when working with this population.

Whether during assessment, treatment, or closure of therapy, counselors need to be aware of their perspective on spirituality and the inherent biases of that perspective. Without such sensitivity toward your bias, counselors may inadvertently neglect the welfare of the client, thereby doing at least passive harm. The awareness of bias can, as with other forms of self-awareness, allow counselors to enter into the spiritual realm trusting that the dance of therapy can be done in a manner of respect and care for the client's well-being. The awareness of bias can build bridges between therapy and spirituality as occurred in the laughter described in the story at the beginning of this chapter. In sum, counselors can facilitate a helping relationship with regard to spiritual issues simply by being aware of their own perspective.

Bridges between Spirituality/Religion and Therapy

Bridges between spirituality/religion and therapy, like the barriers, also have a long history. Yet, Vande Kemp (1996) states that at least one group of mental health professionals, traditionally trained psychologists, may not realize that psychology and religion have a history of significant overlap as well as the divergence discussed earlier. This section explores the roots of both psychology and counseling for evidence of the bridges between spirituality and therapy.

A number of historical bridges exist between the counseling and religious fields. First, religion, like counseling, can help people change, develop, and make positive contributions to society. Related to this is the idea that religion can encourage people to function at a higher level by providing a framework by which to live, just as counseling does. Third, religion, like counseling, helps people develop a sense of self and a maturity. Finally, just as with counseling, religion can help or hurt an individual's potential.

Richards and Bergin (1997) pointed out the aspects of psychology that embraced the spiritual experiences of clients. This is the descriptive approach described in the overview section of this chapter. The descriptive approach was more sympathetic and inner-focused with regard to religion (Wulff, 1997). It emphasized what happened inside the client that helped him or her change and develop. Given this different slant toward religion and spirituality, a more cooperative, collaborative relationship emerged between these two fields. Some of the writers who emphasized this perspective were James, Jung, Allport, and Fromm.

Wulff (1996) reported that even when psychology emphasized science, three concurrent movements contrasted this perspective: psychologists who wrote about religion (James, Jung), humanistic-existential psychology (Allport, Fromm), and cognitive psychology. A brief summary of these movements follows.

James (1985) viewed religion as necessary to life. He believed that intellect and inspiration combined could assist people in achieving a high level of being that would result in others also attaining higher levels of being, thereby making the world a better place.

HISTORICAL FIGURES IN DEVELOPING LINK BETWEEN SPIRITUALITY AND PSYCHOLOGY

William James (1842–1910) was born in New York City where his father was a theologian. James married in 1878 and had five children. He received a medical degree from Harvard University in 1869. He was a psychologist, philosopher, writer, and teacher (Albright, 2001).

Carl Jung (1875–1961) was a Swiss psychiatrist whose father was a priest. Jung obtained a medical degree in 1900 and married in 1903. Freud saw Jung as a successor, but they had a break initially based on sexuality and the nature of the personal unconscious. Jung's most popular concept was the collective unconscious (*Carl Gustav Jung*, 2001).

Gordon Allport (1897–1967) was born in Indiana and grew up in Cleveland, Ohio (Evans, 1981). His father was a doctor and he was the youngest of four boys. In 1922, he obtained a doctorate in psychology from Harvard and focused his professional life on social issues and personality tests (Boeree, 1998).

Erich Fromm (1900–1980) was born in Frankfurt, Germany in an Orthodox Jewish family (Hausdorff, 1972). His father was a businessman. He obtained a doctorate in 1922 and became a therapist. His views were a mix of Freud and Marx (Boeree, 1997).

Jung, influenced by James, encouraged psychologists to examine the religious realm of their clients. Jung viewed the traditions of religions as facilitating the development of the self. Jung viewed self as the fulcrum of personality where conscious and unconscious elements are balanced (Jung, 2001).

The Humanistic Psychology Movement began around the beginning of the twentieth century and viewed human beings as having positive potential and incorporating spiritual needs and values that are not necessarily addressed by conventional religions. The *Humanistic-Existential Psychology* Movement viewed human behavior as more complex than the psychoanalytic and behavioral perspectives, although it believed that people's behavior could be explained naturally (naturalism). Allport (1950) was one of the main authors of that movement. He developed scales for religious orientation in terms of intrinsic and extrinsic factors. Allport attempted to assess the mature religious person in terms of six traits: well-differentiated, dynamic, directive, comprehensive, integral, and heuristic.

Fromm (1950) was another humanistic psychologist who believed that religion could be helpful to clients. He saw humans as needing a guiding framework and a place of devotion to cope with the realities of aloneness and death. He described two types of religion:

1. One that was authoritarian that inhibited the potential of the person, and

2. The other that was humanistic and focused on the development of the person's potential.

Bergin (1992) stated that the field of counseling and development, which focused on the growth and health of student populations, was a good match for the humanistic movement. These two areas encouraged one another in their development. Early vocational counseling looked at the individual within the entirety of their life development. Parsons (1909, 1911) viewed religion and spirituality as helping people develop positively. Davis (1914) connected morality with religion and saw a positive correlation between morals and vocational success.

Cognitive psychology, which blossomed in the 1960s, allowed for the idea of self-control, thereby creating another opening for psychology to the inner world of the individual, an inner world that can include the spiritual dimension.

Vande Kemp (1996) provided an excellent overview of the overlap of the mental health field and religion. The author argues that psychology and religion are a legitimate subdiscipline in psychology as evidenced in a name, professional groups, degree programs, journals, research programs, textbooks, treatment centers, internships, and theoretical literature.

Numerous professional societies that emphasize integration are classified into two types:

1. Groups that merged religious and mental health professionals (e.g., Christian Association for Psychological Studies–1953; [National] Academy of Religion and Mental Health–1954; American Foundation of Religion and Psychiatry–1958).

2. Special interest groups within larger groups (Friends Conference on Religion and Psychology within the World Conference of Friends at Swarthmore–1937; Association for Spiritual, Ethical, and Religious Values in Counseling within the American Counseling Association–1950s; Psychological Interpretations in Theology within the American Academy of Religion–1973; Psychology of Religion [Division 36] within the American Psychological Association–1947).

Evidence of this integration also appears in academia. In 1965, Fuller Theological Seminary began to offer doctorates in psychology that were approved by the APA. Other doctoral programs integrating psychology and religion include Azusa Pacific University, Biola University, Boston University, George Fox University, Loyola University, Regent University, and Wheaton College. Numerous masters programs and nonaccredited programs also integrate these two areas of study.

Vande Kemp (1996) also described evidence of the integration in journals. Some of these journals include: *Inward Light: Journal of the Friends Conference on Religion and Mental Health*–1937; *Counseling and Values*–1956; *Journal of Religion and Health Insight*–1961; *Quarterly Review of Religion and Mental Health*–1961; *Journal of Transpersonal Psychology*–1969; *Journal of Psychology and Theology*–1973; *Journal of Psychology and Judaism*–1976; *Journal of Psychology and Christianity*–1982. The existence of such journals speaks to the number of psychotherapists interested in this area of overlap, as does the increasing literature and textbooks, such as this one, being produced.

This section showed that spiritual and religious views can be used as resources to facilitate the client's welfare. The following section discusses some ways counselors can encourage this development. Specific counseling techniques that can be used as bridges in counseling are discussed in Chapter 8.

Common Bridges

The Human Experience. Bergin (1992) argued that spiritual experiences impact the behavior of individuals. The author stated that counselors use interventions with their clients that are value based and that use of the spiritual realm can help people use their values to guide their behaviors. Counselors can use their spiritual views and those of their clients, to guide them in the processing of the human experience.

Abernathy and Lancia (1998) suggested four factors that can be used by counselors to create bridges: being open, being attuned, using consultation, and using interpretation. Openness includes the counselor being aware of personal knowledge and reactions with regard to religion. An awareness of your reactions to a client's story can assist the counseling process. At the end of this chapter, Case Study 1, as well as Exercises 1 and 4, may facilitate your awareness of these concerns. Attunement means being aware of your current and past involvement with religion as well as the client's religion. This is similar to openness, but more specific in the sense of examining your experiences as well as the client's history of experiences. Case Study 2 and Exercises 1, 2, and 4 may help you develop a heightened awareness in this area. Using consultation means involving other professionals in a collaborative effort to ensure that the welfare of the client is the foremost concern. Here the counselor may need to consult with others regarding a case or the counselor may be consulted about a case of a spiritual or religious nature by a supervisee. Case Studies 1 and 2 as well as Exercise 2 can help you explore the use of consultation in working with spiritual issues. Interpretation includes using religious content material as reflecting the inner life of the client. As with any aspect of a client's story, the inner life or inner perspective of the client is reflected in the manner and content in which his or her life is described. Paying close attention to spiritual or religious aspects of the client's story can provide the counselor with invaluable information about how the client sees and approaches the world. Case Study 2 and Exercises 2, 3, and 4 can help counselors become aware of how spiritual material can be used in sessions. These four factors can facilitate the connection of the human experience between the counselor and the client.

Mattson (1994) advocates three *Ps* when working with a religious client: *place*, *person*, and *philosophy*. The *place* is the setting of the counselor that may create a set of client expectations of counseling. The *person* (the client) requires that a counselor know his or her own spiritual or religious values. The *philosophy* is both the counselor's and client's views of religion. The counselor aware of these three areas can facilitate the incorporation of the spiritual or religious dimension of the client in the counseling sessions.

Making Sense of Our Existence

What is the story I will not tell? The story I do not tell is the only one that is a lie. It is the story of the life I do not lead, without complication, mystery, courage, or the transfigurations of the flesh. Yes, somewhere inside me there is a child always eleven years old, a girlchild who holds the world responsible for all the things that terrify and call to me. But inside me too is the teenager who armed herself and fought back, the dyke who did what she had to, the woman who learned to love without giving in to fear. The stories other people would tell about my life, my mother's life, my sisters', uncles', cousins', and lost girlfriends'—those are the stories that could destroy me, mock and deny me. I tell my stories louder all the time: mean and ugly stories; funny, almost bitter stories; passionate, desperate stories— all of them have to be told in order not to tell the one the world wants, the story of us broken, the story of us never laughing out loud, never learning to enjoy sex, never being able to love or trust love again, the story in which all that survives is the flesh. That is not my story. I tell all the others so as not to have to tell that one. (Allison, 1995, p. 10)

It is the client's story that is at the core of the therapy. It is both the source of the pain and the cure. It is the story that guides our lives and helps us make sense out of them. It is the stories of others' lives as well as our own that teaches us how to live. The spiritual realm is one area that can help us in making sense of our lives and guide how we want to live them. Counseling is an arena for people to tell their stories that can provide them with a sense of hope. Many times, a core theme of these stories consists of a religious or spiritual nature. Therefore, the counselor needs to complete an assessment, even if it is a broad one, of the spiritual life of the client in order to facilitate the counseling process by acknowledging spiritual wounds and strengths of the client.

Zeiger and Lewis (1998) stated that conflicts of a religious nature may be present for clients, especially those whose religious identity is so strongly connected with how they view themselves. In this case, to understand the client's story of his or her life, it is critical to complete an assessment of these concerns. Clients' religious beliefs, in part, reflect how they organize themselves and make sense of the world about them. Such an assessment does not need to occur in the session, but can occur simply by the counselor encouraging clients to examine this area of their lives.

Henning and Tirrell (1982) highlighted that the therapist does not need to be an expert in the religious area to work with the client, but does need to be open to discussing these issues with the focus on the general development of the client. When clients introduce spiritual concerns as a focus of therapy, Zeiger and Lewis (1998) have some specific suggestions for responses. First, it is important to clarify the focus of therapy and the role of the counselor in that work with the client. The next step is to develop trust by being interested in the client's religious views, coming to understand the client's views, and the client's concerns with exploring those views. The counselor needs to facilitate this on an ongoing basis by being aware of self and religious dynamics in the session. As with other areas of concern, the counselor needs to work with the transference of the client. These approaches by the counselor that focus on the welfare of the client, allow clients to tell and process their stories as they relate to their overall development, including the spiritual dimension of self.

To facilitate understanding of the common bridges, specific theoretical and religious perspectives are examined here in relation to counseling. These perspectives are not meant to be exclusive of psychological or religious perspectives not discussed, but are meant to provide examples of similar perspectives between these areas.

Psychological Perspectives. Object relations theory is a more recent development in *psychoanalytic* counseling approaches. In this theory, object relations are the interpersonal relationships (real and imagined) of the client that stem from the client's inner psyche. The object is that person or thing that meets the client's need (Corey, 1996). Another term for the incorporated object is an *introject*. This theoretical approach readily integrates the spiritual or religious realm.

Rizzuto (1979) began this integration through her case studies. She believed that a person's perception of God reflected his or her primary introjects and that this perception of God changed as new experiences were incorporated into one's internal perspective. Carr (2000) states that the bridge between spirituality, religion, and mental health, from this psychological perspective, is the *transitional object*, the object that has irrational power (e.g., a child's security blanket). Such objects are typically left behind by a child as he or she matures, but the transitional object of God is not discarded.

From an *object relations* perspective, Hall, Brokaw, Edwards, and Pike (1998) proposed that an individual's developmental maturity, in terms of a relationship with God, is related to their relationships with others. In their study, they defined spiritual maturity in terms of the quality of the client's relationship with God. They found support for their theory in that less mature individuals showed more pathology in relation to God. Based on their findings, the authors suggest that during assessment, the counselor take a religious history to look at the client's perception of God and the development of their object relations because such examination can assist in determining the client's spiritual struggles as well as their struggles in relation to others.

Suler (1993) states that psychoanalysis, in general, attempts to help people learn about and develop themselves, which is similar to such Eastern views as Buddhism. In both psychoanalysis and Buddhism, there is a search for answers about who you are and the meaning of suffering with the intent of examining assumptions that may result in a different organization of your perspective and changing self (Suler, 1993).

From a *Taoist* perspective, Suler (1993) reports a number of similarities with psychoanalysis. First, it examines change. Second, truths are hidden in images (e.g., the unconscious emerging in dreams). Third, polarities (*yin* and *yang*) are a part of change. Fourth, *wu wei* is the use of nonaction creatively letting things unfold as they are intended. Finally, *Te,* means harmony, naturalness, and spontaneousness that express the Tao, how things are to be.

Suler (1993) also recommends that we integrate Eastern and Western ideas simultaneously looking for overlap where similarities can be emphasized while clarifying the conflicts between the perspectives so we can fill in what is missing in each perspective from the other perspective. He describes this process as neither "here nor there territory" (p. 14). He encourages a "beginner's mind" in this approach that allows us to discover.

From the *humanistic* perspective, Hermsen (1996) reviews the complimentary aspect of Rogers' Client-Centered therapy and Taoism. Rogers' idea of the *actualizing tendency* is that of living beings trying to preserve or better themselves. To create this opportunity, the counselor must be congruent, have unconditional positive regard, and experience empathy. Rogers, encouraged the liberation of a client's nature similar to the Taoist perspective.

Again from the humanistic perspective, Das (1989) discusses the similarity of both Maslow and Rogers to Vedandic Hinduism and two schools of Buddhism (Theravada and Mahayana). Both of these individuals emphasized self-actualization and saw it as a being's tendency to express or better itself while in an environment that assists or inhibits that expression. In a supportive environment, self-actualization is almost spontaneous.

Maslow believed that people would develop their talents and abilities once their more basic needs (physically and psychologically) were met. Rogers called it the actualizing tendency where the self is not fixed, but changes as it learns and matures. People have a natural need for positive regard. According to Maslow, the counselor helps the client take away the external constraints of growth and learns behaviors that help him or her self-actualize (living fully, taking risks and responsibility, developing talents, having peak experiences, and being open to the everyday occurrences with wonder). According to Rogers, the counselor facilitates the process and meets the need for positive regard by being genuine and providing unconditional positive regard and empathy to the client.

Das (1989) describes Hindu and Buddhist concepts as follows. In Hinduism, self-realization is the goal of a human's life, but this is the spiritual self where self-realization is a result of being liberated through disciplined behavior. In Buddhism, self-realization is a way to solve life's problems with the ultimate goal being Nirvana, which is achieved by the Eightfold Path that guides behavior. Both Hinduism and Buddhism view the self as an illusion, that you need to transcend self, and practice a long, hard discipline to be liberated.

Das notes the differences between these religious perspectives and humanistic psychology. Humanistic psychology only deals with the phenomenal self, not the spiritual self. It prescribes only the development of your individuality rather than a specific path. It emphasizes spontaneous self-actualization rather than discipline. Finally, morality is perceived to evolve more naturally than through training. The Eastern views add a spiritual dimension and more responsibility on the individual to develop. The commonalities between Hinduism and Buddhism and humanistic psychology include being self-aware, being open to experiences, and being sensitive socially (not so culturally bound).

Religious Perspectives. De Silva (1993) charges that the Buddhist perspective applied to counseling can help people live with their problems and improve their well-being even if they are not Buddhist. He outlines four ways of using the Buddhist perspective in counseling:

1. With Buddhist clients because of the match with beliefs.
2. With clients in general because Buddhist communities have experience with having a counseling role in the lives of their practitioners.
3. To help people focus on daily living concerns.
4. To involve behavior change strategies.

De Silva (1993) expands on items 3 and 4 as follows. In terms of daily living concerns (3), Buddha encouraged people to live in a manner that facilitated their well-being and that of others which meant living ethically according to one's obligations. In terms of behavior change (4), Buddhism involves the following concepts that are a bridge to counseling: rewards and punishments, graded exposure to reduce fear, modeling, self-monitoring, stimulus control, aversion (overt, covert), drawing on one's family to change behavior, and avoiding cognitions through distraction and over-exposure. De Silva (1993) also notes that Buddhism advocates detachment and not trying to accumulate material resources, which can result in a person being less likely to have daily living problems.

Daya (2000) states that Buddhism does not see a self that exists in the sense of being "separate, permanent, and distinct" (p. 261) and physical illness is related to one's mental state. The author describes counseling as a place where the counselor takes abstract ideas about how people work and assists clients in making concrete application of theory to their lives. Changes are a result of the clients' breaking out of illusions and using techniques (such as meditation to become aware) and concepts (such as impermanence or process) to help them become flexible about their sense of self, live in the present, experience without judgment, have compassion for others, be open, see oneself as interdependent, and experience suffering.

Ehrlich (1986) describes the counseling process as one that blends well with a Taoist perspective. From this perspective, a trust in oneself, a knowing of oneself is encouraged in counseling. The counseling process is a liberating one for clients. Taoism encourages clients to *be* rather than *do* and access reality through our senses; the meaning of life then is being connected with our present experience living. Counselors are attempting to help clients feel a connection to their environment, learn to use their senses, and thereby, be less self-conscious and more free and liberated. Counselors encourage people to be spontaneous by trusting their ability to regulate themselves and by being nonjudgmental, the counselor helps people accept and trust themselves more.

From a *Christian* perspective, Farnsworth (1996) urges Christian counselors to examine how much of both psychology and theology they put in their counseling. He describes three types of Christian counselors. The first are those that are Christian only in name (CNO: Christians in Name Only) and these individuals rely on psychology and do not use theology very much or at all. The second type are Bible-grounded and Bible-guided (BGG) and use the Bible to describe the problem and the solution while distrusting psychology. The third type are those he describes as true Christian counselors who are "Christ-centered, Bible-based, and Spirit-inspired (CBS)" (p. 123). This last group of individuals dedicates their counseling to Christ, follow Biblical principles, and use the Holy Spirit to determine the best procedures to honor God. The use of the Holy Spirit means that each counselor has different gifts, maturity, and knowledge that are both Biblical and secular available to him or her in the addressing of issues.

Farnsworth (1996) states that Christian counseling is psychological and spiritual as well as involving both ministry and business aspects. He recommends each counselor develop a framework that incorporates both keeping in mind that theology emphasizes the moral aspects (values come from Scripture) while psychology emphasizes a person's needs and tendencies in terms of their strengths, weaknesses, and developmental levels). Hesselgrave (1988) adds that the counselor needs to remember that Christian counseling is more than behavior change and that the counselor may need to address the issue of sin in counseling.

These various psychological and religious perspectives provide examples of similarities between the counseling and spiritual and religious realms that counselors can use in the incorporation of spirituality in counseling. While there is no formula for such integration, these examples provide evidence that counselors can find perspectives in both areas that are complimentary to one another thereby making the incorporation an easier process.

Case Studies

CASE STUDY 1

You are supervising a counselor who is interested in integrating counseling and spirituality more actively in his private practice. His concern is that while he has an interest in more actively incorporating spirituality into his practice, he does not want to become labeled as a religious counselor. He presents you with two questions: (1) How can I integrate these areas without being labeled as a religious counselor? and (2), What is the best way for me to begin this integration process? As you form your responses to his questions, keep in mind:

1. Possible ways he can prepare himself for stereotypes that may form about him.
2. Resources (professionals, training) he may use to facilitate this integration.

CASE STUDY 2

You have a client who is of the same religious orientation as you are. Your client has openly talked with you about her spiritual beliefs. She is presently in a crisis regarding her marriage and you have an urge to talk with her about her concerns within the context of her beliefs and to intervene in her struggle in a spiritual manner such as praying with her in a session. What stops you is the agency for which you work. Your agency has a strict policy regarding the separation of church and state and you work for a state agency. You are confused about what to do in this session and future sessions with regard to her spirituality.

1. Where do you begin to sort out your confusion?
2. Who is the best person for you to talk with at your agency?
3. What are the barriers both within and outside of you that inhibit your integration of the spiritual with your clinical work?
4. What are bridges that support your integration of the spiritual with your clinical work?

CASE STUDY 3

You are working with a family in counseling. The family is blended in terms of religious beliefs: the mother is devout in her religious beliefs while the father is an atheist. Although they have never specifically explored these issues in their sessions, you believe they are core critical issues in the family dynamics because the mother mentioned these religious differences in the first session.

1. How would you explore the possibility of this religious conflict in the marriage and the family?
2. How would you explore the impact of these differences on the children?

3. Where would you draw the line on such exploration viewing it as outside of your area of expertise?

Exercises

Exercise 1

Make a chart of your own development of the spiritual aspect of your counseling (if you are a student, make a chart that covers the time frame of your training). Include in this chart the following areas that influenced your emphasis of the spiritual realm in counseling:

1. Personal experiences.
2. Classes taken.
3. Training taken.
4. Instructors.
5. Professional organization involvement.
6. Professional journal involvement.
7. Significant personal books.
8. Significant professional books.

On completion of this time frame, present this information to another student or colleague for discussion of your awareness. As you discuss your experiences, make sure you mention the amount of influence you believe comes from the personal arena and how much comes from the professional arena.

Exercise 2

In this exercise, choose a partner and spend time discussing these questions:

1. How much of my counseling has an emphasis on the spiritual dimension of my clients?
2. Where does this emphasis begin? In assessment, in treatment, in crisis, in closure?
3. How does this emphasis become introduced in counseling? By me? By my client?
4. Am I satisfied with the amount of spiritual emphasis I place in my counseling?
5. If I want to increase the emphasis, how do I plan to do this?

6. What are the barriers I experience or anticipate experiencing as I address the spiritual dimension with my clients?

7. Which of these barriers are within me?

8. Which of these barriers came out of my training as a counselor?

9. Which of these barriers are related to the environment in which I work or anticipate working?

10. What are some bridges that I believe will make it easy for me to integrate spirituality into my counseling practice?

Exercise 3

Take a moment to consider the clientele with whom you work or plan to work. Write down your ideal, general approach of working with them on their spiritual issues. Then write answers to the following questions:

1. Would their spiritual issues be separate from other issues in their lives or an inherent part of all or most of their concerns?

2. What are the main components of the framework of your approach?

Now write down the reality of working with them on their spiritual issues. Frame this section by dividing a piece of paper in half. On one side, write down all the barriers you have experienced both within and outside your self (real or anticipated barriers) and on the other side, all the bridges you have experienced both within and outside your self (real or anticipated barriers). Finally, write down three ways you can work on spiritual issues with your clients without having the barriers stop you.

Exercise 4

Get into a dyad with another student or colleague. Enter into a dialogue with the following incomplete statements as a guide:

1. I define spirituality as . . . .

2. I rely on my spirituality to help me . . . .

3. My best experience in addressing spiritual issues in counseling was . . . .

4. My worst experience in addressing spiritual issues in counseling was . . . .

5. The main concern I have in addressing spiritual issues in counseling is . . . .

Exercise 5

Choose one of the previous four exercises to use in a dialogue with a mental health counselor who you respect. Following the mental health counselor's involvement in the exercise, ask him or her:

1. General reactions (positive and negative) to the exercise.
2. Awareness of the possible impact of this exercise on his or her clinical work.

Suggested Readings

Richards, P. S., & Gergin, A. E. (1997). *A spiritual strategy for counseling and psychotherapy.* Washington, DC: American Psychological Association.

Vande Kemp, H. (1996). Historical perspective: Religion and clinical psychology in America. In E. P. Shafranske (Ed.), *Religion and the clinical practice of psychology* (pp. 71–112). Washington, DC: American Psychological Association.

Western or Monotheistic Religions

Chapter Objectives

1. What are the main Western religions?
2. Which religions come from similar doctrines?
3. What are issues that may arise in counseling in relation to the different religions?

Overview

In Chapter 1, we reviewed the growing American interest in spirituality and religion and discussed how individuals, counseling clients, professional organizations' divisions, and counselor training reflect this tendency. Chapter 2 described the barriers as well as the bridges between spirituality/religion and therapy. These topics lead us naturally to a discussion of different religions and the possible impacts of these religions on counseling. Chapter 3 describes the major Western or Monotheistic religions and their possible impact on counseling and Chapter 4 describes the major Eastern religions and examines their possible impact on counseling. Prior to examining these religions practiced in the United States, we need to look at the history of religion in the Americas.

Most world religions are practiced in the United States and religion played a core part in European settlement the eastern United States and Spanish settlement in the Southwest (Neusner, 1994). Green (1994) provides a summary of the United States' constitutional history as it connects to religion. The United States was a pioneer in separating church and state as a part of its foundation through the First Amendment, thereby, providing religious freedom. The First Amendment reads, "Congress shall make no law respecting an establishment of religion, or prohibiting the free exercise thereof; or abridging the freedom of speech, or of the press; or the right of the people peaceably to assemble, and to petition the Government for a redress of grievances." (This application of the federal government was extended to state governments when in two cases, *Cantwell v. Connecticut,* 1940 and *Everson v. Board of Education,*

1947, the United States Supreme court included the First Amendment in the Fourteenth Amendment thus holding all states accountable to the First Amendment.) The First Amendment assures Americans that there will be more than one religion in America and therefore, no religion can say it is the only American religion and direct people's behavior accordingly. Religious minorities are protected and different religions can coexist in the United Sates. This background on religious freedom encourages a multicultural perspective in relation to religion.

In discussing multicultural approaches to various religious and spiritual beliefs, Siegel, Choldin, and Orost (1995) argue that Christianity is closely woven into the North American culture and legal fabric. They state that there is an influence culturally and legally from the conservative Christian groups that settled the colonies that have impacted different groups (e.g., women being viewed as weak, more easily impacted by evil, needing men to dominate them). They also state that because of its dominance in North America, Christianity has discriminated against other religions. "Christian privilege" based on the dominance of the religion may be held by Christian Americans who are not aware of the privileges they receive simply by being Christian in the United States. Finally, because of the dominance of Christianity, non-Christian religious individuals may experience discrimination in numerous subtle or obvious forms through the stereotypes held about them, religious holidays recognized within the culture, metaphorical language used, and so on. Counselors working in the United States with clients on religious or spiritual concerns need to have an awareness of how the dominance of Christianity may impact the therapeutic relationship.

As we begin this multicultural examination of the various religions, a story by Suler (1993) seems an appropriate starting point:

> I once had a dog, Duncan, who loved to bark (in a befriending way) at cats outside our front door. When I saw one, I would energetically motion to the door with my finger, hoping to direct his attention to the cat. Invariably, he would sense the excitement in my voice and stare at my finger. There is a bit of Duncan in all of us. (p. 15)

This story reminds us to avoid being too concrete as we focus on the different religions discussed. One of the difficulties in learning about different religions, to work more effectively as counselors, is that we, like Duncan, become too focused. Paradoxically, we can develop a rigid perspective on practicing a flexible counseling framework. Perhaps the best approach is to view these two chapters as a place where the reader can develop hypotheses with regard to working with various religious perspectives. In this manner, the reader will not develop dogmatic absolutes about counseling clients from specific religions, but rather propose hypotheses about working with clients from different religious perspectives. We need to be different from Duncan and use the religious descriptions in these chapters to point us in the *direction* of how to work with clients from these various religious perspectives.

A second difficulty in learning about religions is the amount and type of coverage of different religions. Some religions may be left out of the discussion because major religions practiced in the United States have been chosen for exploration. Also, chapter summaries may leave out important aspects of the religion or important areas of debate or distinction within the religion. With regard to this latter concern, a religion can contain different philosophical approaches that reflect disagreement. For example, in a classroom where there was a discussion on spirituality and counseling, a student was willing to engage in a difficult dialogue regarding the integration of spirituality in counseling. The dialogue went as follows. In response to my lecture comments, the student said, "I am a Christian and I am comfortable identifying myself as a Christian counselor with my clients. I believe that I am qualified to work with Christians in counseling on their religious issues because we have the same beliefs." I asked her what her Christian denomination was and she responded, "Baptist," and went on to describe a denomination that is quite conservative. I asked her what she knew about Lutherans and she said, "Very little," and about a specific Lutheran denomination and she said, "Nothing." I pointed out that while both groups are Christian, there are significant differences in how they interpret and practice Christianity. I encouraged her to reconsider her statement that she could work well automatically with all Christians because she was Christian and also encouraged her to examine what she would need to know about another Christian's perspective before assuming they spoke the same "Christian language." There can be tremendous variations in perspective even when the counselor and client generally identify with the same religion.

While Chapters 3 and 4 are limited in these ways, you are encouraged to use these chapters as containing "religious fingers," as discussed in the story about Duncan the dog. We can be different from Duncan by letting the religious fingers point to the spiritual and religious perspectives of our clients rather than becoming too focused on the religious fingers themselves.

A general description of the major religions is provided so therapists may use these chapters in their work with clients. The essential features of a religion are included in these chapters; however, an in-depth description is not given. Hopefully the limited presentation of various religions will assist in the counselor's sensitivity in counseling individuals of other religions. The counselor needs to remember, however, that these descriptions are general and that each client's interpretation and application of his or her religion to his or her life may be idiosyncratic. Clients may be in a specific developmental phase religiously or may have incorporated only certain aspects of the religion into their lives. Some clients may not absolutely identify with only one religion, but may treat the realm of spirituality as more of a buffet, for example, they take a bit of Christianity and mix it with some Buddhist concepts. Finally, depending on the counselor's location, certain religious groups may dominate the local culture. In understanding a client's idiosyncratic interpretation, a counselor may need to ask such questions as: What religious perspectives does the local religious group or leader provide to our client? How does the client respond to these views and practice them in daily living? You are encouraged to use the questions below and on page 94 in Chapter 4 to clarify a client's views on religion or spirituality.

Web sites are provided as an additional resource for counselors who wish to learn more about a religion or provide information to their clients. The Web sites listed can be used to link with other Web sites on the topic area and are not inclusive of all Web sites for these religions. The Web sites can be a resource for clients in a number of ways. For clients who are interested in a specific religion, they can easily obtain information about that religion and contacts for the religious groups through the Web site. Web sites, particularly those with chat rooms or other mechanisms for connecting believers, can be especially helpful for clients who live in areas where they are isolated from other individuals who share their beliefs. For example, a chat room for Buddhists may provide an individual who is Buddhist and who lives in the South, a source of important

---

QUESTIONS TO FACILITATE COUNSELOR AWARENESS OF A CLIENT'S RELIGIOUS OR SPIRITUAL VIEWS

1. What spiritual or religious label does the client use to describe this aspect of self?

2. What do I know of this religion or spiritual perspective in general?

3. What is the impact of the client's spiritual or religious perspective on his or her daily living?

4. What is it like for the client to have that spiritual or religious orientation in the area in which he or she lives?

5. What does the client know of the historical treatment of his or her spiritual or religious group in the United States and in the world? How does that knowledge impact the client's view of the world, spiritual or religious practice, and interactions with others?

support. A Web site that provides information on Native American religions may be useful to someone who wants to learn more about this religion but lives in an area where no one practices these beliefs.

Finally, these chapters examine the possible impact of these religions on counseling. Although counselor reactions to these various religious beliefs are not examined in this chapter, possible issues related to the religious beliefs of clients are examined. This chapter, prior to summarizing Western religions and how they may impact counseling, looks at working with individuals across different perspectives, and examines specific factors influencing these perspectives (gender, age, and disability). Ethnicity is not discussed in this section because it is discussed in some of the specific applications of different religions.

Gender

A woman's identification with her religion might be complex and conflictual because it is mixed with class and ethnicity (Siegel et al., 1995). As Spelman (1988) states, "All women are women, but there is no being who is only a woman" (p. 102). The counselor working with women on spiritual or religious concerns needs to remember that a woman's identification in this area may be complicated. Therefore, the counselor needs to be careful to avoid assumptions regarding a woman's comfort level with her religion. For example, a woman may be comfortable with most aspects of her religion, but struggle with specific doctrines that impact her daily life. While each woman has a unique story of her spirituality, there are common tendencies about women related to the spiritual realm, the impact of patriarchal religions on them, and the use of spirituality to cope with oppression they experience, that a counselor also needs to remember in his or her clinical work with female clients.

J. B. Miller (1976) describes a woman's process of understanding herself by the relationships she creates and maintains in her life. It is her connectedness with others that helps her understand herself and her morals (Surry, 1985). A woman, then, needs to be understood by as well as to understand those people in her life who are important to her in order to know about herself. Also, she may define her power in the world as her ability to care for others (McClelland, 1979). This self-in-relation perspective in terms of self-knowledge, values, and power applies to the spiritual life of a woman. Ballou (1995) notes that feminist spirituality is a part of a woman's ordinary life; a woman knows her spirituality through her experiences and her relationships and connectedness with other people. Her spirituality is a result of her reflections on her experiences in relation to herself, others, and her community. Her spirituality is a natural part of her life. The risk of a woman denying this process in herself is outlined in the following quote:

It is when we define ourselves by what we do or measure ourselves by outside standards that we must beware. We think these will empower us. In reality they have caused us to lose the center, the core of self. This shunning of our own internal feminine energies and principles has been costly. It has been a selling out of intuition, instinct, and life energy, a sacrifice of our gifts to those who judged these qualities inferior. (Hogan, 1986, p. x)

In looking at women in the context of world religions, K. K. Young (1994) finds that women have higher religious, economic, and social status in societies that are small and contain feminine symbolism. This symbolization diminishes when there is a shift to the patrilineal, agricultural and trading societies, or the formation of states of larger societies where reform (including religious reform) occurs that is helpful to women until stress is present. Siegel et al. (1995) specifically present information on how patriarchal religions impact women. They state that these religions define gender roles (dress codes, food-related issues such as preparation and restriction, observances, and rituals) and the family unit (heterosexuality, sexual partners, male household ownership of women and children), and establish reproduction rules and the male hierarchy in both the family and religion. The authors continue that patriarchal religions teach women to be silent, to be economically dependent, to avoid identification with the divine in a feminine, to be cooperative or to exhibit a peaceful manner, to prevent alliances with women different from themselves, to create negative stereotypes of others that are not a part of her religion, and to justify the control of her body by society.

Fukuyama and Sevig (1999) provide a summary of Christ's (1995) feminist spirituality approach in living with oppression. Christ uses the poetry and prose of women on their spiritual journey and describes the journey in a spiral model that involves the experiences of nothingness, awakening, insight, and new naming. The nothingness experience consists of emptiness, self-hatred, or struggle that comes from living in a patriarchal world that is abusive to women. At this stage of the journey, a woman lets go of her view of self and reality as she has been conditioned. The awakening experience can involve connections with nature, a general way of operating in the world that is in tune with her femaleness (e.g., caring for others), connecting with movements of social justice, or having a mystical experience. This awakening is the process of self-empowerment. The insight experience is where the woman becomes more self-aware and confident and thereby more authentic. The new naming experience encourages the woman to find words to describe her own spiritual experience rather than in a traditionally male fashion.

In an applied context, G. Miller, Evans, and Youngblood (1998) suggest that women need to practice self-care spiritually to live with the oppression they experience. They metaphorically describe this practice as "breathing under water." They suggest that women find a place to tell their story, practice meaningful activities, and become involved in enjoyable activities. They describe the places to tell her story as being both formal (counseling, women's support groups) and informal (contact with friends). Meaningful activities include quilting, needlework, cooking, and other creative activities that allow her to express herself and provide her with a sense of pride and accomplishment. Enjoyable activities are those where she loses her sense of time and forgets about her worries.

At this point, there needs to be a discussion of male spirituality and development within the context of male socialization. While women may experience oppression due to their gender, males may be locked into specific roles through their socialization process. This socialization process can keep them from developing their potential as human beings and specifically inhibit them in the area of spirituality.

The socialization process for males may inhibit them from coming to, and being involved in, counseling in general. Granello (2000) states that men react differently to male socialization so the counselor needs to be sensitive to the socialization impact on each male client and be flexible enough to work with these variations. The impact of socialization in the male may appear as hesitancy about being involved in counseling, experiencing shame or embarrassment about his vulnerabilities, having restricted emotions, or being afraid of intimacy with the counselor. The author recommends that counselors be aware of their own gender bias, look for themes of socialization, help men reframe, or let go of, these themes of socialization, support and challenge them in therapy, and change therapy to respect each male client's expression of his gender.

Sensitivity to males' potential counseling issues assists in the exploration of their spirituality. In working in the spiritual area for males, Harris (1997) states that the spiritual side of men is understudied, resulting in a view of maleness that is incomplete. For the counselor to assist men in developing this spiritual aspect of themselves, sensitivity to the barriers to therapy work can facilitate the spiritual development of the client.

Harris argues that spirituality and religion impact how men live their daily lives and practice their beliefs—that men can use this aspect of themselves to find greater life meaning where life becomes a quest for this meaning. Harris proposes ten tenets of male spirituality:

1. Finding inner wisdom.
2. Searching for truth.
3. Speaking from the heart.
4. Confronting the dark side.
5. Loving.

6. Working for a better world.
7. Passing a test.
8. Belonging to something great.
9. Following scripture.
10. Believing in destiny. (p. 34)

These tenets of spirituality can result in men having a sense of purpose and direction where they are connected to some essence bigger than themselves and in turn draw higher moral standards of behavior from them.

Williams and Myer (1992) describe the mythopoetic approach of the men's movement as one way of helping men individually or in a group explore who they are outside of gender roles. This approach connects with men's emotions and draws on the healing energy of the male psyche through "ceremony, drumming, storytelling/poetry reading, physical movement, and imagery exercises designed to create a 'ritual process'" (p. 395). F. E. Rabinowitz and Cochran (2002) recommend some of these same approaches as ways to assist men in their spiritual development in a group counseling context:

1. Tell stories: Here the male tells the story of his life and describes his relationship with his father.
2. Read inspirational passages: In the group, a male can read what it means to be male or act out an image of maleness.
3. Use metaphors: This can help the male connect with his emotions if he uses a metaphor to describe himself.
4. Drum: This shared activity in a group can help a male access his emotions and give him a sense of belonging.
5. Meditate: This process will allow the male to get in touch with his emotions and his body.

The use of such approaches can assist the male client in both being emancipated from gender role stereotypes and developing a stronger spirituality. These two areas may overlap in the process of counseling male clients.

Age

Youniss, McLellan, and Yates (1999) found that adolescents/young people who were religiously oriented were more likely to be involved in community service as volunteers and were overall more flexible and open-minded than typically stereotyped. Elkind and Elkind (1962) found that adolescents might turn away from their religious institution, but this did not mean that they were turning away from religion. Rather their religious expression was becoming a personal, private relationship with God who was their confidant expressing a shift from the institution to the personal. S. L. Lovinger, Miller, and Lovinger (1999) discuss how religion helped two adolescents in object relations therapy deal with their respective issues, a turbulent life and depression. Their belief is that relationship with God reflects parental relationships and the self-object comes out of religious relationships. Working with adolescents in therapy with regard to religious concerns ethically involves the consent of the legal guardians, however, in the cases where consent is given, the counselor may be able to use the resource of religion as a coping strategy with the adolescent client.

As with any group, older adults (individuals over 65) are a diverse group of individuals (APA, 1998). With regard to religious involvement, older adults are most commonly involved in religious affiliation in terms of participation in organizations and prevention outreach may include houses of worship (APA, 1998). About 52 percent of them attend religious services each week or more frequently and over 75 percent say that religion is important to them according to the Princeton Religion Research Center (1994). Barna's (1991) survey results showed private involvement with religion among this age group: reading the Bible at least weekly (61%), praying (95%), and watching TV programs involving religion (58%).

Many older adults state that religion is a coping behavior that helps them address their physical and mental problems (Koenig, Larson, & Matthews, 1995). Koenig et al. reviewed a number of studies with older adults and found that those involved with some aspect of religious practice (attending church, praying, reading) were overall a healthier, happier, and more satisfied group and coping behaviors of a religious nature helped them with depression and physical problems (blood pressure, strokes, coronary heart disease, length of survival). Koenig et al. present eleven psychological and spiritual needs that older adults have that may need to be addressed in therapy:

1. Meaning, purpose, and hope.
2. Transcending circumstances.
3. Maintaining identity and self-esteem.
4. Integrity and worthiness.
5. Continuity.
6. Religious participation.
7. Expressions of anger and doubt.
8. Loving and serving others.
9. Cultivating thankfulness.

10. Forgiving and being forgiven.
11. Preparation for death and dying.

The authors state that a religious history of a client can determine if religion is a possible source of coping, if it has been used in the past to cope with stress, if it can be used in the present, if past experiences that were negative can be addressed so it can be used as a resource, and how it may be used in the future in terms of counseling. Religion may be used as a part of supportive therapy to increase the defenses and coping of the older adult and enhance their sense of self-sufficiency. Koenig, George, and Peterson (1998) found that intrinsically motivated religious faith (religion is a core motivator in directing their behavior and decisions) among older adults resulted in an increased ability for them to cope with physical and living situation changes. They explained these results as due to self-esteem and well-being. For some older adults, then, involvement of religion may be an effective coping device as they age.

Disability

Byrd (1998) presents suggestions on how Christianity can be used in counseling to assist people who have disabilities. The author states that disabled clients may be able to experience spiritual healing through their church or a rehabilitation professional who is concerned about the spiritual nature of clients and elaborates on how specific counseling theories may assist in that application.

While Byrd speaks from a Christian perspective, the recommendations to counselors working with the disabled population could reasonably be applied to other religions. These recommendations are that counselors encourage clients to:

1. Join a religious organization that strengthens their faith and possibly results in improved physical and emotional functioning as a result of the client's mind-body-spirit interaction.
2. Find individuals with similar spiritual values who can provide a sense of fellowship and support.
3. Find other disabled individuals who have adjusted to their disability through their faith and belief.

The author states that while counselors may take these actions in general with their clients, an emphasis on the spiritual realm may be especially important for the disabled population that may struggle with the question of "Why me?" and the feelings related to that question. A strengthened relationship with God or their Higher Power may provide them healing in adjusting to their disability.

Working across Differences

The Hasidic Rabbi Susya illustrated the very same theme when, just before dying, he said, "When I get to heaven, they will not ask me why you are not Moses? Instead they will ask, 'Why were you not Susya? Why did you not become what only you could become?'" (Ehrlich, 1986)

This quote can serve as our guide in discussing how to work across different spiritual perspectives. Sometimes as helping professionals, we are encouraged to believe that if only we work harder on ourselves, we can learn to work effectively with all populations of clients. This fallacy does not account for how difficult it may be for us at times to separate our personal values from our professional work. Particularly, this may arise with clients who have different perspectives from us spiritually. We need to take into account our reactions to various spiritual perspectives and, as in the preceding story, become what only we can become as a multicultural counselor in this area rather than an ideal multicultural counselor who proposes to work well with clients from all spiritual perspectives equally well. Therefore, as well as understanding our own spiritual and religious perspective, we need to understand our own comfort with the spiritual and religious perspectives of our clients, and determine the spiritual and religious arenas in which we are comfortable working as a counselor. We need to become the counselor that only we can become in the unique context of our clinical work.

G. Miller (1999b) describes multicultural counseling as that which attempts to bridge the differences between people: the counselor encourages the development of a bridge by being aware of himself or herself, the other, and the various cultural influences on the counselor and client. Because we are all "something" in terms of gender, ethnicity, and so on, that means that there is something that we are not, therefore, all counselors need to learn how to work across differences. Fukuyama and Sevig (1999) describe multiculturalism as "a state of being, a process, an ebb and flow of kinetic forces that is aimed at inclusivity and the valuing of people for who they are" (p. 69). Therefore, the authors argue that multicultural learning encourages spiritual evolving which encourages multicultural learning.

Working within a spiritual and religious perspective is an integral part of multicultural counseling (Fukuyama & Sevig, 1997). As previously stated, the counselor needs to invite the bridging across the spiritual or religious perspectives through awareness of his or her own perspective,

---

**SUGGESTIONS FOR WORKING WITH
COUNTERTRANSFERENCE**

1. Examine the nature of the discomfort in self in terms of:

   Values

   Philosophy

   Own spiritual beliefs

2. Discuss the nature of the discomfort with a trusted colleague or supervisor with the following questions in mind:

   a. Can I continue to work with this client given my own countertransference issues?

   b. Do I *want* to continue to work with this client?

   c. In working with this client, what limits will I set on how I will address this concern in counseling?

   d. In working with this client, how much of my own struggle with these religious views do I need to share?

   e. If I decide I cannot work with this client, who will I refer the client to for counseling? How will I bring up the referral with the client?

---

awareness of the client's perspective, and how their respective views influence how they perceive and operate in the world. These differences are a core part of the dynamics of counseling because both the counselor and client are a result of their spiritual worldviews.

As Atkinson, Morten, and Sue (1993) state about general multicultural counseling, even the intervention strategies must fit the client's culture. If a counselor working with a client does not have an understanding of the client's spiritual or religious perspective, the counselor may be less effective in counseling because a strategy may be chosen that does not fit the client. Bishop (1992) concurs that a counselor who does not understand or accept the values of a client's religion may upset their value system or develop unrealistic goals for therapy. The counselor, for example, may simply suggest to her client that she use yoga as a relaxation technique, but given her client's perspective, this may be viewed as "devil's work" and the counselor may lose the therapeutic trust whether the client states her reaction or not. Had the counselor known the client's spiritual views more clearly, she may not have even presented yoga as an option, but may have focused on exercises such as deep breathing as a relaxation technique.

G. Miller (1999b) outlines steps for counselors to take to create a dialogue friendly atmosphere with clients. These steps have been adapted to a spiritual orientation as follows:

1. Know the religious or spiritual culture of the client's life and the impact of that culture on the client in order to avoid stereotypes.

2. Use Rogers' (1987) interpersonal factors of genuineness, empathy, and unconditional positive regard by being genuine in discussions of religion and spirituality, having empathy for the struggles of the client, and viewing the client positively as he or she discusses these views.

3. Be compassionate rather than critical when conflict arises between counselor and client during discussions of the client's spiritual or religious world. When this occurs, focus on the client's view of the session conflict in terms of what happened and how that impacts the counseling relationship rather than who is to blame for the conflict. If appropriate, the counselor may need to apologize to the client for his or her part in the conflict.

4. Use "common sense" approaches of questioning that communicate respect:

   a. What spiritual or religious label does the client prefer to use to describe this aspect of self?

   b. What is it like to have that spiritual or religious perspective in the client's daily life?

   c. "What has happened?" can be asked in a counseling session when the counselor senses the client is no longer engaged in the process.

5. Avoid operating out of ignorance and fear with regard to the client's spiritual or religious perspective.

6. Be aware of the historical treatment of the client's spiritual or religious group in the United States.

7. Ask the client to teach you about his or her spiritual or religious perspective.

8. Turn to other counselors for support in addressing the religious or spiritual concerns of clients.

Now we examine specific Western or Monotheistic religions and how they may impact counseling. Each religion has a general description of its current state, an overview of its beliefs including its historical development (Figure 3.1), and possible impact of these beliefs in counseling.

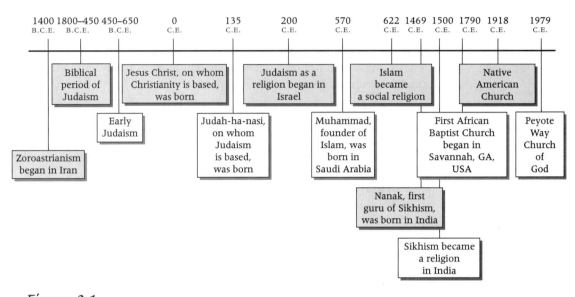

Figure 3.1

Timeline of Western Religions

Judaism

Of the major world religions, Judaism is the oldest and the first to focus on believing in one God (Schiffman, 1999). There are 5,996,000 Jews in North America (Encyclopedia Britannica, 2001) and about 13 million Jews in the world (Schiffman, 1999). Most Jews live in the United States. A few Jewish congregations, consisting of a few thousand people, immigrated to America in Colonial times, and later immigrants were encouraged by the Bill of Rights' freedom of religion. These early settlers had mainly emigrated from central Europe. Their numbers increased substantially in the nineteenth century, when Jews arrived in the United States mainly from Eastern Europe (DeLange, 2000).

Overview of Beliefs

There is debate about when Judaism actually began, in part because it is a historical religious culture and also because there are diverse forms of Judaism. Some texts discuss the "Biblical Period" of Judaism from about 1800 B.C.E. to 450 B.C.E. that presents the biblical stories as based on eyewitness or historical accounts of events. Others call the period of 450 B.C.E. to 650 B.C.E. "early Judaism" where there were different Judaic worlds that formed Judaism. After this period, the diverse Judaic worlds began to form an "international rabbinic culture" (Jaffee, 1997, p. 20).

Judaism began as a formal religion around the year 200 C.E. with the scholar, saint, and political/religious leader named Judah ha-Nasi, who lived in Galilee. He was born in 135 C.E. His followers called him rabbi, which means teacher. He became Patriarch of Judea and tried to negotiate a peaceful relationship with Rome that occupied Jewish land. He created the six-volume Code, called the *Mishna* (teaching), that covers legal, value, ethical, and worship concerns. The *Mishna* was written by the Tannaim rabbis. These formed the basis of the Talmud—the oral law used to interpret the written law (Torah). The Amoriaim and Seboraim rabbis' discussions, called the *Gemara* (learning), were included with the Talmud. The Talmud was edited by the *Stamaim* (anonymous men), a group of scholars. Currently, the name Talmud usually refers for the combination of the *Mishna* and *Gemara* together. It is not known who compiled and edited it in its entirety (Solomon, 1996).

While prayer is considered communication between the individual and his or her God, Jews also engage in communal prayer that occurs in synagogues. There are three daily services: *Maariv* (*Aravit*)—evening; *Shacharit*—morning; and *Mincha*—afternoon. An additional service, *Musaf,* is observed on Sabbath days, festival days after the morning service, and *Ne'lah* on the day of atonement. These services are focused on two main prayers: *Shema* (three scriptural readings about God's Unity) and *Amida* or *Shemone Esreh* (containing the elements of praise, petitions, thanksgiving; Solomon, 1996). The holidays as described by L. Miller and Lovinger (2000) are:

- The Sabbath (Saturday, a day of rest and rejuvenation).
- Three festivals (Passover—a Spring festival that focuses on the Exodus; Feast of Weeks or Pentecost—celebrates receiving the Ten Commandments; Booths—recognizes the wilderness sojourn).
- The New Year (*Rosh Hashana*).
- The Day of Atonement (*Yom Kippur*).

Hanukkah became more celebrated because it was near Christmas and helped parents with the competition of the Christmas celebration with regard to their children (L. Miller & Lovinger, 2000).

The relationship between Jews and God is one based on love shared between them. There is no official creed of Judaism, which makes it hard to describe this relationship. Jews who do not believe in God are still thought to be Jews, and God is thought of typically as unknowable. The Bible, made up of the books of the Christian Old Testament, is one of Judaism's main texts even though Jews do not necessarily believe it was inspired by God.

While Christianity uses the Old Testament and New Testaments, Jews have not and do not use the Christian Bible (New Testament) as a religious text (Siegel et al., 1995). In American Judaism, God is thought of more as an idea than a supernatural being. Jewish life is usually focused around the family and the community. There are three main denominations: Orthodoxy, Conservatism, and Reform. The latter two are considered modern movements (DeLange, 2000). Reconstructionist Judaism began in 1968 and encourages full equality for women (Solomon, 1996).

God is considered holy and to be obeyed—one to be believed in, loved, and feared. Jews are to be righteous, to be concerned about the well-being of all. They are to avoid evil and do good. Jews believe that people are rewarded or punished after death for their behavior in this life. There is no clear belief about the Messiah or the Messianic Age, although in the Bible it was thought to be a time when the Israeli people would be returned to Israel (Zionism) and there would be justice for all in the world (DeLange, 2000).

Possible Impact of Beliefs on Counseling

Because one may identify with Judaism ethnically rather than religiously, a counselor needs to ask a Jewish client if his or her identification is of an ethnic, cultural, or religious nature. As Siegel et al. (1995) state in their summary of Grossman and Haut (1992): "We range from being secular, areligious, or antireligious Jews, to being casually or occasionally observant of religious customs, to being religiously affiliated and actively observant within a Reform, Reconstructionist, Conservative, or Orthodox congregation" (p. 112). Making this type of self-identity clarification with a client can reduce the tendency of the counselor to assume the presence or absence of religious issues. In addition, understanding the type of Jewish identity may help the counselor determine the amount and type of support or anguish related to the counseling issue presented. For example, a Jewish couple coming for marital counseling may identify as Jewish ethnically while close family members on both sides identify religiously and tell the couple they would have fewer marital problems if they were more religiously involved. Here the marital issues are not of a religious nature, but the religious identification of the couple and their families is related to their issues.

If the client does identify being Jewish religiously, then the counselor needs to know the type of Judaism and the ramifications of these views on their life. For example, an Orthodox Jewish woman may feel caught in very traditional gender roles where she is expected to defer to the male figures of her religion (Siegel et al., 1995). For all religiously practicing Jews, even though Jewish customs and attachment (religious, historical) to Jerusalem and the Holy Land may remain the same, because

Jewish families have lived in various host countries, some customs may be different because of the host country's culture in which they lived (Siegel et al., 1995). An example of this is Yiddish language. Yiddish language is fourteenth- century German with some Hebrew and local language combined. As a result of cultural mixes, the counselor needs to be sensitive to the unique manner in which the Jewish customs are practiced for a client.

Jewish clients may come to counseling because of problems they are experiencing within their family or community. L. Miller and Lovinger (2000) state that Jewish clients may struggle with feelings of responsibility toward family members because of the importance of being responsible for and committed to family. The closeness of family may result in boundaries that are confusing for individuals. Siegel et al. (1995) state that Jewish families are stereotyped as consisting of men who are "gentle scholars" and women who are "selfless mothers." Within this stereotype, marital violence may be missed by the counselor or encouraged to not be discussed outside of the family because of anti-Semitic views. There also may be other marital related struggles. As a result of the Holocaust, there may be a pressure to marry and have children and a discouragement of intermarriage. Due to early customs regarding menstruation and childbirth, both men and women may struggle with a sense of uncleanliness or body shame. For Orthodox Jews, issues with male masturbation and homosexuality may be present because they are not permitted.

In terms of women, Siegel et al. (1995) outline a number of issues facing them. First, when Jewish women came to the United States, they lost their roles outside of the home (e.g., shopkeepers) and respect in the home (criticized for caretaking). Second, negative stereotypes such as "Jewish mother" and "Jewish American Princess" evolved and females were compared to impossible standards of beauty. Third, Jewish girls are traditionally not as valued in a family as Jewish boys. Fourth, women have often been excluded from religious activities. Siegel et al. label the issues facing a Jewish woman as "double oppression" because she experiences sexism and patriarchal views within her religion and sexism and anti-Jewish views from those outside of her religion. If she confronts such issues of sexism or racism, she may experience isolation from others. She may have a tendency then to attribute the cause of her anger or mixed feelings as her fault rather than cause problems for herself or her loved ones within or outside of the Jewish community. Counselors working with a Jewish woman may need to explore these possible gender related issues in terms of her past, present, and future relationship with her religious identity.

Jewish clients may come to counseling because they are experiencing discrimination related to their ethnicity or religious practices in the community in which they live. The counselor working on any types of counseling issues may be well advised to approach the issues with sensitivity for how these issues may be impacted by the Jewish client's experience of discrimination.

Christianity

There are 256,882,000 Christians in North America. This number breaks down into these groups: 69,536,000 Roman Catholics; 69,437,000 Protestants; 4,852,000 Orthodox; 3,260,000 Anglicans; 83,519,000 other Christians; and 34,204,000 unaffiliated Christians (Encyclopedia Britannica, 2001). Christians are the largest world religious group (about 1-billion people) living in Europe, the Western Hemisphere, Australia, Africa, and Asia (Bowdein, 1999). Christianity was brought to the United States in the seventeenth century by individuals who had experienced religious persecution mainly in Europe (McGrath, 1997). The majority of Christians are Eastern Orthodox, Roman Catholic, or Protestant with Roman Catholics being the largest religious group in the United States (Shafranske, 2000).

Overview of Beliefs

Christian beliefs describe God as a father, creator of the world, and a part of a trinity (Father, Son [Jesus Christ], and Holy Spirit). Christians are encouraged to develop a personal relationship with God. One can be reconciled with God by accepting Jesus as His Son and following the Bible (Siegel et al., 1995). The Bible, the main text for the Christian faith is divided into the Old Testament and New Testament (McGrath, 1997). Although the Christian Old Testament contains the same books as the Jewish Bible and the Christian church grew out of the Jewish tradition, Christians believe that Judaism is fulfilled in Christ's life as evidenced in the New Testament (McGrath, 1997). The New Testament contains the gospels, the four books that primarily describe the life of Jesus by four of his disciples, Matthew, Mark, Luke, and John.

Christianity, then, is based on the life and teachings of Jesus Christ and while each Christian group has different beliefs, all Christians focus their views on Jesus Christ, whom they view as their savior, the Son of God (Bowdein, 1999). It is not known exactly when Jesus was born, but his birth is celebrated on December 25. The traditional story of his birth is that he was born to the Virgin Mary in a stable manger in Bethlehem, where she and Joseph, her betrothed, had traveled because of the Roman Census court. His conception is described as divine and at his birth shepherds and wise men visited him. In the Old Testament, there is discussion of a messenger from God who was sent to prepare the way for God. Christians believe this messenger was John the Baptist and that Jesus himself was the human embodiment of God. (McGrath, 1997)

Jesus was baptized as a young man by John the Baptist in the River Jordan and it is then that his ministry began. For 40 days and nights he was alone and confronted with temptations that resulted in his power and glory because he did not succumb to them. Jesus lived in Judea (Palestine) and was seen as a teacher, a healer; and a performer of miracles. He was criticized by Jewish leaders, rejected by the Jews and crucified by the Roman authorities about 30 c.e. Most Christians believe that he was raised from the dead after three days (McGrath, 1997).

Jesus means "God saves" in Hebrew and Christ means "Messiah"; therein lies the description of Jesus Christ as the savior of Christians. Most Christians believe that Jesus was sent into the world by God to save the world and that Christians can be saved from their sins through their belief in Jesus. His death is viewed as freeing humans from the bondage of sin and death and reconciling them with God. Jesus is also seen as following God's will, and Christians view his life as the example of how all people should strive to live (McGrath, 1997). Christians are urged to replicate his behavior during Lent (which comes before Easter, the acknowledgment of his death and the celebration of his resurrection).

Salvation from one's sins is important because most Christians believe in heaven and hell. Heaven is the place where one is happy and living in the presence of God without sin. The traditional view of hell is one where Satan, a fallen angel from heaven, causes sinners to suffer (McGrath, 1997). At the end of each individual's life, God judges the individual's life to determine whether he or she will go to heaven or hell for eternity (Siegel et al., 1995). Belief in Jesus Christ as one's savior results in salvation of one's soul meaning that the individual will go to heaven. Note that Catholics believe in purgatory, which is an intermediate place where individuals can rid themselves of their guilt before going on to heaven.

While the majority of Christians are Roman Catholic, Eastern Orthodox, or Protestant, Catholicism is the largest church of Christianity. The Pope in Rome is the head of the church government. Only men can become Catholic priests because women do not represent Christ's maleness appropriately (Siegel et al., 1995). The Orthodox Church is Greek or Russian and connects strongly with the early Greek church and its liturgy and doctrines. Protestantism stems from the sixteenth-century European Reformation, yet is strongly connected with the early church. Protestant groups include Anglicans, Baptists, Lutherans, Methodists, The Reformed Churches, Evangelicals, and the Charismatic Movement (McGrath, 1997).

Possible Impact of Beliefs on Counseling

The counselor working with a Christian client needs to know to which of the main types of Christianity he or she identifies, as well as the specific group in that category. The counselor then needs to understand how the Christian practices these beliefs and the rituals associated with them. For example, a Catholic client may struggle with issues such as abortion or divorce, two actions that the Catholic church generally forbids. In general, Christians may be concerned about the quality of their relationship with God or if they are living according to the practices of their denomination. Because of the predominance of Christianity in the United States and the integration of that religious perspective in the cultural and legal fabric of the United States, a more extensive review of the beliefs of the Eastern Orthodox, Catholic, and Protestant religions are provided here as well as the possible impact they may have on counseling issues.

For each type of Christianity discussed, the counselor needs to remain sensitive to the diversity of the individual client with regard to the beliefs and practices presented. Also, when working within the context of each religion, the counselor may need to assist clients in integrating their religious views with the reality of their lives as they process their mental health issues. Finally, it may be useful to assess the level of sexism experienced by female clients within the context of their Christianity. For example, Siegel et al. (1995) state that women have had the choice of being like Mary, Jesus' mother, who represents asexuality and being separate from the world or being like Eve in the Garden of Eden (the creation story where God created Adam and from his rib created Eve who later took an apple from the tree of life, thereby, resulting in their being banished from the garden) and produce new babies as a way of saving herself. Such dichotomous perspectives on being female may be difficult and limiting for some female clients in terms of their life choices.

Eastern Orthodox

T. R. Young (2000) provides an overview of the beliefs of this religion:

1. One must be living a holy life to please God.
2. Divorce and remarriage are generally forbidden although there are some allowances for divorce such as abuse.
3. Birth control is left up to the couple although the religious doctrines condemn it.
4. Abortion is not allowed and even has to be considered when the mother's life is in danger.
5. Homosexuality is a sin.

Generally clients may present themselves in counseling as struggling because they are not living a holy life according to their religious beliefs. They may also present struggles with how to live a holy life as they may be addressing specific issues such as divorce, remarriage, birth control, abortion, and homosexuality. T. R. Young (2000) also mentions the importance of finding out if they are first generation immigrants to the United States because their native culture may have more of an influence on their mental health issue and there may be language barriers that need to be addressed in counseling.

Catholic

Shafranske (2000) summarizes some of the clinical issues that may arise for Catholics in counseling. Catholic clients may struggle with these three areas as they attempt to sort out mental health issues in counseling: (1) there is an emphasis in the Catholic faith on personal freedom, (2) the church's moral views, and (3) God's voice to help individuals discern what action to take in a situation.

Shafranske (2000) outlines four areas that may emerge as clinical issues.

1. *Authority:* Conflicts between the individual and the church may be very difficult for the client requiring assistance in helping the client sort out values. Also, the counselor needs to be aware of possible immature attachments to the church by the client resulting in being inhibited, acting out, or having a childlike dependency on the church. Because struggles with authority may substantially impact the other three areas listed here, a counselor would be well advised to do an assessment of a client's attachment level to the church.

2. *Sexual Ethics:* Premarital sex, birth control, and homosexuality are prohibited by the church. In assisting clients with these issues, it may be helpful to encourage clients to find places in addition to the counseling sessions where they can safely address these concerns.

3. *Marriage:* Interreligious marital issues may emerge within the context of children's religious education and not being fully involved in the sacraments. Premarital counseling may assist with these issues, however, if a counselor is currently working with an intermarriage couple, these issues require the same theoretical counseling approach the counselor would use in addressing any marital concerns. Divorce is not an option and one cannot remarry within the church if there is a divorce, however, clients can file for an annulment of the marriage stating that the marriage sacrament is invalid. Separation and divorce issues, then, need to be approached in counseling with an awareness of the seriousness with which they are viewed by the church.

4. *Abortion:* Women who have abortions may be ostracized through the church. Counselors working with women contemplating abortion or working through postabortion issues need to ask the women clients about both their internal dialogue and the external religious messages

they are receiving with regard to the abortion. This same approach applies to working with their heterosexual partners or to parents whose children are struggling with abortion issues.

5. *Suicide:* Suicide is considered a serious offense within the church. As with abortion, when the issue of suicide is raised with regard to a client or the client's loved ones, the counselor needs to sensitively explore the internal dialogue and external religious messages being received.

Protestant

This section of Christianity is described by Keller (2000) as the Mainline Protestants (Episcopalians, Lutherans, Presbyterians, Methodists) and the Upstart Protestants (Evangelical, Pentecostal, Denominations with American Roots—The Church of Jesus Christ of Latter-day Saints (Mormon), Jehovah's Witness, and the Seventh-Day Adventist Church).

The Mainline Protestants consist of the Lutherans, Episcopalians, Presbyterians, and Methodists. McCullough, Weaver, Larson, and Aay (2000) discuss the similarities of these four groups in that they: emerged from Europe's Protestant Reformation in the sixteenth century, were impacted by the liberalism of the twentieth century, and have some basic beliefs in common. The four religions evolved from the Protestant Reformation as follows. The *Lutherans* were led by Martin Luther, who was a German, Roman Catholic monk. Luther believed that salvation comes from the grace of God through faith and that the Bible is the final source of authority, not the church. The *Presbyterian* church was started by Zwingli and Calvin, the latter believing that God has complete control over the individual's life. The *Episcopal* church evolved out of a desire for political changes resulting in the Church of England separating from Catholicism. The *Methodist* church was started by Wesley who began an evangelical movement to renew the Church of England.

The churches were impacted by the liberalism of the twentieth century in three ways. First, they developed a more optimistic perspective on human nature. Second, they began a questioning of scripture (literalism of the Bible) and tradition (distinctions of denominations were not as stressed). Third, they were open to scientific findings.

The common beliefs of the churches may be related to counseling issues of clients. The common beliefs in four areas are:

1. *Marriage:* The churches are tolerant of divorce even though marriage is expected to be lifelong. As a result of this general attitude of tolerance, this may or may not be an issue for clients of these religions.

2. *Sexuality:* Premarital sex is discouraged although it is recognized as occurring outside of marriage. Homosexuality is debated among the

churches. Although premarital sex may not be a concern, the diverse perspectives on whether or not homosexuality is a sin make a difference in whether this is a counseling related issues for clients who are homosexual or bisexual as well as their family members and loved ones.

3. *Contraception:* This is an accepted practice, therefore, there are minimally related counseling issues in this area.

4. *Abortion:* There is a general discouragement of abortion although some exceptions are granted (e.g., saving the life of the mother). Because of the discouragement of abortion, these issues may need to be addressed in counseling in a fashion similarly discussed under the Catholic religion.

Siegel et al. (1995) report that Episcopal, Presbyterian, and Methodist denominations have allowed women to have important roles in the church, such as being involved in social justice issues and being a clergy member. Women in these denominations may find church involvement to be an empowering experience.

The Upstart Protestants consist of the Evangelicals, Pentecostals, and those denominations with American roots—The Church of Jesus Christ of Latter-Day Saints (Mormon), Jehovah's Witness, and the Seventh-Day Adventist Church. Each of these groups is examined separately. The *Evangelicals* consist of the Evangelicals and the Fundamentalist Protestants as described by Thurston (2000). The largest group of churches in this denomination is the Southern Baptist Convention. The Evangelicals are moderately conservative, striving to reform the world, while the Fundamentalists are very conservative, tending to want to separate from the world. Both groups believe that they need to preach and witness to others because Christ will come to earth someday without warning and judge people on the Last Judgment Day determining whether they will go to heaven or hell forever. They tend to be against homosexuality, abortion, extramarital sex, alcohol and drug use, and divorce and remarriage (except when divorce has involved infidelity). The Fundamentalists have a more extreme stance on these issues and tend to encourage obedience to the church. All of these areas, then, may emerge as religious related issues in the counseling session.

While typically Fundamentalists are more suspicious of mental health counselors, Thurston (2000) describes general counseling issues that may arise in working with both Evangelicals and Fundamentalists. Specifically, they may struggle in four ways: (1) concern that the counselor resembles a pastor with whom they had negative experiences, (2) concern that their core religious beliefs may be harmed, (3) concern for how they will appear to others since their problems were not solved within the context of the family or the church, and (4) concern whether or not the counselor is

"saved." The counselor needs to be aware that the client may try to triangu-
late the counselor into his or her struggle with the church hierarchy. Also,
the counselor needs to be aware that the client may try to "save" him or her
if it is perceived that the counselor has not been saved. Specifically with
Fundamentalists, counselors need to be aware of how gender differences
may play out in the authority structure of the counseling sessions (e.g.,
male counselor, female client) due to the hierarchal nature of the church.

Two other general issues may emerge in working with Evangelicals
and Fundamentalists in counseling (Thurston, 2000). There may be a struggle with perfectionism in that they cannot be good enough or do enough to
satisfy God. There also may be a rigidity in thinking and behavior. Specifically the Fundamentalists may bring a bias of behaving authority and being
isolationist while the Evangelicals may have a lot of "don't" rules.

Sloat (1990) outlines dysfunctional roles that Evangelical clients may
resort to in response to their church's stance: rebel, surface pleaser, struggle
(the struggle with the church occurs inside the person), and obedient (negative feelings remain inside the person). The counselor may use these roles
to understand the response style of the client in reaction to the church.

Siegel et al. (1995) discusses some of the impact of the fundamentalist churches on women. The authors state that five negative impacts on
women are:

1. *Fear:* There may be a fear of death and being judged by God causing
   women to focus on serving others and not developing themselves.
2. *Caregiving and Guilt:* Women are viewed as being responsible for everyone's happiness and are made to feel guilty if situations do not
   turn out as hoped, once again, causing women to focus on serving
   others at the cost of not developing themselves.
3. *Powerlessness:* Women have been taught that they are weak and
   therefore, cannot challenge God, do not learn how to judge situations, and are not responsible for decisions.
4. *Isolation:* Sects may keep women isolated in terms of what they read
   and with whom they have contact.
5. *Dualistic Thinking:* The church encourages this type of thinking
   which can be difficult for women who have to live out their lives in
   more complexity.

The counselor can assess these negative impacts on women clients.
Siegel et al. (1995) recommend that counselors help women address their
anxiety under their religious views. The authors also suggest that it may
be helpful for a counselor to respond in religious language to a woman
who speaks mainly in that language. Finally, they suggest that counselors
encourage women to have contact with other women so they are less isolated and more exposed to other ideas and role models.

The *Pentecostal* Protestants are described by Dobbins (2000). This group believes that prayer for the sick and healing are a part of the church and baptism is of the Holy Spirit. Baptism involves the one who is "baptized" (Celebrant), the "baptizer" (Communicant), and the element involved in the "baptism" (Element). These three components are a core part of this religion that applies to baptism in a broad sense. For example, someone who is a believer is the Celebrant, who in the presence of Jesus the Communicant experienced the presence of the Holy Spirit (the Element). The Assemblies of God is one main denomination of this group.

Although there are different types of Pentecostal Protestants, there are some common beliefs:

1. Scripture is infallible.
2. Sex can only occur in marriage.
3. Homosexuality is wrong.
4. Birth control, while okay for a married couple to use, is not to encourage premarital sex.
5. Abortion is opposed.
6. Substance abuse is not allowed.
7. While there are different views on divorce and remarriage, they are generally discouraged.

A client struggling in any of these areas in counseling would potentially have these as religiously related issues.

In addition to these common concerns, Dobbins (2000) reports five more concerns that may emerge with these clients as a part of therapy: (1) They may believe that there is something wrong in their relationship with God if they are sitting in a counseling office; (2) they may feel guilty if something bad has happened to them believing that somehow they have displeased God which is why this has occurred to them; (3) their image of God may be like that of their parents; (4) they may view the body as evil and have sexual issues as a result (e.g., masturbation, repression); (5) finally, they may struggle with managing their anger.

American-Based Denominations

Keller (2000) describes the similarities and differences between the three main churches in this category, *The Church of Jesus Christ of Latter-day Saints (Mormons), Jehovah's Witnesses,* and the *Seventh-Day Adventist Church.* There are two similarities among them: (1) They all began when people believed Jesus Christ was returning to earth and (2) they believe that either God or Christ will rule for a millennium (1000 years) of peace. The differences between them are as follows.

The Mormons believe in:

1. The existence of the Father, Son, and Holy Spirit, but not as one as in the Trinity.
2. Involvement in the world and politics.
3. God speaking through prophets of the Church.
4. The Bible and other texts, for example, *Book of Mormon,* as the Word of God.
5. Spirit gifts.
6. Avoiding the use of specific substances (alcohol, tobacco, tea, and coffee).
7. Using temples to save the dead.
8. The family as a place of practice for the Mormon religion.

Jehovah's Witnesses believe:

1. God (Jehovah) created Jesus and the Jehovah's influence is expressed in what Christians call the Holy Spirit, but that spirit is not a separate entity.
2. In avoiding involvement in the institutions of the world.

Seventh-Day Adventists believe in:

1. The Trinity and the creation of the world from nothing.
2. Avoiding the use of tobacco and alcohol.
3. Acknowledging the Sabbath on the seventh day of the week (sundown Friday up to sundown Saturday).

Ulrich, Richards, and Bergin (2000) provide a history of the Mormon religion. The Mormon Church was founded by Joe Smith, who in 1823 was visited by a spirit who told him where metal plates of ancient spiritual texts were buried. It became an official religion in 1830 when the *Book of Mormon: Another Testament of Jesus Christ* (1981) was published; this book came from divine translation of the spiritual texts through Joe Smith. Ulrich et al. describe the title of the church: "It purports to be a latter-day restoration of the original church established by Jesus Christ among the *Saints,* as his followers were called in the ancient world" (p. 187).

Brigham Young led the Mormons to Utah in 1847 after years of moves across the United States in response to persecution. The Mormon hope was that no one would want the Utah territory because of how hard it was to get there. The largest group of Mormons is still in the Utah-based church that consists of both liberal and conservative Mormons. There is a smaller church of Mormons in Missouri called the Reorganized Latter-Day Saints.

The family is very valued by this religion. Women are considered equal, encouraged to be educated, but also encouraged to not work when their children are young.

With regard to specific religious practices:

1. Polygamy was legally stopped as a religious practice in 1890 by a U.S. Supreme court ruling.
2. Only men can be priests in this religion.
3. Sex outside of marriage, masturbation, acting on homosexual urges, and abortion are prohibited.

There are therapy-related organizations within the church. Latter Day Saints (LDS) Family Services provides counseling. The Association of Mormon Counselors and Psychotherapist (AMCAP) began in 1976 and has its own journal and conventions. Mormons tend to want to see counselors who share their faith. However, Mormons who see non-Mormon counselors may struggle with trust issues or not want to speak about religious concerns with them. Yet, some Mormons might want a counselor who is not of the same faith.

Ulrich et al. (2000) specify the following issues as possibly being religiously connected for Mormon clients:

1. Perfectionism/shame.
2. Authority abuse (both in the church and family in terms of perpetration and victimization).
3. Sexual problems with regard to masturbation, homosexuality, abortion, and sex outside of marriage (note that LDS Family Services provides sexual reorientation therapy for homosexuals).
4. Anger problems (having difficulty expressing it directly).
5. Gender role conflict (sexism).
6. Divorce/single status (divorce is equivalent to failure and it may be difficult to be single in a religion that places such a strong emphasis on marriage).
7. Social pressure/conformity (one might feel intruded on within such a close-knit religion).

Jehovah's Witnesses believe that they are the only ones who will be saved when the world ends. They disapprove of: postsecondary education (unless it is vocational), smoking, oral sex, premarital sex, extramarital sex, and individual interpretation of the Bible. You can be kicked out of the church if you are not active enough or are too deviant. It is a closed, patriarchal society so it is difficult to obtain information about it. Typically, members do not seek therapy. However, individuals may come to therapy after leaving the church and clinical issues facing the client may be related to the personal reactions of leaving such a closed society (Keller, 2000).

R. J. Lovinger (1996) calls Christian Science a New Scripture church. The author states that Christian Science views reality as being spiritual while the physical realm is both evil and an illusion. In this religion, illness is believed to be caused by incorrect thinking so other than allowing for bones to be set, Christian Science practitioners use prayer and helping a person think differently to heal from illness. Typically, these individuals come to therapy only when they are leaving or have left the church, so like Jehovah Witnesses, the client's issues may focus more on the thoughts and feelings related to leaving the church.

Black Church

L. N. Lincoln (1999) reports that black religion in the United States stems from the black experience in America rather than America's religions. In the early years of the Republic, African Americans were allowed limited involvement in the nation's churches. Therefore, the Black Church focused on African Americans getting to know God and refusing to cooperate with slavery. In coping with racism, membership in the Black Church was not "tallied" as in white churches to protect its members from people in the community who did not want them to attend church (C. E. Lincoln & Mamiya, 1990).

Overview of Beliefs. In 1790, Andrew Bryan, a slave, started the First African Baptist Church of Savannah. In 1803, and then again a few years later, a Second African Church and a Third African Church respectively were started by black pastors. In the South during slavery, black churches were legally bound to be supervised by whites. After slavery was abolished, blacks had more authority over their churches, particularly in the north (Raboteau, 1999).

During the time of slavery, worship services were a combination of African traditions and revivalistic Christianity. The preaching style reflected this type of worship and sermons were called "chanted" sermons because their rhythm and tone resulted in interaction between the preacher and the congregation. Because the law kept African Americans from learning to read and write, they had to learn the Bible auditorily. Spirituals and songs brought aspects of the Bible to life. These spirituals in combination with the chanted sermon and the need for conversion were core aspects of this religion. Many of the slaves were Protestant and a few were Roman Catholic and Muslim. The church created a sense of community for the black members. Black churches were political in nature, involved in stopping slavery, and active in the civil rights movement (Raboteau, 1999).

The preaching style, spirituals, and songs are still the same as in the early days of the Black Church. Also, the church remains a core of social support for African Americans in America today. It helps families stay together, provides a release for pain and negative emotions, and provides spiritual support for coping with stress. The church remains a center for politics, spiritual resources, and intellectual discussions as it has always been for African Americans (McFadden, 1999). Participating in the church helps individuals cope as well as identify socially (G. Miller, Fleming, et al., 1998).

Possible Impact of Beliefs on Counseling. When working with African American Christians in counseling, the counselor needs to be sensitive to the sense of community within the Black Church. This community can be used as a resource for the client. The church may provide: social support (for the individual and his or her family); a place to release pain and negative emotions; spiritual support; political support; intellectual discussions; and self-identity.

However, the counselor also needs to determine what kind of information the church is giving the individual with regard to the issues with which he or she may be struggling. For example, the church may have a different view of addiction; rather than seeing it as a disease, it may view it as a moral problem. For an addicted individual in recovery, this could send a confusing message about what is wrong with him or her and what action needs to be taken to break out of the addictive habit.

The counselor may want to use a model to assess the type of Black Church to which the client belongs. Such a model is described by C. E. Lincoln and Mamiya (1990). In this model, the authors describe the Black Church in what they call a six pair dialectical model where there is tension between opposites. They argue that these opposites are present in the Black Church:

1. Priestly functions (worship and spiritual life) and prophetic functions (political and community).
2. "Other worldly" (heaven and eternal life) and "this worldly" (political and social world involvement).
3. Universalism (Christianity) and particularism (racial history).
4. Communal (involvement in all aspects of a member's life) and privatistic (religious needs only).
5. Charismatic (speaking abilities) versus bureaucratic (keeping records of numbers).

6. Resistance (affirming cultural heritage) versus accommodation (being influenced by mainstream culture).

The authors believe that this is a more accurate description of Black Churches because it is broader and more dynamic. It does a better job of accounting for the changes within the church in response to changing social conditions. The counselor can use this model to enhance understanding of the Black Church to which the client belongs rather than be caught in stereotypes of the Black Church.

Morris and Robinson (1996) outline some specific suggestions for counselors in working with clients who belong to the Black Church. They suggest that the counselor examine his or her attitude toward race and religion, which can facilitate an accurate assessment of the role of religion in the client's past as well as current life. They also suggest that the counselor reflect the client's religious terminology. In addition, they suggest the counselor use a systemic approach where the church is used as a potential resource for the client and provide an example of the counselor assigning homework that involves other church members. Finally, they recommend that counselors develop an awareness of how racism can operate within a system.

Islam

Islam is the next most widespread world religion after Christianity, with about 850 million to one billion followers (Gordon, 1991). There are 4,349,000 Muslims in North America (*Encyclopedia Britannica*, 2001).

Overview of Beliefs

Islam became a social religion when Muhammad emigrated during the *Hijra* (Great Emigration) of the Muslims from Mecca to Yathrib in 622 C.E. Prior to the emigration, Muhammad had been a prophet encouraging the belief in one God and the repentance of immorality. After the emigration, Islam developed complex laws and Muhammad became a religious figure (Elias, 1999).

Muhammed was named Ahmad by his mother and Muhammad by his grandfather; his father had died before he was born. When he was a child, he, like typical children in his culture, was sent to a foster family of a nomadic tribe to live. While he was with them, he was visited by two angels who removed his heart and washed it with snow in a golden basin. Following this experience, he returned to Mecca. Shortly after his return, his mother and grandfather died and he was raised by his merchant uncle. As an adult, he worked as a merchant and married when he was 25. At age 40 when meditating in a cave, he was again contacted by an angel, an event that occurred throughout his life. Over time, he became convinced that he was a prophet of God.

The Great Emigration occurred when Muhammad decided to move from Mecca to Yathrib to be a judge because his followers were persecuted by leaders of Mecca. He died in 632 c.e. without a successor. The Islamic leaders after him were called *Caliphs*, which means representative. Typically Muslims (men and women who believe in Islam as a religion), think of the first four Caliphs as the virtuous ones who were "rightly-Guided," which ended when the first Islamic dynasty, the Umayyads, came into power. There are two main sects of Islam based on the subsequent leadership struggles: the *Sunni* and the *Shi at Ali* (or Shi). The latter has three main branches called the Twelvers, Isma ilis, and Zaydis. Most Muslims are Sunni, except for those in Iran, in which the Shi are prevalent (Elias, 1999).

In terms of their beliefs, Muslims view God as a merciful, compassionate being. They typically believe in angels, who are to watch over and keep track of people. They believe that we are judged in the afterlife for our behavior on earth and that at the end of the world everyone is judged to go to heaven or hell. In terms of prayer, the *adhan* is the Islamic prayer call that is given five times a day and can be done in a mosque or at home. Muslims believe that God uses prophets, such as Jesus, to communicate with people. Four scriptures thought to be used by God to communicate are the Torah, the Psalms of David, the New Testament of Jesus, and the Koran (Elias, 1999).

The *Qur'an* (Koran) is the scripture believed to be the literal word of God that was revealed to Muhammad by God (or Allah in Arabic); Arabic is the language used in prayer/liturgy. The Koran provides guidelines on how to live and is written in rhymed prose in 114 chapters (*suras*) and then into verses (*ayat*). It was a number of years after Muhammad's death that the *Fiqh*, was put together. The Koran gives rules on a variety of areas for living, but a system of laws was created for those situations not covered by the Koran. *Fiqh* has four principles (Usul al-fiqh, Principles of Jurisprudence) that can be used to develop rules for living. These four principles are the Koran, *Sunna* (tradition, the way Muhammad lived his life), *Quyas* (analogous reasoning), and *ijma* (community consensus). Only in the absence of clear direction in the Koran can other avenues be explored (Elias, 1999).

Sufism is a mystical form of Islam that views its origins in the Koran and Muhammad. Sufis desire a union with God that eventually results in the individual no longer having an individual identity. Each believer has a master that guides the follower along the Sufi path beginning with repentance of the past, to getting rid of earthly belongings, and joining a monastery. Three main Sufi orders are: Chishti, Mevlevi, and Naqshbandi (Elias, 1999).

In the eighth century, Muslims exerted military power across North Africa (Parrinder, 1971). Slaves brought Islam to the Americas so African Americans today sometimes view Islam as an authentic religion to their people. Islam became more popular during the Civil Rights era because it was seen as coming from Africa and being different from Christianity that was viewed as "white" (Elias, 1999).

Possible Impact of Beliefs on Counseling

In counseling, issues may arise with clients with regard to how to apply traditional practices in a modern world, setting off a debate of what is genuine Islam (McCloud, 1995). Another area of concern is the differences that may exist between Islamic law, which is considered the highest law, and government laws (McCloud, 1995). Counselors may need to work with clients in counseling about how to apply their religion in their current lives and which laws they are most comfortable adhering too. A willingness to listen and process such concerns with clients within a non-judgmental and safe context can facilitate the problem-solving approach of the client.

McCloud (1995) outlines some additional concerns that may emerge in marriage counseling. First, no extramarital sex is allowed. Second, there may be struggle with the Koran's statements of male superiority. Third, women who are educated or divorced may have difficulty finding partners, whereas unmarried women without children would not have difficulty. Divorce is not encouraged, but is allowed in Islam, with men experiencing less stigma than women. A related issue for divorced women is if the marriage was both Islamic and civil in nature because if divorce occurs, this can impact the process. For example, the divorce may not be recognized in Islamic law.

These marriage related concerns may need to be processed in counseling. What does a couple do when an extramarital affair occurs? The counselor may need to assist the clients in determining if and how they can reconcile such an infraction of their religious beliefs. The issue of male superiority may be a struggle in sorting out the gender roles and rights of the couple. The counselor may need to negotiate these issues related to sexism within the context of the marital relationship and the couple's religious beliefs. Women who come to counseling who are divorced may have a need to discuss the stigma they experience with regard to the divorce. The lack of recognition of the divorce within Islamic law may pose an issue for both male and female clients. A counselor needs to be able to work comfortably within the religious perspectives of clients on these views.

With regard to discrimination, there may also be a struggle with a stereotype of an Islamist being connected with some extreme group (McCloud, 1995). Muslims may also struggle with traditional education systems in terms of prayer absence; a competitive, materialistic culture; lack of information about Muslims and Islamic culture; and an orientation toward Judeo-Christian beliefs (McCloud, 1995). Counselors may need to process the discrimination experienced by clients with them in the session. Such stressors may have a significant impact on the counseling issues being addressed.

Zoroastrianism

Three thousand Zoroastrians live in North America. Approximately 200,000 Zoroastrians exist worldwide, largely concentrated in Iran and India (*Encyclopedia Britannica,* 2001). Clark (1998) indicates that the membership numbers are diminishing.

Overview of Beliefs

Zoroastrianism is thought to have begun in 1400 B.C.E. (about 3,500 years ago) within Indo-Iranian tribes who settled in Iran (Dastoor, 1994). There is not agreement as to when and where Zarathustra (Zoroaster), a priest-prophet after whom the faith was named, was born (Clark, 1998). Zarathustra was a priest, hymn composer, and an educated individual who wanted peace after watching Indo-Europeans take cattle from villagers (K. K. Young, 1994).

When he was twenty, Zoroaster went to Mount Ushidarena where he had a spiritual experience during meditation. The god Ahura Mazda showed him how to create the peace, justice, and order he wanted in the world (K. K. Young, 1994). At 30, Zarathustra (he of the Golden Light) began his missionary work (Dhalla, 1998). In his work, *Gathas,* which consists of seventeen short hymns, the philosophy of the religion is expressed along with a description of how the prophet viewed that the world should be (Clark, 1998). The hymns are primarily a discourse between the prophet and the god, Ahura Mazda, which means the Lord of Wisdom (Clark, 1998). The hymns were kept alive orally in ancient Sanskrit until they were converted to writing and are today a part of the religion's scriptures, *Avesta* (Dastoor, 1994). Zarathustra did not really start a new religion, but introduced his ideas into the current religious framework known as Mazdayasnan (Clark, 1998). He encouraged a religion that embodied wisdom and conscience rather than blood/flesh offerings, rituals, and magic (Dastoor, 1994).

Mazdayasnan involved the worshiping of Mazda, the all-knowing, as well as natural forces and other deities (Dhalla, 1998). Zarathustra made his God, Ahura Mazda, the highest deity, the creator and universe ruler, who creates everything through His Holy Spirit. The dualism of this religion appears in the presence of the Holy Spirit (Spenta Mainyu) and the Evil Spirit (Angra Mainyu). The Holy Spirit is the force of life and the Evil Spirit the force of evil and destruction. Each is in conflict with the other until ultimately the Holy Spirit wins when man is resurrected and the universe is renovated. *Asha,* which governs creation, is thought to be the Eternal Truth, the plan used by Ahura Mazda to create the universe. Zoroastrians are to follow Asha rather than *Druj* (the Lie). Because humans have free will, they need to choose between these dualistic forces. The *Amesha Spentas'* (Holy Immortals) doctrine represents six aspects of God's nature that humans should aim to achieve (the first three are masculine and the last three are feminine): (1) Asha Vahista, the Best Order that guides the universe; (2) Vohu Manah, the good mind, which involves being kind to others; (3) Khshathra Vairya, the omnipotence to assist the universe; (4) Spenta Armaiti, which is the devotional power; (5) Haurvatat, spiritual wholeness; and (6) Ameretat, immortality, who are "twins," a spiritual pair bound together (Dhalla, 1998). The three females were to help Ahura Mazda in his fight with Angra Mainyu (K. K. Young, 1994). *Yazatas* are other female deities that were added to the religion to help protect the earth, the water, and the plant life (Young, 1994). Zoroastrianism encourages harmony with nature, light is considered the nature of God, and one is to serve others (Dhalla, 1998).

Originally, women were involved in religious activities, educated in religious schools, and participated in rituals to the point of being priests in minor rituals (K. K. Young, 1994). Religion was home-based and women were its teachers; marrying and having children were seen as sacred and even housework was viewed as prayer. Although men were the head of the household, women had rights socially, economically, and legally. A shift toward male dominance in the religion occurred around the tenth century c.e. when it became a minority religion in Iran and Zoroastrians went to India to escape persecution by Muslims and temple worship became conducted by priests (Young, 1994).

Clark (1998) describes the different types of ceremonies. There are inner (can be attended only by Zoroastrians and occurs in Iranian and Indian fire temples where priests conduct the ceremonies) and outer ceremonies in Zoroastrianism. The three inner ceremonies are *Yasna, Vendidad,* and *Visperad.* Yasna is the highest ceremony that celebrates a certain deity, although praise is given to all spiritual beings. This ceremony is performed at the sun's rising (symbolic of getting rid of darkness) and 72 chapters of the Yasna are recited from memory as rituals are performed. The purpose is to purify the world, strengthen the connection between the spiritual and physical worlds, and praise Ahura Mazda and other good spiritual beings. The orthodox members believe that the world will dissolve into chaos without this daily celebration. The Vendidad is the nocturnal celebration of the Yasna while the Visperad uses the Yasna and the Vendidad in addition to other later material.

Some outer ceremonies are the *Afrinagan* and the *Navjote*. These ceremonies can be held in any clean place and attended by both Zoroastrians and non-Zoroastrians. The Afrinagan is a ceremony where Ahura Mazda is praised for the blessings he has given the world, connections are strengthened between the spiritual and physical worlds, and community blessings are requested. The Navjote ceremony is to affirm a child's belief in the religion. Children are viewed as not being able to "sin" until age seven because they cannot make decisions, so this ceremony is performed around that age. The child receives sacred garments, a *Sudre* (a thin, white garment symbolizing purity and innocence that, according to the orthodox, is always worn under outer clothes except when doing something like bathing) and a *Kushti* (a sacred wool cord that has 72 threads like the 72 chapters of Yasna and is to be worn at all times wrapped around the body three times to symbolize good thoughts, words, and deeds).

Ahuric is all that is good and *Ahrimanic* is "not life," all bad comes from this when it enters the domain of Ahuric. The *menog* is the plane of the spiritual (immaterial) while the *getig* is the physical plane (material). The ethics of Zoroastrianism involve good thoughts, good words, and good deeds. People have free will to choose between ethical behavior, asha or Truth, and falsehood. The Ahura Mazda has given human beings five tools to help them choose Truth:

1. *Mind*—the ability to make a decision.
2. *Desire*—the want of truth.
3. *Conscience*—the acceptance of the revelation as provided by Ahura Mazda.
4. *Perception or Insight*—the intuition or innate intelligence that ritual can help develop.
5. *Wisdom*—the natural result of the use of insight and intuition when focused on the correct path; it is the parallel growth to truth.

Possible Impact of Beliefs on Counseling

Zoroastrians live in Iran and most major Western cities (Nigosian, 1996). Some are not attached to their religion, but are involved in their communities and visit temples, whereas others have blended their views with other religions and still others are very traditional (Nigosian, 1996). Clark (1998) describes two types of Zoroastrians as *Catholic* and *Protestant*. The Catholic ones are the more orthodox ones who believe that ritual is important and the texts from the beginning of the religion throughout its development are important. The Protestant ones are less orthodox, emphasizing less ritual and texts and instead encouraging a focus on the *Gathas*. The Protestant perspective became more popular in India in the nineteenth century when Western scholars and missionaries encouraged this more challenging thinking. This perspective became popular in Iran in the 1920s while rural India and Iran remained more orthodox in their views. Usually, those in the West have made their religious practice fit in with the culture in which they live. Typically, those individuals from Iran have a more liberal perspective (Clark, 1998).

Due to this wide range of religious practices, a counselor would be well advised to assess what Zoroastrianism means to an individual who considers him or herself Zoroastrian. This would mean assessing the level of traditional values and practices as well as assessing the level of community support for the religion and the client's need for that support. In addition, knowing if the client is from an Iranian influence may assist in determining the level of orthodoxy of his or her views.

Clark (1998) provides a summary of the perspective on marriage and family. Marriage is viewed as a place where you can develop your righteous and good thoughts, raise children, and keep property. There is an encouragement to marry within the religion and although forced marriages are rare, a marriage will rarely occur without parental approval. The traditional writings of *Gathas* sent an egalitarian message, but until quite recently, the roles for women have been very traditional (wife, mother, homemaker, low profile in religious life). Recently, room has been made for educated women to express their views although the priesthood is still only open to males. Also, in 1991 the Association of Inter-Married Zoroastrians was formed to support women who have married outside of the religion to be accepted into the religious community with the same rights as a woman who married within the community.

A counselor working with Zoroastrian clients needs to determine how orthodox they are in order to understand the level of traditional gender roles and the impact of these roles on the marriage. Also, being aware of a woman's educational level and her husband and religious community's comfort level with her education may assist in the assessment and treatment of issues. Finally, because of the encouragement to marry within the religion, the counseling needs to be sensitive to inter-marriage issues that may be present.

Clark (1998) outlines five issues specific to young people within the religion. First, their use of tobacco is forbidden from the orthodox perspective. Second, there is a tendency to only wear the sudra and the kushti during religious occasions. Third, the priesthood is not drawing young men. Fourth, if Western born, they tend to not see India or Iran as either their ethnic or spiritual home and may challenge any tendencies of the religion toward solidarity and exclusiveness. Fifth, they may tend to question the rituals that they see encouraging an outdated mythology. These five issues may play out in a Zoroastrian family's dynamics. To be sensitive of these shifts within young people and how they impact the family can assist the counselor in addressing the multicultural issues present.

In general, clients may come to counseling out of a concern for not being in harmony with nature or not being of service to others in a manner that is meaningful to them. They may view themselves as not practicing ethical behavior in terms of their thoughts, words, or deeds, of not choosing truth or using the five tools they have been given. The counselor, by having a basic knowledge of the religion and asking clarifying questions to understand how the client applies the religion to his or her daily behavior, can determine some possible points for interventions on the religious issues.

Sikhism

There are 498,000 Sikhs in North America. Sixteen million Sikhs live in India with the majority in the northern state, Punjab, although communities also exist in England, Malaysia, Singapore, and East Africa (Encyclopedia Britannica, 2001; K. Singh, 1998).

Sikhism is a main religion of India. In the early twentieth century, Sikhs began to move to the United States to work primarily as lumberjacks on the west coast. In 1910, the United States began to block their migration and did not loosen it again until after the Second World War (McLeod, 1997).

Overview of Beliefs

Sikhism started about 500 years ago in India and most Sikhs (disciples) still live there. The first guru was Nanak, born in 1469 c.e. Nine other gurus followed and their words are in the *Guru Granth Sahib,* their sacred text that is written in verse. Nanak's family was Hindu and Hinduism and Islam were the two religions in the Punjab when he was born. When he was 28, Nanak bathed in a river, disappeared, and returned on the third day telling people he had been communing with the Divine One. He left his wife and two children and for 25 years carried his message to others.

Sikhism began as a combination of Hinduism and Islam (Birodkar, n.d.). *Sikh* means student, so all Sikhs are students of God (Fisher, 1994). They believe in God, *Waheguru* (Great Teacher), who reveals himself to individuals who are ready at the time of God's choosing (Breuilly et al., 1997). This God transcends everything and encompasses all other gods and views (N.-G. K. Singh, 1993). K. K. Young (1994) states that Sikhism helped change women's lives because it set marital standards that were not based on material goods and status and it allowed women to be involved in religious activities (studying, being initiated, participating in, and leading). In this religion, men and women are considered equal and are expected to be willing to do any kind of work (Breuilly et al., 1997).

N.-G. K. Singh (1993) describes some of the traditions of Sikhism. Every man has a surname of *Singh* (lion) and every woman has a surname of *Kaur* (princess); each wears a steel bracelet around the right wrist. Men have beards and turbans as a religious symbol. They do not use tobacco or intoxicants, but they do not believe in self-denial. Most are vegetarian, but they will only eat nonslaughtered animals (Breuilly et al., 1997).

Keller (2000) states that the focus of the religion is to make life better on earth and ritual is not the heart of the religion, but service to others is. Rights of passage include birth, marriage, initiation, and death (Breuilly et al., 1997). One such ritual is joining the Khalsa, which was founded by the Guru Gobind Singh to defend the oppressed individuals in the world (Keller, 2000). Individuals can join if they are both spiritually mature and willing to dedicate their life to their religion. Breuilly et al. describe the initiation ceremony of *amrit sanskar.* Boys from fourteen to sixteen years of age join Khalsa, the community of Sikhs committed to defending their faith and the weak. Girls can join, but it is not very common. At the ceremony, each of the five Khalsa members present give one of the "five Ks" to the initiate: *kesh* (uncut hair), *kanga* (comb), *kara* (steel bangle), *kirpan* (small sword), and *kacchera* (short trousers). Festivals are held at the same time as Hindu festivals, but they focus on quiet meditation and activity. Examples of festivals include the birthdays of the nine gurus and *Baisakhi,* a harvest festival. Their temple is called a *gurdwara* and is considered the home of Guru Granth Sahib. Services happen any time without any special worship day (Breuilly et al., 1997).

N.-G. K. Singh (1993) describes their main beliefs. *Seva, sangat,* and *langar* are at the core of their beliefs. Seva means to labor in one's community of *Sikhs.* Sangat is a Sikh community or a gathering of Sikhs. They focus on living their faith with others; community and relationships are very important. They have a strong work ethic. They believe in hard work, equality, being of service to their community, and being involved in the Sikh family. *Langar* is the community meal and kitchen where a vegetarian meal is served by men and women after every major service (Breuilly et al., 1997).

They believe that everyone has divine truth in them, but *Haumai* (egotism) keeps them from experiencing this truth and causes suffering. Reincarnation and rebirth are due to being attached to the material world and you are not reborn if at death God says the person's soul is satisfactorily pure (Breuilly et al., 1997). One can overcome this state by hearing the Divine Word, having faith in the Divine Word, and being full of love. Ultimate Reality can be achieved through five stages: duty, knowledge, art, grace, and truth (N.-G. K. Singh, 1993).

Possible Impact of Beliefs on Counseling

As with the other religions discussed in this section, the counselor needs to evaluate the level of acculturation of the client to determine possible contributing factors to the counseling issues presented. The client may have issues with others in the Sikh community or the surrounding local community, making it difficult to practice the values of community service and involvement. Sikhs may experience some discrimination because they are people of color, their religion is not known, and their dress is different (N.-G. K. Singh, 1993). However, the author also states that people tend to respect them for their hard work and values.

Sikhism may have an impact on counseling if a Sikh comes in to therapy to resolve some inconsistencies in his or her life. In particular, these inconsistencies may emerge in the areas of work, addictive substances, or involvement in the community. For example, the client may be having struggles with working hard at a job because of on-the-job conflicts, thereby resulting in a conflict with his or her values. Or a client may be addicted to nicotine or alcohol and feel a tremendous amount of shame and guilt for not living within the tenets of his or her religion. The counselor must understand how these problems impact the strong sense of work and community and evaluate any recommendations for change within the context of those values.

K. K. Young (1994) states that Sikh women do well comparatively within Indian culture: They are "cherished in private and treated with respect in public" (p. 38). Keller (2000) reports that women and men are considered equal and the family is central in this religion. These strong values may minimize the marital and family issues presented in counseling. However, as with any cultural immersion, the mixing of western values with the religion may result in marital and generational issues that need to be explored further in counseling.

Native American Religions

There are about 2.3 million Native Americans in the United States and they vary as a people in terms of acculturation, tribal groups, and living settings (rural, urban, reservation) (Garrett, 1998). Approximately one-third live on reservations and one-half in areas near the reservations (Cadwalader, 2001). Currently, there are 557 tribes recognized by the federal government and each tribe has its own distinct spiritual practices and beliefs (McFadden, 1999).

Because spiritual practice is seen as a part of daily life that helps one stay in balance, many Native American languages do not have a word for religion (Garrett, 1998).

Overview of Beliefs

Although there are differences in tribal practices, there are some core beliefs that cross-over the various religions. First, spiritual beings and forces are seen as impacting people's lives and it is important for followers to try to find out how to please them and have contact with them for knowledge, power, and protection. Second, a spirit power connects the natural and supernatural worlds and is the source of knowledge and abilities (Bonvillain, 1996). Third, four common values are: (1) "to be," (2) relate well with others, (3) live in the present, and (4) live in harmony in the world. Living in harmony means not being aggressive or competitive, using a neutral person to resolve disagreements, being generous, and believing in an inherent justice in the world. Fourth, medicine is seen as the life force in all living beings (Garrett, 1998).

Usually the beliefs state that the world has always existed, but that it was transformed to its current state. This change is reflected in a discussion of relationships and moral lessons. Native American religions teach that respect should be shown between humans and all other living things and provide prayers and rituals for animals and plants that give life to humans. Native American religions believe that spirit power lives in every living thing and contains knowledge and abilities. This power can be channeled through prayers and songs. It can also live in objects.

Fukuyama and Sevig (1999) discuss the importance of the circle in Native American spirituality. The circle symbolizes the life cycle, the importance of being in balance, harmony, and connection with the life force in all beings, and the Medicine Wheel (the four directions) that looks at the relationship between the body, mind, spirit, and nature. One stays healthy by staying in balance in these directions. As Garrett states (1998), "When we honor the Circle, we honor all that is, all that has ever been, and all that ever will be" (p. 57). People, like nature, develop in cycles, which the circle represents (Garrett, 1998).

Dance is an important part of ceremonies (Bonvillain, 1996). Ceremonies exist for normal life stages such as birth, naming, puberty, marriage, and death that acknowledge and celebrate the transition. There are also healing ceremonies dealing with the issues of suffering and death. Some illnesses may be believed to be caused by spiritual or supernatural concerns. For example, it may be believed that foreign objects must be taken out of the body in order for the individual to be healthy again (Bonvillain, 1996). Everything is viewed as being alive and deserving respect (McFadden, 1999).

Rituals are practiced within one's community and the Creator for the purpose of helping you become more spiritually developed (Fukuyama & Sevig, 1999). Garrett (1998) describes some of the rituals used. The pow-wow celebrates life and relationships between all living beings. The dancing and singing are prayers that result in healing power. The drum represents the heartbeat; the drum is considered to be made up of the actual drum and the singers and thought of as a prayer. The powwow is held in a circle that has been blessed and is representative of beings existing in harmony and balance. A second ritual is called a *giveaway* where you thank others publicly or privately by giving away material items to them. You are respected for giving in an unselfish manner without any expectations. The talking circle allows people to express how they think and feel without judgment from others. A "talking stick" is used to give all people a chance to talk. The facilitator starts by holding the stick and then passing it to others who speak without interruption or criticism. It is usually passed around two to three times and then put in the middle for anyone who wants to say more.

One distinct church in the Native American culture is the Native American Church that began in 1918 in Oklahoma City. Its founder, Jonathan Koshiway, had been influenced by the Church of Jesus Christ of the Latter Day Saints (LDS) (more commonly known as the Mormon Church), Protestantism, and his Native American spiritual culture. Peyote was used in Native American Church religious ceremonies. In some places, this religion can be practiced only by Native Americans who can prove they are at least 25% Native American and their spouses. In 1979, the Peyote Way Church of God was formed by Reverend Immanuel Pardeahtan Trujilo because he did not like the racial discrimination required for membership. This Peyote Way Church of God's doctrine believes that peyote can reveal the divine. Under the 1978 American Indian Religious Freedom Act, the Native American Church can legally use peyote in its religious practices. However, this exemption has not been passed on to the Peyote Way Church of God because the exemption was not viewed by the court as including non-Native use of peyote (Rigal-Cellard, 1995).

Possible Impact of Beliefs on Counseling

If a counselor is addressing Native American religious issues in counseling, it is probably with clients who consider themselves to be Native American by ethnicity. With these individuals it is necessary to determine to which tribe they belong or with which tribes they identify. Then, it is important to find out about their religious practices and how these relate to current counseling issues. Because Native American religions emphasize balance and harmony, the individual may have come to counseling in an attempt to understand how his or her life is out of balance or harmony.

The client may believe that spiritual beings or forces are impacting his or her life in a negative way and may be concerned about how to please them in order to obtain their protection. The client may also report having problems connecting with the spirit power that gives him or her the knowledge and abilities to live. Physical or mental illness may be viewed as being caused by the spiritual realm. Finally, the use of peyote may be a concern for the client if he or she belongs to the Native American

Church or the Peyote Way Church of God. Understanding the tribe and its religious practices may assist the counselor in clarifying these issues and the counselor can promote wellness by working within the client's Native American perspective (Garrett, 1999).

Garrett (1999) offers seven guidelines in working with Native Americans that can facilitate a trusting relationship in counseling:

1. Give a gentle handshake greeting if giving one at all.
2. Be hospitable.
3. Begin the session with silence.
4. Assess the client's acculturation level.
5. Avoid eye contact.
6. Be true to your word.
7. Make suggestions, but do not direct the client.

Case Studies

CASE STUDY 1

You work in a predominantly Christian community. There are no religions practiced in your area outside of Christianity and Judaism. Your client is a middle-aged, educated (has a masters' degree) man who is struggling with the meaning in his life. He has come to counseling to address his "middle age crisis," which includes difficulties in his intimate relationship and at his job. He was raised Christian in the community in which he lives, but he reports that he never felt a kinship with the spiritual beliefs of Christianity or with the church in which he was raised. He wants to explore other religions, but he is not sure how to do this and does not want to upset others around him with his search which is in part why he came in for counseling. He considers counseling to be a safe place where he can explore his views without offending anyone. He sees his mid-life crisis as strongly linked to the lack of meaning in his life and his lack of a "spiritual home." He asks you for guidance on where and how to begin such a search.

1. Before entering into a discussion with him about his search, what would you want to know about his spiritual/religious history?
2. Would you be hesitant to work with him on a spiritual search? If so, what would make you hesitate?
3. How would you expose him to the various religions in this chapter?
4. As he continues his spiritual quest, what role do you see yourself playing in this process?

5. What would concern you about your lack of knowledge or expertise with regard to different religions?

CASE STUDY 2

Your clients consist of a family that has come to counseling because of problems with their adolescent son. They describe their son as rebellious and going against their religious practices. The family is deeply religious and has worked on their struggles with their local religious leaders but this approach has been ineffectual. They have come to you for counseling as a last resort. The family consists of a father, mother, son (of the father), and daughter (of the mother). The other parents of the children are not involved with the daily parenting, but have contact with the children only on religious holidays.

Use the case study with all of the religions discussed in this chapter: Judaism, Christianity, Islam, Zorostrianism, Sikhism, and Native American. Ask yourself the following questions based on _____ (each type of religion):

1. What types of rebellious behavior might the son be engaged in?
2. What might be some marital problems underlying the family issues?
3. How might gender roles be impacting the problem?
4. Does ethnicity of the family affect the problem?
5. Could the family be experiencing discrimination within or outside of their religious community that could be causing more stress on the family system?
6. How would your knowledge of this religious practice guide your clinical work with this family?

Exercises

Exercise 1

1. Which Web site provides basic information on the following religions:
   —Christianity
   —Judaism
2. Which Web site offers access to various chat rooms for the following religions?
   —African American Christian
   —Christianity
   —Zoroastrianism
   —Sikhism

3. Which Islamic Web site provides information on building Muslim character?

4. Which African American Islamic Web site is directed to jail and prison inmates?

5. Which Native American Web site provides information on different tribes?

Exercise 2

1. Which of these religions would you find difficult to work with in counseling? Why?

2. What is the value conflict you are experiencing with this religion?

3. Do you find certain views threatening to your religious views? If so, which ones?

4. Do you find certain views repulsive or offensive? If so, which ones?

5. How would you address these difficulties:

   —With your client?

   —With your colleagues?

   —With your supervisor?

Exercise 3

Go through this process with a discussed religion with which you feel comfortable.

1. Why would it be comfortable for you to work with these views?

2. What is the value congruence you are experiencing?

3. Which views compliment your religious views?

4. Which views do you find congruent with your own views?

5. Could your congruence with these views cause any difficulties in working with your client? If so, what difficulties would you anticipate?

6. How would you address these difficulties:

   —With your client?

   —With your colleagues?

   —With your supervisor?

Exercise 4

Contact a mental health counselor who has experience with integrating spiritual and religious issues in counseling. Use Exercises 2 or 3 in an interview with the counselor and contrast your responses with that of the counselor you are interviewing.

Suggested Readings and Web Sites

Readings

Billingsley, A. (1999). *Mighty like a river: The black church and social reform.* New York: Oxford University Press.

Bonvillain, N. (1996). *Native American religion.* New York: Chelsea House.

Clark, P. (1998). *Zoroastrianism.* Portland, OR: Sussex.

Cole, W. O., & Sambhi, P. S. (1995). *The Sikhs: Their religious beliefs and practices* (2nd ed.). Portland, OR: Sussex.

DeLange, N. (2000). *An introduction to Judaism.* Cambridge, England: Cambridge University Press.

Dhalla, H. B. (1998). The message of Lord Zarathustra. *Dialogue & Alliance, 12,* 5–19.

Elias, J. J. (1999). *Islam.* Upper Saddle River, NJ: Prentice-Hall.

Fisher, M. P. (1994). Sikhing for truth. *Areopagus, 7,* 26–29.

Fukuyama, M. A., & Sevig, T. D. (1997). Spiritual issues in counseling: A new course. *Counselor Education and Supervision, 36,* 233–244.

Garrett, M. (1998). *Walking on the wind: Cherokee teachings for harmony and balance.* Santa Fe, NM: Bear & Company.

McCloud, A. B. (1995). *African American Islam.* New York: Routledge.

McGrath, A. E. (1997). *An introduction to Christianity.* Cambridge, MA: Blackwell.

McLeod, H. (1997). *Sikhism.* New York: Penguin.

Raboteau, A. J. (1999). *African American religion.* New York: Oxford.

Richards, P. S., & Bergin, A. E. (1997). *Handbook of psychotherapy and religious diversity.* Washington, DC: American Psychological Association.

Singh, N.-G. K. (1993). *Sikhism: World religions.* New York: Facts on File.

Solomon, N. (1996). *Judaism: A very short introduction.* New York: Oxford University Press.

Web Sites

Judaism

www.zipple.com. At this Web site, you can obtain information on Israeli history, Jewish people, and guides to Israeli cities. There are many channels on this Web site that focus on food, arts and entertainment, singles' scenes, and sports in relation to Judaism. You can also learn Hebrew and Yiddish. This site may be viewed as more current and less traditional in its focus.

www.4judaism.com. This site describes how to become involved in Judaism, provides an overview of Jewish beliefs, traditions, holy days, Jewish organizations, rites of passage, and higher education.

www.jewsforjudaism.org. This Web site was organized in response to the efforts of missionaries and cult groups to convert Jews. It offers counseling services, classes, and seminars as well as a calendar of events with regard to speakers. It also has two forums: one on Judaism, spirituality, and traditions, and another related to differences between Christianity and Judaism.

Christian Based

www.christianitytoday.com. This Web site has information on churches/ministries, Christian life, schools/jobs, communities (that focus on women, marriage, parenting, singles, teens), chat rooms almost every hour and some that focus exclusively on women, as well as a Christian travel center.

www.suite101.com/welcome.cfm/christian_women. This Web site includes information on politics and minorities, healthy living, regional humor, articles for Christian women, current news, and links to other Christian women Web sites that focus on programs for women such as those in domestic violence situations or who are pregnant.

www.christianity.net.au. This Web site is designed for individuals who are interested in obtaining basic information on Christianity, Jesus, and the "meaning of life." Short audio talks on Christianity are also available. The site features an interactive component where one can ask a missionary a question and receive a Christian perspective on current issues. Individuals can order a free copy of the New Testament from this site.

The Church of Jesus Christ of Latter-Day Saints (Mormons)

www.mormons.org. This extensive site explains the beliefs and practices of the Church of Jesus Christ of Latter-Day Saints such as how the Mormons should live their lives, articles of faith, scriptural writings, and interfaith relationships. The site includes Young Men and Women's Corners and a Singles' Corner, LDS humor, and a response to outside criticism.

www.lds.org. This is the official site of the Church of Jesus Christ of Latter-Day Saints; providing explanations on basic beliefs, scripture and gospel. It also offers church history, publications, and family resources.

www.geocities.com/SouthBeach/ponte/5279. At this site you can find a description of the LDS church, pictures of important LDS sites, hymn pages, a chat room, and Mormon humor.

Jehovah's Witness

www.jehovahs-witness.com/forum/. This Web site includes a variety of chat rooms, for example, a place for Jehovah's Witnesses from around the world to meet, sources of entertainment, news and events, health, and so on.

www.watchtower.org. This is the official site of the Watch Tower Society, the legal arm of the Jehovah's Witnesses. It includes information on their beliefs and activities, current topics, and sources for Jehovah's Witness publications.

www.jw-media.org. This is the Web site of the public affairs office of the Jehovah's Witness. It explains their defense of human rights, current events worldwide, the role of Jehovah's Witnesses in society, and so on.

Black Churches

www.churchfolk.com. This Web site offers an interactive Internet site for the African American Christian community. There are a variety of chat rooms (children, adults, pastors, singles); a focus on Christian education (Bibles, study programs); church folk recipes; calendars of events, festivals, sermons, plays; information on historically black schools and colleges; and links to African American churches.

www.ame-today.com. This Web site provides an examination of the African American Methodist Episcopal church. There is information on its history, chat and discussion groups, audio sermons and meditations, as well as sermon helpers and inspirational stories.

Islam

www.islamworld.net. This extensive Web site provides a substantial amount of information about Islam. This Web site has a special section devoted to non-Muslims that provides information about Islam and the process of becoming Muslim. The *Koran* has been translated into different languages on this site. The site also provides prayers, the Islamic calendar, and information on fasting, the role of women, and how to build Muslim character.

www.addawah.com. This Web site provides past and current scholarly articles, events, publications, monthly quotes, relevant news, recommended reading, and links to other sites about Islam.

www.isprin.com. This Web site provides information about Islamic beliefs and is dedicated to debating with Christians on major areas where viewpoints differ from Islam.

African American Islam

www.noi.org. This Web site includes a Nation of Islam study center, a self-improvement study course, and articles and speeches by Louis Farrakhan. There is general information on the history of the Islam nation and the Muslim program. Also included are events and announcements related to Islam.

www.geocities.com/mikailtariq. This Web site is an introduction to Islam that is particularly focused on jail and prison inmates. Here, information is provided on how one can become a Muslim as well as information on the religion and its groups in America. There is discussion on topics such as drug use, crime, and sexual behavior.

www.islam.org/mosque/Intro_Islam.htm. This Web site introduces Islam to non-Muslims. It provides very basic information in an easy-to-read format.

Zoroastrianism

www.zoroastrianism.com. This Web site describes the basics of the religion including explanations provided by Zoroastrian priests. It has links to other sites and includes a religious novel that is popular within this group. It also includes a matrimonial page where individuals are encouraged to describe themselves in order to find a good marital match within the faith in order to save the religion.

www.delphi.com/zoroastrianism1/start/. This Web site is a discussion forum. A summary of discussions is provided. Individuals can begin their own discussion or enter a chat room.

www.zoroastrianism.homepage.com. This Web site provides basic information on Zoroastrianism. Individuals can hear prayers, subscribe to a mailing list, or link up with other sites.

Sikhism

www.sikhs.org. This Web site explains the religion and its principles, origins, and philosophy. It also makes available information on names, essays, the alphabet, lifestyle, and the roles of women.

www.sikhnet.com. In this Web site, information is focused on the culture of Sikhism. There is a live chat room that has strict rules for entering that include identifying yourself and either being a member, being referred by a member or faxing copies of identification.

www.srigurugranthsahib.org/. This Web site includes a video, audio, quotations, articles, and information about gurus. This appears to be a site for individuals who are familiar with the religion.

Native American Religions

www.native-american-online.org. This Web site is by Native Americans for Native Americans. There is a chat room that is open to anyone regardless of race or religion. There are also job listings, stories, poems, and food recipes available.

www.press-on.net. This Web site is maintained as a Native American newspaper dedicated to exposing corruption and demanding accountability from state and federal governments.

www.geocities.com/heartlandprairie/8962/index.html. This Web site allows the viewer to click on the tribe or nation to obtain specific information about that tribe. There are many links to other sites.

Eastern Religions

Chapter Objectives

1. What are the main Eastern religions?
2. Which religions are closely related in philosophy?
3. What are issues that may arise as counseling issues in relation to the different religions?

Overview

This chapter examines Eastern religions. Once again, each of the religions is described in a shortened summary with statistics on the number of individuals in America who practice the religion; Web sites are also provided; and the possible impact of these religions on clients is addressed. As a prelude to this chapter, you may want to review the section in Chapter 3 that describes the multicultural issues present in counseling individuals with various religious perspectives (Figure 4.1); use the box titled *Questions to Facilitate Counselor Awareness of a Client's Religious or Spiritual Views* on page 48 to facilitate this counseling process.

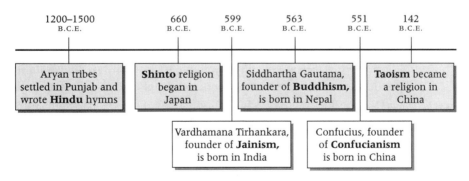

Figure 4.1

Timeline of Eastern Religions

**SUGGESTIONS FOR WORKING WITH
COUNTERTRANSFERENCE**

1. Examine the nature of the discomfort in self in terms of:

   Values.

   Philosophy.

   Own spiritual beliefs.

2. Discuss the nature of the discomfort with a trusted colleague or supervisor with the following questions in mind:

   a. Can I continue to work with this client given my own countertransference issues?

   b. Do I *want* to continue to work with this client?

   c. In working with this client, what limits will I set on how I will address this concern in counseling?

   d. In working with this client, how much of my own struggle with these religious views do I need to share?

   e. If I decide I cannot work with this client, who will I refer the client to for counseling? How will I bring up this referral with my client?

Hinduism

Today, there are 1,266,000 Hindus in North America (*Encyclopedia Britannica,* 2001) and about 750 million in the world, with most of them living in Southern Asia (Gordon, 1991). Hinduism is the main religion in India and Nepal. Hinduism is difficult to define, but most often involves a belief in reincarnation, *karma* (actions have effects), and salvation, which means that one is freed from the cycle of reincarnation and karma (Flood, 1996). In the nineteenth century, some American scholars became interested in Indology, which is the study of Sanskrit texts; Christian theologians began to dialogue about the concepts; and some Westerners began to visit Indian gurus for spiritual truths. The Theosophical Society, which became the channel for numerous Hindu ideas, was founded in New York in 1875 (Flood, 1996). Hinduism also played an important role in India's developing as a nation; it was a bonding force through its symbols and ideals (Shattuck, 1999). Gandhi mixed Hinduism and nationalism resulting in an ethical Hinduism that focused on the principles of tolerance, peace, and truth (Flood, 1996).

In the 1960s and 1970s during the cultural shifts in America, many Indian gurus came to the West (Flood, 1996). Shattuck (1999) expands on this process of immigration. Beginning in the 1960s and continuing through the present day, the Hindu immigrants primarily consist of urban, middle-class, educated professionals who speak English. They move to large metropolitan areas of the United States and the world because India does not have enough job opportunities for them. Generally they move to suburban, middle-class areas.

Overview of Beliefs

Hinduism derives from the word *Hindu,* which was used by Muslims in medieval times to describe people living around the Sindu River and later became the term for everyone living in India. It was between 1500 B.C.E. and 1200 B.C.E. that Aryan tribes came to India and wrote Hindu hymns (Parrinder, 1971). The term *Hinduism* is used to describe the indigenous Indian religion.

Siegel et al. (1995) states that for approximately 3,000 years, Hinduism has believed in social classes, *varnas,* that consist of castes, which have rules of conduct for the individual. It is believed this system was divinely inspired. Untouchables were below the lowest class although this was outlawed in 1950 and all people were legally given the same civil liberties. Yet, Shattuck (1999) reports that for modern, middle-class Hindus, religion and social concerns have merged to the place where they try to help Untouchables and some current gurus say that God is an impersonal Absolute that sees no castes.

There is no god, teacher, or scripture viewed as the core of Hinduism. Hindus hold no uniform perspective of God because they believe each individual is different and, depending on one's level of consciousness, each person will view God differently. Wangu describes the gods of Hinduism as follows: some say there are thousands of Hindu gods while others suggest that only one god, *Brahma,* the World Soul is the only god and the other gods are a part of *Brahman.* The three main sects of Hinduism each focus on one god, Shiva (Shivaism), Vishnu (Vaishnavism), and Shakti (Shaktism) (Wangu, 1991).

Breuilly, O'Brien, and Palmer (1997) state that there are four typical ways to lead a spiritual life, *yogas,* and each person needs to choose the path that best fits him or her. Many individuals also have a guru who guides their path. These four paths are: bakhti (devotion to a specific god), karma (perform good works), jnana (knowledge of the truth behind the philosophy), and meditation and spiritual discipline (systematic training of the body, heart, and mind).

Hinduism has two types of sacred writings as described by Fowler (1997). The first is *Sruti,* which is the oldest and the most sacred teachings.

It is considered to contain universal laws consisting of four *Vedas* and numerous *Upanishads* of which 13 are considered the most important. The second is *Smrti,* which is the most popular literature currently. These teachings use symbolism and mythology to convey its message. Three of the most popular of the Smrti are the: *Mahabharat* (a poem), *Bhagavad Gita* (a story), and *Ramayan* (a story). Each of these three involve an *avatar,* which is God in a human form who acts as an intermediary between God and humans.

Shattuck (1999) describes the Hindu practice as follows. The temple is viewed as the place where the divine and mortal meet because it is where the deity lives and the temple architecture replicates the universe (the Brahma, the three spheres of gods, humans, and demons). Priests perform temple rituals with the core one being the *puja,* which is a daily practice. The *puja* is the ritual worship of the *murti,* the temple icon, where the icon is treated as a royal guest. The ritual is done in an attempt to honor and please the gods so they will offer protection. In addition to temple worship, each home has a place set aside for worship that may involve the worship of a number of deities. The puja is often involved in rituals or sacraments of the Hindu faith that are called *samskaras* (perfecting). These sacraments include birth, *upanayana* (a child becoming a student), female puberty, marriage, and death. There are also numerous festivals connected with deities, two of which are the *Ganesha* (an elephant-headed god who can create and remove obstacles in one's life) and the *Navarati* (a nine-night, ten-day festival at harvest time).

Shattuck (1999) discusses how immigrants from India since the 1960s have needed to accommodate their religious practices. Initially, they were concerned about their culture so there was a tendency to set up cultural centers. As they began to raise families, they began to create temples because in the past grandparents passed on the religion, but this resource was often lost in the immigration process. Some of the accommodations included: having numerous deities in temples, celebrating festivals on weekends rather than their normal calendar dates to facilitate attendance, providing religious camps and classes for children, and publishing educational literature especially in the English language for second generation immigrants. Finally, more women are religious leaders (gurus, priests) because of the shortage of male priests (this tendency occurs in South Asia also, but it is more prevalent outside of South Asia).

Hindus believe in reincarnation, and they believe there are two parts to a person: the *jivatman* (personality that changes and can be reincarnated) and the *atman* (part of self that is permanent, that is Brahman). Hinduism is a way of living (Siegel et al., 1995). All actions are seen as having religious bearing. *Dharma* is the correct behavior in terms of religion and social context (Shattuck, 1999). For example, there is a teaching of inherent emptiness in all things and the practitioner uses this teaching by being aware that all things present in the world have an inherent emptiness and applies this awareness to his or her day-to-day living. They believe that *karma* is what shapes an individual's state in the next life. That is, one's actions and thoughts are saved up and impact the future life. To have good karma, one must live right (i.e, live according to dharma). This means doing what is right for the person, his or her family, class, and the universe. The goal is to end the process of reincarnation, which is what happens when there is no karma, that is when the jivatman has disappeared and only the atman exists. *Moksa* is the liberation from *samsara*, the cycle of reincarnation (Fowler, 1997).

Some other Hindu perspectives are described by Sharma (2000). The cow is considered sacred. Many Hindus are vegetarian. Women may wear red dots, a *bindi*, on her forehead to indicate the third eye import of the *chakra* of intuition or to signify marriage, but now it is worn as an adornment whether a woman is married or not.

Possible Impact of Beliefs on Counseling

As discussed with the previous religions in this section, because many Hindus live in Southern Asia, the counselor may need to do an assessment of the Hindu client in terms of level of acculturation and the impact of it on the client and the presenting issue. In particular, Indian identity may need to be assessed. At the same time, Sharma (2000) cautions counselors to avoid assuming that someone from India is Hindu.

The counselor needs to be aware of the difficulty it has taken for the Hindu client to come in for counseling. There is a strong value that the family takes care of its own and if a Hindu client comes for counseling there is the strong possibility that the problem is quite severe or the person does not feel comfortable addressing it within the family (Sharma, 2000).

In general, the client may struggle with the karma of his or her life. Sharma (2000) states that karma belief implies a belief that you are personally responsible for your life and nothing is random, both of which can be useful in therapy. However, the author also states that some clients may take it passively. Allowing for the expression of concerns may help the counselor and client clarify the goals that need to be accomplished in counseling. The counselor can assist the client in working with the concept of karma by helping him or her choose the right course of actions for his or her life.

The counselor needs to be aware of Indian family tendencies (Sharma, 2000). First, the family tends to value education to the point of having high expectations for children and that medical professions are valued the highest. Second, there may be some guilt by the client for leaving family members in India. The author suggests that counselors assess the developmental level of the client with regard to his or her family in order to understand the impact of family dynamics on the counseling issues presented. Sharma adds that the counselor should always assume that the family is present because of the importance of the family. Therefore, the counselor should evaluate the family's expectations of the client, the current struggle's impact on the family, the client's family role, the level of importance of the family to the client, and the possible resources of the family for client support.

Marriage has typically been arranged, matching individuals from the same area, language, and caste that have compatible horoscopes (Shattuck, 1999). Typically, the woman moves in with the man's family (Sharma, 2000). In counseling a couple, the counselor needs to ask about how they met as a couple in order to understand the historical dynamics of their relationship. Sharma outlines the struggles for men and women from Indian culture in this area since many of them come to America as students and single. Overall, they come from a culture that does not involve dating. Living in the West challenges men because they are typically encouraged to have fun with Western women, but to marry an Indian woman who is chaste while Indian women face needing to marry to have a place in Indian culture, but marriage means that she gives up power. It is also important to assess the level of sexism the woman experiences within the context of her marriage and the local Hindu community.

Siegel et al. (1995) describe the historical dynamics of oppression for Hindu women. In traditional views, the woman can only be saved and fulfilled through her husband who she is to place first in her life. Because the marriage cannot be broken and widows cannot remarry, divorce and remarriage tend to be rare. The male head of the household has absolute power. Men are seen as rational, therefore, they are to be in charge of women. Women are expected to be pure in their thoughts as well as their actions and if they violate this expectation, it may be at a price for both them and their families.

Women are restricted in their movements, economically, and sexually. Movements may be restricted physically or socially as decided by the men in her family. The physical restrictions may include where she can go or how she dresses (the *purdah* covers a woman except for netting over the eyes and the *dupatta* is a scarf that covers the shoulders and breasts and sometimes the head and facial features). Economically, men have all the control including the decision if the woman is allowed to work outside of the home. The Hindu Succession Act (1955) let women inherit the property of their parents, however, there are many loopholes in the act that keep women from this right. Also, a dowry keeps a daughter from her land rights because by giving the dowry gift to the husband and his family, no claim on the daughter's family's land can be made. Sexually, a girl's virginity is important so typically she marries young and if she is not a virgin, for example, she is raped or molested, she is disowned. A counselor working with an immigrant woman may be able to help her by helping her understand what and how religious views are impacting her and her issue(s) in counseling.

Sharma (2000) states that other marital struggles include having children. The couple's status goes up when they have children so childless couples may struggle with this area. A second area of struggle is with the bonds of loyalty: typical loyalty is between mother and son rather than between husband and wife so a male may struggle with his role conflicts as son and husband. Third, the issue of domestic violence may be hidden because of a concern for how it will make Hindus look and the woman may not even be able to consider leaving the marriage as an option.

Other sensitive family issues include sexual abuse and aging (Sharma, 2000). Sexual abuse may be a problem for the same reason as domestic violence, how it makes Hindus look in the broader community. The aging issue may emerge because of the conflict between the traditional Indian view of the aging being respected and the American view of the aging being discriminated against. How the elderly are cared for may be a family struggle.

Other generational issues include no dating being allowed, young adolescent girls not feeling attractive because they do not meet American standards of beauty, and children who are not academic (Sharma, 2000). Also, there may be struggles between the generation in various forms around religious beliefs and practices and young people may not recognize the regional or caste differences (Shattuck, 1999).

Within a community context, Shattuck (1999) notes some additional problems that may be present:

1. A lack of communication between Hindus and mainstream culture. The religion may be seen as a cult. It may also be viewed as made up of extremists. There may be neighborhood concerns about temples or cultural centers in terms of noise levels.

2. Temple support. There may be difficulty obtaining funds for the upkeep of temples. Also, as Hindu communities expand, there may be a tendency toward separation into regional and cultural groups within the larger Hindu community.

These problems may have an impact on presenting client problems because of discrimination and community relations.

Shintoism

There are 55,000 Shintoists in North America (*Encyclopedia Britannica*, 2001). It is difficult to estimate the number of followers accurately both in North America and the rest of the world because primarily the Japanese are involved in this worship and its followers typically follow Buddhist beliefs also (Breuilly et al., 1997).

Overview of Beliefs

Shinto means "the way of the gods (*kami*)" in Japanese: *shin* (kami, gods) and *to* (way) (Picken, 1994). It comes from an agricultural society dating back to 660 B.C.E., (Sprunger, n.d.), but in the B.C.E. 500s when Buddhism came to Japan, it received its name, Shinto, in order to separate it from the new religion (Childress, 1998). It can be seen as a religion because of its ability to bind people together within a society, however, it has no founder, scriptures, belief statements, or guides for behavior, which is why it is thought of as a "way" (Picken, 1994). It is an indigenous religion, a religion of experience that cannot be taught and one that is more community and family oriented than individual. Picken describes Shinto as caught rather than taught, perceived before believed, and felt more than thought.

Picken (1994) provides an excellent summary of Shinto history. Shinto is very bound to Japan, although it can be found overseas among Japanese communities. Japanese ethics are based on Shinto with contributions also coming from Buddhism and Confucianism. Originally, Shinto began as a prehistoric folk religion when the Japanese worshiped *kami,* divine spirits that controlled nature. Ancestors also were worshiped as kami. The kami of Shinto are believed to guard and protect Japan. Shinto is focused on this life being better and having correct relations between the kami and humans (Reader, 1998). Main books that discuss the myths and history of the kami are: *Kojiki* (*Records of Ancient Matters*), *Nihongi* (*Chronicle of Japan*), and *Kujiki* (*Chronicle of Old Matters of Former Ages*) (Northrup, 1998).

Picken (1994) elaborates on the Shinto perspective. Early worshiping was intended to make sure the gods (kami) would look favorably on the world and be helpful to humans since the kami were viewed as being in charge of natural events and as giving and maintaining life. There is not a hierarchy of kami; kami pertains to the essence of the divine that expresses itself in different forms (people, places, animals, rocks, etc.). All of the kami share the same essence, therefore, kami does not mean a number of gods, but rather the essence of the divine expressed in different forms. Shrines are sacred areas built to honor the kami of the location; *jinja,* the place of the kami, means shrine in its literal translation (*jin* means kami and *ja* means place).

Shinto has been kept alive through attitudes and rituals. Unfortunately, Shinto rituals were used by the government to encourage nationalism during the Pacific War (1941–1945) resulting in Shinto being seen as a strong contributing force in the war. However, in reality, some of its priests were not supportive of State Shinto or the war. After World War II, Shinto was not under state control or receiving state support and the choice for practicing the religion became an individual one.

Breuilly et al. (1997) describe some of the festivals involved in Shinto. *Matsuri* means daily worship and being open to the kami by visiting the local shrine or praying or meditating at home at the beginning of the day. However, matsuri also means the Shinto festival where activities (dance, music, chants, prayers) are used to make contact with the kami. One main festival is New Year's Day and a famous one is the Cherry Blossom Festival.

Shinto's main rituals focus on impurity (*tsumi*) and purification (*oharai*). Shinto believes that somehow people came from the kami so the divine is a part of people allowing them to distinguish good from evil if humans are following their basically good nature. *Kannagara* means the natural order law or the way of the kami. People who follow the way know how to live as well as know both the divine and the human. Even though it does not have rules to guide people's behavior, it does have morals and values such as being sincere and honest. They believe the following four parts of the soul (*tama*) are controlled by one spirit: wild, primitive (*ara-tama*), peaceful, refined (*nigi-tama*), happy, creative (*saki-tama*), and mysterious, concealed (*kushi-tama*). The power of the soul is called *tamashii*.

In Shinto belief, humans have the capacity to live with the divine and with nature in harmony, but because impurity distorts this capacity, one needs to become purified. An example of a purification ritual is the *misogi* where one plunges into a freestanding waterfall; Picken (1994) describes it as a union with nature that is immediate: "For the truly adventurous, I suggest making the journey to a mountain shrine to plunge into an ice cold waterfall at midnight with crisp, frozen snow on the ground" (p. xxxii).

Some additional Shinto beliefs are:

1. Humans can see and experience the divine in the midst of life.
2. People need to be thankful and work hard.
3. Humans need to find a purpose (mission) to which they can commit themselves (duty, responsibility) so they can meet their destiny.
4. Death is "simply a stage in a longer process" (Picken, 1994, p. 345).

Picken suggests that Shinto makes six significant contributions:

1. Having reverence for nature.
2. Seeing humans and nature exist in harmony.
3. Lacking a dualistic perspective.

4. Viewing each moment as having value (*naka-ima* means "in the middle of the present").

5. Using purification to renew a person.

6. Emphasizing the process of life and the need for purification.

Possible Impact of Beliefs on Counseling

If a client is Shinto, he or she is probably of Japanese descent. It may be critical for the counselor to determine the level of acculturation of the client in order to understand some of the issues possibly present in day-to-day living related to being Shinto. For example, the client may be receiving pressure from his or her children not to practice the religion in the United States or the client may be in a cultural context where there is no one else practicing his or her religion and may be struggling with a sense of aloneness. This aloneness may be especially heightened in a religion that is so community and family based.

Issues in counseling related to Shinto may relate to a concern that you do not have proper relations with the kami of the area or your ancestors who are kami. These improper relations would reflect impurities that may show up in:

1. Having difficulty distinguishing good from evil.

2. Struggling with being sincere, honest, or thankful.

3. Feeling out of flow with the natural order of life.

4. Having problems seeing the divine in life.

5. Believing that you are not meeting your destiny.

The counselor may need to work with a client on clarifying these concerns and how they can be effectively addressed. These resolutions may need to be framed as related to the purification process that is essential in the process of living.

Jainism

Jainism is the oldest of the Eastern religions and most Jains live in India (Zydenbos, 1993). *Jinas* means spiritual victors and *Jain* means Jinas' follower (Breuilly et al., 1997). In the late 1980s, there were only twenty local Jain groups active in the cities of New York, Chicago, Dallas, and Houston. However, that number grew to three times as many by the mid-1990s, and new temples were added each year (Cort, 1997).

Today, seven thousand Jains live in North America (*Encyclopedia Britannica*, 2001). Over three million Jains live in India and communities are also active in East Africa and Europe as well as the United States and Canada. It is the sixth largest religious group in India (Lal & Lal, 1999). Breuilly et al. (1997) describe the three factions of Jains. The Digambara live mainly in northern India, believe in complete nudity to show no material attachment (although they currently wear robes in public), and will not let women into monastic life because they believe women need to be reborn as men in order to be enlightened. The Shvetambara primarily live in southern India, wear white robes, and allow women into the monastic life. The Sthanakavasi are a small group that focuses on practicing rigorous discipline and no worshiping of images. Breuilly et al. state that the main holidays celebrated are the Mahavira's birth and enlightenment and the Paryushana (eight days of fasting, confessing, and addressing forgiveness issues).

Overview of Beliefs

Hinduism, Buddhism, and Jainism developed at about the same time in the same part of the world and as a result, use some common terms. The founders of Jainism and Buddhism distinguished their views from Hinduism in terms of ritual, sacrifice, and caste (*Hinduism in Transition [600 B.C.–322 B.C.]*, n.d.). Jainism is the oldest of the three religions and does not acknowledge the concept of caste or the practices of deity worship or sacrifice as incorporated in Hinduism (*Hinduism in Transition [600 B.C.–322 B.C.]*, n.d.).

Vardhamana, given the title of Mahavira (Great Hero), the twenty-fourth Tirthankara, was born in India in 599 B.C.E. around the time of Buddha. He lived with his clan for 30 years and then gave up all of his possessions and began to wander with a focus on questions about existence and the universe as well as how to detach from possessions and the birth/rebirth cycle. Twelve years later he obtained a state of perfect omniscience where he was aware of the universe and everything occurring in it at all times. After this experience he began teaching others the five vows of abstaining from violence, lies, stealing, possession, and sex. The ideas of being responsible for your spiritual destiny, separating yourself from your family, karma, and striving for perfect knowledge and release from the world became important concepts in this teaching (S. K. Jain, 1997).

Jainism developed the concept of karma before Buddhism and Hinduism. Your actions produce karma that directs the course of rebirths in the future. Individuals are caught in the birth and death cycle, but we can shape destiny by our karma, which is soul residue from our mental, vocal, and physical actions of the past that will have an impact on our current and next lives. The goal is to get rid of karma so the soul can live forever in bliss. There is no god that created the world or that judges humans (Zydenbos, 1993). The aim of Jainism is to free people from suffering. It is believed that attachment and delusion are the cause of our suffering. Attachment and hatred lead to karma (delusion is at the core of this) and karma is based on birth and death, the cycle that causes misery. The goal is *moksa*, which is a perfect, purified soul, free from impurity and the birth/death cycle (S. J. Jain, 1995). You achieve moksa, a state of bliss, by doing good deeds and letting go of material desires (Breuilly et al., 1997). Emancipation means that you realize your true nature; right knowledge and faith, renunciation, discipline, and yoga are the way to achieve that state. In other words, right knowledge, right belief, and right conduct are the three-fold liberation path (Jain, 1995).

Jainism is a practice of faith and worship; a *Jina* is a person who is victorious over passions and an enlightened man is called a *tirthankara*, the *tirthankas* help men and women cross over to death (Breuilly et al., 1997). There is a code of conduct to guide Jains in this victory over passions. It is considered a natural religion because it looks at what is essential and the characteristics and feelings of people, but it is not a revealed religion because no supernatural being brought it into existence or has power over nature or humans. Rather, nature's laws control the universe. Followers of Jainism do believe that every person has a soul. In Jainism, the universe and time, like Jainism itself, has no beginning or end (S. K. Jain, 1997). It believes in renouncing possessions and being freed from the birth and death cycle (S. J. Jain, 1995). It is strongly rooted in nonviolence (*ahimsa* meaning noninjury) and encourages compassion for all living things (therefore, they are vegetarian). It also teaches that an object has many aspects, so the truth may be or may not be (Gandhi, 1997).

There are five principles in this religion:

1. *Ahimsa*—avoid harm.
2. *Satya*—be truthful (think before speaking with the intent to not harm others).
3. *Asteya*—avoid stealing, greed, exploitation of others.
4. *Brahmacharya*—practice chastity (celibacy for monks and nuns; monogamy and faithfulness for lay followers).
5. *Aparigraha*—material detachment (Breuilly et al., 1997).

Possible Impact of Beliefs on Counseling

As with the Shinto religion, Jains are predominantly connected to a country, in this case, India. Therefore, the counselor working with a Jain needs to assess the level of the acculturation of the client in order to determine the struggle between daily living and religious beliefs. Issues that may be heightened for Jains in counseling are attachment and delusion. Jains may want to examine how they are attached to or deluded in their thinking with regard to certain aspects of their lives. They may view counseling as a way to break out of the binds of attachment and delusion, thereby becoming free of their suffering, free of their karma. In particular, they may be searching for ways to become free of the passions that bind them.

While they may see themselves as having the right knowledge and belief, they may need assistance in counseling with the right conduct. For example, they may be caught in a habitual pattern of behavior such as smoking cigarettes and be unable to quit. Counseling may be a place where they can learn some coping mechanisms to help them break out of this attachment, to help them with the right conduct.

Other counseling issues may focus on some of the other four principles of Jainism: avoid harm, be truthful (think before speaking with the intent to not harm others), avoid stealing, greed, exploitation of others, and practice chastity (celibacy for monks and nuns; monogamy and faithfulness for lay followers). Some counseling issues, such as a marital affair, may be viewed by a Jain as violating all four of these principles. Such a violation of these basic principles of Jainism might result in negative thoughts and feelings related to yourself that need to be addressed in counseling.

Violation of these principles may arise as issues for a family also. For example, adolescents in a stage of rebelliousness may intentionally violate these principles making it difficult for the parents to live with such behavior. As discussed in Chapter 3, these struggles need to be addressed from a family systems perspective.

It may be very important to Jains in counseling that their religious beliefs and daily living behaviors match. In addition, this religion's emphasis on nonviolence may not match the culture in which they live. The counselor needs to assess the level of difficulty for the client to apply such a principle for daily living *within* their daily living. For example, issues may be present around such themes as assertiveness and boundary setting. The client's comfort level in learning such coping skills may need to be carefully integrated within the client's religious perspective in a collaborative fashion between the counselor and the client.

Buddhism

There are 2,445,000 Buddhists in North America (*Encyclopedia Britannica,* 2001) and about 330 million in the world. There also are Buddhists in India, China, Tibet, Korea, Japan, Sri Lanka, Thailand, Burma, Cambodia, Vietnam, Europe, and Australia. Buddhism conforms well to different cultures (Reynolds, 1999, p. 668). Lester (1987) describes the development of

Buddhism. In the late nineteenth century it was revived in India, in the early twentieth century in Southeast Asia when Burma monks revived mindfulness training, in the 1930s in Japan, and in the 1950s in Indonesia.

Lester (1987) also describes how the major forms of Buddhism (Pure Land, Zen and Nichiren Mahayana, Theravada and Tibetan Tantrayana) are all present in the United States. Pure Land came to Hawaii and the West Coast in the late nineteenth century via immigrants from China and Japan. Zen came via a Japanese roshi speaker, Soyen Shaku, at the 1893 World Parliament of Religions. Two of his disciples established centers in San Francisco while another disciple published books in Illinois. Nichiren started in California in 1960. Theravada has been present in the United States since 1966. Tibetan Mahayana came by way of Tibetan refugees who emigrated to the United States starting in 1959. The author also states that the different types of Buddhism tend to draw different types of people: Pure Land attracts Japanese Americans, Meditation (Zen and Tibetan Mahayana) draws highly educated Americans, and Nichiren invites the disenfranchised Americans.

Buddhism began more than 2,500 years ago in India. Buddha was born Siddhartha Gautama in Nepal. Like Jainism, Buddhism distinguished its views from Hinduism in terms of ritual, sacrifice, and caste (*Hinduism in Transition [600 B.C.–322 B.C.]*, n.d.). Buddhist practices vary from Hindu ones and sacrifice and caste are not involved in the religion. Jainism and Buddhism have similar concepts. First, there is the same idea that individuals are suffering due to possession and karma. Second, there is an emphasis on nonviolence in both religions.

Overview of Beliefs

Buddhism was founded by Siddhartha Gautama. The Buddha story that has been told since the second century B.C.E. is that Gautama (C. 563–483 B.C.E.) was an unhappy Indian prince born in Nepal; he married when he was sixteen, and they had a son. At 29, after riding at his father's palace, he saw people suffering and he renounced his royal status to become a wandering monk in search of a resolution of suffering and death. Six years later he became Buddha, The Enlightened One, when sitting under a fig tree refusing to rise until he found the answer to his question (Lester, 1987). After becoming enlightened, he chose to share his enlightenment with others rather than simply end his own suffering. He began his teaching in a deer park (Wangu, 1993). Buddhism does not stem from Hinduism, yet Buddha came from a culture strongly influenced by Hinduism, so some of the terminology used by both religions may be the same. However, Buddha developed a different stream of thought and practice in terms of view of reality.

There are two major Buddhist traditions, *Theravada* and *Mahayana*. Theravada means "the way of the Elders" and follows Buddha's teachings more literally. Mahayana means "the Great Vehicle" (Lester, 1987). The Mahayana tradition has numerous sects, each of which emphasizes a different aspect of Buddhism (Pure Land, Meditation School, Tantric) (Wangu, 1993). Buddhism does not have a god. Although different sects have developed their own creeds and specific ceremonies and rites, common beliefs and works operate throughout the different sects of Buddhism. As a result, it is very adaptive to various cultures (Wangu, 1993). Buddhist literary works include: the Three Baskets (*Basket of Discipline* about the *Sangha*; *Basket of Discourses* about the *sutras,* sermons/stories of the Buddha and devotional songs of nuns; and *Basket of Metaphysics,* which is comments on the Buddhist teachings); the *Jatakas* (tales of the Buddha's former lives); the Way of Righteousness (sayings of Buddha); the *Milindapanha* (questions between two historical individuals); the Lotus Sutra (Buddha teachings of the disciple Sariputra); Chinese Dedication Messages (a message explaining the motivation of the individual who paid for a scripture or sutra copy that was made); Zen Stories (anecdotes about Zen masters); and the Tibetan book of the Dead (spiritual manual to assist lamas in helping a dying person stop the cycle of rebirth) (Wangu, 1993).

Buddha believed that desire is what causes human suffering; therefore, the solution was to eliminate suffering by right thoughts and actions guided by the Eightfold Path, which is an ethical code. These eight areas are the "right" view, intention, speech, action, livelihood, effort, mindfulness, and concentration (Gethin, 1998). They are not stages, but components of your behavior that depend on one another and describe a way of living (Gethin, 1998). Buddha called this view the Middle Way. Buddha prescribed self-denial and meditation as the means to live the right thoughts and actions. Eventually, following the Eightfold Path leads you to *Nirvana,* which is not really heaven, but means "blowing out" hatred, greed, and delusion. When these elements are blown out of the individual, the individual becomes a part of the universe free from suffering. The cause of suffering is seen as karma, that is the words, deeds, and thoughts of the individual impacting his or her current life and future lives by creating an energy force. There is good (meritorious) and bad (demeritorious) karma. This lifecycle of death and rebirth stops when desire has ceased, when the individual is free from karma, rebirth, and suffering (Lester, 1987).

You begin the path to enlightenment and Nirvana by taking refuge in the Three Jewels: the Buddha, the *Dharma* (the law of Buddhism that shows how Nirvana can be reached), and the *Sangha* (the community of monks and nuns teaching the religion). The Buddha's initial teachings consisted of Four Noble Truths:

1. Life is full of suffering.
2. The cause of suffering is human desire.

3. The cessation of suffering is attainable.
4. The eightfold discipline is how you achieve Nirvana.

Taking refuge means to follow the example and to rely on the power of the Three Jewels. It is the result of taking refuge in the Three Jewels that produces good karma (Lester, 1987). Buddhism emphasizes kinship with all living beings, compassion, and wisdom (Wangu, 1993).

Possible Impact of Beliefs on Counseling

Because of the similarity of beliefs between Buddhism and Jainism, there is similarity in their impact on counseling. The similar themes of attachment and delusion with regard to the client's life may emerge. The client may be seeking counseling in order to find a middle way to become free of suffering and karma. The client may also be searching for assistance in learning how to match your religious beliefs and your daily actions. The struggles with assertiveness and boundary setting may also be present due to the religion's stress on nonviolence and the client not being sure how to apply these techniques to daily living situations.

There are a number of ways that Buddhist thinking can impact counseling. Initially, the counselor may need to clarify the type of Buddhism with which the client is involved to understand the emphases of their form of Buddhism. For example, for some Buddhists, Zen stories may be used as a short form of bibliotherapy in order to stress a specific point. In general, the idea that all humans suffer can be helpful for Buddhist clients who think they are alone in their suffering. When clients or counselors become caught in the idea of "measuring" suffering or feel that they are the only ones suffering, this perspective acknowledges that we are all suffering and all have the capacity to break free of it. Counseling can assist the client in finding ways to break out of his or her form of suffering and karma by helping the client find the right thoughts and actions, the Middle Way, through such practices of self-denial and meditation. Finally, knowing the amount and type of community of support clients have or believe that they need to have as they develop spiritually is helpful so it can be determined if this is an issue that needs to be addressed in counseling. For example, knowing who the client's teacher is and what they are hearing from their teacher may assist the counselor in clarifying the client's problems from a Buddhist perspective.

Confucianism

No Confucian groups have been identified in North America (*Encyclopedia Britannica*, 2001). However, approximately six million Confucianists live elsewhere in the world. The majority of them live in East Asia. Those who do live in other places are typically Asian (Hoobler & Hoobler, 1993).

Overview of Beliefs

Confucius lived from 551 B.C.E. to 479 B.C.E., and Confucianism is based on his teachings. He was a descendent of royalty, and his father died when he was three. Early in his life he was a tax collector, and he eventually established a school focused on his teachings. When he was about 50 years old, he left his home state and traveled for the majority of the rest of his life trying to find a ruler he could influence. At the time of his death, he thought he was a failure and described himself as a "hidden orchid." However, he has had great influence on Chinese perspective as a sage and a teacher. Confucianism was the official state religion during the Han dynasty (202 B.C.E.–220 C.E.), and it formed the basis of the educational system for two thousand years. The main texts are the *Five Classics* (basic texts that are the oldest Chinese literature and were edited by Confucius) and the *Analects* (497 verses assumed to be written by the second generation of his disciples). Confucianism shaped the Chinese government as well. Today, these values are evident in a commitment to family, work, and education (Hoobler & Hoobler, 1993).

Confucius focused on a moral code of ethics, humanity, and love. He believed people should live in order and harmony with one another, thereby, developing a system for organizing personal relationships and government. His view was that by understanding your role in life and living by this role, harmony could exist in the family, the government, and then in society. He advocated five virtues: courtesy, magnanimity, good faith, diligence, and kindness. The basic principle of *Jen* is to treat others as you want to be treated. The family was viewed as patriarchal and the link between the person and the culture. This is why three of the human relationships discussed (father/son, husband/wife, older brother/younger brother) focused on the family. The other two relationships are friend/friend and ruler/subject (Hoobler & Hoobler, 1993).

As with Taoism, there is debate over whether Confucianism is a religion. This stems in part from how the Chinese look at religion, which is different from other cultures. In this perspective, religion is a form of education where the purpose is to place and encourage moral values in the person. *Chiao* is a Chinese word that is used for both religion and education. Within this definition, then, Confucianism can be considered a religion, but it has no public worship, no relationship with god, and no creed to follow (Hoobler & Hoobler, 1993). The Confucian Way is a way of living (Berthrong & Berthrong, 2000).

Confucianism is an East Asian tradition that plays itself out in a variety of contexts (philosophy, politics, ethics, culture, religion; Yao, 2000).

Yao also points out that it is a religion of a humanistic type that looks for the sacred in an ordinary, disciplined life; you are to cultivate and transform yourself by fulfilling ethical and moral duties. The Way (*dao*), or the meaning of human existence, is to maintain/restore the world's harmony. These are expressed in the Way of Heaven (yin and yang), Way of Earth (yielding and firm), and the Way of Humans (humaneness and righteousness), three forces that interact with one another. Yao also reports that even though there have been numerous changes in East Asian culture, Confucian ethics are still useful and its religion is a part of spirituality whose moral and spiritual values are still of import. It is a Humanistic philosophy (Berthrong & Berthrong, 2000).

Tan and Dong (2000) state that it encourages a submission to the family, proper relationships between the young and old, and a wife obeying her husband. In particular, children are to obey and respect their parents even after they are married, and the oldest male in the family is the authority figure.

Possible Impact of Beliefs on Counseling

As a result of its inner weaving with East Asian culture, Confucianism may appear in counseling more as a part of a cultural experience for clients rather than as a religion per se from a Western perspective. Clients of an East Asian culture may need to articulate their perspective on the Confucian influence on their lives, and counselors working with those clients need to keep this influence in mind. As G. Miller, Yang, and Chen (1997) state in their discussion of counseling Taiwanese Americans, these traditional values may present in the following behaviors: showing proper and respectful behavior to others, having meaningful relationships, and following authority, structure, and roles. Both the traditionalism of the client and the client's family may need to be examined for bicultural conflicts that can result in passivity, internal shame, and isolation. Issues that may bring this type of client to counseling may be relationship oriented or career and educational (Miller et al., 1997).

The counselor may need to examine how the client is receiving support for his or her Confucian views that are of a religious or philosophical nature. The importance of harmony and the lack of it in a client's life may be of great concern to the client. In addition, the client may be struggling with understanding his or her life role, the living of his or her moral code, and practicing an ordinary, disciplined life that reflects Jen. Finally, the impact of these values on the client's family life need to be examined in terms of their impact on counseling issues. For example, a couple strongly influenced by Confucian ethics may believe they need to follow their parents' wishes, however, their different sets of parents may have different wishes thereby causing marital conflict for the couple.

Although it is not a religion per se, the counselor who has a sense of Confucian ethics can assess the influence of this belief system on clients of Asian American descent in counseling. Such sensitivity can facilitate the assessment and treatment of the client's issues in counseling.

Taoism

There are about 20 million Taoists, most of whom live in Taiwan. In North America, there are about 30,000 (Robinson, 1995). In the previous section on Confucianism, the difficulty of defining religion was discussed. The question "What is Taoism?" (Thompson, 1993) explores the debate of whether Taoism is a philosophy or a religion. Thompson indicates that this distinction is a Western one trying to understand Chinese philosophy and that there is a lack of clarity regarding the definition of Taoism due to these cultural contexts. Although there is a debate regarding whether or not Taoism is a religion, it has had such a strong influence on Eastern religions that it will be included in this discussion on Eastern religions.

Overview of Beliefs

There is no one founder of Taoism as with some other religions. Rather, it has masters who have written about Taoism or about the writings on Taoism. Taoism is believed to have begun in the sixth century B.C.E., but it has also been traced to the Yellow Emperor Huang Di, who is believed to have founded China around 4000 B.C. and who went to the mountains to consult with a wise hermit and returned with information about life and how governments should operate.

Laozi's (also known as Lao Tzu) teachings are a core basis for Taoism. It is unclear if he existed or if he is an amalgam of individuals. A man named Li Ehr, who is thought to be Laozi, which stands for "The Master," lived at the same time as Confucius who was born about 551 B.C.E. He worked in the royal archives of the Zhou dynasty and many people talked with him about his views on religion and politics. Upon deciding to leave the province when he was over 90, he was asked by a guard to write down his wisdom, which became the manuscript, *Tao Te Ching*, The Book of the Way and Its Power. In reality, it is believed that this book of 81 short poems, originally written for rulers, is a collection of works of many people. Zhuangzi was another Taoist master who lived from 369 to 286 B.C.E. His works, *Zhuangzi*, are also debated as to whether he, or a combination of individuals, wrote them. He wrote his perspectives in stories that could be understood by everyday people. A third classic text, *Huainanzi*, "Masters of Huainan," stems from the teachings of eight Taoists who visited the court of Liu Ann, the grandson of the first Han dynasty emperor. It contains a mix of Taoist and Confucianist views.

Taoism became a religion in the second century (142 C.E.) with the appearance of the god, Taishang Iaojun, who is the *Tao*, as well as Laozi's mythological development to Zhang Dao Ling (Kohn, 1993). The religion has many gods. Its followers believe that everything that exists has a god and also views heroes and ancestors as gods. Taoism is similar to Confucianism and Buddhism in that worship services are not practiced creeds that must be believed. Breuilly et al. (1997) report that the most popular gods currently are those that are associated with concerns of childbirth, wealth, and health. The festivals of Taoism center on keeping a balance between the heaven and the earth, caring for the dead by making sure they are buried correctly and therefore are not upset with the living, obtaining mortality for yourself, and keeping the deities alive (Breuilly et al., 1997).

Taoism emphasizes being moral and improving yourself (Hartz, 1993). The author elaborates on the importance of the "three treasures" of life, which are vitality (*jing*, the physical function), energy (*chi'i*, movement), and spirit (*shen*, intellect, spiritual) all of which rely on one another. The physical life as well as the intellectual and spiritual life of a person is important in Taoism. Taoist masters developed acupressure and acupuncture in light of the importance of physical health. Diet, exercise, and meditation also are important. Meditation is thought to extend life and having a long life is important to have an increased chance of being in harmony with *Tao* (Hartz, 1993).

The Tao is indescribable, an order under all that exists, yet, an order that is organic in its form (Kohn, 1993). Hartz (1993) explains Taoism as follows. Tao means "the way," that is the way of nature in Chinese. Tao is thought to be the beginning of everything, the Great Void, that resulted in the One that resulted in the *yin* and *yang* (forces that are opposite) that resulted in the universe's forces of heaven, earth, and humanity. Breuilly et al. (1997) describes the yin and yang as being present in everything in a constant struggle where the yin is the feminine and the yang is the masculine. Humanity is expected to keep a balance between heaven and earth, but people's behavior can upset this balance so prayers and offerings are used to ask forgiveness from the god.

Hartz (1993) explains that nature and its changes are considered to be reflections in earth of a powerful universal force. People who consider themselves to be Taoists try to be in harmony with Tao. Individuals are encouraged to be like nature (i.e., neither right nor wrong, but simply be; Hartz, 1993). People try to live in harmony with others and not confront issues directly (Tan & Dong, 2000). Two main concepts of Taoism include nonbeing and nondoing. Nonbeing means that something is given the space to exist, like the emptiness of a cup, whereas nondoing means doing only actions that are natural and in harmony with the world. Together they support a nonviolent approach to life (Johanson & Kurtz, 1991).

Possible Impact of Beliefs on Counseling

When a client identifies himself or herself as a Taoist, it is important to understand what exactly that means to the individual. Because there are no formal worship services or creeds that one must follow, understanding the client's perspective is critical. Also, it may be helpful to find out what caused the client to identify himself or herself as Taoist. There may be no cultural markers for becoming Taoist, such as studying with a master or being baptized; therefore, an individual may feel hesitant with this self-definition or be challenged with regard to these views.

It may be beneficial to come to understand the views of Taoism with which the client identifies. For example, if the client is concerned with harmony, how does this play out in his or her life? Is the client so concerned with getting along with others that he or she has difficulty setting limits or being assertive? Or if the client believes in self-discipline and regulation, is the client out of balance with this perspective? Also, the client may be concerned with regard to his or her physical life being out of balance in terms of diet, exercise, or meditation.

Finally, it may be helpful to examine how the client finds support for these views. Can the client access a temple or does the client rely on a meditation book? Is the client able to attend some retreats that focus on similar views such as Buddhism? It is important to find out how the client sustains his or her views since the client may feel isolated in a country that has few Taoists.

Johanson and Kurtz (1991) discuss the application of Taoism to counseling. Therapists can use some of these perspectives in counseling. For example, practicing and teaching a client mindfulness requires being aware in the moment. Being aware that life is about change and that we need to work with these changes is important. Lahav (1996) talks about the application of Taoism to counseling, which he calls "philosophical." In this form of counseling, individuals come to know their "lived understanding," which means understanding the statements they make of their views in terms of how they act toward self and their world. In this form of counseling, the client comes to understand his or her philosophy of life by looking at how it is woven into his or her life context.

At this point, it seems appropriate to discuss the relationship between Buddhism, Confucianism, and Taoism in terms of their impact on Asian Americans. Although not all Asian Americans (Chinese, Japanese, Korean, Filipino, Asian Indian, Southeast Asian, and Pacific Islander) are Buddhist, Confucian, or Taoist, the influences of these religions on Asian Americans is strong because they are woven into their culture, their values, their beliefs, and their behaviors. Tan and Dong (2000) speak of cultural tendencies for the counselor to remember when working with this population:

1. Underuse of the services of mental health resulting in problems being more severe when they do come to counseling.
2. Experiencing stigma for having mental health issues (personal or family failure and punishment for sins).
3. Somatizing because of a belief that there is no separation between the mind and the body so if the physical is treated, the emotional problems will disappear.
4. Turning to family first, then community people (elders, leaders in their spiritual community, healers, doctors).

Tan and Dong (2000) also recommend that counselors assess them for the following concerns:

1. Acculturation issues related to losses and role conflicts.
2. Different religions practiced by different family members.
3. Somatization of problems.
4. Secondary status of women.
5. Obedience to parents.
6. Intergenerational conflicts such as a concern for a loss of tradition, involvement in extracurricular activities, and independence by parents.
7. Posttraumatic Stress Disorder among refugees.

The authors suggest that counselors use natural community supports, a problem-solving focus, and collaboration with religious leaders to assist Asian American clients as they address their issues in counseling.

Case Studies

CASE STUDY 1

Your client comes to you stating she is a Taoist. She says that she is having problems in her marriage in part because of her spiritual views. Her partner is Christian, and she attends church with her partner; however, her partner wishes that she were more of a believer in Christianity. Your client believes she can attend the Christian church with her partner without a conflict with her beliefs, but she does not believe that she needs to espouse all the beliefs. Her partner believes that unless they have the same Christian beliefs, they cannot grow together as a couple. Your client says she wants counseling in order to find a balance around these perspectives. She says that her partner will not come in for counseling, but wants her to come in order to "get her head straight." As you listen to the client, you become concerned that throughout the relationship she has had trouble setting boundaries for herself. When you ask her about this situation, she seems to describe herself as "going with the flow" and not seeing the point for small amounts of conflict with her partner. You have had a few sessions with her where both of you seem comfortable with one another and you want to confront her more strongly on this issue of setting some limits with others.

1. List four questions you would ask her to better understand the pervasiveness of her struggle.
2. What would you like to know about her relationship with her partner that could give you information about the struggle she has on setting limits?
3. How would you know if you were challenging what appears to be a personal limitation or her religious perspective on life?
4. How would you address her spiritual views and their impact on her relationship?

CASE STUDY 2

A family comes to you for counseling. The family is concerned about their youngest child who is a boy. They have three children: an adolescent daughter, a latency-age son, and a five-year-old child. They are having difficulties disciplining their son. However, as you talk with the family you pick up both strong religious tones and marital problems. Take each religion discussed in this chapter (Shintoism, Jainism, Hinduism, Buddhism, Confucianism, Taoism) and discuss what are possible issues present for the family in these areas:

1. Marital.
2. Parenting.
3. Acculturation.
4. Discrimination.

Brainstorm how you might approach these issues with the family in a manner sensitive to their religious culture.

Exercises

Exercise 1

1. Which Web site provides basic information on the following religions:
   —Hinduism?
   —Buddhism?
   —Jainism?
   —Shintoism?
   —Confucianism?
   —Taoism?
2. Which Web sites offer chat rooms for the following religions?
   —Hinduism?
   —Confucianism?
   —Taoism?
3. Which Web site is directed to female Buddhists?

Exercise 2

1. Which of these religions would you find difficult to work with in counseling? Why?
2. What is the value conflict you are experiencing with this religion?
3. Do you find certain views threatening to your religious views? If so, which ones?
4. Do you find certain views repulsive or offensive? If so, which ones?
5. How would you address these difficulties:
   —With your client?
   —With your colleagues?
   —With your supervisor?

Exercise 3

Go through this process with a religion discussed with which you feel comfortable.

1. Why would it be comfortable for you to work with these views?
2. What is the value congruence you are experiencing?
3. Which views compliment your religious views?
4. Which views do you find congruent with your own views?

5. Could your congruence with these views cause any difficulties in working with your client? If so, what difficulties would you anticipate?

6. How would you address these difficulties:

—With your client?

—With your colleagues?

—with your supervisor?

Exercise 4

Contact a counselor who identifies himself or herself as a religious counselor. In a dialogue with this counselor, engage the counselor in Exercises 2 and 3. After the interview, compare the counselor's answers to the questions in terms of values, viewpoints, and approaches to addressing difficulties.

Exercise 5

Search for Web sites that interest you regarding different Eastern religions. As you read about these religions, look for similarities and differences between them. Then ask yourself which religions would you be comfortable working with in counseling and why? Which religions would you be uncomfortable working with in counseling and why? How would you work with a religion for which you experience discomfort?

Suggested Readings and Web Sites

Readings

Cort, J. E. (1997). Recent fieldwork studies of the contemporary Jains. *Religious Studies Review, 23,* 103–110.

Flood, G. (1996). *An introduction to Hinduism.* Cambridge, England: Cambridge University.

Fowler, J. (1997). *Hinduism: Beliefs and practices.* Portland, OR: Sussex.

Hartz, P. (1993). *Taoism: World religions.* New York: Facts on File.

Hoobler, T., & Hoobler, D. (1993). *Confucianism: World religions.* New York: Facts on File.

Jain, S. K. (1997). *Glimpses of Jainism.* Delhi, India: Motilal Banarsidass.

Johanson, G., & Kurtz, R. (1991). *Grace unfolding: Psychotherapy in the spirit of the Tao-Te Ching.* New York: Bell Tower.

Lester, R. C. (1987). *Buddhism.* San Francisco: Harper & Row.

Picken, S. D. B. (1994). *Essentials of Shinto: An analytical guide to principal teachings.* Westport, CT: Greenwood Press.

Reader, I. (1998). *The simple guide to Shinto.* Kent, England: Global Books.

Sharma, A. R. (2000). Psychotherapy with Hindus. In P. S. Richards & A. E. Bergin (Eds.), *Handbook of psychotherapy and religious diversity* (pp. 341–365). Washington, DC: American Psychological Association.

Singh, D. (1997). Human harmony through Sangat and Pangat. *Journal of Dharma, 2,* 187–196.
Wangu, M. B. (1991). *Hinduism.* New York: Facts on File.
Wangu, M. B. (1993). *Buddhism: World religions.* New York: Facts on File.

Web Sites

Hinduism

www.indiadivine.com. This Web site explores folklore, natural healing, mystical experiences, meditation, scriptures, culture, traditions, and alternative medicine. The focus of the Web site appears to be less traditional and more spiritual in nature.

Shintoism

www.jinja.or.jp/english/index.html. At this Web site, you can explore the basic terms of the Shinto religion, beliefs, and concepts. This is primarily an informational site for areas such as Shinto priesthood, festivals, worshiping rites, sins, and ethics.

www.egroups.com/group/shintoml. In this Web site, there is a forum for the discussion of Shinto. It focuses on the theory and practice of Shinto and fluent English is not required.

Jainism

www.jainnet.com. This Web site provides an introduction to Jainism in terms of beliefs and traditions as well as a forum to discuss Jainism; however, it is more appropriate for individuals already familiar with this religion.

www.jainsamaj.org. This Web site contains information on temples, saints, history, festivals, and institutions. There are also sections for children and matrimony and links to other Jainism sites.

www.jainsansaronline.com. In this site the philosophy and concepts of Jainism, such as being a vegetarian, are available. It provides information on matrimony, cooking, and news. It also offers free, online courses.

www.jainworld.com. This site might be considered more traditional, where information about the beliefs of Jainism (philosophy, society, literature, education, food, speakers) is available. Also, there is information on how Jains have made contributions to history, yoga, psychology, the environment, and other areas.

Buddhism

www.tricycle.com. This Web site provides an introduction to Buddhism, basic information on Buddhism, the life of Buddha, and general information on meditation. There is also a forum on many different topics. Finally, there is a "personals" section, and information on news and events as well as dharma centers.

www.livingdharma.org/index.html. In this Web site, common misconceptions about Buddhism are discussed, such as it being a pagan religion, that followers must endure grueling meditations, that all Buddhists are required to wear robes, and Buddhism's portrayal by the media. In addition, information on upcoming events, a glossary, children's pages, and youth groups are provided. Finally, it has numerous links to other Buddhist sites.

www.members.tripod.com/~lhamo. This Web site is for women active in Buddhism. It has information on activists, teachers, scholars, and events. Also listed are projects and groups. Dharma teachings available on the net are provided.

Confucianism

http://thespiritualsanctuary.org/Confucianism/Confucianism.html. This Web site provides general information on Confucianism as well as information from Confucian texts, beliefs and practices, analects, and the role of women. This is more of a reference Web site rather than a personal one that involves chat rooms and discussions.

www.chineseculture.about.com. This Web site features a chat room focusing on Chinese culture and customs as well as information about Confucius. One can obtain a free newsletter from this site.

Taoism

www.taorestore.org. This Web site is dedicated to the rebirth and rehabilitation of Tao traditions out of concern that the culture is vanishing. This site explains the religion and provides both a question and answer page and a library.

www.clas.ufl.edu/users/gthursby/taoism/index.htm. In this site, information is available on classical texts, martial arts, language and culture, and acupuncture.

Theoretical Integration with Cultural Implications

Chapter Objectives

1. How might transference provide information on a client's spiritual or religious issues?

2. What are some indicators that countertransference is present in a counseling session?

3. What are the three different types of integration of spiritual and religious concerns in counseling?

4. What are four counseling orientations to incorporating spiritual and religious issues in counseling?

5. How can counselors use their knowledge of their clients' religious or spiritual cultures to insure the welfare of the client is protected through the assessment, treatment, or referral process of counseling?

Therapy Integration

Suffering . . . Certain people adore her and talk about her as if knowing her gives them a special status. Other people despise her; when they see her across the aisle at the supermarket, they look the other way. Even though Suffering is considered a formidable instructor, she is actually quite compassionate. She feels lonely around students who dislike her. It is even more painful to be around those who idealize her. She is proud only because she recognizes the value of her lessons. (Gendler, 1988, p. 31)

As this story implies, your view of suffering impacts how suffering is incorporated into your life. Assisting clients in understanding their lives means assisting them in understanding the suffering that is a component of their lives, the problem that has brought them to counseling, and then integrating this suffering into the framework of their lives. The counselor who has done (and continues to do) his or her work around suffering provides sensitivity to the client on addressing these concerns and making them a part of the client's life. Assisting clients in integrating their suffering into their lives may require a more in depth exploration of the client's and the counselor's spiritual and religious views. To explore these spiritual and religious views, a counselor needs to be aware of counselor and client attitudes that may inhibit such exploration and be prepared to respond to such attitudes.

Kochems (1993) discusses isolationist attitudes by both clients and counselors that may inhibit the exploration of spiritual and religious views in counseling. In terms of clients, the author reports that they may isolate religion in their lives in two extreme forms: In one, religion is kept out of your life and in the other, religion is kept away from others. Both keep the religion from being integrated into your experience psychologically. This individual isolation may also be reflected in an interpersonal isolation in the therapy or a cultural isolation, such as American culture's emphasis on utilitarianism and individualism or psychotherapy's views on objective measurement or reductionistic views. Not to ask a client about religion, then, is to collude with these individual, interpersonal, or cultural isolationist tendencies.

One of the ways to overcome individual isolation attitudes is for the counselor to self-examine, and possibly to examine with the client, a distinction between spirituality and religion. The invitation to such examination could be a question as simple as "Do you have a spiritual presence that could help or does help you in your day-to-day life?" When using this type of question with a client, the counselor would then follow the client's lead and the client's knowledge and concerns regarding spirituality. Factors such as religious beliefs (atheist, fundamentalist) and age may influence this aspect of counseling. For example, the counselor may need to discuss with the parents of the child being seen in therapy the limits the parents want to set around discussing spiritual issues.

In terms of interpersonal isolation, the counselor needs to examine his or her biases around spirituality with a sense of how his or her worldview influences the spiritual perspective. The interpersonal isolationist approach may be avoided by substituting an "O.K. human being" approach (G. Miller et al., 2001). Here the counselor is an Open learner and a Kindred spirit to the client. The counselor approaches the spiritual world of the client with these two emphases in place, thereby allowing for a collaborative, supportive approach in the counseling context. This approach is similar to Abernathy and Lancia's (1998) approach of being open and attuned in the counseling process as discussed in Chapter 2.

Another integration approach that can reduce interpersonal isolation has been called the "3 Rs": refuge, rituals, and resources (G. Miller et al., 2001). Here the counselor looks at the spiritual realm as: a refuge both in- and outside of counseling for the client, a source of rituals that may assist clients in "catching their breath" and learning to care for themselves, and a source of various resources both within and outside of the individual that may sustain him or her in the process of therapy. Framing the spiritual or religious realm of the client in this fashion may assist the counselor in being able to facilitate the integration of the spiritual or religious realm in counseling and reduce interpersonal isolation through a connectedness in counseling with the counselor and out of counseling with a spiritual or religious community with the possible use of rituals within both contexts.

It is legitimate for you to ask about the limits of such open approaches to working with the spiritual and religious realm: Where does a counselor "draw the line" regarding such openness? Cults may be a good example of an extreme situation where a counselor needs to set a limit. Hoge (2000) states that the word "cult" is an example of a word in this area that has different definitions and meanings for individuals. Cults, here, will be defined on the five criteria outlined by Fielding and Llewelyn (1996):

1. The group has a common set of beliefs deviant from mainstream culture.
2. The group is cohesive and cut off from mainstream culture.
3. There is pressure to conform to group norms.
4. The group or the leader of the group is seen as divine.
5. The religion is deviant from the dominant religion.

While it would be unlikely that someone from a cult would come in for counseling because his or her needs are probably being met by the cult (unless they are planning on leaving the cult), a counselor may work with someone who: (a) is connected with someone belonging to a cult (partner, spouse, child, parent), or (b) seems to have "cultish-like" behavior in their group involvement.

In the first example, the counselor may need to begin by understanding the views of the client with regard to the cult involvement. Are they involved in the cult in some way? Is this involvement comfortable for them? If not, what about it makes them uncomfortable? Does any involvement with the cult (direct or indirect) impact the issues that have brought them to counseling? These types of questions will help clarify the extent to which the cult is a problem and possible intervention steps necessary. If possible, it may be most effective for the counselor to keep any struggle regarding the cult with the client. The ambivalent feelings toward the cult can be more readily confronted if the counselor avoids taking a position that causes the client to take the opposite position resulting in a power struggle between counselor and client. Rather, the counselor can ask the client to discuss the pros and cons of such involvement as perceived by the client, leaving the struggle within the client rather than between the therapist and the client. Obviously, if a child's custodial parent(s) are involved in a cult, the counselor needs to consult with a colleague, supervisor, licensing board, agency attorney, or the Department of Social Services regarding if, or what, ethical action needs to be taken in such a situation.

In the second example, the counselor needs to first examine his or her bias toward the "cult." Is it a cult, or is it simply a spiritual or religious perspective with which the counselor is unfamiliar? Encouraging the client to talk more about the group can help the counselor determine if there is a need for concern. Also, the counselor is faced with the value-based decision: Even if the behavior seems "cultish" to the counselor, is it a counseling issue if the client is being helped by involvement in it and the client does not bring it up as a counseling issue? Again, as in the first example, consultation with others in combination with keeping the client active in processing ambivalent feelings can facilitate any confrontation required.

To avoid cultural isolation, the counselor needs to be aware of his or her culture, the culture of the client, and the workplace "culture" with regard to the integration of spirituality. At the end of this chapter, cultural influences of the counselor and the client in general are explored. Some notations about the workplace culture are needed here.

Counseling agencies vary in terms of formal and informal rules regarding the discussion of spirituality. In the United States, for example, there generally is a separation of church and state where counseling agencies, unless specifically labeled a religious affiliated agency, do not typically explore spiritual or religious concerns of clients in depth. For example, a counselor in the United States school setting may need to be very careful regarding words that are used, as well as, techniques used in counseling. While this separation of church and state may have at its basis a commitment to avoid the oppression of religious beliefs, it may also make the exploration of such beliefs difficult or awkward for both counselor and client because of the separation. To reduce such awkwardness, the counselor needs to be familiar with the workplace culture as it relates to discussing and exploring the spiritual or religious area with a client. Understanding the acceptable parameters of your counseling role and the discussion of such a potentially sensitive topic can facilitate the respectful integration of spirituality into counseling. Clarifying dialogues regarding both formal and informal agency policy with colleagues and supervisors can provide a solid foundation on which the counselor can begin a respectful integration of spirituality in counseling. Chapter 7 further explores the ethics involved with clients or their legal guardians around such exploration.

Other spiritual or religious related issues in the workplace culture may be with colleagues or supervisors who are extreme in their personal and professional views on spirituality and religion. These issues may be stated directly or indirectly and may have an important influence on even the discussion of this topic in the counseling setting.

This aspect of the workplace culture is beyond agency policy and involves the "personality" of the workplace as well as the attitudes of other employees. The workplace personality may be one that encourages openness around spirituality or religion. People may openly wear religious symbols, have pictures displayed of religious figures, or have religious literature in the waiting room. Other agencies may be void of such blatant images of religion. If the spiritual or religious area is important to the counselor, from beginning contact (e.g., job interview), the counselor may want to openly discuss this area. The box below provides some examples of questions the counselor may want to ask.

A caution here is that if a counselor raises these questions at a job interview, the counselor risks being stereotyped as a religious counselor, which may be positive or negative. Such a stereotype may result in the counselor experiencing undesirable expectations of his or her behavior. It may also result in the counselor not obtaining the job if the stereotype is negative.

Perhaps the safest approach for the counselor is to enter the job interview with an awareness of environmental cues that encourage or discourage such discussion. Based on the information obtained through observation, the counselor can shape the questions in the box to more sensitively fit the situation.

Colleagues and supervisors will vary in their openness to the spiritual or religious area being addressed in counseling. Casual conversations with others at the agency may elicit information that the counselor can

---

QUESTIONS TO ASK IN DETERMINING AGENCY OPENNESS TO EXPLORATION OF SPIRITUALITY

1. Because the spiritual and religious area is important to me as a counselor, could you tell me how open the agency is with my discussing this area with clients as we work on their mental health concerns?

2. What are the limits of the agency as I explore these areas with clients in the context of counseling?

3. What are the formal agency policies regarding the discussion of the spiritual or religious realm in counseling?

4. How much does your agency collaborate with local spiritual and religious leaders as you work with people in counseling?

find useful in determining how open they may be about this area in counseling clients. However, there may be a point at which a counselor needs
to directly let others know how important it is to him or her to discuss
such concerns in counseling. Such directness can be beneficial for the
counselor and the agency in three ways:

1. The counselor does not need to feel as though he or she is "sneaking
   in" the spiritual or religious perspective in counseling.
2. By being open, the counselor may role model the safety of such dialogue within the setting.
3. The agency may be willing to explore this topic as one of import both
   as a staff and as a facility in terms of using it as a healing resource for
   clients.

This discussion of the exploration of spiritual and religious views in
counseling requires an extension of the discussion of the themes of transference and countertransference that began in Chapter 2. Such a discussion is necessary because transference and countertransference can
facilitate or inhibit the exploration of spiritual and religious views.

Transference Issues

Transference means the projections of the client on the counselor. It consists of the client's expectations of the counselor based on the client's history in the world. In counseling, these projections are addressed so that
the client is aware of the projections and has a choice as to how much they
impact his or her interactions with others (Cornett, 1998). These projections on the counselor may be based on:

1. How we look and conduct ourselves as counselors.
2. Our office appearance or location.
3. Our job title.
4. Client knowledge of us (*idealizing transference,* where the client uses
   information to create a story about the counselor so the counselor is
   not a stranger to him or her) (Kochems, 1993).

As a result, of transference, the counselor becomes too much of an ideal,
too valued, and all-knowing, like the client's version of the divine (Spero,
1985), or the counselor receives the client's negative projections in the
form of anger and resentment (Pattison, 1965).

Cornett (1998) defines transference as the "projection of unresolved
familial patterns" (p. 147) that distort the therapeutic relationship in a

manner similar to distortions in other relationships the client has. Shafranske (1996) expands on the concept of transference from a Jungian perspective. The transference is a reflection of how the client relates to his or her unconscious in two ways. First, a client's unconscious is connected with parents, the adults, who showed him or her the world and how to be in it. In counseling, the client typically has similar expectations of the counselor as with the client's parents. Second, the client becomes aware of the unconscious and its impact on his or her perception of the world. Coming to understand and recognize the distortions, initially, with the therapist and then with others, frees the client from the dysfunctional distortions hurting his or her relationships with others (Cornett, 1998).

These distortions can show up specifically in the spiritual realm. Abernathy and Lancia (1998) provide an example of Ms. R who wanted to know the religious faith of her counselor and eventually requested to work in therapy with a counselor of similar religious beliefs because of the intensity of her transference: She believed a "like-minded" counselor could be more helpful to her. In my own work as a counselor, I worked with a client who had strong transference with me in terms of the spiritual realm in counseling. This client believed in what might be labeled "new age spirituality." After four months of counseling, where we developed a strong, trusting relationship, she brought me a crystal and requested I use it to cleanse my "third eye" before my sessions with her so I could work with her more clearly (G. Miller, 2000). She projected on to me the capacity to address her spiritual concerns in an improved fashion if I was assured of being spirituality clear in a manner that was understandable to her. She projected on me an increased ability to assist her as a counselor by participating in a ritual that she viewed as empowering an individual, me. I fueled her transference by agreeing to cleanse my "third eye" before our sessions thereby strengthening her perception of my ability to assist her.

Understanding the impact of these distortions on the spiritual realm of the client, can help the client have more satisfactory experiences with the spiritual realm (Cornett, 1998). In the discussion of a case study with a client who addressed spiritual issues as a part of counseling, Cornett reports:

> *Therapy with James lasted almost three years. At its conclusion, he related that a great deal had changed in his life for the better. In addition to the positive changes in his relationships, his spirituality had moved in a more affirming direction. His god no longer simply viewed James as "stupid." Like James himself, his god became more curious and empathic. (p. 155)*

Even bringing up the topic of spirituality may cause our clients to view us from a specific perspective. Richards, Rector, and Tjeltveit (1999) report that bringing up value issues with clients may result in unnecessary transference reactions such as dependency, confusion, and hostility. Therefore, counselors who bring up the spiritual or religious realm for discussion in counseling need to be prepared for transference issues to arise.

Abernathy and Lancia (1998) describe two types of transference: *interreligious* and *intrareligious.* Interreligious is where the client perceives different religious backgrounds while intrareligious is when the client perceives similar religious backgrounds. Both types of transference can be beneficial or limiting to the therapeutic process. The authors recommend, as described in Chapter 2, that counselors work with transference by being open and attuned and using consultation and interpretation.

Cornett (1998) states that it is important to examine and work through the transference issues of a spiritual nature because these issues can help the client: (a) be more clear about interpersonal relationships, (b) enhance his or her spiritual development, and (c) assist the counselor in understanding how the client views God or his or her concept of a Higher Power. Kochems (1993) states that understanding how a client views God can reflect his or her "defenses, identity, intrapsychic structure, sense of self, and interpersonal relationships" (p. 40). For example, the case study of Ms. Y (Abernathy & Lancia, 1998) describes how the client's view of God resulted in transference. Her view of God was a reflection of her perception of her father. This similar view of God and her father shaped her anticipation of her counselor's reactions toward her. She expected the same reactions from her counselor that she expected from her God and her father as a result of her transference. A wealth of information about the individual, and the possible ramifications on the counseling process, can be obtained by an examination of the client's perceptions of the spiritual or religious realm.

Countertransference Issues

In Chapter 2, countertransference issues in the spiritual or religious realm are introduced. These projections may stem from personal experiences or professional experiences (education, training, supervision) that result in positive or negative biases toward the client's perspectives on spirituality or religion. Abernathy and Lancia's (1998) interreligious (counselor perception of different religious backgrounds) and intrareligious (counselor perception of similar religious backgrounds) framework on countertransference indicate that extreme views on the counselor's part can result in a negative impact on the client's spiritual well-being. These countertransference reactions can result in a misinterpretation of Existential questions, as well as impact the assessment and treatment process for clients. Assessment may be inaccurate and treatment interventions may be inappropriate depending on the degree of bias of the counselor. These issues are further explored within the perspective that the counselor does not need to get rid of countertransference, but simply be aware of it and work with it so it does not harm the client.

West (2000) points out that religion or spirituality cannot be avoided in counseling because this realm is important to many clients. Many clients have spiritual experiences that they need to process in therapy, have had negative experiences with religion that need to be examined, or are facing specific issues such as bereavement or illness that cause them to examine their spiritual or religious views. Yet Kelly (1995) warns that the spiritual or religious dimension of counseling is especially susceptible to reactions outside of counselor awareness. Strong potential for countertransference exists because this area tends to be an intense combination of emotions, significant relationships, significant events, and positive or negative opinions about religion in general or specific religions or practices.

Genia (2000) describes common countertransference reactions as general responses to religiousness, work with evangelizing clients, and experiences of relief when dogmatic clients change their religious views. Cornett (1998) describes two ends of the continuum in terms of countertransference. One is being afraid to explore it because the counselor considers it to be an unknown mystery and the other is when there is no mystery for the counselor because the counselor believes that his or her spiritual or religious views are the "true" ones. Both extremes require that a counselor be willing to explore his or her reactions to the spiritual realm of counseling to find a balanced perspective when addressing the spiritual or religious realm in counseling. If the counselor does not explore the impact of spirituality and religion on his or her personality, there is an increased danger of the counselor's values and beliefs impacting the well-being of the client and therapy through the unconscious processes of the counselor (Burke et al., 1999).

Zeiger and Lewis (1998) describe negative countertransference as occurring in two main ways when counselors appear to have the same religious beliefs as their client's:

1. Their beliefs are different in terms of their source or how they are used.
2. The counselor identifies too strongly with the client's religious struggles.

Spero (1981) states that countertransference may be present when the counselor views the client as irrational, has fantasies of rescuing the client, or has difficulty with the client's questioning with regard to spiritual or religious matters. R. J. Lovinger (1984) described six behaviors that may indicate countertransference:

1. Being involved in discussions of philosophy that are not related to therapy.
2. Becoming involved in arguments with clients about religious beliefs.
3. Avoiding or relabeling client's religious concerns.
4. Translating spiritual or religious concerns into psychological concerns too quickly.
5. Not seeing shifts in the client's religious orientation.
6. Viewing a client's change in religious orientation positively or negatively without the necessary exploration of the meaning behind this change.

Kelly (1995) advises addressing countertransference by being clear about spiritual and religious attitudes and values and having a willingness to consult with experienced colleagues in this area. Spero (1981) suggested that counselors know the difference between belief systems that are mature and immature; examine your views; avoid being anxious or too familiar when working with clients who have similar religious views; know the difference between being committed to religious values and using them to avoid exploring religious areas; focus on those views of the client that are related to therapy. West (2000) recommends that counselors be actively involved in:

1. Examining positive and negative views toward spirituality and religion.
2. Being familiar with literature regarding spirituality and religion as it pertains to counseling.
3. Experiencing a religion different from his or her own.
4. Becoming familiar with assessment issues related to spirituality and religion.
5. Being familiar with spiritual development models.
6. Learning implicit and explicit counseling approaches to spirituality.
7. Understanding differences and similarities between spirituality and counseling.
8. Being involved in a spiritual development of your own.
9. Arranging for supervision in this area.

Supervisors of counselors need to be alert to when spiritual or religious concerns are not being addressed. Cornett (1998) recommends that supervisors explore three areas with counselors who tend not to examine client spiritual concerns: how comfortable the counselor is with not knowing answers, how much the counselor needs to be an expert, and where the counselor may be stuck in his or her own spiritual development.

Types of Integration

The positive relationship between religion, spirituality, and mental health stresses the importance of the integration of spiritual and religious concerns in counseling. Richards and Bergin (2000) summarize the findings of this positive relationship as follows. First, religious coping behaviors assist people during stress and illness. Second, religious people have a greater physical health, life length, surgical recovery, and sense of well-being, as well as more life satisfaction, moral behavior, empathy, and altruism. Third, they have less anxiety related to death, worry, neurotic guilt, depression, and suicidal tendencies; are less likely to divorce, use or abuse alcohol or drugs, have premarital sex or teenage pregnancies (if the religion prohibits premarital sex), and delinquency. This summary indicates the powerful resource religious beliefs and practices can be to clients in counseling and the importance of integrating this area in counseling.

Tan (2000) describes three types of integration of spiritual or religious concerns in counseling: implicit, explicit, and intentional. Implicit and explicit integration are placed at opposite ends of a continuum of addressing these issues in counseling while intentional is more of a description of the counselor's process of integrating these concerns. Specific interventions in relation to the implicit and explicit types of integration are discussed in Chapter 6.

Implicit integration is at the covert end of the continuum. It does not involve the stimulation of discussing religious or spiritual ideas. It also does not use spiritual resources (prayer, texts) in a direct or systematic manner in counseling. Yet, this end of the continuum does recognize that values are a part of counseling and clients may need assistance finding meaning for their lives. Also, clients may discuss concerns related to spiritual or religious perspectives.

Explicit integration is at the overt end of the continuum addressing spiritual or religious views in counseling. The counselor, in a systematic manner, does address spiritual or religious concerns directly as well as use resources such as prayer, texts, religious practices, or referrals to religious leaders or institutions.

Intentional integration is where the counselor decides to use implicit or explicit integration with a client depending on the following factors: the client, the client's needs, the client's problems, the counselor's training, and the counselor's inclinations. The counselor is professional, ethical, and sensitive with regard to the welfare of the client as the spiritual and religious concerns are addressed in counseling. This means that the client has provided the counselor with consent to address these issues based on being informed by the counselor that they are being addressed.

Counselors need to examine where they fit on the continuum of integration. There is no inherently correct way to address these issues in counseling. However, an ethically competent, professional counselor has a clarity of where he or she falls on the continuum and provides clients with this information so that an informed consent to work on these

---

SPIRITUALITY COMPETENCIES

The professional counselor will be able to:

- Explain the relationship between religious, spiritual, and transpersonal phenomena, including similarities between the three types of phenomena.

- Describe religious, spiritual, and transpersonal beliefs and practices from the perspective of diversity.

- Engage in self-exploration of one's religious, spiritual, and/or transpersonal beliefs to foster self-understanding and acceptance of one's belief system.

- Describe one's religious, spiritual, and/or transpersonal belief system.

- Explain one or two models of human religious, spiritual, and transpersonal development across the lifespan.

- Demonstrate empathy for, and understanding of a variety of religious, spiritual, and transpersonal communication.

- Identify limits to one's tolerance of religious, spiritual, and/or transpersonal phenomena; in case of intolerance, demonstrate appropriate referral skills and generate possible referral sources.

- Access the relevance of the religious, spiritual, and/or transpersonal domains in the client's therapeutic issues.

- Be receptive to, invite and/or avoid religious, spiritual, and transpersonal material in the counseling process as it befits each client's expressed preference, when it is relevant for counseling.

- Use a client's religious, spiritual, or transpersonal beliefs in pursuit of the client's therapeutic goals as befits the client's expressed preferences, or admit an inability to do so in such a way that honors the client. (*Spiritual competencies*, 2000, p. 6)

Source: Interaction, Volume 4, No. 1. Copyright Winter 2000. Reprinted by permission of editor.

issues in counseling can be given. The Association for Spiritual, Ethical, and Religious Values in Counseling of the American Counseling Association provides guidelines for spiritual competencies for the professional counselor (see box on page 132).

Cultural Implications

The following is a conversation between a mother and her son:

> [O]ne afternoon on the way home from church I asked her whether God was black or white. A deep sigh. "Oh boy . . . God's not black. He's not white. He's a spirit." "Does he like black or white people better?" "He loves all people. He's a spirit." "What's a spirit?" "A spirit's a spirit." "What color is God's spirit?" "It doesn't have a color," she said. "God is the color of water. Water doesn't have a color." (McBride, 1996, pp. 50–51)

This story emphasizes that working with cultural differences requires the counselor to look for what is common across cultures. In this story, the color of water is the common thread of a Higher Being that crosses over differences of ethnicity. Counselors need to find similar bridges in working with clients who come from different religious or spiritual cultures, but counselors also need to find the idiosyncratic aspects of each client's religious or spiritual culture. Incorporation of the spiritual or religious realm of the client in counseling requires an examination of spiritual or religious values as a part of the client's culture (Bishop, 1992). Bishop states that all cultures have a value system and shared ideas and patterns of behavior, therefore, for a counselor to work effectively with a client's values, the counselor needs to understand the cultural context of those values. Further, Bishop claims that counselors and clients do not necessarily have to have the same religious or spiritual values to work together and that counselors do not have to change their values to work with a client of a different spiritual or religious orientation.

There are four different counselor orientations to addressing religious and spiritual concerns in counseling that may assist counselors in determining an effective cross-cultural counseling approach: rejectionist, exclusivist, constructivist, pluralist (Zinnbauer & Pargament, 2000). The latter two are viewed as being the best approaches for working in the areas of religious diversity.

The authors describe the *rejectionist* approach as one that is similar to Freud's in that it has an antagonistic, reductionistic perspective on religious and spiritual concerns in counseling. Basic concepts such as God are denied existence and religion is viewed as a defense psychologically or a disturbance, thereby preventing religious or spiritual views as accepted for their own merit. The authors report that this perspective can be found in psychoanalytic, behavioral, and existential theories. They summarize three problems with this perspective: difficulty establishing a therapeutic alliance with clients who are religiously committed, inconsistency with research findings regarding religion and mental health, and the importance ethically for mental health professionals to incorporate religious diversity.

The exclusivist approach incorporates the perspective that there is one true reality in terms of religion or spirituality and that counselors need to share the same views as their clients in these areas. This approach also encompasses beliefs such as God existing, behavior resulting from spiritual experiences, and texts of a religious or spiritual nature containing values that are final. The problems with this approach include counselors working with a limited pool of clients or attempting to convert clients to their religious or spiritual perspective, being intolerant of other religious perspectives, and inhibiting the stress coping strategies of clients.

The *constructivist* approach, the first of two presented here that may be most adaptable in working with spiritual and religious diversity, acknowledges that clients can construct their own meaning and reality even if there is not an absolute one. Counselors do not have to be religious to work out of this orientation because the option of having God or a Higher Power as part of one's perspective on the world is up to the client. It is the quality of the client's perspective that matters to the counselor; quality in the sense that the perspective is consistent and helpful in living and coping in one's environment. Counseling is done within the client's perspective, thereby showing a respect for the client's beliefs and values. The criticisms of this approach include the belief that client and counselor need to agree on the worldview spiritually or religiously, the use of religious or spiritual metaphors may seem hollow, the counselor may not be authentic because of a lack of a religious tradition, and given its flexible perspective, it may be difficult to determine what is mentally healthy and what is not in terms of the client.

In the final approach of the *pluralist,* the counselor believes in a spiritual or religious reality but also believes that there are numerous ways to reach that reality allowing for differences among clients and cultures in terms of spiritual or religious perspectives. Here the counselor has his or her own spiritual or religious views and, yet, allows the client to have unique spiritual or religious views. While this approach is a flexible and respectful one, the counselor needs to know himself or herself well in terms of beliefs and biases and their potential impact on counseling. If the counselor and the client share religious or spiritual perspectives, there is a danger that they will assume that they share similar beliefs beyond that which they truly share.

The constructivist and pluralist approaches are important to consider when incorporating spiritual and religious issues in counseling. Their flexibility allows for respectful, yet, effective interventions in counseling in terms of diagnosis, assessment, and treatment of clients. Zinnbauer and Pargament (2000) suggest that counselors examine themselves in terms of their beliefs and values in order to choose the counseling approach that fits them best. The authors also recommend that counselors assess clients in terms of the spiritual or religious realm, obtain training, experience, and knowledge to be able to practice counseling in this area of competence, know their values and beliefs (including a resolution of conflicts in this area and what they view as healthy and unhealthy models in both the psychological and spiritual realms), and provide clients with informed consent. The authors state that informed consent includes providing the client with information on the values and models (as discussed previously) used by the counselor so the client can make an informed decision about counseling.

Bishop (1992) provides guidelines for counselors to include the client's spiritual or religious culture (that embodies the client's values, thoughts, feelings, and behaviors). In terms of a general orientation, Bishop recommends that the counselor be knowledgeable on different religious cultures and how they may overlap with counseling, become involved with different religious cultures, explore one's own religious culture, and include direct discussions of religious culture with clients. These general approaches assist the counselor in making a culturally fair, yet, professionally appropriate, diagnosis of the client's situation. The author recommends that the counselor send messages to the client that religious values can be a part of counseling and be involved in setting goals that include what the client perceives as healthy mental health functioning for himself or herself. This approach increases the likelihood of the client following through on goals set and make the counseling more relevant in terms of the client's day-to-day life.

Counselors need to remember that religious values can be a part of the solution for the client's difficulties as well as a part of the problem. The general approaches discussed in the previous paragraph can also assist the counselor in choosing appropriate treatment interventions. For example, counselors may be able to use the religious community of the client as a resource in counseling. When encouraging a client to use any type of outside resource, it is necessary for the counselor not to make assumptions about the level of support available or potentially available to the client from the community. Rather, it is more effective to assess the level of religious community based on client perception and counselor knowledge of the resource.

This same approach of balancing client perception and counselor knowledge can be applied to referral situations when a counselor believes it is in the best interest of client welfare to be referred to a religious professional in the community for more appropriate assistance with the client's problem. An example of such a referral in my own clinical work was with a female client who struggled with the death of her father. We worked in counseling on her grief issues for a number of sessions until she made resolution with her grief except for a specific concern with regard to her father in the afterlife. Her concern was that he could watch and judge her every move as an angel. I told her we were beyond my professional competence in discussing such a concern and we talked about leaders in her religious community who she trusted and with whom she believed she could safely process her concern. Through our dialogue she decided to talk with a local minister about her issue and since this was her only remaining concern regarding the death of her father, we ended therapy. Although I did not know the religious leaders in her community, I was able to assist her in discussing the different individuals available to her and help her determine those individuals she trusted.

Case Studies

CASE STUDY 1

Your client has come to you for counseling, but has made no mention of his spiritual or religious views. You, as a typical part of your counseling approach, ask the client in the intake interview about his religious orientation. Your client becomes enraged and tells you that he came to counseling to look at his difficulties on the job not to talk about "whether God exists or not." Your client threatens to leave the session and report you to the ethics board of your helping profession.

1. What is your first internal reaction to the client's intense emotional explosion?
2. What is your first comment to your client in response to his comments?
3. What would be your goal with regard to exploring the spiritual and religious realm of the client?
4. Would you consult with a colleague or supervisor following the session? If so, what would you want to address.

CASE STUDY 2

A woman comes in for counseling with regard to her marital issues. During your second session with her, she tells you that her husband had an affair and she forgave him for it. She tells you that according to her religion, she could have divorced him for the affair, but since she had forgiven him and reconciled with him, that divorce with regard to that affair is no longer an option in the eyes of her church. Then she tells you that now she is convinced he is having another affair, but he learned from the last one how to hide it better and she cannot obtain any proof to give to her religious leaders of the second affair and no church action can be taken with regard to the first affair in support of divorce. She tells you also that her husband has openly told her, "You won't catch me this time and you can't divorce me for the last time." She wants to divorce her husband, but she will not divorce him without the approval of her church. She reports feeling trapped and unsure of what to do. This religion is not one with which you are affiliated and you experience countertransference as you listen to her story.

1. What emotional reactions do you have as you listen to her story?
2. What reactions do you have to her church doctrine as she describes it?
3. What would be your therapeutic approach with her issues in counseling?
4. Would you require supervision or consultation with a colleague in order to proceed in therapy with her? If so, what specific areas would you need to address?
5. How would you prevent your countertransference issues from interfering with her therapeutic process?

CASE STUDY 3

You are a counselor and have a professional friend who is also a mental health counselor. He has called you for some advice about a work situation. He is facilitating a counseling group for individuals who have very difficult life situations. He himself relies heavily on his spiritual beliefs to cope with life struggles. A couple of times a few individuals in the group have raised the topic of spirituality in group sessions. Your friend wants to directly discuss this area as a possible source of empowerment for group members, but he is concerned about his clients' reactions, the reactions of his colleagues, and his supervisor's reaction to his raising the topic of spirituality.

1. How would you advise him to proceed in this situation?
2. What concerns would you have for him in approaching this topic with his clients?
3. How could he make the situation most safe for himself and his clients?

Exercises

Exercise 1

Once you have answered the questions under Case Study 1, find a partner and receive feedback on your reactions. Discuss openly the pros and cons of each of your approaches. Remember there are no right or wrong answers, simply different ways of handling a difficult situation.

Exercise 2

Find a different partner and receive feedback on your reactions to Case Study 2. As with Exercise 1, discuss the pros and cons of your approaches. With your partner, develop a list of common issues that are legitimate concerns for this woman in therapy. Discuss how you would handle these concerns without the interference of your countertransference.

Exercise 3

Choose Case Study 1 or 2 to use in a dialogue with a mental health counselor. Summarize you and your partner's reactions to the cases and ask the mental health counselor for feedback on your approaches.

Exercise 4

Create a group of three or four individuals and appoint someone to be a recorder of comments in response to the following:

1. The context in which I counsel (or anticipate counseling in) is (will be): _____.

2. Three cultural barriers to discussing or working with spiritual concepts in my work setting are (may be):

   _____

   _____

   _____

3. Three ways I can overcome these cultural barriers are:

   _____

   _____

   _____

Exercise 5

Take a few moments to answer the following questions for yourself to enhance your understanding of your religious culture.

1. In what religious or spiritual perspective was I raised? (If not raised a specific religion, answer these questions from the perspective of general experiences and people that taught you values.)

2. What did that religion or spiritual perspective teach me in terms of values?

    —How was the concept of a Higher Power portrayed in religious or spiritual services, texts, and various other materials?

    —What did I learn about me as a person from that religion or spiritual perspective, for example, how am I to act if I am "good" or what is "bad" behavior?

    —What did I learn about what would happen to me if I were "good" or "bad"?

    —What did I learn about how to treat myself?

    —What did I learn about how to treat others?

    —What did I learn about forgiveness toward myself and others?

    —What did I learn about the world and how it works?

3. What is my current spiritual or religious community?

    —How is it different from that of my childhood?

    —How is it similar from that of my childhood?

    —Within this culture, what are the concepts of:

        —A Higher Power (God)?

        —"Good" or "bad" behavior?

        —Consequences of being "good" or "bad"?

        —How to treat myself?

        —How to treat others?

        —Forgiveness?

        —How the world "works"?

4. The person in my childhood who most embodied the "good" values of my spiritual or religious culture was _____ because _____ . As an adult, the person who best embodies the "good" values of my spiritual or religious culture is _____ because _____.

5. How do these values play out in my personal life? My professional life?

6. How do my spiritual or religious cultural experiences impact how I work as a counselor today?

Exercise 6

1. Explore the terms "transference" and "countertransference" in regard to religion and spirituality. Look for common issues raised in both areas as well as suggestions on how to handle these issues in counseling.

2. Examine the resources on the Internet for counselors interested in religious or spiritual cultures of their clients. How can such resources be found? What makes it difficult to locate them?

Suggested Readings

Cornett, C. (1998). *The soul of psychotherapy.* New York: Free Press.

Randour, M. L. (Ed.). (1993). *Exploring sacred landscapes.* New York: Columbia University Press.

Tan, S.-Y. (2000). Religion and psychotherapy. In A. E. Kazdin (Ed.), *Encyclopedia of psychology.* Washington, DC: American Psychological Association/Oxford University Press.

West, W. (2000). *Psychotherapy and spirituality.* Thousand Oaks, CA: Sage.

Zeiger, M., & Lewis, J. E. (1998). The spiritually responsible therapist: Religious material in the psychotherapeutic setting. *Psychotherapy: Theory, Research, Practice, Training, 35,* 415–424.

Zinnbauer, B. J., & Pargament, K. I. (2000). Working with the sacred: Four approaches to religious and spiritual issues in counseling. *Journal of Counseling & Development, 78,* 162–171.

Counseling Focus Integration

Chapter Objectives

1. What are some general approaches in assisting a client in developing a spiritual identity?

2. What are some specific guidelines counselors can use when incorporating the spiritual or religious dimension in the supervision process? The assessment process? The treatment process?

3. What are some of the main avenues of counseling that have historically incorporated a spiritual dimension?

6

Chapter

Helping Clients Develop a Spiritual Identity

In Chapter 1, there was a discussion of incorporating spirituality in counseling. G. Miller focused this incorporation around three questions (1999a, p. 501):

1. "How do we help people develop a spiritual identity?"

2. "Do we have a right and an obligation to help people develop a spiritual identity?"

3. "How does context impact application?"

This chapter examines the first question in depth while Chapter 7 explores the second and third questions regarding counselor responsibility and the context of the application.

In helping clients develop a spiritual identity, it is necessary to look at their current level of spiritual development. One model of development is Fowler's (1981) faith development. The six stages that make up this developmental model are preceded by the prefaith stage, from one to three years, where trust and mutuality are developed (Fowler, 1981, 1991):

1. *Intuitive-projective (3 to 7 years):* This stage focuses on imagination where the child can be affected by the faith of adults around them.

2. *Mythic-literal (7 to puberty):* This stage is where the person takes in the beliefs and symbols of their religious community in a literal way.

3. *Synthetic-conventional (puberty to adulthood):* The person is involved in interpersonal faith, but tends to conform to beliefs and values of their community with an emphasis on authority.

4. *Individuative-reflective (young adulthood):* There is more personification of beliefs, symbols, and meanings, and one is committed to these meanings.

5. *Conjunctive:* A person tries to integrate opposites, sees a community that is inclusive, and exerts self in conjunction with beliefs.

6. *Universalizing:* The focus is on loving others at a universal level and goes beyond one's specific faith.

Because faith is the representation of the client's view regarding life meaning and value, these stages can be used by the counselor to assist in determining the client's developmental stage (Kelly, 1995). Such determination can help the counselor and client determine how the client's faith may need to become more personalized to help the client through the crisis or transition at hand. To make such an accurate determination, the counselor needs to clarify his or her spiritual or religious perspective.

As discussed in Chapter 5, counselors need to understand their motivation and biases to determine how they may impact the process of assisting clients develop a spiritual identity. This is critical as you work both with transference and countertransference issues as they arise in the counseling process. However, while working with transference and countertransference issues is important, developing a spiritual identity is broader than that. A spiritual identity is a result of exploring the spiritual and religious dimensions of the client. It evolves in an overall counseling goal of assisting the client in developing the most fitting spiritual perspective for him or her. How then does a counselor do this? A counselor does this by taking into account the client, the problem, and the situation being addressed within the context of supervision, assessment, and treatment.

Supervision

Supervision of clinical work is one place where this process begins. The supervisor of the counselor needs to examine how he or she sets a tone of openness to the discussion of spiritual matters since this can "trickle down" and have an impact on the counseling process. R. J. Lovinger (1996) provides an example of supervisor countertransference. In this situation, the client had converted from Christian Science to Christianity and the therapist was Jewish. While Lovinger was not able to work through his own countertransference as a supervisor, another supervisor was able to process the struggles of the counselor allowing the counselor to effectively work with the client. This example exemplifies the powerful impact supervision can have in "freeing" the client and counselor in working with spirituality issues in counseling.

The supervisor can take a number of approaches in attempting to assure the presence of the spiritual domain in the counseling process. One is to ask himself or herself the following questions with regard to the supervision process:

1. Am I creating a safe place in supervision where spiritual and religious views can be discussed?
2. Am I encouraging avoidance of religious or spiritual stereotypes?
3. What are the "dangers" of incorporating a spiritual dimension in counseling for me, my supervisee, and his or her clients?

Miller, Lassiter, Gardner, and Hamilton (1999) make specific suggestions in response to these questions. In terms of question 1, the supervisor needs to have an openness for these discussions even to occur and when they do emerge, to establish some ground rules with the supervisee regarding discussion of this topic, for example, no "bashing" of religions is allowed. Also, the supervisor may need to explore with the supervisee any biases about religion and spirituality that are emerging (or may emerge) with regard to clients.

A way to examine bias is to apply a framework that can be used to assess where the supervisor, supervisee, and the client stand, providing some common terminology for the supervisor and supervisee to use when discussing spiritual or religious concerns in supervision. An example of such a framework is Batson and Ventis' work (1982) describing three spiritual continua: quest, ends, and means. No one person fits into each of these types perfectly which is why they are continua. A person ranges between high and low on each. Examples of individuals who may fit on the high end of each continuum follows (G. Miller, 1992):

1. *Quest:* A philosopher who loves the questions and the process of examining the questions.
2. *Ends:* Someone who goes to the same church each day or week and believes that he or she will be saved by following church guidelines; who is involved in religious behaviors because they are important to them.
3. *Means:* A business person who attends church because it looks good for business.

Metaphorically these continua are like three borders of a weaver's loom creating a tapestry of spirituality. The tapestry is a result of the continua (quest, ends, means) interacting. This framework can be used in supervision to describe generally where the supervisor, supervisee, and client fit along these continua.

For example, a supervisor might introduce this terminology into the supervision session explaining the concepts to the supervisee. The supervisor could provide an example by describing her spiritual beliefs and how they apply to clients: "I think of myself as high on the quest continuum because I really enjoy discussions on spirituality where there is not necessarily a decision made on a topic, but many ideas are discussed. I believe I am low on the ends continuum because I do not adhere to a specific religion or attend a place of worship. I also believe that I am low on the means continuum because I am not concerned about how my spiritual beliefs appear to others."

Discussion of where the counselor can be placed along these continua can lead to discussions in supervision of potential areas of conflict between the counselor and current and potential clients, depending on their spiritual tapestry (G. Miller, 1992). The supervisor could continue: "As a result of where I place myself on the continua, I am aware of clients with whom I have matched well in therapy and those with whom I have matched poorly. Those good matches have been ones where dialogue was easy about spirituality because they were similar to me (high on quest, low on ends and means). Those difficult matches have been where dialogue was harder because they were low on quest and higher in terms of the ends or means continua. I struggle more with those who are high on the means continuum because I do not value a spirituality that is based on appearances. I do not struggle as much with those high on the ends continuum because they are practicing their spirituality in a genuine fashion that makes sense to them. It is simply easier for me to discuss spirituality with clients more likely to engage in the process of exploring the unknown without resolution. As a counselor, I need to be careful to stay focused on the spiritual issue at hand when I work with a high-quest client so we do not become lost in discussion. When working with a high-ends person, I need to work on not being disappointed with what may appear to be a lack of interest in exploring spiritual questions. In clinical work with a high-means person, I need to not judge them for their spiritual practice."

These examples are meant to illustrate how easily this continuum can be used in a supervision session to enhance the counselor's awareness of his or her spiritual views. An awareness of potentially good and poor matches between counselor and client can enhance the likelihood of helpful counseling as well as reduce the likelihood of counseling that is not helpful.

In response to question 2 on page 141, the supervisor and supervisee need to be aware that there may exist a potential for actual disrespect of differences between them, the clients, or within the agency; too much or too little interest in this area could overshadow or eclipse critical areas of counseling. Disrespect of differences may stem from stereotypes held by the supervisor or supervisee in terms of religion or spirituality. Stereotypes can be avoided by an awareness of self and your religious or spiritual perspective, suspension of judgment in the supervision session, and participation in a genuine dialogue. The presence of these dynamics can lead to an appreciation of differences between the supervisor and supervisee rather than a debate of "rightness" or "truth." This openness can be passed on to the clinical work between counselor and client.

A final area to be noted in supervision is that supervisors and their supervisees risk being stereotyped or ostracized for their spiritual or religious perspectives by clients or colleagues. Depending on the context of your work situation, these experiences may vary. Clients or coworkers may be of a majority spiritual or religious belief and may struggle with the counselor's spiritual or religious beliefs. Research, presentations, or discussions about the spiritual or religious realms may be viewed as inferior or odd and may prevent counselors from employment or educational opportunities. Although these experiences may not be openly or formally stated, they may still operate in the individual counselor's professional life. By being aware of such possible negative experiences, the counselor interested in incorporating spirituality in counseling may be able to reduce the personal hurt that comes from such experiences and, instead, anticipate and prepare for the possibility that others may struggle with such incorporation.

Assessment

Lukoff, Lu, and Turner (1995) report that psychiatry has had a tendency to not address or view religious and spiritual client issues or to view them as pathological. The authors label that tendency as a cultural insensitivity. Further, they state that clients may come to counseling for specific religious problems (faith issues, denomination or religion changes, increased religious practice, involvement in a new religion or cult) or specific spiritual problems (mystical or near-death experiences, uncontrolled spiritual phenomena, meditation effects, illness). The counselor needs to be prepared to do an assessment of the client's religious and spiritual views because of a possible related impact on the presenting problem or because the presenting problem is spiritual or religious in nature.

Richards and Bergin (1997) recommend that an assessment of religious or spiritual views be done (a) to understand the perspective of the client; (b) to obtain knowledge as to how healthy that perspective is and how it influences counseling issues; (c) to determine possible resource of beliefs and support groups; (d) to determine possible interventions that can be used in counseling; and (e) to clarify the level of need to address spiritual or religious views in counseling. Making an assessment of a client's spiritual or religious views requires that a number of factors be addressed. Family history of spiritual or religious areas are core in this assessment process (Genia, 2000). Specifically, exposure to certain spiritual or religious views in the client's upbringing may impact him or her now and the problem being addressed by the client in counseling. For example, if there was an emphasis in choosing a partner of the same religion, a client may have difficulties with having chosen someone of a different religion (Genia, 2000).

Additional areas of current impact from past experiences with religious or spiritual perspectives may include sexual behavior or orientation, messages about the client's inherent goodness, and acceptance of roles in the family of creation even if they are harmful to the client or others (e.g., domestic violence). Genia (2000) also states that religious conflicts may arise when certain issues present themselves: "death of a significant other, suicidal urges, an illicit sexual affair, divorce, or a life-threatening illness" (p. 215). Lukoff et al. (1995) add other types of religious problems, which include denominational membership change, conflicts between current and past lifestyles for new converts, and involvement in cults. They also add spiritual problems such as an experience of a mystical nature or near-death, spiritual emergence (gradual development) or emergency (sudden and uncontrollable), and medical or terminal illnesses.

Kelly (1995) recommends that counselors incorporate the spiritual dimension by making it a normal part of the intake, determine the issues that arise that need to be addressed, and make clinical decisions regarding the use of spiritual assessment instruments. One example of an assessment tool is Spilka's (1986) framework of secondary religious control that can help counselors understand the purpose of a client's religious views. Although Spilka describes these as forms of religious control, these types of control (predictive, vicarious, illusory, and interpretive) can be viewed as types of control you use in daily living. G. Miller (1992) provides examples of these types of control:

1. *Predictive:* The individual believes that if some spiritual action is taken, a positive outcome will result, such as with prayer.
2. *Vicarious:* This control comes from identifying with a type of Higher Power through a process such as meditation.
3. *Illusory:* The person sees reality as a result of the will of the divine.
4. *Interpretive:* The individual tries to obtain meaning from problems.

The counselor who understands the client's tendency to use religion to experience one of these types of control may understand how this control influences the client's current functioning and may cause him or her problems in life. For example, if a client adheres to a specific religion where prayer is an important ritual, the client may believe that his prayers about his father being cured of alcoholism should result in a cure for his father's illness. The client may struggle in counseling with trying to understand why all of the praying is not having an impact on his father's drinking. The counselor's understanding of this type of control may assist in selecting a counseling intervention, for example, information about the causal factors of alcoholism.

Pargament, Smith, Koenig, and Perez (1998) and Pargament et al. (1988) provide a similar style only within a coping-style, problem-solving context. The four styles the authors present are:

1. *Self-Directing:* The client views himself or herself as the one who needs to solve the problem (the self is at the control center);
2. *Collaborative:* The client considers God a partner in the problem solving;
3. *Deferring:* Because God is thought to be the one who has all power, personal responsibility does not exist;
4. *Pleading:* God is asked to intervene so what the individual wants is obtained.

This framework does not need to be viewed as only within a specific religious framework or religious terminology. For example, the word *God* could be replaced with the term *Higher Power* or whatever word connoting some presence larger than you. As with Spilka's framework (1986), this framework can assist the counselor in determining the client's perspective on how the problem needs to be handled and by whom, thereby assisting in the clarification of the type of counseling intervention needed. In the situation where the son is worried about his father's drinking, if the son has a deferring problem-solving style, the counselor may want to introduce the concept of *enabling* to the client to assist him in taking some action with regard to his father's drinking. Such a translation would be shifting the focus from God making an intervention to the client beginning to examine through the counseling process any action he may be able to take to address the problem.

R. J. Lovinger (1996) provides ten markers of religious pathology that counselors can use to determine if a client is "out of balance" in terms of the application of his or her religious principles. These are:

1. Demonstrating to others how much they adhere to their religious principles.
2. Viewing religion as a means of making life easier for them.
3. Being overly concerned with not committing a sin or making a mistake.

4. Not being responsible or being overly responsible.
5. Expressing emotions intensely without control.
6. Continuing to change churches.
7. Expressing religious enthusiasm without thought or awareness of the context.
8. Experiencing "love" that has been hurtful within the religion.
9. Using the Bible to guide every day life.
10. Reporting an experience of possession.

These pathology markers need to be considered within the context of the client's life as well as the intention of the client in practicing them. They do not automatically indicate pathology, but are simply observable indicators that a counselor can use to flag potentially pathological behavior. For example, number nine, "Using the Bible to guide every day life" is not necessarily pathological (note that any religious or spiritual text could be listed here, not just the Bible). A woman may read her Bible every day for support as she struggles with raising her children in poverty. A counselor would not view this as pathological, but rather as a coping skill, a resource the woman uses to help her in her daily living. Contrast that description with another female client who uses the Bible to determine essentially every decision she makes in a day and, if confronted on her behavior by others, practices no self-reflection but aggressively defends herself through the statement of a Biblical quote. In this scenario, the counselor may note reading the Bible daily as a marker that intrapersonal pathology is played out in interpersonal struggles. These scenarios illustrate that the daily reading of the Bible, or any religious literature, alone, is not pathological. Markers are simply punctuation points the counselor can use to do a further assessment of the client's spiritual framework to understand how the marker operates in the rest of the client's life.

R. J. Lovinger (1996) also describes five indicators of mature religious adjustment that a counselor can use in the assessment process. These are:

1. Being aware that religious literature and traditions are both complex and ambiguous.
2. Making a choice of religious affiliation that reflects his or her inner beliefs (not necessarily that of his or her parents).
3. Demonstrating congruence between values and behaviors.
4. Being aware of his or her shortcomings in a realistic, balanced manner.
5. Respecting the religious perspectives and boundaries of others.

These indicators of mature adjustment can be combined with the pathological markers to make a more in depth assessment. Staying with the previous examples of reading the Bible daily, both women could be asked questions to clarify their level of maturity given these five indicators. While the first story may indicate number three (congruence between values and behaviors), the counselor would want to ask questions to clarify that congruence and to determine where she is in relation to the other four indicators. Regarding the second example, the counselor would want to obtain information about all the items particularly emphasizing her interactions with others.

Although these frameworks are more descriptive in their nature, they provide a useful framework that counselors can use to guide their assessment of clients in the spiritual or religious domain. Such a framework can provide the counselor with terminology that can be used in a dialogue with the client about the spiritual or religious concerns that need to be addressed in counseling.

Treatment

Counseling that incorporates the spiritual dimension can help clients have a sense of hope, view their issues from a different perspective, become more focused on what is important to them, help them discover who they are, and provide them with a sense of "other" resulting in their feeling less alone in the world. Chapter 1 of this text describes some of the approaches needed to create a sacred place for clients: no interruptions, a sense of safety, and honor of the client's story. Chapter 1 also describes how counselors can encourage a spiritual practice for their clients by encouraging them to have a refuge of spirituality, if that seems appropriate, to assist them in coping with changes in their lives. Encouragement of developing a refuge can be accomplished by asking them questions, such as what helps them "catch their breath" in life, what rituals are or might be helpful to them, where are safe places in their daily living where they can take refuge, and who provides them with a sense of community.

Other general counseling approaches were described in Chapter 5. These include: awareness of self and biases, the "O.K. (Open learner and Kindred spirit) human being" approach, the "3 Rs" (refuge, rituals, and resources), and resolution of transference and countertransference issues. Tan's (2000) description of three types of integration (implicit, explicit, intentional) also are general counseling approaches that can be used by a counselor when addressing the religious or spiritual realm of the client. The *implicit end* of the integration continuum allows for the counselor to be sensitive to religious themes (covert) while the *explicit end* involves direct addressing of the religious themes with religious resources (overt);

intentional integration is using covert or overt means to act in the best interests of the welfare of the client.

Kelly (1990) describes four categories describing the relationship of religion with certain issues presented by the client in counseling and how a counselor may intervene in these issues. These four categories of issues are:

1. Religious issues such as losing faith, having committed a sin, being unsure about a commitment to a religious vocation.

2. Nonreligious issues such as converting to a different faith due to marriage or hiding one's religious views to enhance one's professional career.

3. Nonreligious issues with possible connections to religion such as life meaning, afterlife, a sense of universality that emerges with issues of death, family problems, pregnancy, public humiliation, financial problems, illness, and alcoholism.

4. Nonreligious issues with no real connection with religion such as job problems, weight loss.

While basic counseling and listening skills can be used to facilitate responses in clients in each of these areas, religiously oriented responses are appropriate for the first category (religious issues), possibly the second and third (nonreligious issues, nonreligious issues with possible connections to religion), but not for the fourth category (nonreligious issues with no real connection with religion). Kelly (1990) also provides the following taxonomy to understand how open clients may be to counselor responses that are religiously oriented. The first four are described as responsive to religiously oriented responses while the last four are not.

1. *Religiously Committed:* These clients have a deep, personal religious conviction that impacts all ways in which they think and act and also impacts how they grow spiritually (Stem, 1985).

2. *Religiously Loyal:* These clients have received the expectations of their families, communities, and society that impact how they think and act, but not necessarily in the same way developmentally as the religiously committed client (Albany, 1984).

3. *Spiritually Committed:* This type of client may be committed to the spiritual dimension of life, but not be identified with any specific religion.

4. *Religiously and Spiritually Open:* This client does not have a commitment to either the religious or spiritual realm, but through counseling does become more open to these areas.

5. *Superficially Religious:* These clients show religious beliefs or affiliation, but do not have an inner conviction that plays out in their lives.

6. *Religiously Tolerant and Indifferent:* These clients tolerate religion in general and individuals' religions, but in their own lives do not appear to have any need for it.

7. *Nonreligious:* This group of clients do not view religion or spirituality as necessary and reject it.

8. *Hostile to Religion:* This group of clients have a hostile attitude toward religion and its influences on others and society.

While the counselor needs to avoid typecasting clients, this description of different types of clients may assist the counselor in making a choice about the appropriateness of a religiously oriented statement, question, or intervention in response to the client's life story. It can also assist in helping the counselor determine the form of expressing such a response. For example, a counselor may be comfortable talking with a spiritually committed client about the general concept of how he keeps his spirit "alive," but avoid making any comments about a specific religion. The same counselor working with a client who is hostile to religion may want to explore the hostility, but again avoid any comments specific to a religion.

Awareness of factors such as age, literacy level, and terminology may facilitate the incorporation of spirituality in counseling. Some adolescents may be limited in how they can work with their spiritual or religious beliefs because of developmental issues or stages. Some clients may be limited in their work in this area because of their literacy level (e.g., bibliotherapy resources may not be an option for them). Some clients may be limited on wording they can tolerate when discussing spiritual or religious concerns (e.g., given past trauma, some clients may struggle with the word "ritual" and be more comfortable with words such as "activity").

Case Application

A counselor meets regularly with her supervisor, but has never discussed spiritual or religious concerns with him. Because her supervisor has a history of being respectful toward her, she decides to open the next supervision session by discussing a male client with whom she is struggling: She and the client seem to have very different spiritual/religious perspectives.

Her supervisor tells her that while he has had some training in this area, he does not consider himself an expert on spiritual matters. Yet, he tells her he is open to discussing this area of concern. He asks her how he can make it comfortable for her to discuss her concerns in supervision. She says her only request is that he avoid critiquing her own personal spiritual views. He agrees to her request.

Before discussing the case, the supervisor suggests they place themselves on the quest, ends, and means continua. After the supervisee agrees and the supervisor explains the basic concepts, they describe themselves as both being high on the quest continuum, but low on the other two. The supervisee has an "AHA" experience in that she says she believes the client she is about to discuss is high on the ends continuum and low on the others, thereby indicating a possible source of friction between her and him.

She said that normally she does not bring up religious or spiritual concerns so readily with a client, but her client quoted the Bible and used biblical metaphors so frequently in the first session that she believed she needed to ask him about his religion. The client told her he was a recent convert (last six months) to a fundamentalist Christian religion, and he came in for counseling because his girlfriend of two years is threatening to leave him unless he examines his issues with control. Because his religious views were discussed in relation to his problem, he said he had been praying to God to fix his problem with his girlfriend (predictive control), but God had not yet fixed it (deferring problem solving). He said he was confused about this situation because he reads his Bible every day for explicit direction on how to proceed in problem situations with his girlfriend, but when he quotes the direction to her from scripture, she becomes silent or angry that he will not talk with her without his Bible present (religious pathology marker #9).

The supervisee believes she treated him respectfully in the session (O.K. human being approach) and would like to examine his religious perspective that is so important to him as a source of strength for him (3 Rs: refuge, rituals, resources), however, she wants to do this in more of an indirect manner because that is more comfortable for her style of counseling (implicit integration). She believes her client has nonreligious issues of a relational nature that sound connected to his recent conversion. She views him as being a very devout Christian (religiously committed).

She acknowledges that her countertransference struggle is in relation to the Biblical quotes he reportedly says to his girlfriend when he wants her to "obey." The supervisee said she does not necessarily believe in the existence of God, in fact, if she were to label herself, she would probably label herself a Taoist. She said she is mainly unsure if she can work with him given his views of women and his strong adherence to a religious perspective that he believes supports his views of women. She also acknowledges that she has a limited knowledge of the Bible so she cannot determine the accuracy of the quotes her client reports to her.

Her supervisor applauds her willingness to be honest with him about her struggles with this client. He suggests that they spend some time in the supervision session talking about the extent and manageability of her countertransference with this client to determine if she can effectively work with him in therapy. The supervisee agrees and acknowledges appreciation that her supervisor has been willing to process this struggle with her.

This case application demonstrates how the different aspects of counseling (supervision, assessment, treatment) can incorporate a spiritual or religious dimension. The process of supervision can lay the groundwork for sound, effective incorporation of this dimension in therapy.

Counseling Avenues

While this discussion is not an exhaustive review of available avenues of counseling that incorporate spirituality, it is an overview of three that have an inherent spiritual dimension. These avenues, as a result, may provide examples to counselors for incorporating the spiritual dimension of counseling. Specific spiritual and religious techniques, some of which are related to counseling theories, are discussed in Chapter 8.

Addiction Recovery

The addictions counseling field has frequently used a 12-step program that incorporates spirituality since the beginning of Alcoholics Anonymous (AA), a self-help addiction recovery group, in 1935 (Judge, 1994). In fact, one of the criticisms of the 12-step treatment recovery model is that it has a spiritual/religious dimension and, in particular, one that is based in Christianity (Judge, 1994). The 12 steps, in part, were derived from concepts from the Oxford Group, a nondenominational Christian group (Kurtz, 1988). The addiction counseling approach that has used the 12-step model has been called the *Minnesota Model* where professional addiction counseling is fused with AA's 12 Steps and the counselors are frequently recovering from their own addiction (O'Dwyer, 1993).

The 12 Steps are living guidelines for the addicted individual that were confirmed at the First International Conference of Alcoholics Anonymous in 1950, although they were first published in 1946 (Alcoholics Anonymous World Services, 1953). Small variations in these steps are made for the self-help groups of Narcotics Anonymous and Cocaine Anonymous (G. Miller, 1999b).

Spirituality in AA is viewed as affinity in terms of yourself, others, and a Higher Power (Brown, Peterson, & Cunningham, 1988). W. R. Miller and Kurtz (1994) describe the AA model as a spiritual one that guides a way of life based on abstinence and character development. The spiritual dimension in AA can be seen in the steps of the program as outlined in the box on page 154.

TWELVE STEPS OF ALCOHOLICS ANONYMOUS*

1. We admitted we were powerless over alcohol—that our lives had become unmanageable.

2. Came to believe that a Power greater than ourselves could restore us to sanity.

3. Made a decision to turn our will and our lives over to the care of God, *as we understood Him.*

4. Made a searching and fearless moral inventory of ourselves.

5. Admitted to God, to ourselves and to another human being the exact nature of our wrongs.

6. Were entirely ready to have God remove all these defects of character.

7. Humbly asked Him to remove our shortcomings.

8. Made a list of all persons we had harmed, and became willing to make amends to them all.

9. Made direct amends to such people wherever possible, except when to do so would injure them or others.

10. Continued to take personal inventory and when we were wrong promptly admitted it.

11. Sought through prayer and meditation to improve our conscious contact with God, *as we understood Him,* praying only for knowledge of His will for us and the power to carry that out.

12. Having had a spiritual awakening as the result of these steps, we tried to carry this message to alcoholics, and to practice these principles in all our affairs.

*The Twelve Steps are reprinted with permission of Alcoholics Anonymous World Services, Inc. (A.A.W.S.). Permission to reprint the Twelve Steps does not mean that A.A.W.S. has reviewed or approved the contents of this publication, or A.A.W.S. necessarily agrees with the views expressed herein. A.A. is a program of recovery from alcoholism *only*—use of Twelve Steps in connection with programs and activities which are patterned after A.A., but which address other problems, or in any other non-A.A. context, does not imply otherwise.

Steps 2, 3, 5, 6, 7, and 11 specifically mention the concept of a Higher Power or God and step 12 mentions a "spiritual awakening." The emphasis in the recovery program on spirituality is quite evident. This emphasis on spirituality for clients can be both a strength or a weakness depending on the client and his or her previous experiences with spirituality, religion, or self-help groups (G. Miller, 1999b).

ADDICTION SUPPORT GROUP INFORMATION

1. Alcoholics Anonymous
World Services Inc.
P.O. Box 459
Grand Central Station
New York, NY 10163
(212)870-3400
www.alcoholics-anonymous.org

2. Sixteen Steps (16 Steps)
Many Roads, One Journey PACKET
362 N. Cleveland Avenue, Suite 1
St. Paul, MN 55104
(608)249-9076
members.aol.com/empower16/steps.htm
empowere16@aol.com

3. Women for Sobriety (WFS)
P.O. Box 618
Quakertown, PA 18951-0618
(215)536-8026
www.mediapulse.com/wfs
WFSobriety@aol.com

4. Al-Anon Family Group Headquarters
1600 Corporate Landing Parkway
Virginia Beach, VA 23454-5617
(757)563-1600
(800)4AL-ANON
www.alanon.alateen.org

Although AA or one of the other 12-step programs (see box) may not work for all clients (Le, Ingvarson, & Page, 1995), it may work well with a number of clients recovering from addiction because it provides an increase in support (Flores, 1988), a decrease in isolation (Talbott, 1990), and an increase in self-regulation (Khantzian & Mack, 1994). Counselors using this model with clients need to know the "personality" of the various community self-help groups, how his or her counseling theory fits with the self-help groups, and the client's reaction to involvement with such groups.

One of the strengths, as well as the limitations of these groups, is the involvement of spirituality. Although the groups typically advocate a

Higher Power of your choosing, individual groups may open with the Serenity Prayer, close with the Lord's Prayer, and during the meeting talk about their Higher Power with a definition that may be too religious in orientation for the client (G. Miller, 1999b). A counselor, using this as a potential source of additional support for a client, needs to be aware that it is critical to match the client with a group that is most fitting for the client. Miller provides suggestions for counselors on matching a group with client needs.

One possibility is to explore other national, abstinence-based, self-help groups that may be a resource for clients spiritually. Other groups that involve a spiritual component are Women for Sobriety (WFS) that focuses on emotional and spiritual growth and Kasl's 16 Steps that emphasizes empowerment (G. Miller, 1999b).

Also, counselors may use such avenues as bibliotherapy of a spiritual nature in working with addicted clients (Alpers, 1995). The author provides examples of daily meditation books, stories of recovering people, the main text of the self-help group, daily prayer books, step guides, historical literature, special populations in recovery, and general books on spirituality. Other techniques include prayer and mediation, which are often viewed respectively as talking and listening to God by recovering addicts (Kus, 1995).

Another possible resource for clients who are family members or friends of addicted individuals is Al-Anon. Al-Anon, which began in 1948, focuses on assisting these individuals in their addiction-related recovery issues. It uses the same 12 Steps as AA, except the word in the twelfth step, *alcoholics,* was replaced with *others.* These groups can provide an excellent community resource for support in addition to counseling. Once again, there is a spiritual emphasis to these groups.

Chapman (1996) advocates looking at alcohol dependence as being a disorder that includes a spiritual dimension and that counselors can incorporate this dimension by examining the worldview of the client and examining the client's recovery from a spiritual, mental, and physical perspective. This area of counseling has historically incorporated the spiritual dimension relatively successfully. Counselors interested in integrating this dimension would be well advised to study how addiction counselors have worked with this area.

Wellness/Positive Psychology

Wellness is about more than the body (Hermon & Hazler, 1999). Wellness is for all people and is more than not having a disease, but also having the presence of indicators that a person is functioning well (Cowen, 1994). Formally, psychology showed its interest in this area at a 1978 conference in the United States on this topic and by forming a division within the American Psychological Association (APA) in 1979 (Pitts, 1998).

Ogden (1996) outlines some of the main views of health psychology. People and illness are viewed as complex with no one thing causing illness. Rather, illness is a result of biological, psychological, and social components—a biopsychosocial perspective. The whole person needs to be treated, and the person is responsible for playing a part in the illness as well as the treatment and recovery. Health and illness are viewed as a continuum with the mind and body interacting. Psychological factors are viewed as both causing and resulting from illness. Health psychology looks at how behavior has a part in illness, and unhealthy behaviors can be predicted. Psychological factors are a part of both illness and its treatment. Health psychology tries to promote healthy behavior and prevent illness.

Health psychology or wellness in terms of spirituality began in the health care field as a core aspect of a person's life (Curtis & Davis, 1999). Westgate (1996) identified four components of spirituality from a wellness perspective: life meaning, internal values, belief in a Higher Power, and involvement in a like-minded community in terms of values and beliefs. Religion/spirituality can help people in daily living and coping with stress (Bibbins, 2000) as well as recovering from physical problems such as disability (Byrd, 1997).

These core components emerge again in positive psychology that examines how normal people cope (Seligman & Csikszentmihalyi, 2000). The aim of this avenue is to build on the positive qualities of individuals and enhance what is good and positive in their lives rather than what is wrong (Kogan, 2001). Positive psychology is about valued experiences, individual traits, and civic values. Values experiences include a sense of satisfaction when looking at the past, a sense of happiness with the present, and hope and optimism with regard to the future. Individual traits that are positive include a sense of spirituality; some other examples of positive traits are forgiveness, wisdom, courage, and capacity for love and vocation. Civic virtues include altruism, responsibility, and nurturance.

Seligman and Csikszentmihalyi (2000) discuss the mental health, illness buffers supported by research findings. These buffers include faith, optimism, and hope which may be derived from a spiritual or religious domain in one's life. D. G. Myers (2000) examined three factors that can contribute to a sense of happiness: money, relationships, and religion. The findings on religious faith indicate that religious people are better at handling life crises, have more social support, have a meaning and purpose in their lives, and experience hope in facing life's existential questions (G. Miller, 2001).

Health psychology and positive psychology help people draw on the religious and spiritual domains in their lives that help them cope with issues from the past, present, and the future. It emphasizes what works for an individual that can be encouraged or further developed in the process of counseling.

Wounded Healer

The wounded healer framework of counseling does not directly address spirituality but indirectly does so in its perspective of the counselor and his or her wounds. In this framework, the typically polarized relationship between being a wounded person and being a healed person, as described by Remen, May, Young, and Bertand (1985), is nonexistent. This polarity usually expects counselors not to have vulnerabilities of any kind, particularly those in the psychological, spiritual, or emotional areas (G. Miller, 1999b).

The wounded healer is more like a bridge between two worlds, the world of wellness and the world of illness (Remen et al., 1985). As a bridge between these worlds, the counselor brings a compassionate *spirit* to the counseling setting. This compassion emerges from the transcending of the counselor's difficult life experiences because compassion cannot come from wounds that have not yet healed (G. Miller, 1999b). Therefore, to be a wounded healer, the counselor needs to know his or her "soft spots" and places of vulnerability, and then address and work through these issues in their counseling.

The counselor's skill as a therapist, in part, emerges from an understanding of his or her vulnerability and how difficult it is to heal and live with these vulnerabilities partially healed (since no therapy is perfect). The counselor is essentially a role model for the client about living with your wounds. By being attentive to his or her vulnerability, the counselor shows more empathy and understanding with clients because they share wounds (G. D. Miller & Baldwin, 1987). Sorting out personal issues and struggles with oppression help counselors be sensitive, supportive, and respectful toward their clients (Wolgien & Coady, 1997).

The wounded healer framework is a bridge between the use of psychological knowledge and skill and the spirit of the counselor as a result of addressing and living with his or her wounds.

Case Studies

CASE STUDY 1

You work as a supervisor in a community mental health agency. You have a supervisee who tells you that her clients are "too religious" for her. She complains to you weekly that she is sick of working with all of these Christians who have more faith in their ministers than her professional training as a counselor. You know that your supervisee really cares about her clients and that some of her clients are involved with a local minister who practically directs them on how to live their lives each moment of each day. You also know that your supervisee was raised in a very strict, fundamentalist Christian religion and that she makes sarcastic comments about Christianity at times.

1. How would you raise your concerns about your supervisee's work with clients and their spiritual or religious views?
2. What would be the pros and cons of your approaches in raising your concerns in terms of your relationship with your supervisee? Her relationships with her clients?
3. How would you balance your awareness of the local community with your supervisee's personal struggles with religion in terms of interventions you choose?

CASE STUDY 2

Your client comes in for counseling because her family is concerned about the intensity of her involvement with a local church. She tells you that she believes that God's will directs her life and that God will solve all of her problems.

1. What type of religious control (according to Spilka, 1986) might she be using?
2. What type of coping style, problem-solving approach (Pargament et al., 1988, 1998) might she be using?
3. What could be the pros of her using such religious control and problem-solving approach in her daily living?
4. What could be some cons of her using this type of control and approach in her daily living?

CASE STUDY 3

The same client in Case Study 2 comes in for her second session with her Bible held tightly to her chest and she is wearing a large cross necklace. She begins the session by telling you that she has never missed a day of church attendance or church choir practice in five years since she converted to Christianity, but she has had to change churches every few months because she has yet to find a minister and a congregation who are as committed to the practice of Christianity as she is. When you ask questions about how she lives her life daily, she quotes directly from her Bible.

1. Which pathological markers of Lovinger does your client show?
2. How would you work with her on this pathology in counseling?
3. What would be your hypotheses about her family's concerns in terms of these pathological markers?

4. Would you explore having the family join the counseling? If so, what steps would you take to include them in the counseling sessions?

Exercises

Exercise 1

Answer the following questions keeping in mind that you are a supervisor:

1. Am I creating a safe place in supervision where spiritual and religious views can be discussed?
2. Am I encouraging avoidance of religious or spiritual stereotypes?
3. What are the "dangers" of incorporating a spiritual dimension in counseling for me, my supervisee, and his or her clients?

Now answer similar questions as a supervisee:

1. How can my supervisor create a safe place in supervision where spiritual and religious views can be discussed?
2. How can my supervisor avoid encouraging religious or spiritual stereotypes?
3. What are the "dangers" of incorporating a spiritual dimension in counseling for my supervisor, for me, or for my clients in the counseling setting I currently work or one in which I anticipate working?

Examine the similarities and differences in your answers. Find a dyad partner and discuss these similarities and differences.

Exercise 2

Draw a diagram of the quest, means, and ends continua with examples of behavior describing each end of the three continua (Batson & Ventis, 1982). Place yourself on these continua. Find a partner and discuss how your placement on these continua may impact your work as a counselor.

Exercise 3

Write out the answers to the following questions:

1. What type of religious control do you use in your daily living (Spilka, 1986)?

2. How does this control impact you personally and professionally?

3. How might it impact your work with your clients in therapy?

4. What type of problem-solving approach do you use in your daily living (Kaiser, 1991)?

5. How does this problem-solving approach impact you personally and professionally?

6. How might this problem-solving approach impact your work with clients in therapy?

Now, in small groups, discuss your answers.

Exercise 4

Using Kelly's (1990) framework of religious and nonreligious issues in counseling, write down examples of religious issues you would be comfortable addressing with a client in counseling. Then write down examples of nonreligious issues you would be comfortable addressing that may have a connection with religion. Now do the same for issues of both a religious and nonreligious nature that you would be uncomfortable addressing in counseling.

Exercise 5

Kelly (1990) describes eight types of clients in two categories: those who might be responsive to religiously-oriented comments and those who might not. Choose a type of client from each of the two categories. Then choose a religious issue and a nonreligious issue from Exercise 4 for each of the two clients. What might be a religiously-oriented response you would be comfortable giving each client on each issue? Write down an example of a response for each issue and receive feedback from a partner on the pros and cons of your statements.

Exercise 6

Choose one of the areas of counseling that historically has used spirituality in its counseling approach: addictions, wellness/positive psychology, wounded healer. With the approach you choose, answer the following questions:

1. Why would this approach be comfortable for you?

2. How would this approach be a good match for you in terms of raising spiritual and religious concerns in your counseling?

3. What would you anticipate to be some drawbacks in your use of this approach?

Exercise 7

On the Internet, look up the words "supervision" and "spiritual counseling" or "religious counseling." What are Web sites that you may access for assistance in working in this area?

Exercise 8

On the Internet, look for the topic areas of assessment and treatment in terms of religious and spiritual counseling. What Web sites are available that you feel comfortable accessing for information in your work as a counselor? Would these be different Web sites from those you would be comfortable accessing personally for information?

Suggested Readings

Lovinger, R. J. (1996). Considering the religious dimension in assessment and treatment. In E. P. Shafranske (Ed.), *Religion and the clinical practice of psychology* (pp. 327–364). Washington, DC: American Psychological Association.

Miller, G. A. (1999). *Learning the language of addiction counseling.* Boston: Allyn & Bacon.

Seligman, M. E. P., & Csikszentmihalyi, M. (2000). Positive psychology: An introduction. *American Psychologist, 55,* 5–14.

Shafranske, E. P. (Ed.). (1996). *Religion and the clinical practice of psychology.* Washington, DC: American Psychological Association.

Ethical Issues

Chapter Objectives

1. What are some core ethical issues when incorporating spirituality in counseling?
2. What are some general approaches a counselor can use to prevent ethical dilemmas?

7

Chapter

Overview

A Native American elder once described his own inner struggles in this manner: "Inside of me there are two dogs. One of the dogs is mean and evil. The other dog is good. The mean dog fights the good dog all the time." When asked which dog wins, he reflected for a moment and replied, "The one I feed the most." (Native American Folk Tale)

This quote summarizes the general struggle with incorporating spirituality in counseling. Counselors need to work hard within themselves to determine the right therapeutic approach that anchors itself in the welfare of the client, a fundamental ethical consideration. The "dog" that wins in this struggle is the one that is fed the most by the counselor. This chapter examines ways to enhance the ability of the counselor to have the "good dog win."

Previous chapters have addressed these concerns to some degree. Chapter 1 generally addressed the rights and obligation of therapists incorporating spirituality in counseling with clients. This involves creating a sacred space (no interruptions, clients feel safe, clients' stories are honored), encouraging self-care (teaching clients to reassure themselves, reinforcing the spiritual experience), and encouraging spiritual practice (creating a refuge, having rituals, creating safe places, having a sense of community). Chapter 5 explored issues related to transference and countertransference, recommending that counselors be aware of both their own and their clients' spiritual views and beliefs in order to more effectively work with these projections. Chapter 5 also examined the different ways of integrating spiritual and religious concerns in counseling (implicit, explicit, intentional).

This chapter explores some of the pragmatic ethical concerns to create a more fluid incorporation of ethical guidelines and treatment practices (see Figure 7.1). Prior to exploring specific ethical concerns, it may be beneficial to keep in mind some general recommendations for counselor practice. Each mental health profession has guidelines for its practitioners. You are encouraged to refer to the respective guidelines for your profession as seen in the Appendices.

Counselors may address ethical concerns overall by:

1. Being aware that there is a fine line between exploring the views of a client and being judgmental toward him or her.

2. Obtaining informed consent to discuss the spiritual and religious realm with clients.

3. Obtaining skill or training to work in this area and be aware of your values and those of the client.

4. Observing clear roles and boundaries between counselors and religious leaders (Bergin, Payne, & Richards, 1996).

Informed Consent

Prior to discussing informed consent, some basic aspects of assessment need to be discussed. Assessing this dimension with the client represents a holistic counseling approach that encourages the welfare of the client (Birdsall, 2001). To enhance the incorporation of the spiritual and religious aspect of the client's life in counseling, the counselor needs to sensitively address these concerns and invite such a discussion. Barnett and Fiorentino (2000) recommend that an assessment be done that includes the client's secular and religious history. If religious or spiritual issues arise in this process, they recommend that the counselor talk openly with clients about the use of religious or spiritual interventions chosen (specific intervention techniques are reviewed in Chapter 8). Such dialogue can inhibit any negative impact on the trust in the therapeutic relationship as well as limit the counselor's values being pushed on clients (Barnett & Fiorentino, 2000). In this dialogue, informed consent must be given by the client for the use of such interventions (see Figure 7.1).

Hawkins and Bullock (1995) summarize common aspects of consent forms as having seven areas. These areas: address confidentiality, describe the counselor, explain financial guidelines for therapy, provide emergency information, describe therapy, provide information on termination, consultation, and supervision, and state possible referral and

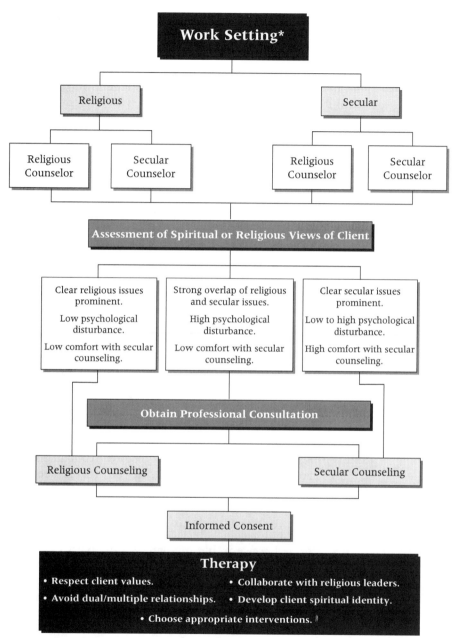

*In a secular setting where there is a strict separation of church and state, the counselor needs to proceed with caution in exploring the client's spiritual and religious views.

Figure 7.1

Ethical Decision-Making Tree

treatment options. They state that describing the counselor, describing the therapy, and stating possible referral and treatment options can be especially applied to work with religious clients.

The informed consent can be explicit about the religious or spiritual perspectives of the counselor as well as intervention techniques that may be used; it can allow a counselor to work with a client of a different religious perspective as long as this different perspective is obvious to the client (Barnett & Fiorentino, 2000). The informed consent needs to talk about therapy and how religious beliefs and issues are addressed (Yarhouse & VanOrman, 1999). Chappelle (2000) recommends that counselors obtain informed consent every time a spiritual or religious intervention technique is used in counseling, whether it is used inside or outside of the session, and that the consent includes talking about other options for treatment. Examples of consent forms the counselor may use are shown on pages 167 and 169.

Counselors, in practice, may feel legitimately overwhelmed at reading such a recommendation. The individual counselor may say, "Now I need to remember to have another consent form signed?" Some suggestions on adapting this important recommendation into your counseling practice are:

1. Have a specific consent form signed at the beginning of counseling for all clients or those with whom spiritual or religious issues arise during the assessment process.

2. Incorporate aspects of the specific consent form for spiritual and religious issues into the standard client consent form used by the counselor.

3. Use the specific consent form only when explicit spiritual interventions are used and find a way within your record keeping to flag the need to have a consent form signed, for example, put a blank one in each client's file so when charting, the blank consent form serves as a reminder to the counselor to have it signed.

An informed consent and dialogue with clients can prevent ethical dilemmas that may arise as the counselor attempts to incorporate the spiritual dimension in counseling. Further recommendations to counselors that may prevent ethical dilemmas are document spiritual interventions used in counseling, make financial arrangements clear (with both clients and funding sources, particularly when spiritual or religious interventions are used as a core part of counseling), and always keep in mind that the client be safe in therapy (Chappelle, 2000).

A counselor who wants to work with spiritual or religious issues implicitly in counseling does not need to have much concern regarding informed consent if he or she makes decisions based on the welfare of the client and in dialogue with the client. In addition to these suggestions, counselors who want to work more explicitly in the spiritual and religious area with a client are well advised to include the following in an informed consent agreement:

1. Open discussion with the client has occurred about how the spiritual and religious realm will be addressed in counseling.
2. The counseling approach is based on an assessment done with the client that examined the type of client issues, level of client disturbance, and client preference for secular or religious counseling.
3. A clear statement of fees.

As with any intervention technique, it is wise clinical practice for the counselor to document interventions used with clients and the rationale for their use.

SAMPLE INFORMED CONSENT FORM

PROFESSIONAL DISCLOSURE STATEMENT

I welcome you as a new client and look forward to working with you. The purpose of this form is to inform you of my counseling approach, what you can expect from counseling with me, and my background. The form will also give you an opportunity to give consent for counseling.

In my view of counseling, [theory of counseling explanation]. In counseling I use strategies that are primarily [major category of intervention techniques]: [types of techniques explanation]. These strategies will be used both during and between sessions. I work primarily with [population and type of counseling].

In [type of counseling] counseling, you will be encouraged to express your views and concerns in order to better understand your situation and to help you learn new ways to address your problems. The risk involved for you is that you may be uncomfortable at times in counseling as you examine yourself and your life. I am committed to providing you with an accurate, fair assessment (diagnosis) that will assist in planning your treatment (setting goals). This will become a part of your treatment record. We will discuss the assessment and treatment process throughout counseling.

Everything you discuss with me will be kept confidential by me, except matters pertaining to: (1) suicide and harm to another person;

(continued)

PROFESSIONAL DISCLOSURE STATEMENT (Continued)

(2) physical/sexual abuse or neglect of minors, persons with disabilities, and the elderly; (3) legal activity resulting in a court order; and (4) to anything else required by law. For those matters, legally and/or ethically, I would have to break confidentiality and involve others. I am willing to share information about our counseling sessions with any other professional or agency that you wish, provided that you sign my Release-of-Information form. Ethically guiding my behavior is the [professional organization] Code of Ethics, published by the [professional organization and its national headquarters], and legally, I adhere to U.S. and [state of residence] statutes.

In terms of my background, I have worked in the mental health field since [date]. I earned my [highest level] degree from [university and location as well as date of degree]. I am a [licensure title and number]. I am a member of [professional organizations].

I charge [fee] for counseling. Sessions typically last [length of time].

I have attached a business card to this letter; please feel free to leave me a message on my answering machine if I am not available and I will get back to you. In the event of an emergency, do not hesitate to call 911 or to go to the nearest emergency room.

I hope that you find counseling to be helpful and I thank you for taking the time to read this statement. [state name and degrees here]

Contact Information:

[State Licensure Organization]

[National Professional Organization]

(Note: You do not have to sign this; you have a right to refuse counseling.)

I, _____ , fully understand what I have just read and offer my consent for counseling free of any pressure to do so. Here is my signature and the date of that signature (expires one year from now):

_____ (Signature of Client) _____ (Date)

_____ (Signature of Parent or Guardian) _____ (Date)

**SAMPLE INFORMED CONSENT FORM STATING
SPIRITUAL/RELIGIOUS PERSPECTIVE**

PROFESSIONAL DISCLOSURE STATEMENT

I welcome you as a new client and look forward to working with you. The purpose of this form is to inform you of my counseling approach, what you can expect from counseling with me, and my background. The form will also give you an opportunity to give consent for counseling.

In my view of counseling, [theory of counseling explanation]. In counseling, I use strategies that are primarily [major category of intervention techniques]: [types of techniques explanation]. These strategies will be used both during and between sessions. I work primarily with [population and type of counseling]. I believe that the spiritual and religious realm is an important part of counseling. Therefore, I am willing to explore issues of this type with you. I may also recommend specific spiritual or religious practices or interventions that will assist you in counseling if these practices or interventions complement your values and beliefs. You always have the right to refuse to participate in any practices or interventions that I recommend in counseling. A part of the assessment process will include a spiritual and religious assessment and possibly the administration of an assessment test(s) to clarify your concerns.

In [type of counseling] counseling, you will be encouraged to express your views and concerns in order to better understand your situation and to help you learn new ways to address your problems. The risk involved for you is that you may be uncomfortable at times in counseling as you examine yourself and your life. I am committed to providing you with an accurate, fair assessment (diagnosis) that will assist in planning your treatment (setting goals). This will become a part of your treatment record. We will discuss the assessment and treatment process throughout counseling.

Everything you discuss with me will be kept confidential by me, except matters pertaining to: (1) suicide and harm to another person; (2) to physical/sexual abuse or neglect of minors, persons with disabilities, and the elderly; (3) to legal activity resulting in a court order; and (4) to anything else required by law. For those matters legally and/or ethically, I would have to break confidentiality and involve others. I am willing to share information about our counseling sessions with any other professional or agency that you wish, provided

(continued)

PROFESSIONAL DISCLOSURE STATEMENT (Continued)

that you sign my Release-of-Information form. Ethically guiding my behavior is the [professional organization] Code of Ethics, published by the [professional organization and its national headquarters], and legally, I adhere to U.S. and [state of residence] statutes.

In terms of my background, I have worked in the mental health field since [date]. I earned my [highest level] degree from [university and location as well as date of degree]. I am a [licensure title and number]. I am a member of [professional organizations]. In the spiritual/religious area, I have received specific training by [type of training such as classes, workshops, training institutes, readings, consultations].

I charge [fee] for counseling. Sessions typically last [length of time].

I have attached a business card to this letter; please feel free to leave me a message on my answering machine if I am not available and I will get back to you. In the event of an emergency, do not hesitate to call 911 or to go to the nearest emergency room.

I hope that you find counseling to be helpful and I thank you for taking the time to read this statement.[state name and degrees here]

Contact Information:

[State Licensure Organization]

[National Professional Organization]

_____

(Note: You do not have to sign this; you have a right to refuse counseling.)

I, _____ , fully understand what I have just read and offer my consent for counseling free of any pressure to do so. Here is my signature and the date of that signature (expires one year from now):

_____ (Signature of Client) _____ (Date)

_____ (Signature of Parent or Guardian) _____ (Date)

Determination of Secular or Religious Counseling

Following the assessment, Genia (2000) recommends that the counselor dialogue with the client who has a religious commitment, about whether the client would prefer counseling that is secular or religious in its basis. The author recommends that three factors be taken into account: the *type of religious issues* the client has (the client may have very specific religious concerns best addressed by a religious counselor), the *amount of disturbance* the client has (the more disturbed the client, possibly the greater need for secular counseling), and the client's *comfort with secular counseling* (the client may have concern that his or her religion may be undermined by the therapeutic process).

If the counselor determines that the client's religious issues are best addressed by a religious counselor, then a referral to a religious counselor would be appropriate and in the best interests of the client. Such a referral may be based on the counselor's assessment that an expert in this area would be helpful to the client. This approach would involve the same decision-making process for the counselor used in making an expert referral about any aspect of a client's life. Some questions the counselor may ask himself or herself in determining if a referral is necessary are:

1. Do I believe I lack the necessary information about the religious or spiritual perspective needed to address this concern?
2. When I imagine obtaining the information needed to help my client in this area, do I become overwhelmed with my lack of time to obtain such information or my extensive lack of knowledge in this area?
3. Is my client's concern so focused that I cannot respond within my area of competence?

If the counselor's response to any of these questions is affirmative, a referral to a religious or spiritual expert of the client's view may be appropriate.

Referral to a religious or spiritual expert requires knowledge of the various types of training of religious counselors or leaders in your area. In addition, while religious counselors and leaders can have a wide variation of counselor training, they also range on the continuum of conservative to liberal perspectives of their religion. Therefore, the referring counselor needs to know who the possible referral sources are, the type and amount of counselor training they have had, and their religious perspective. A counselor may not be able to have knowledge of all of the religious counselors or leaders available to clients, but by having a professional network, a counselor may be able through contacts with colleagues, mental health professional licensure boards, and helping professionals be able to make these assessments for an appropriate referral.

With regard to *amount of disturbance,* because of the range of counselor training among religious counselors and leaders, the amount and type of counselor training may be a significant factor in the referral process. Therefore, the referring counselor needs to know the amount of psychological disturbance the client has and the amount and type of counselor training the religious counselor or leader has to make the best possible referral match. The more disturbed the client, the more the counselor may work at reducing the psychological disturbances of the client until a referral to a religious counselor or leader seems timely. Also, the client may require the psychological issues be at a more manageable level before the spiritual or religious issues are addressed.

The client's *comfort with secular counseling* also needs to be examined. The client may be most comfortable with a religious counselor and the secular counselor may then need to make a referral. If this is the core basis of the referral, the counselor would need to inform the client of possible limitations of the referral (without making damaging statements about the other counselor, but rather talking about possible realistic limitations with regard to training level of the counselor) and chart this information in the client's file. For example, a client may decide to work with a religious leader or counselor, but the referring counselor knows that this religious counselor has limited training in working on the client's specific mental health problems. In this situation, the counselor could make the referral at the client's request, but inform the client that while the religious concerns may be addressed, the other mental health concerns may not be addressed as extensively.

Another option may be that the client is open to working with the secular counselor on the mental health concerns and simply be referred to the religious counselor for a consult of a few sessions. This type of referral may effectively address both areas of concerns.

If the counselor assesses that his or her professional and personal competence is adequate to address the type of religious issues and the amount of client disturbance, and the client is comfortable with secular counseling, the counselor may begin to explore the client's development of a spiritual identity.

Development of a Spiritual Identity

Richards and Bergin (1997) define spiritual identity as a "person's sense of identity and worth in relation to God and his or her place in the universe" (p. 178). The authors propose that assessing a client's spiritual identity is critical because it can help them heal and grow, and that if clients do not have a spiritual identity that is positive, this lack may be contributing to their personal problems. Counselors can encourage clients who have a positive spiritual identity to use it as they address their counseling concerns while counselors can use interventions, as discussed in Chapter 8, to assist clients in developing a spiritual identity.

In assisting clients in accessing or developing a spiritual identity, counselors need to choose approaches and techniques carefully. This means taking into account the client, the problem, and the situation. The counselor needs to use only techniques that fit with the client (Yarhouse & VanOrman, 1999). One example of respectful exploration of this area is in a modification of Multimodal Therapy (Curtis & Davis, 1999). While Multimodal Therapy uses the BASIC ID (behavior, affect, sensation, imagery, cognitive, interpersonal relations, drugs, and biology) in assessing the problems of clients, the authors add spirituality (Sp) to this assessment process. They suggest that counselors begin with a closed-ended question simply asking clients if they have spiritual or religious beliefs and then follow-up a "Yes" answer with these types of questions:

1. Tell me about your spiritual and religious beliefs.
2. What role do your beliefs play in your life?
3. Tell me about any beliefs, rituals, or prayers that you find particularly comforting.
4. Tell me about any of your beliefs that cause anxiety or confusion. (p. 204)

A careful selection and application of interventions is necessary to enhance the welfare of the client. Richards and Bergin (1997) offer some general suggestions for using interventions in counseling that can minimize the advent of ethical dilemmas (see box on page 174).

In summary, to help a client make use of his or her positive spiritual identity or develop one in counseling, the counselor needs to:

1. Decide on techniques based on a careful assessment of the client's spiritual and religious realm.
2. Choose techniques that fit the client, the client's problem, and the life context of the client.

In addition to ethical issues related to informed consent and spiritual development, Richards and Bergin (1997) cite some potential ethical dilemmas for counselors attempting to integrate the spiritual dimension in counseling. These dilemmas (creating dual relationships, undermining the

**GENERAL PROCESS SUGGESTIONS FOR USING
RELIGIOUS AND SPIRITUAL INTERVENTIONS***

1. Therapists should inform clients during their informed consent procedures that they approach therapy with a spiritual perspective and sometimes (when appropriate) use religious and spiritual interventions.

2. Therapists should assess clients' religious and spiritual background and current status before using religious and spiritual interventions.

3. Therapists should establish a relationship of trust and rapport with clients before using religious and spiritual interventions.

4. Therapists should consider carefully whether religious and spiritual interventions are indicated (or contraindicated) before using them.

5. Therapists should clearly describe religious and spiritual interventions they wish to use and obtain clients' permission to do so before implementing them.

6. Therapists should use religious and spiritual interventions in a respectful manner, remembering that many of the interventions are regarded as sacred religious practices by religious believers.

7. Therapists should work within their clients' value framework and be careful not to push their own spiritual beliefs and values on clients, although they should challenge and help clients examine beliefs that are clearly irrational or self-defeating and linked to the presenting problem.

8. Therapists should not apply religious and spiritual interventions rigidly or uniformly with all clients but use them in a flexible, treatment-tailoring manner.

9. Therapists who believe in God and in the reality of transcendent spiritual guidance should seek spiritual enlightenment and inspiration to guide them in what interventions to use and when to use them (Richards & Bergin, 1997, p. 256).

*Copyright © 2001 by the American Psychological Association. Reprinted with permission.

Source: A Spiritual Strategy for Counseling and Psychotherapy by P. Scott Richards and Allen E. Bergin (Washington, DC: American Psychological Association). Copyright 1997 by the American Psychological Association. Reprinted with permission.

religious leaders of clients, imposing your religious or spiritual values, and violating the boundaries of your clinical work setting) are explored in this section.

Avoidance or Minimization of Dual or Multiple Relationships with Clients

Dual relationships or multiple relationships can pose problems for the counselor and client. A counselor may have a number of professional roles (counselor, expert witness, evaluator) with a client or a combination of professional and personal roles with a client (family, social, friendship, business) that may occur at the same time or follow one another in time (Sonne, 1999). Sonne states that multiple relationships cause problems when three dynamics of the counseling relationship are negatively impacted. These three dynamics are the *relationship and role expectations* of the counselor and client (e.g., the welfare of the client), the *emotional relationship* between the counselor and the client, and the *unequal power* in the counseling relationship. Therefore, when the relationships and role expectations are blurred or conflictual, the client can experience emotional struggles or harm or the multiple relationships can result in the counselor having his or her own needs met because of the unequal power.

With dual or multiple relationships, G. Miller (1999b) advocates having as few roles as possible with a client. The author recommends a list of questions a counselor can ask himself or herself in an attempt to clarify the relationships with the client:

1. What are my different roles with this client?
2. Are these roles in conflict or potentially hurtful to my client?
3. What are the fewest roles I can have with this client?
4. What is the most important role I need to have with my client?
5. Am I trying to have any of my own needs met in this (these) roles with my client?
6. Who else can meet the needs of my client with regard to this (these) roles?
7. Do I need to refer my client to another counselor?
8. Is a collegial consultation necessary to clarify my roles with this client?
9. Am I counseling someone I am too close to personally?

Some small community settings, such as rural or small "communities" focused on a commonality as addiction recovery or sexual orientation, really emphasize the struggle with dual or multiple relationships. Schank and Skovholt (1999) state that in small communities, social, business, and family relationships may overlap as well as working in counseling with more than one family member or clients who are friends with one another. The authors state that overlapping relationships are a reality for therapists in small communities and that the counselor needs to look at professional ethical standards within the context of the community. They also recommend that expectations and boundaries be clear, consultation with colleagues about cases occur regularly, and knowing yourself as well as having a personal life can provide both clarity and balance in trying to sort out multiple roles.

These dual or multiple relationships can emerge in a unique fashion with regard to the spiritual or religious arena. First, a counselor cannot effectively be a client's religious leader and counselor. Barnett and Fiorentino (2000) warn that such relationships may confuse clients and not take into account their welfare. This dual relationship is clear when the counselor has a religious position and provides counseling for his or her clients. The problems involved in such a situation are outlined by Richards and Bergin (1997): (a) being involved in activities that are only designed for the religious position, (b) having clients feel safe to express some of their issues that may require religious sanctions, (c) having possible conflict of interest, (d) knowing too much about other people involved in the religion, and (e) needing to report child abuse in one role but not the other. The authors recommend that counselors who want to do both roles provide free counseling in their religious setting as a part of their religious role and have an agreement with the client that the counseling is limited to spiritual and religious concerns.

Second, Richards and Bergin (1997) also state that dual relationships can occur for the counselor who does not have a religious position, but is involved in the same religious or spiritual community. Here the dangers include client avoidance of the spiritual community because of what the counselor knows about the client's life, accidental violation of confidentiality, and clients raising concerns about counseling in the community setting. The authors state that if a counselor does provide counseling in this context, the counselor should consult with a supervisor or colleague as to whether this action is in the best interests of the client (having consultation on an ongoing basis until the counseling is terminated) and set up boundaries that are explained to the client.

In summary, if a counselor is a religious leader providing counseling to a client, the counselor may want to:

1. Provide free counseling to the client.
2. Limit the focus of counseling to religious and spiritual concerns of the client.

If the counselor is involved in the same spiritual or religious community of the client, the counselor may consider:

1. Obtaining an ongoing consultation relationship with a colleague or mentor that focuses on the counseling from the perspective of the best interests of the client.
2. Setting firm boundaries with the client about interactions within the spiritual or religious community.

Collaboration with Clients' Religious Leaders

As stated in the section on determining if religious or secular counseling best fits the client, knowledge of possible referral sources of religious leaders or counselors is necessary to serve the best interests of the client. This is a point where a counselor may need to examine his or her biases toward or against specific spiritual or religious perspectives.

If a counselor is open to a particular spiritual or religious perspective, naturally the counselor may have more of a knowledge base on this perspective regarding information or contacts that can be given to a client. If a counselor is neutral toward a spiritual or religious perspective, the issue may be more of a practical one of taking the time or energy to find out information or contacts to assist the client. However, if a counselor has personally or professionally obtained information about a spiritual or religious perspective that runs counter to the counselor's values, the counselor needs to carefully sort out biases against this perspective because of their potential negative impact on the welfare of the client.

Negative biases may play themselves out directly or indirectly in counseling sessions. Directly a counselor may make derogatory comments about a client's religious leader. Chappelle (2000) states that undermining a client's religious leader in general is unethical. Also, the author points out that if a counselor makes such statements to clients, clients may be hurt by what the counselor says because they respect their religious leaders.

Indirectly, these biases against a religion or religious leader may also emerge. In an indirect fashion of underestimating the impact of religious leaders on clients' lives, counselors may not consider networking with religious leaders for the welfare of their clients or may be biased against such networking. However, a component of professional responsibility involves consultation and referrals to others, which includes religious leaders (Yarhouse & VanOrman, 1999). Counselors who have relationships with spiritual leaders may be able to enhance the welfare of their clients by turning to these leaders for support, consultation, and referral purposes (Barnett & Fiorentino, 2000). Such networking may increase knowledge of and access to community resources that can be helpful to the client. In addition, contact with spiritual and religious leaders can educate them about the counselor and his or her clinical work as well as hear their concerns about counseling (Yarhouse & VanOrman, 1999). Such dialogue can enhance the counseling work with future clients as well as create a possible bridge for religious leaders to refer clients for counseling.

Richards and Bergin (1997) provide some suggestions about how counselors can collaborate with religious leaders. One is that the counselor determines if the client views the religious leader as a source of support and if so, talk with the client about collaborating with the leader. If the client agrees, then have the client sign a release so the counselor can talk with the religious leader and vice versa. Second, they suggest that in the conversation with the religious leader the counselor identify himself or herself and the client as well as the purpose of the call, and talk about only the concern of import with the understanding that there may be contacts in the future.

Richards and Bergin (1997) underscore the importance of talking with religious leaders with respect. Religious leaders are professionals in their own right and have or potentially have a powerful impact on the client's life. A counselor who treats a religious leader with respect can build a trust and rapport with that leader that may assist in the development of a therapeutic alliance with the client as well as a professional link that can be helpful with both the current and future clients' therapeutic work.

Respect for Clients' Religious or Spiritual Values

In general, religious clients may be concerned about how the counselor will react to his or her religious views, particularly that their beliefs will be ignored or seen in a negative light (Yarhouse & VanOrman, 1999). This may be a concern for any client who has strong spiritual or religious views. Therefore, counselors need to be especially respectful and sensitive when discussing this domain with clients. For example, Haug (1998) suggests counselors use language that fits with the client's language and is not offensive. Terminology needs to be carefully selected by the counselor when discussing spirituality and religion, with the counselor being sensitive to both verbal and nonverbal cues of the client that indicate discomfort. Such sensitivity can provide the opportunity for a respectful dialogue between the counselor and the client that assures the client that the counselor will not be imposing spiritual or religious values on the client.

Chappelle (2000) describes several ways a counselor may impose values on a client. First, the counselor may try to shift the client's spiritual or religious values to be more like the counselor's values. Second, the counselor may focus on goals that do not fit with the values of the client.

Finally, counselors may try to shame or condemn their clients, which can hurt the client as well as the therapeutic relationship. These may be done out of awareness or a lack of awareness on the counselor's part. Both, however, are ethical violations. A crucial aspect of counseling is that the counselor respect and work within the client's value system. This is why it is important when working within the spiritual and religious realm that a counselor has a high knowledge of self and the areas of potential or actual countertransference.

One approach to avoiding the imposition of values in the process of counseling is for the counselor to examine how he or she looks at the client's religious or spiritual beliefs. Neusner (1994) describes four ways that individuals may look at other religions. A counselor may use this framework to understand his or her view of the client's religious or spiritual perspective. The first view is the *exclusivist* where the believer believes that his or her religion is the only true one. The second is the *inclusivist* where the believer has more of a relativist view that proposes each person's religious beliefs are true for him or her. The third is the *pluralist* view where every religion is believed to hold some truth. The fourth, which the author recommends in the reading of the text, is the *empathetic interest in other people* where each religion can teach us about being humans. Counselors who can employ the *empathetic interest in other people* view in relation to their clients can communicate a respect for the religious or spiritual beliefs of the client in the sense of how they assist the individual in living in the world as a human being. Such an attitude can communicate a respect for diversity that Birdsall (2001) describes as a critical aspect of counseling.

Another approach that the counselor can use to avoid value imposition is to view the spiritual or religious world of the client as a cultural influence or a culture to which the client belongs. In that sense, cultural values and norms are operating for both the counselor and client as clinical decisions are being made. Values impositions may be made in an obvious fashion (attempting to convert clients to your religious beliefs) or an indirect manner (judging, focusing on certain statements, making nonverbal gestures) (Birdsall, 2001). Counselors may especially experience this tension when they assess the spiritual or religious views of the culture as negatively impacting the mental health of the client. Sparks and Park (2000) speak of this general counseling conflict from a feminist perspective:

> *If a clinical decision is made to support the client's wish to adhere to her or his indigenous cultural beliefs, practitioners may feel that they are violating feminist principles by not actively addressing the oppression sanctioned within the client's culture. However, if practitioners decide to confront and challenge the client's cultural values and norms, practitioners may feel that this also constitutes a violation of feminist principles because they are not supporting the woman's values and beliefs. (p. 212)*

This quote describes the bind any counselor may experience when viewing a client's situation from a different value system: "Do I stay with the client's perspective even though it appears oppressive to the client's mental health or do I confront the client's values and beliefs which may negatively impact the therapeutic alliance and the welfare of the client?" The authors make four specific recommendations to counselors sorting out these complex ethical dilemmas: understand the *context of the culture*, be aware of the *history of oppression*, be *aware of yourself*, and be *flexible in problem solving*. These recommendations made with regard to women in domestic violence situations can be extended to exploration of the client's spiritual or religious culture.

The counselor needs to understand the *context of the culture*. Understanding the strengths and weaknesses of the culture can assist the counselor in avoiding stereotypes about the spiritual or religious culture of the client. The culture may be both oppressive and supportive to the client in his or her current situation.

Awareness of the *history of oppression* can be two-fold in the spiritual or religious culture. The history of the spiritual or religious practice in the United States may help the counselor understand some of the dynamics of the client's spiritual or religious community. For example, a religious group that has experienced discrimination may be a closed system in terms of "outsiders." A second way oppression may express itself is in relation to your client. The counselor needs to be sensitive to how the client's gender, sexual orientation, and so on may have resulted in the client's experiencing oppression within his or her spiritual or religious culture.

Awareness of self as a counselor has been discussed previously in this book. The more aware the counselor is of his or her values and beliefs spiritually and religiously, the less likely countertransference will operate negatively toward the client. The more self-aware the counselor is, the better the counselor can protect the welfare of the client in sessions.

Flexibility in problem solving can assist the counselor in avoiding dichotomous approaches with clients. Rather, the counselor and client can collaborate in a brainstorm fashion regarding spiritual or religious values of the client when mutual trust and respect are present.

Because counseling is value-based and the counselor may influence the spiritual and religious views of the client, the counselor needs to be careful about imposing values (Lannert, 1991). Hawkins and Bullock (1995) make specific suggestions to prevent values imposition:

1. Talk openly with the religiously oriented client about his or her spiritual or religious orientation and your expertise within this area.

2. Discuss therapeutic goals in terms of your perspective that will be discussed in counseling (e.g., divorce).

3. Present additional options for counseling for the client if appropriate.

A thoughtful approach to working with a client's values can enhance the possibility of clients having a trusting therapeutic relationship with his or her counselor and having therapy that is in the client's best interests.

Boundaries of the Counselor's Work Settings

Chappelle (2000) states that counselors need to consider the setting in which they work when choosing interventions. The setting's response to incorporation of spirituality or religion in counseling may vary due to agency policy, supervisor or collegial preference, agency "personality," or community influences on the agency. These various influences in combination with one another impact the comfort level of the counselor in addressing this area as a part of the counseling process. They also have potential impact on how publicly or directly the counselor incorporates the exploration of this domain in counseling. For example, an agency may have a policy that separates church and state, thereby limiting what the counselor can address in counseling or how those issues may be addressed. The counselor may, in such a situation, discuss the spiritual or religious area by using "safe" terminology with the client such as discussing resources for hope and meaning in one's life rather than asking directly about spiritual or religious resources available to the client. The counselor in this context and approach would be acting in the best interests of the client as well as within the bounds of the agency.

Richards and Bergin (1997) further discuss the impact of the separation between church and state on counselors in public, tax-supported settings in the United States where First Amendment rights apply. They state that counselors have two basic rights: the right to explore spiritual issues with clients when both the counselor and the client agree that this area is related to the counseling problem and the right to tell clients of their religious views if clients ask about them. However, they state that legally, counselors cannot pressure clients to accept their (counselors') religious views. One example of self-disclosure from a religious perspective is Guinee's (1999) elaboration on Christian counselor disclosure in a secular counseling agency.

Chappelle (2000) recommends that prior to incorporating any interventions of a spiritual or religious nature in such settings, the counselor tell both clients and supervisors about the type and purpose of the intervention in a written document. Richards and Bergin (1997) recommend that in settings where there is a separation between church and state, the counselor obtain permission from the client and the counselor's supervisor to use specific, explicit spiritual or religious interventions as a part of counseling. The authors stress that these suggestions are especially important when working with adolescents. Chappelle (2000) adds that when working with individuals such as adolescents or those mentally challenged, the counselor needs to sensitively involve those individuals' guardians in the consent process.

Such documentation of spiritual or religious interventions for clients would be the informed consent while a document for supervisors may be a supervision contract. However, if a counselor anticipates working within the spiritual or religious realm frequently, the counselor may consider informing his or her supervisor of this integration in his or her counseling approach via some type of documented correspondence, for example, letter, memo, or e-mail.

Counselors need to consider the context of their work when using spiritual or religious interventions in counseling. A counselor who wants to incorporate a strong spiritual or religious component in their counseling needs to consider the impact of such incorporation on himself or herself, the client, the clinical work, and the agency or community in which he or she works. A careful incorporation of the spiritual dimension in counseling can increase its effectiveness and minimize any negative outcomes. Overall, if the counselor respects the client's value system and has a written consent for spiritual or religious interventions used, the counselor is relatively safe in the incorporation of spirituality in counseling (Richards & Bergin, 1997).

Counselor's Area of Competence

Mental health professionals have an ethical commitment to being reasonably aware of current professional information in the area in which they work as well as make a commitment to being competent in interventions employed in therapy. To practice outside of your competency may not only hurt your client, but also your integrity as a counselor (Chappelle, 2000). Therefore, counselors need to use techniques in which they have been trained and should be careful in using techniques with clients who cannot give consent alone, for example, adolescents (Barnett & Fiorentino, 2000). If the counselor believes he or she would be working outside of their knowledge and training, he or she needs to obtain consultation to continue such work or make referrals to experts. W. B. Johnson, Ridley, and Nielsen (2000) suggest that counselors should be educated, trained, and experienced in working with issues of religion as well as willing to obtain consultation to most effectively address these concerns if they plan to integrate religious content in counseling.

Counselors also need to be clear about services they can provide for clients (Yarhouse & VanOrman, 1999). In terms of competence, Yarhouse and VanOrman recommend that counselors working with a religious client have knowledge of the client and his or her values and how values have impacted personality theories in psychology. This knowledge means understanding what religious beliefs mean to the client, different spiritual and religious assessment instruments that may be used by the counselor with this client, how effective religious techniques may be with this client, and the slants of personality theories.

While these are legitimate guidelines for the counselor to follow, they can create a dilemma for counselors. There is limited training in the spiritual and religious area for counselors, yet a counselor may see this as an area that needs to be addressed in counseling (Lannert, 1991). So what does the "typical" counselor do when facing a client who has issues in the spiritual or religious realm that need to be addressed in counseling?

Current counselors or counselors-in-training have typically had few if any counseling courses on working with clients from different religious groups. Those who have done readings or trainings in the United States may have primarily been exposed to information from a Judeo-Christian perspective. With these possible limitations, should these "typical" counselors always refer clients to spiritual or religious experts? Does the counselor have an obligation to the client to obtain more training in this area when the counselor does not see himself or herself typically working within this domain?

These are some of the hard, important questions for each counselor to address when facing the integration of the spiritual or religious area in counseling. It may be helpful to examine these concerns in supervision or in discussion with colleagues. The counselor may use the following questions as guidelines in answering such questions and dilemmas:

1. How much do I plan to work on the spiritual or religious issues of clients?
2. What are the limits that I need to ethically place on myself as I work within such domains?
3. How do these limits apply in terms of my own countertransference?
4. How do these limits apply in terms of various spiritual or religious practices?
5. To work on this area with this client or clients in general, do I need more training?
6. If I need more training, how much training and in what areas do I need training to consider myself competent?
7. From whom can I receive consultation on these issues?
8. How may I feasibly receive such consultation in terms of type of contact (in-person, phone, mail, e-mail) and frequency?

Each counselor needs to be a careful consumer when choosing trainers and consultants in the spiritual and religious realm. As with any specific area of counseling, there is a wide range of quality available to the mental health professional in terms of trainers and consultants. Choosing an effective, current avenue of information in this area may be best accomplished by being in contact with your licensing or certification board or the division of your professional organization that focuses on spiritual or religious areas of counseling. Also, the mental health professional may find it helpful to discuss possible recommendations with trusted colleagues and supervisors who are current in this area of counseling.

In summary, counselors, to practice within their area of competence, need to:

1. Be aware of current professional information on spirituality and religion as they relate to counseling.
2. Be trained in spiritual or religious interventions techniques they use in counseling.
3. Have clients sign a consent form after they have been clearly informed about the counseling they will receive.
4. Refer clients to spiritual or religious experts as appropriate.
5. Understand both the spiritual and religious values of the client and the biases of psychological theories in terms of personality.
6. Obtain training and consultation from qualified professionals in this area.
7. Set appropriate limits for yourself in working in this area in terms of knowledge, skill base, and personal biases.

Case Studies

CASE STUDY 1

As a part of your assessment process with a client, you use Multimodal Therapy BASIC ID (behavior, affect, sensation, imagery, cognitive, interpersonal relations, drugs, and biology) with the spirituality (Sp) section added. Your client answers your question with regard to having spiritual or religious beliefs with "Yes"; so you are comfortable asking some additional questions. In asking about his spiritual and religious beliefs and the role they play in his life as well as beliefs, rituals, and prayers, your client finds comforting, your client begins to tell you about some of the beliefs related to his spiritual/religious practice that make him anxious. You are not familiar with his spiritual/religious beliefs or any religious leaders in the community related to those beliefs.

1. Would you be comfortable exploring such concerns with your client?
2. Where would you begin exploring your client's concerns?

3. What additional information would you need about your client to effectively intervene on his concerns?

CASE STUDY 2

You have attended the same spiritual or religious community since you have practiced counseling in the area. You are at one of the services in your community when you notice one of your clients attending the service for the first time. You have worked with this client for a few sessions and anticipate your client will be returning for counseling. While you knew your client had some spiritual concerns, you did not believe that they were related to the counseling problem so you did not do a thorough assessment regarding the client's spiritual or religious history and you do not advertise yourself as a spiritual or religious counselor. You are surprised your client is at the service.

1. How would you handle this situation in the social context at hand?
2. What would you do in the next session with your client?
3. Would you refer the client to another counselor, continue in therapy with the client as is, or stop your involvement in the spiritual/religious community?
4. If you felt it were necessary, who would you contact for consultation regarding this dual relationship and what would be the focus of the consultation?

CASE STUDY 3

You have been contacted by a local religious leader to present a series of mental health topics to his religious community. The leader has a reputation of being quite closed to the mental health field and you have heard him publicly make derogatory comments about counselors. You believe that it would be beneficial to make a connection with him in terms of educating him about the benefits of mental health counseling for members of his religious community, but you are hesitant because you do not know much about this religion and you are unclear about his expectations given his request on your answering machine.

1. What would be your overall plan in this possible community outreach situation?
2. What would be your first approach in this situation? What would be the possible pros and cons of this approach?
3. What additional information would you want to have about the religious leader, the community, and who would you contact to receive such information?
4. What, if any, ethical guidelines would you follow in providing this request for mental health services?

Exercises

Exercise 1

Write a professional disclosure statement using the form on page 167 as a sample. Then write a professional disclosure statement that explicitly states a spiritual/religious dimension to counseling using the form on page 169 as a sample. Then answer the following questions:

1. Was it difficult for me to write a professional disclosure statement that included the spiritual/religious dimension? If so, what was difficult for me in writing such a statement?

    —Concern about stating my spiritual/religious orientation so openly?

    —Concern about how such a statement may influence how I am perceived by my clients?

    —Concern about how such a statement may influence how I am perceived by the local community?

    —Concern about how such a statement may influence how I am perceived by my colleagues?

    —Concern about how such a statement may influence how I am perceived by my professional community?

Exercise 2

In your community, you would like to network with different religious and spiritual leaders because the area of spirituality is an important one for you and you want knowledge of community resources in this domain on which your clients can draw. Answer the following questions with regard to this goal:

1. Which religious and spiritual communities locally am I interested in working with?
2. Who would I begin to make such contacts with?
3. How would I make such contacts (phone, letter, e-mail, in person)?
4. How would I describe myself and my clinical work with these professionals?
5. What information would I want to know about them and their view of counseling?

Exercise 3

You receive a phone call from a client's loved one (parent, partner, and so on) and the person says (very emotionally): "I do not like what you are doing with my _____ in counseling because I believe those interventions are disrespectful of our religion."

A. How would you respond to the caller?
B. What would be the rationale you would have for your response?
C. How would you shape your response based on:
    —Welfare of the client?
    —Your theoretical orientation to counseling?
    —Your spiritual or religious orientation?
    —Clinical setting?
D. Would your response hinge at all on the specific religious denomination mentioned by the client?

Exercise 4

In your work setting, you have openly told colleagues that you are a member of [specific religious or spiritual group]. You have never told this to clients because you have been concerned about how you might be perceived by them. You also are unclear about the agency policies regarding your use of spiritual or religious interventions in counseling. Discuss with another person the following areas:

1. How to incorporate spiritual or religious interventions more as a part of your counseling approach.
2. How you might bring this up with supervisors, colleagues, and clients.
3. The pros and cons of incorporating a more distinct spiritual or religious approach as a part of counseling in terms of supervisors, colleagues, and clients.

Exercise 5

Your client asks you in your first session, "Are you a member of [specific religious denomination]? I will only talk with a member of [specific religious denomination] counselor."

A. How would you respond to the client?
B. What would be the rationale you would have for your response?
C. How would you shape your response based on:
    —Welfare of the client?
    —Your theoretical orientation to counseling?
    —Your spiritual or religious orientation?
    —Clinical setting?

D.   Would your response hinge at all on the specific religious denomination mentioned by the client?

Exercise 6

Contact a local mental health counselor and ask for an opportunity to interview him or her about the connections made professionally with the local religious communities. Tell him or her you would like to know:

1.   The nature of the contacts in terms of being formal or informal.
2.   How contacts with the religious communities were made.
3.   The types of outreach done with the various religious communities.
4.   If there are no local contacts with the religious communities, is that a conscious decision on the counselor's part?

Exercise 7

Find the ethical standards for your professional group (psychologists, social workers, counselors, and marriage and family therapists) as stated in their national professional Web sites. Determine which of their standards relate to the area of spirituality/religion.

Suggested Readings

Bergin, A. E., Payne, I. R., & Richards, P. S. (1996). Values in psychotherapy. In E. P. Shafranske (Ed.), *Religion and the clinical practice of psychology* (pp. 297–325). Washington, DC: American Psychological Association.

Richards, P. S., & Bergin, A. E. (1997). *A spiritual strategy for counseling and psychotherapy.* Washington, DC: American Psychological Association.

Specific Treatment Techniques

Chapter Objectives

1. What are some specific religious practices that can be used in counseling clients?
2. What are some general spiritual practices that can be used in counseling clients?

8

Chapter

Overview

This chapter examines the use of specific techniques that can be used to facilitate the development of the client's religious/spiritual life as well as the development of skills and resources in the spiritual domain for the client to access. In the review of these techniques, terminology may be used that does not apply to all religions or spiritual practices. For example, the word "God" may not apply to a client who is a Taoist. However, the reader is encouraged to look beyond the language to discover how the technique may be respectfully and appropriately used in counseling.

The use of the technique depends on whether the client is ready for the technique and if the counselor has the ability to use the technique (Sollod, 1993). In terms of client readiness, the counselor needs to be sure the client is comfortable with the approach if it is religiously or spiritually based (Sollod, 1993). An example of an eight-category taxonomy of client responsiveness to interventions was provided in Chapter 6 (Kelly, 1990): religiously committed clients, religiously loyal clients, spiritually committed clients, religiously and spiritually open clients, superficially religious clients, religiously tolerant and indifferent clients, nonreligious clients, clients hostile to religion. Keeping in mind that a taxonomy of this nature may assist the counselor in selecting an appropriate intervention technique.

Sollod (1993) advises counselors to be skilled and trained in the use of these critical techniques. Although this may seem like a basic suggestion, how do you learn these spiritual techniques and when is enough training enough for use of the technique (Sollod, 1993)? Is it enough to attend a course or go to one workshop? Is a spiritual practice necessary to learn about a technique to provide a depth to the technique and a context for understanding it?

Using the ethical guidelines of practicing within your area of competence and focusing on the welfare of the client may guide your counseling through this confusing ethical maze. Currently, there are no clear guidelines with regard to competence in working with spiritual or religious values in counseling. This reality places the counselor in a dilemma regarding the determination of practicing within your area of competence. As described in Chapter 7, the counselor may consult with colleagues or supervisors who have experience working within this area, licensing boards, or divisions of professional organizations that focus on religious and spiritual issues for guidance. Also, counselors may use peer supervision or study groups to hone their intervention skills (Fukuyama & Sevig, 1999).

With regard to the welfare of the client, the counselor needs to determine what the client needs and wants in therapy. In Chapter 7, *type of religious issues, amount of client disturbance,* and *comfort with secular counseling* (Genia, 2000) were used as a guide for religious or secular counseling. These same parameters can be used in choosing intervention techniques with clients. The counselor may determine that the *type of religious issues* require specific religious interventions that the counselor feels competent using or the counselor may determine that the type of religious issues may require a referral to a religious expert in keeping in mind the best interests of the client. If the client has a high *degree of psychological disturbance,* the counselor may want to not use any religious techniques at that time in counseling or use them cautiously in a metaphorical manner. The *comfort with secular counseling* can be adapted to techniques by determining if the client is more comfortable with the use of religious or secular techniques in counseling. One way to facilitate such comfort is to use the spiritual or religious language of the client to communicate respect and a nonjudgmental attitude (Haug, 1998). These three factors need to be considered in relation to one another as indicated in the ethical decision-making tree in Chapter 7. As with the use of any techniques in counseling, the counselor needs to choose the technique based on the client's needs and wants, the timing of the use of the technique in counseling, and the context of the use of the technique which, in this case, involves the spiritual or religious area of the client.

This combination of needs and wants requires the counselor to discuss intervention techniques with the client prior to their usage in counseling. Also, before using the technique, the counselor needs to inform the client that they can stop the technique usage in the session simply by letting the counselor know that they want to stop. They need to be reminded that they can do the same outside of the session when they are using a technique and it becomes overwhelming or uncomfortable for them. Such respectful collaboration around the use of techniques strengthens the therapeutic alliance and assures the welfare of the client when working in such a sensitive area for many of our clients.

A final point is the importance of being sensitive to using an intervention technique that fits the client's culture. As discussed in Chapter 3, choosing a strategy that does not fit the client can result in the client being upset or therapeutic goals being unrealistic. To facilitate the therapeutic alliance and the healing process of therapy, intervention strategies require that the counselor take into account the culture of the client in choosing a technique. This "culture" includes the client's spiritual or religious orientation, age, gender, class, and ethnicity. What is important is that the counselor finds a balance between a standard "cookbook" spiritual intervention approach in counseling (no matter who the client is, they receive the same approach) and a haphazard spiritual intervention approach (choose a technique without thought or plan) (Fukuyama & Sevig, 1999).

The remainder of this chapter examines specific techniques that can be used in working with clients within the spiritual or religious areas of their lives. The chapter is divided into religious practices, general practices, and religious and general practices. Each of the interventions needs to be carefully examined by the counselor and client in collaboration to find the most appropriate match for the client. These interventions may require adaptation to the religious or spiritual views of the client also.

Religious Practices

Prayer

Prayer is a core part of religious practice and prayer has many different forms due to individual differences and cultural differences (Wulff, 1997). As McCullough and Larson (1999) state, prayer is made up of actions, thoughts, and attitudes that connect a person to the sacred realm. Prayer can be viewed as talking and the act of praying may cause the client to slow down his or her busy life and find that he or she receive information about or answers to his or her life questions (Becvar, 1997).

Poloma and Pendleton (1989, 1991) describe four types of prayer that they label *meditative, ritualistic, petitionary,* and *colloquial. Meditative* is related to worship (being in God's presence), *ritualistic* is prayer involved in rituals, *petitionary* is asking specific things, and *colloquial* is relational to your Higher Power in the sense of gratitude or requests for guidance (more conversational than petitionary). McCullough and Larson (1999) add a fifth type, *intercessory,* which is to ask for healing for others (Poloma and Pendleton include this in petitionary prayer). These five types of prayer may be practiced by the counselor or the client either in or outside of the session. It may be helpful for the counselor and client to examine the type of prayer the client is using or the type of prayer they are using together in session to determine if another form would be more beneficial for them. For example, a client who struggles with self-centeredness may be engaged in petitionary prayer yet intercessory may be more beneficial to the client in terms of his or her issues. Or another client who struggles with a negative, pessimistic perspective may benefit from colloquial prayer. Therefore, asking the client about their prayer in terms of content may assist the counselor in choosing the type of prayer intervention that best fits the client.

In addition to the types of prayer, the counselor may approach the use of prayer differently in the counseling setting. Canda (1990) outlines three forms of prayer that may be used in relation to the counseling setting. These three forms include praying for the client, referring or working with religious leaders to facilitate the client's prayer interests, or praying with the client in the session.

The technique of praying for clients is one of implicit integration (Tan, 2000) as discussed in Chapter 5. Implicit integration means that prayer is involved in the counseling process, but not in an intrusive or obvious manner. However, a decision facing counselors is whether to let clients know they are praying for them. When a counselor decides to tell a client that he or she is praying for the client, the counselor needs to be aware that this technique is now explicitly involved in the counseling process and requires that the counselor weigh the pros and cons of such a disclosure prior to making it. This caution fits in with West's (2000) general caution to counselors regarding disclosure in session about the counselor's spiritual or religious views: There needs to be a trusting relationship; the client needs not to be overwhelmed by the disclosure; and it needs to be done tentatively.

When counselors pray for their clients, this act of prayer may arise from different motivations of the counselor. Some of these motivations are:

1. The counselor may pray for his or her clients in general because of religious or spiritual beliefs.
2. There may be some clients in especially difficult situations for whom the counselor prays.
3. The counselor may pray for difficult or unlikable clients because it is harder to have resentments toward someone for whom one prays (McCullough & Larson, 1999).
4. The counselor may work with clients in such difficult or dangerous situations that prayer is a critical part of self-care as a counselor. For example, some counselors create what they call a "Higher Power box." In this form of prayer, a counselor writes the first name or a symbol of the client on a sheet of paper, places it in the "Higher Power box," and

puts the lid on the box. When the counselor worries about the client (after having done as much as clinically possible), the counselor can reassure oneself that the client has been placed in their Higher Power's hands since they are in the "Higher Power box."

With regard to referring or working with religious leaders to facilitate the client's prayer interests, the counselor needs to know the religious resources available in the community. Depending on the client's religious affiliation, the counselor may want to match up a client with a religious leader in the community that can act as a consultant regarding possible forms of prayer groups available to the client given his or her religious faith. The counselor needs to encourage the client to be a "wise consumer" so the client feels comfortable ending the connection with the religious leader if it proves to be an uncomfortable or bad match for the client and not assume that he or she needs to remain connected with that religious group simply because the counselor made the referral.

Praying with clients in the session is explicit integration of the religious or spiritual views in counseling. McCullough and Larson (1999) state that prayer might help people feel better, more hopeful, more comfortable in counseling, and more open to working on their issues in counseling, as well as help counselors see how clients view the world through the process of praying. Prayer may also show the client that the counselor cares, increase the client's trust in the counselor, and reduce the client's loneliness and increase his or her hope (Koenig & Pritchett, 1998).

Various authors make recommendations for the use of prayer in counseling. Kelly's (1990) guidelines include using prayer in counseling when:

1. It may help a client change and the client has asked for prayer or the counselor believes the client is open to it.

2. The counselor believes in prayer and can use it in a manner that matches the beliefs of the client.

3. The counselor and the client are a good match spiritually and the use of prayer does not conflict with agency policies.

McCullough and Larson (1999) stipulate that prayer only be used in counseling when the client asks for it, an assessment leads the counselor to believe that boundaries would remain intact, and therapeutic care is being provided in addition to rather than replaced by prayer.

Koenig and Pritchett (1998) warn that praying with clients, particularly psychiatric patients, may impact the therapeutic relationship in unpredictable ways. Prayer could break the trusting relationship, make the counselor less objective, and impact the client's stability (especially if the client has poor boundaries). Kelly (1990) also outlines some concerns about the use of prayer in counseling. These include:

1. Prayer in counseling can be an avoidance technique of the client.
2. The counselor's religious values may be intrusive on the client's views.
3. Use of the religious practice of prayer in a counseling setting that is secular may be problematic.
4. Use of prayer by a counselor who is not using prayer appropriately in general or specifically for the client's needs is inappropriate.
5. Counselors may believe that prayer is ineffective.

Koenig and Pritchett (1998) make some specific recommendations to counselors regarding the use of prayer in sessions. First, they suggest that counselors not pray on a regular basis with clients and if counselors are at all uncomfortable with praying with their clients, they should refer them to a religious leader for prayer. Second, they recommend prayer if the client uses religion to cope, asks for prayer or does not hesitate when the counselor mentions it as an option, and has good boundaries. Third, they recommend its use if it looks as though prayer would be helpful to therapy and if both client and counselor have experienced the same religion. Fourth, they suggest brief prayer where the client does the praying or the counselor, if asked by the client to pray, makes it a general, positive prayer, and that this experience of praying together is processed in the next session.

Tan (1996) suggests a specific type of prayer that can be used in counseling: *inner healing prayer* which is particularly useful for unresolved past traumas. While some counselors suggest the use of guided imagery as a part of this prayer, for instance, Jesus comforting the client in the past situation, Tan suggests that the prayer itself be more emphasized and provides an outline of seven steps for a healing prayer. These seven sequential steps are as follows:

1. Having the counselor pray to God for healing.
2. Helping the client relax.
3. Leading the client back to the trauma visually (while processing the experience).
4. Having the counselor again pray to God.
5. Waiting for God to respond to the client with regard to the memory (again processing the experience).
6. Closing with a prayer from both counselor and client.
7. Debriefing the client.

Another prayer technique, *praying through,* where the client finds new ways to look at the past, is described as a four step process by Dobbins (2000). In the first step, the client talks to God about the pain in an honest fashion such as writing a letter. In the second step, the client adds emotion to the experience, for example, reading the letter intensely. In the third step, the client meditates, and in communication with God, asks for another way to look at the pain. Finally, the client expresses gratitude to God for the healing. The author suggests these steps be repeated until resolution is complete. Although the author does not comment on the location of this intervention, it seems that it could be used either in or outside of the therapy session.

Finally, Richards and Bergin (1997) caution counselors about praying with their clients in session or encouraging clients to pray outside of sessions. They note that counselors need to be very careful about working within the belief structures of clients and avoid imposing their own beliefs on clients. Generally, they suggest that counselors refer clients to religious leaders for guidance about prayer if the client has specific questions or concerns in relation to the process of prayer.

Counselors also need to be respectful to themselves personally when engaging in prayer with clients. The counselor may be uncomfortable praying with clients and simply need to set that limit professionally. This discomfort may be due to a counseling style of the counselor that does not incorporate prayer easily even if the counselor prays outside of sessions. Also, the counselor may set the limit on praying in sessions because of different religious or spiritual beliefs from the client. Even if a counselor is comfortable praying with a client, the counselor needs to be aware that prayer will reveal a lot about the counselor personally (concept of a Higher Power, comfort with prayer, focus of prayer, manner of prayer, and so on) and may shift the dynamics of the therapeutic relationship in a direction that the counselor does not want. Prior to introducing prayer into a session, a counselor may want to anticipate the pros and cons of including prayer in a session with this particular client. Counselors may have different reasons for declining to incorporate prayer in sessions or for incorporating prayer in sessions. Whatever motivates a counselor to pray or not to pray with or for clients needs to be tempered by the ethical guideline of the client's welfare. In addition, the counselor needs to carefully examine his or her motivation to use prayer in sessions, always keeping in mind what is in the best interests of the client.

Sacred Writings

A part of counseling may involve the use of religious bibliotherapy (West, 2000). West recommends talking with individuals early in therapy about their religious beliefs to determine if using scriptures or other readings as a part of therapy would be helpful to them. As a part of the assessment process, the counselor can easily ask the client what spiritual or religious readings does or has the client used to sustain or support him or herself; which readings provide hope, meaning, and a sense of safety in living. Such a simple question can assist the counselor in understanding the client's spiritual history and how important the spiritual or religious realm is or could be in terms of a resource of strength for the client. Also, finding out the types of readings the client actively engages in can cue the counselor as to some of the client's spiritual or religious struggles. For example, the client, daily, may read literature as a part of his or her religious practice with which he or she may fundamentally disagree yet feel bound to read because it is a part of the religious practice. The counselor may need to assist the client in such a situation to determine if the client wants to continue the reading or not and how to make that a comfortable decision for the client. If the client continues the reading, can he or she talk with a trusted religious leader about the struggle or can the client engage in self-talk that makes the reading more tolerable ("That text was written in [date], so the views are dated and do not directly apply to my situation"). Or if the client continues the reading, can a religious leader be consulted or self-talk employed by the client.

Richards and Bergin (1997) report this is the most common spiritual intervention used by counselors and recommend the use of writings that fit with the client's beliefs. They state that counselors quote, interpret, indirectly refer to, and discuss stories related to spiritual writings as well as use them to challenge beliefs of clients and encourage clients to memorize or read and study them. This intervention can be used even if the counselor and the client have different spiritual or religious beliefs (A. Rabinowitz, 2000). Sperry and Giblin (1996) recommend the use of scriptures with clients if the counselor believes it will assist in the therapy process. The authors state the benefits of such use can assist clients in viewing their problems differently, experiencing a sense of normalcy about their struggles, and feeling less isolated about their issues. Richards and Bergin (1997) report that clients may enjoy, be comforted by, and experience insight or the presence of their Higher Power by reading sacred writings. The authors also state that using these writings may help clients change their beliefs, look at their problems differently, understand their sacred writings better, and seek their Higher Power.

The counselor needs to be clear about his or her limitations theologically (West, 2000). Also, counselors need to set clear limits in this regard so they remember that they are using these writings in the context of therapy and that they are not a religious leader to the client (West, 2000). Tan (1996) makes some additional cautions to the use of sacred writings: Do not use writings in an authoritarian manner or in a simple manner, and be aware of possible different interpretations of the text by the counselor and client. Finally, Richards and Bergin (1997) recommend that counselors do not debate sacred writings with their clients and refer their clients to religious leaders if they believe the clients' beliefs about the writings are dysfunctional.

All of these comments on the use of readings have in common that stories can teach us how to live. As Garrett (1998) states: "In the traditional way, there is no one moral to a story. The power of it lies in the listener's subjective experience of the story" (p. 16). The power of the readings are in what the client hears in the story, what meaning the client derives from the story. The counselor can assist the client by engaging in a discussion of what the readings mean to the client and help the client use the readings that are healing and let go of those readings which are not. The counselor may also make use of consultation with religious or spiritual leaders to find readings for the client that are beneficial.

Religious Community

West (2000) suggests that counselors work closely with religious leaders in the community in the best interests of clients. He states that this might seem to be an unusual idea unless it is placed in the context of consulting or collaborating with another professional. From this perspective, the spiritual or religious leader is viewed as an expert with whom the counselor consults. Specific suggestions for working ethically with leaders are outlined in Chapter 7.

One advantage of such contacts is the enhancement for appropriate referrals. In addition, Tan (1996) states that a referral to a religious community may elicit numerous group resources that can be supportive to a client. This resource may be especially important for clients who have limited financial means or whose therapy is constrained by managed care limitations. Also, these communities can also help clients feel that they belong and provide them with a structure of support (emotional, financial, employment; Richards & Bergin, 1997).

Thurston (2000) makes suggestions for psychologists who want to network with Evangelical and Fundamentalist Christian religious communities that could be expanded as suggestions for counselors who want to network with religious and spiritual communities. These suggestions are to: Conduct retreats or programs on issues that cross over between the spiritual and psychological realms; consult with religious leaders on cases where they are doing counseling; and help religious leaders develop church programs on pertinent counseling issues, for instance, domestic violence. All of these approaches create bridges between the counseling and spiritual or religious communities. Such bridge building can create a firm foundation for collaboration especially when working with difficult issues or clients that cross over between the two areas. Whenever there is an overlap of two perspectives, individuals from both areas can learn and grow both personally and professionally which can assist counselors with both current and future clients.

One of the questions facing the counselor in referral or access to spiritual or religious communities is the health of the community. An assessment tool of the community's "personality" that a counselor can use in the referral or access process can be found in the box below.

Such an assessment can open up a dialogue with a client to determine the health and support of the religious or spiritual community in general, as well as, assess specific aspects of the community in terms of strengths and weaknesses.

A second question is how to make connections with a spiritual or religious community. Working with a specific client may motivate a counselor to make contact with the client's spiritual or religious leader or community. Also, a counselor may decide that he or she wants to make more connections with the local spiritual or religious communities

---

ASSESSMENT OF A RELIGIOUS/SPIRITUAL COMMUNITY'S HEALTH

1. What is the client's perception of the religious/spiritual community overall?

2. What is the general atmosphere or tone of the community?

3. How do individuals within the religious community typically treat the client?

   —The religious leader.

   —The "body" (members of the community).

4. How does the client feel after contact with the community?

5. Are there certain aspects of the community (activities, rituals) that help the client feel better about self, his or her life, and his or her outlook?

6. Are there certain aspects of the community (activities, rituals) that make the client feel worse about self, his or her life, and his or her outlook?

7. Does the client feel a respected part of the community? If so, in what ways and by whom? If not, in what ways does the client feel disrespected and by whom?

in general. Some suggestions in addition to Thurston's (2000) outlined previously are:

1. Be aware of your biases toward or against specific leaders or communities.
2. Determine with which spiritual or religious leader(s) or community(s) contact is desired.
3. Determine through contact with clients, colleagues, supervisors, licensing boards, or spiritual or religious divisions of professional organizations, who are local leaders who can be approached and how to best approach them.
4. Approach all contacts in a friendly, open manner that conveys a willingness to collaborate.
5. Work with those leaders who are open to working with counselors.
6. Attend local gatherings that involve leaders.

General Practices

Bibliotherapy

Bibliotherapy refers to the use of books or other reading material to assist clients in their healing process. Goldstein (1990) discusses three approaches in using bibliotherapy in helping people heal: self-help/educational, psychosocial support, and interactive. In the self-help arena, the leader may not be a helping professional, but assigns people readings with little or no discussion. In the psychosocial support arena, the readings are given by a helping professional and may involve discussion of how they apply to the individual. The interactive use of bibliotherapy is the form that is typically used in counseling. Goldstein states that it is the interaction between the counselor and the client about the material that is important. This interaction is based on the client's response to the reading material and that response guides the dialogue between the counselor and the client.

The counselor suggests the readings to guide or intervene in the client's life (Cohen, 1994). The intervention on the client's life can involve counselors using readings as assignments for clients or as discussion "kick-offs" in the therapy session (Cohen, 1994). The counselor may also use a shortened form of bibliotherapy by introducing a proverb or a saying read to or by the client for discussion in the session. This type of intervention can assist in explaining a concept in a simple, yet focused fashion.

Shrodes (1950) viewed bibliotherapy as allowing the client's emotions to be freed by reading the material. Shrodes believed that the reading

BIBLIOTHERAPY QUESTIONS

For the Counselor:

1. What is the main purpose of the reading material(s) I want to give the client?
2. Would it be best to provide these materials in the session or outside of the session?
3. What are the reading material options?
4. Which of these options seems best suited to my client in terms of:
   _____ a. Reading ability.
   _____ b. Time commitment.
   _____ c. Values.
5. Where can my client access these materials?
6. If I am lending out these materials, am I comfortable if the client never returns them?

For the Client:

Before the assignment:

1. Are you interested in reading some materials outside of the session?
2. Do you have time to read such materials?
3. Do you have the money to buy such reading material?
4. Will you stop reading if the material feels overwhelming to you or conflicts with your values?

After the assignment:

1. What did you think/feel about the reading materials?
2. What part(s) made sense to you?
3. What part(s) did you agree with? Disagree with?
4. Overall, how does this material fit with your spiritual perspective?

could be effective in the process of diagnosing and treating problems of an emotional nature because the client could identify with the material, have a cathartic experience, and then have insight. The change experienced by the client is one of an existential nature related to the meaning of his or her life.

One example of changes experienced by clients as a result of biblio-therapy is Cohen's (1994) study in which participants described changes in *ways of feeling and ways of knowing.* Participants reported feeling less alone (reading felt like a shared experience with the protagonist or author), validated (both their life experiences and reactions to them were okay), comforted, hopeful about their situation, inspired to address their situation (motivation), and relieved (catharsis). In terms of knowing, they reported gaining information that was empowering to them. With regard to both feelings and thoughts, they stated they gained insight, awareness, and clarity in both areas. Finally, participants reported that their experiences were very individual, supportive, and a form of healthy escape.

Because it is a means of self-exploration, bibliotherapy is a technique counselors can use to assist clients in developing their spiritual/religious life. Readings that focus on a spiritual theme of counseling, specific spiritual issues, or new spiritual concepts for the client can be chosen and assigned. Readings must be chosen carefully, however, to compliment the client's values and provide metaphor that is meaningful to the client. The counselor can use the questions on page 200 to assist in the choosing of materials and assisting the client in applying the material to his or her life.

Focusing

Hinterkopf (1998) describes the focusing technique as one that can be used in counseling to facilitate the integration of spirituality in counseling. Focusing is defined as the "vague, bodily, wholistic sense of a situation such as a problem, creative project, or spiritual experience" (p. 19). It is a way of being connected to what the author describes as a "felt sense." The felt sense is the experience we feel in our bodies with a sensation that is vague. Focusing is a technique where clients learn to listen to themselves without judgment, but with an openness, and a curiosity toward the unknown that facilitates new growth. Grounding clients in their bodily sensations can help them identify and label both their feelings and how their feelings express themselves in their bodies. It assists people in making the connection between the mind, body, and spirit.

Prior to using the process, Hinterkopf (1998) suggests that both the client and the counselor are comfortable and relaxed physically. There are six steps in the technique that Hinterkopf labels as follows:

1. *Step 1: Clearing a Space:* The client is asked how he or she feels (how that feeling is experienced in the body), to imagine setting aside the problem, and the feeling experienced in not having the problem.

2. *Step 2: Getting a Felt Sense:* The counselor asks the client to experience the bodily reactions by having a "felt sense" of the entire problem.

3. *Step 3: Finding a Handle:* The client is asked to think of words or images that describe the feelings or bodily reactions in relation to the "felt sense."

4. *Resonating:* The counselor asks the client to make sure that the correct handle words have been chosen to describe the experience.

5. *Asking:* Here the client asks an open-ended question of the felt sense and may have a "felt shift" (the release experienced when there is a match of information that results in the truth) in response to the answer received.

6. *Receiving:* This is where the client applies the experience to his or her understanding of self-in-the-world.

This technique can assist clients in making a connection between their minds, bodies, and spirits. Such a connection allows them to be more integrated human beings.

Journal Writing

There is something about writing things down that is different from talking them out. Writing builds trust in your ideas and beliefs. Writing makes you dig deep inside yourself. Writing reveals the self. Writing connects you to your insides. Because writing and the poetic process have enabled me to know myself in a unique way, it is no wonder that when I became a psychologist, writing became woven into the fabric of my clinical work. (Rabinor, 1998, p. 254)

As described in the preceding quote, journal writing is another technique that can be used in counseling. The journal can be more than a chronological record of events and become a means of exploring oneself (Rainer, 1978). As with bibliotherapy, this self-exploration aspect of journal writing can assist the client in exploring his or her spiritual world.

The intent of the journal is to help the client feel both free and safe, which means that imperfection is a part of the process including, but not limited to, random sentences, nonsensical words, spontaneous writing, and incorrect punctuation or grammar (Linder, Miller, & Johnson, 2000). There is no such thing as wrong writing. Writing is a way for clients to understand the tensions between *telling the truth* and *being good* (Belenky, Clinchy, Goldberger, & Tarule, 1986). The journal writing is a process where clients can express their thoughts and feelings without judgment from self or others. It can help clients achieve goals, have less stress by having a safe outlet for their daily struggles, and have a sense of a friend or a comfort (Linder et al., 2000).

Journal writing can be specifically applied to working in the area of spirituality because clients can learn to trust themselves and can find inspiration. Journal writing can be used to assist clients in exploring spiritual views or existential questions regarding themselves or their lives. For example, Swearingen (1994) describes about half of their participants in workshops on spirituality and creativity as experiencing a "spiritual poverty in their lives" (p. 254) even though they may not have specific religious beliefs or an interest in developing them. In these workshops for women, participants are allowed to be freed from their responsibilities, learn how to dialogue with their inner critics, develop self-images that provide them with meaning, and provide them with a sense of the spiritual.

Some specific suggestions counselors can make to their clients about journaling are as follows (Linder et al., 2000):

1. Use as simple a journal as possible (for example, unlined) to avoid distractions while writing.
2. Use a good pen that facilitates writing.
3. Have a time limit (10–15 minutes) or a page limit (2–3 pages) to facilitate the writing process.
4. Write faster than one can think, have no rules about writing, and do not go back and rewrite.
5. Make a commitment to writing in the journal on a regular basis.
6. Journal after counseling sessions or between them.

**USE OF JOURNAL WRITING TO EXPLORE
THE SPIRITUAL DIMENSION**

1. Have the client write out his or her definition of God or a Higher Power.*
2. Have the client write journal entries to this presence.*
3. Have the client imagine being this presence and writing a response to the client's entries.*
4. Have the client write about his or her core spiritual concern in life and proceed with steps 2 and 3 above.
5. Discuss the journal entries with the client.
6. Have the client read selected journal entries in the counseling session.

*Note: For clients who do not believe in a "presence," steps 1, 2, and 3 could be adapted by having them write out their definition of spirituality and have a journal dialogue in a manner that fits with that definition.

Rabinor (1998) provides guidelines for therapists and journal writers about journal writing that encourage the writer to:(a) use a comfortable pen and notebook; (b) suspend rules allowing for variations in writing, including writing on unusual topics and dreams, freeflow writing, and poem copying; and(c) know your limits as a writer and take risks. The box on page 203 provides some specific examples of spiritually-related journal writing exercises counselors can use with their clients.

Religious and General Practices

Meditation/Relaxation/Imagery

Because spiritual factors may be related generally to your health and sense of well-being (Astin, 1997), interventions on psychophysical well-being can also include a spiritual health dimension. A definition of spiritual health is as follows:

> *A high level of faith, hope, and commitment in relation to a well-defined worldview or belief system that provides a sense of meaning and purpose to existence in general, and that offers an ethical path to personal fulfillment which includes connectedness with self, others, and a Higher Power or larger reality. (Hawks, Hull, Thalman, & Richins, 1995, p. 373)*

Meditation may be a part of your religious or spiritual practice or it may be outside of that realm for you. Meditation is a technique that can intervene on both psychophysical and spiritual health dimensions. Research has shown meditation can result in a variety of positive benefits for the individual. These include an increase in being more relaxed, alert, aware, willing to change, and being more sensitive and empathic toward others (Carrington, 1977; LeShan, 1974; Shafii, 1985). It has also helped with treating stress, insomnia, chronic pain, cancer, AIDS, and emotions such as anger, anxiety, and depression (Benson, 1993; Carrington, 1993). Yoga incorporates meditation and is an attempt to assist individuals in growing spiritually, mentally, emotionally, physically, and intellectually by calming the mind. Posture and meditation (including breathing techniques) are used in this traditionally Indian practice to facilitate these changes. Yoga has shown therapeutic effectiveness with asthma, hypertension, diabetes, and blood pressure (Vedanthan et al., 1998).

Meditation can be viewed as listening (Faiver, Ingersoll, O'Brien, & McNally, 2001). Although there are numerous meditation methods, they share in common an emphasis on a calm, alert attention of the individual that is focused (Kelly, 1995). Meditation helps people stay in the present moment and be less reactive (Daya, 2000). Kelly describes two main forms of meditation: concentration (the person focuses on something inside or outside of self) and mindfulness (the person focuses on everything that goes through the mind without judgment).

One form of concentrated meditation is Transcendental Meditation (TM). In TM, you practice two times a day for 15 to 20 minutes with your eyes closed focusing on an assigned mantra. It originated with Maharishi Mahesh Yogi, but is not affiliated with any religion (Clements, Krenner, & Molk, 1988). This form of meditation has been shown to result in a sense of rest and relaxation. An example of its effectiveness has been with the decrease in the use of alcohol and drugs (Clements et al., 1988).

Marlatt and Kristeller (1999) describe mindfulness meditation as follows: To be mindful is to be completely in the here and now, aware of what is present both inside and outside of self without judgment. In this process, you learn to watch your thoughts and feelings and not necessarily change the thought, but change your relationship to the thought; thoughts do not define who we are. In introducing interventions, they suggest first finding out a client's previous experiences with or knowledge of meditation and addressing any issues or concerns, then having a practice session in the office, and have clients practice meditation outside of the office, working with them on integrating the meditation into their lifestyle. Note that clients can use the technique of being mindful in the present both in and out of the counseling session without ever having to meditate (Daya, 2000).

An example of a stress reduction program using mindfulness meditation techniques is Kabat-Zinn's (1982) Stress Reduction and Relaxation Program (SRRP). In this program, individuals were taught mindfulness meditation techniques in addition to undergoing psychotherapy. The mindfulness meditation technique involves both concentration on something specific like your breathing as well as a nonfocused meditation (Astin, 1997). The attempt is to have the client become attentive consciously to what is happening both within and outside of himself or herself, thereby becoming an observer of his or her life. The focus is on your attention rather than other aspects of cognition, and everything is to be noticed (Astin, 1997).

In-session meditation techniques can be helpful to clients. One meditation technique counselors can readily use with clients either in or outside of session is *How to Elicit the Relaxation Response* (see page 206).

Another shortened form of meditation may be having a moment of silence in the session for a loved one. Finally, an in-session intervention could be done with guided imagery. Becvar (1997) provides an example of asking clients in counseling to take an imaginary journey through the body looking for spots where they are uncomfortable or there is known illness, and talk with that part of the body to obtain information about what can be done to assist the healing process. The client may visualize white

HOW TO ELICIT THE RELAXATION RESPONSE

Some general advice on regular practice of the relaxation response:

- Try to find 10 to 20 minutes in your daily routine, before breakfast is a good time.
- Sit comfortably.
- For the period you will practice, try to arrange your life so you won't have distractions. Put the phone on the answering machine, and ask someone else to watch the kids.
- Time yourself by glancing periodically at a clock or watch (but don't set an alarm). Commit yourself to a specific length of practice, and try to stick to it.

There are several approaches to eliciting the relaxation response. Here is one standard set of instructions used at the Mind/Body Medical Institute.

Step 1. Pick a focus word or short phrase that's firmly rooted in your personal belief system. For example, a nonreligious individual might choose a neutral word like *one* or *peace* or *love.* A Christian person desiring to use a prayer could pick the opening words of Psalm 23, *The Lord is my shepherd;* a Jewish person could choose *Shalom.*

Step 2. Sit quietly in a comfortable position.

Step 3. Close your eyes.

Step 4. Relax your muscles.

Step 5. Breathe slowly and naturally, repeating your focus word or phrase silently as you exhale.

Step 6. Throughout, assume a passive attitude. Don't worry about how well you're doing. When other thoughts intrude, simply say to yourself, "Oh, well," and gently return to the repetition.

Step 7. Continue for 10 to 20 minutes. You may open your eyes to check the time, but do not use an alarm. When you finish, sit quietly for a minute or so, at first with your eyes closed and later with your eyes open. Then do not stand for one or two minutes.

Step 8. Practice the technique once or twice a day.

Source: Mind-Body Medicine: How to Use Your Mind for Better Health by D. Goleman and J. Gurin (Eds.) (Yonkers, NY: Consumer Reports Books). Copyright 1993. Reprinted by permission of Herbert Benson, *The Relaxation Response* (pp. 233–257).

light going into that part of the body or the body being healed. There are numerous variations on guided-imagery available (Faiver et al., 2001) and one such exercise is provided on page 208.

In addition to using a meditation technique such as *How to Elicit the Relaxation Response,* counselors may want to refer clients to readings, trainings, or workshops in a specific form of meditation that compliments their work in therapy. While these interventions may not be used directly in counseling to explore the client's spiritual world, they can be used as an adjunct to therapy to increase personal awareness, to increase coping skills, and to develop a spiritual community outside of the counseling setting. For the religiously committed client, meditation may already be a part of his or her religious practice. In this event, the counselor may simply encourage the client to use this resource during the counseling process.

Rituals

Rituals can be of a religious or secular nature. Ritual is formalized behavior that draws out certain feelings (Denzin, 1974) and provides individuals ways to express their thoughts and feelings in a symbolic fashion (Rando, 1985). Rituals bring meaning and truth to the ordinary as well as a sense of safety.

Rituals can connect people from their everyday concerns to the sacred realm, with the ritual helping the person move from what is known to what is unknown (Fukuyama & Sevig, 1999). B. K. Myers (1997) describes four stages of rituals. In the first stage, a sacred space is created. In the second stage, the person expects a change when the ritual ends (luminality). In the third stage, an elder guides the ritual. In the fourth, the person expects a transcendent experience. Faiver et al. (2001) state that counseling is essentially a ritualistic process that follows these four stages.

Rituals have been used in different theories of counseling. Freudian and Jungian analysis have used ritual in the techniques of catharsis and dream analysis. Existentialists use techniques such as guided imagery and psychodrama and acknowledge that rituals may help people experience life in more manageable portions. Strategic therapy has used ritual as homework assignments (Al-Krenawi, 1999). Rituals can also assist in cross-cultural counseling (Al-Krenawi, 1999). If a client is from a traditional culture, ritual can help the client trust the therapeutic process because it is more integrated into the client's culture and because ritual depends on actions rather than words. Rituals may help therapy by bringing a focus and structure to it that is within the realm of the client's understanding.

GUIDED IMAGERY EXERCISE

Make yourself very comfortable now, relaxing just as fully as you can, and now listen closely and discover that you can relax still more.

Relax your body a bit at a time, beginning with the toes, just let them go very limp and relaxed. Then the rest of the foot, and the ankle, feeling the ankle going limp and relaxed, and that relaxation moving up through your body, to the calves, and the knees, and on up to the thighs, and just going very, very limp in your body as I describe the progression of this deep relaxation to you.

And now on up into the pelvic area, relaxing, relaxing, more and more relaxed. And the abdomen now, and on up to the chest, going loose and limp all over. The fingers, the wrists, the forearms, the elbows, upper arms, and on up to the shoulders now, feel the relaxation, all strain or tension slipping out and away from your whole body. So that the neck feels so loose and limp now, and the jaw, the lips, the cheeks, and the eyes, right on up to the forehead and over the entire head.

The entirety of your body relaxed now, and relaxing even more and more, so that you are just as limp and relaxed as an old rag doll appears to be, and you really are that relaxed, as you listen now to what I have to say to you, and you will want to listen extremely closely, very, very closely please, as you are listening just to me, becoming aware of what is said to you, and of your responses to what is being said to you.

And for a little while now, with closed eyes, remaining relaxed, breathing slowly and deeply, focus your awareness on that breathing, as you breathe in now, and then breathing out . . . in and out, in and out, in and out (about 2 minutes).

Let your eyes remain closed now, be deeply relaxed, and there is something of importance and value to you that I have to say to you now.

So concentrate just upon what I will say to you, very fully concentrated on my words, and on what you will experience when the words are spoken. Remember, and accept without doubt that it is true, and recollect now very realistically a dream that you used to have as a child. You may have forgotten it, but now you remember, and you will recall it most vividly now as I remind you of the details of that dream you used to have, of that dream you are going to have again.

GUIDED IMAGERY EXERCISE (CONTINUED)

At night, when you slept, as a small child, the same dream, recurring again and again, so that you were not sure that it was a dream, although it was not your usual waking reality either.

And beginning always in the same way, as in the dream, you would get out of your bed, walking across the room to the closet, and finding that there is a door in the back of the closet. A door you could never find when you looked for it when you were awake, although often you did look for that door. But now the door opens for you in your dream, and you pass through the door to stand at the head of a stone staircase.

It is a very ancient-looking stone staircase, winding down and around, and in the dim light you begin going down the staircase, not at all afraid, but eager to go down, deeper and deeper, descending on down through the dream, going always deeper as you go down a step at a time, until finally reaching the bottom of the stairway to stand at the edge of what you recognize to be dark water, lapping, where a small boat is tied.

And now, lying on the blankets in the bottom of the boat, the boat adrift and floating in the blackness, dark all around, but rocking gently from the motion of the water, back and forth and rising and falling, gently rocked as the boat drifts on and on, as the boat drifts down and down, as you feel only that gentle rocking, listening to the lapping of the water, nearing an opening where the boat moves along toward a light at the opening, and passes out of the opening and into a warm sunlight.

Still floating, downstream, feeling the warm sunlight, and a soft breeze that passes over you, as you drift down and down, and along the bank the birds are singing, and the fish are jumping in the water, and there is the smell of flowers and of the freshly cut grass in fields that have just been mowed. Feeling a great contentment, serenity, drifting drowsily down and down, down and down, with that gentle rocking, and now just let yourself feel it for a while. Be aware of this whole situation, the movements, the warmth, the sounds, the odors, as you keep on drifting down and down.

Continuing now to float, to rock, gently, drifting deeper and deeper, until your boat approaches the shore and runs smoothly aground at the edge of a meadow. Leaving the boat now, and walking through the meadow, the grass against your legs, the breezes on

(continued)

GUIDED IMAGERY EXERCISE (CONTINUED)

your body, and conscious of rabbits in the tall grass, of the smell of the flowers all around, of birds singing in the trees, of the movements of your body as you walk, approaching a large tree and seating yourself beneath it, in its shade.

As you are sitting in the shade, a sacred object, which brings you a sense of well-being, catches your eye. You reach for the object and hold it near you. While holding the object, you study it and as you do, your sense of peace and wholeness grows stronger. You hold the sacred object while sitting under the tree fully relaxed and content for a few minutes (about 2 minutes).

Now, for a while, just feel your surroundings, be in total harmony with all that exists here in this world out of time, this world without separations, this world where all is one, where you are one with all that is.

I want you to be aware of your surroundings and say goodbye to them. You can leave the sacred object under the tree or bring it back with you. I would like you to come back to the room now. I will count back from 10 to 1. When I reach 1, open your eyes when you are ready. 10-9-8-7-6-5-4-3-2-1. Open your eyes when you are ready.

Source: Mind Games: The Guide to Inner Space by Robert Masters and Jean Houston (Wheaton, IL: Quest Books/The Theosophical Publishing House). Copyright 1972. Reprinted by permission of Quest Books/The Theosophical Publishing House (pp. 8–11).

Religious rituals that have meaning to the client may help the client cope with transitions in life and crises (Kelly, 1990). They may also simply help people cope with their difficult situations (Pargament, 1996). Examples of religious rituals are those that involve purifying, meditating, praying, and confessing (Fukuyama & Sevig, 1999). Jacobs (1992) discusses the impact of specific rituals on individuals. The author states that confession (done individually or within the context of an entire community) breaks shame and allows the individual to reconnect with others. Grief rituals can result in a catharsis for the individual; mourning rituals can help people with feelings of fear, sadness, anxiety, and anger. Finally, there are rituals that can help someone express their anger in general.

Counselors may want to encourage clients to use rituals to heal the past or to assist them with a transition and help clients determine if these rituals may be done alone or with others (Fukuyama & Sevig, 1999). If the counselor is comfortable and it is appropriate for both the client and within the counseling setting, the counselor may assist the client in choosing or creating a ritual to assist in the healing process. If the counselor is uncomfortable discussing healing rituals or it seems inappropriate within the therapeutic relationship or the context of counseling, the counselor may want to consider referring a client to a religious leader who can assist in the practice or creation of a ritual for the client. Richards and Bergin (1997) urge counselors to be cautious about participating in rituals in and out of sessions because of possible role confusion.

The counselor needs to select a ritual that fits the client as well as fits the counselor. This fit needs to take into account the values and beliefs of both the counselor and the client, as well as the context in which they are working in counseling. If the client does not have a ritual that can be used in or out of the session, the client and counselor can collaborate on rituals that may be beneficial to the client. In other words, create his or her personal ritual.

Case Studies

CASE STUDY 1

Your client has been to see you twice and tells you that he or she wants to pray with you about the presenting problem.

1. How would you respond to this request?
2. Would there be some issues that you would want to raise or parameters that you would want to set prior to any statement you make or action you take?
3. What would make this request easy for you to respond to?
4. What would make this request difficult for you to respond to?
5. Would any of the following factors influence the action you take?
   —Client's gender?
   —Client's ethnicity?
   —Client's religious affiliation?
   —Client's type of problem?
   —The degree of similarity between you and your client's spiritual or religious beliefs?

CASE STUDY 2

You have a single parent family (mother, adolescent son) come for counseling because of conflict between them: The mother claims the son will not obey her. They each have the same religious faith, but the son no longer wants to attend the meetings of the young people in their religious community because he finds them too boring. The mother is in agreement with his wish to drop out of the activities as long as he is willing to attend religious services (the son agrees to this) and begin some religious practices in their home (the son does not agree to this).

1. Would there be any additional information you need from them in order to encourage certain practices?

2. How would you begin to explore possible religious practices with them?

3. Are there any particular practices in this chapter that you think would be helpful to them?

Exercises

Exercise 1

Examine the different religious practices described at the beginning of this chapter (prayer, sacred writings, worship/ritual, use of religious community). Then answer the following questions:

1. Which of these practices am I most comfortable using?

2. Which clients would be most conducive to my use of these interventions?

3. Is my current or anticipated work setting conducive to these interventions?

4. What would be my own personal limitations on the use of these interventions?

Exercise 2

Think about a spiritual or religious ritual that has a lot of meaning for you. Write a description of the ritual in detail for a reader that has never practiced the ritual. Then answer the following questions:

1. How was I introduced to this ritual?

2. How long and how consistently have I practiced this ritual?

3. As I imagine practicing the ritual, what feelings am I aware of?

4. What aspects of this ritual do I find comforting? Healing?

5. How does this ritual have meaning for my life?

6. How often do I practice this ritual?

7. What prevents me from practicing the ritual as often as I want? What are some ways I can work around those barriers?

Exercise 3

Choose a partner to work on inventing a new spiritual ritual. Think of a life transition or crisis that does not have a ritual attached to it. Design a ritual for this transition or crisis with your partner that would help you live better through the experience by providing you with a sense of meaning and safety.

1. The life transition or crisis we have chosen to develop a ritual for is: _____.

2. Fill in the blank with an activity of the ritual that will access these senses.

   a. Auditory: _____

   b. Visual: _____

   c. Touch: _____

   d. Taste: _____

   e. Smell: _____

3. The goal of the ritual is:

   _____.

4. The meaning behind the ritual is:

   _____.

5. The ritual will help me cope with the transition or crisis by:

   _____
   _____.

Exercise 4

Interview two mental health professionals—one who identifies as a religious mental health counselor and one who does not. Ask each of them the questions in Exercise 1. Then compare their answers for similarities and differences.

Exercise 5

Explore on the Internet some of the religious intervention techniques available for counselors to use in sessions. Do some of the interventions seem more amenable with some religions than others?

Exercise 6

Chose one Eastern and one Western religion described in Chapters 3 and 4. Do a search on the Internet with regard to counseling techniques that may be a good match for those religions.

Suggested Readings

Becvar, D. S. (1997). *Soul healing.* New York: Basic Books.

Faiver, C., Ingersoll, R. E., O'Brien, E., & McNally, C. (2001). *Explorations in counseling and spirituality.* Belmont, CA: Brooks/Cole.

Koenig, H. G. (Ed.). (1998). *Handbook of religion and mental health.* San Diego, CA: Academic Press.

Miller, W. R. (Ed.). (1999). *Integrating spirituality into treatment: Resources for practitioners.* Washington, DC: American Psychological Association.

Richards, P. S., & Bergin, A. E. (1997). *A spiritual strategy for counseling and psychotherapy.* Washington, DC: American Psychological Association.

Shafranske, E. P. (Ed.). (1996). *Religion and the clinical practice of psychology.* Washington DC: American Psychological Association.

American Association for Marriage and Family Therapy (AAMFT) Code of Ethics[1]

Preamble

The Board of Directors of the American Association for Marriage and Family Therapy hereby promulgates, pursuant to Article 2, Section 2.013 of the Association's Bylaws, the Revised AAMFT Code of Ethics, effective July 1, 2001.

Appendix

The AAMFT strives to honor the public trust in marriage and family therapists by setting standards for ethical practice as described in this Code. The ethical standards define professional expectations and are enforced by the AAMFT Ethics Committee. The absence of an explicit reference to a specific behavior or situation in the Code does not mean that the behavior is ethical or unethical. The standards are not exhaustive. Marriage and family therapists who are uncertain about the ethics of a particular course of action are encouraged to seek counsel from consultants, attorneys, supervisors, colleagues, or other appropriate authorities.

Both law and ethics govern the practice of marriage and family therapy. When making decisions regarding professional behavior, marriage and family therapists must consider the AAMFT Code of Ethics and applicable laws and regulations. If the AAMFT Code of Ethics prescribes a standard higher than that required by law, marriage and family therapists must meet the higher standard of the AAMFT Code of Ethics. Marriage and family therapists comply with the mandates of law, but make known their commitment to the AAMFT Code of Ethics and take steps to resolve the conflict in a responsible manner. The AAMFT supports legal mandates for reporting of alleged unethical conduct.

The AAMFT Code of Ethics is binding on Members of AAMFT in all membership categories, AAMFT-Approved Supervisors, and applicants for membership and the Approved Supervisor designation (hereafter, AAMFT Member). AAMFT members have an obligation to be familiar with the AAMFT Code of Ethics and its application to their professional services. Lack of awareness or misunderstanding of an ethical standard is not a defense to a charge of unethical conduct. The process for filing, investigating, and resolving complaints of unethical conduct is described in the current Procedures for Handling Ethical Matters of the AAMFT Ethics Committee. Persons accused are considered innocent by the Ethics Committee until

---

[1] Reprinted or copied from the AAMFT Code of Ethics. Copyright 2001, American Association for Marriage and Family Therapy. Reprinted with Permission. NO ADDITIONAL COPIES MAY BE MADE WITHOUT OBTAINING PERMISSION FROM AAMFT.

proven guilty, except as otherwise provided, and are entitled to due process. If an AAMFT Member resigns in anticipation of, or during the course of, an ethics investigation, the Ethics Committee will complete its investigation. Any publication of action taken by the Association will include the fact that the Member attempted to resign during the investigation.

Principle 1

Responsibility to Clients

Marriage and family therapists advance the welfare of families and individuals. They respect the rights of those persons seeking their assistance, and make reasonable efforts to ensure that their services are used appropriately.

1.1. Marriage and family therapists provide professional assistance to persons without discrimination on the basis of race, age, ethnicity, socioeconomic status, disability, gender, health status, religion, national origin, or sexual orientation.

1.2. Marriage and family therapists obtain appropriate informed consent to therapy or related procedures as early as feasible in the therapeutic relationship, and use language that is reasonably understandable to clients. The content of informed consent may vary depending upon the client and treatment plan; however, informed consent generally necessitates that the client: (a) has the capacity to consent; (b) has been adequately informed of significant information concerning treatment processes and procedures; (c) has been adequately informed of potential risks and benefits of treatments for which generally recognized standards do not yet exist; (d) has freely and without undue influence expressed consent; and (e) has provided consent that is appropriately documented. When persons, due to age or mental status, are legally incapable of giving informed consent, marriage and family therapists obtain informed permission from a legally authorized person, if such substitute consent is legally permissible.

1.3. Marriage and family therapists are aware of their influential positions with respect to clients, and they avoid exploiting the trust and dependency of such persons. Therapists, therefore, make every effort to avoid conditions and multiple relationships with clients that could impair professional judgment or increase the risk of exploitation. Such relationships include, but are not limited to, business or close personal relationships with a client or the client's immediate family. When the risk of impairment or exploitation exists due to conditions or multiple roles, therapists take appropriate precautions.

1.4. Sexual intimacy with clients is prohibited.

1.5. Sexual intimacy with former clients is likely to be harmful and is therefore prohibited for two years following the termination of therapy or last professional contact. In an effort to avoid exploiting the trust and dependency of clients, marriage and family therapists should not engage in sexual intimacy with former clients after the two years following termination or last professional contact. Should therapists engage in sexual intimacy with former clients following two years after termination or last professional contact, the burden shifts to the therapist to demonstrate that there has been no exploitation or injury to the former client or to the client's immediate family.

1.6. Marriage and family therapists comply with applicable laws regarding the reporting of alleged unethical conduct.

1.7. Marriage and family therapists do not use their professional relationships with clients to further their own interests.

1.8. Marriage and family therapists respect the rights of clients to make decisions and help them to understand the consequences of these decisions. Therapists clearly advise the clients that they have the responsibility to make decisions regarding relationships such as cohabitation, marriage, divorce, separation, reconciliation, custody, and visitation.

1.9. Marriage and family therapists continue therapeutic relationships only so long as it is reasonably clear that clients are benefiting from the relationship.

1.10. Marriage and family therapists assist persons in obtaining other therapeutic services if the therapist is unable or unwilling, for appropriate reasons, to provide professional help.

1.11. Marriage and family therapists do not abandon or neglect clients in treatment without making reasonable arrangements for the continuation of such treatment.

1.12. Marriage and family therapists obtain written informed consent from clients before videotaping, audio recording, or permitting third-party observation.

1.13. Marriage and family therapists, upon agreeing to provide services to a person or entity at the request of a third party, clarify, to the extent feasible and at the outset of the service, the nature of the relationship with each party and the limits of confidentiality.

Principle II

Confidentiality

Marriage and family therapists have unique confidentiality concerns because the client in a therapeutic relationship may be more than one person. Therapists respect and guard the confidences of each individual client.

2.1. Marriage and family therapists disclose to clients and other interested parties, as early as feasible in their professional contacts, the nature of confidentiality and possible limitations of the clients' right to confidentiality. Therapists review with clients the circumstances where confidential information may be requested and where disclosure of confidential information may be legally required. Circumstances may necessitate repeated disclosures.

2.2. Marriage and family therapists do not disclose client confidences except by written authorization or waiver, or where mandated or permitted by law. Verbal authorization will not be sufficient except in emergency situations, unless prohibited by law. When providing couple, family, or group treatment, the therapist does not disclose information outside the treatment context without a written authorization from each individual competent to execute a waiver. In the context of couple, family, or group treatment, the therapist may not reveal any individual's confidences to others in the client unit without the prior written permission of that individual.

2.3. Marriage and family therapists use client and/or clinical materials in teaching, writing, consulting, research, and public presentations only if a written waiver has been obtained in accordance with Subprinciple 2.2, or when appropriate steps have been taken to protect client identity and confidentiality.

2.4. Marriage and family therapists store, safeguard, and dispose of client records in ways that maintain confidentiality and in accord with applicable laws and professional standards.

2.5. Subsequent to the therapist moving from the area, closing the practice, or upon the death of the therapist, a marriage and family therapist arranges for the storage, transfer, or disposal of client records in ways that maintain confidentiality and safeguard the welfare of clients.

2.6. Marriage and family therapists, when consulting with colleagues or referral sources, do not share confidential information that could reasonably lead to the identification of a client, research participant, supervisee, or other person with whom they have a confidential relationship unless they have obtained the prior written consent of the client, research participant, supervisee, or other person with whom they have a confidential relationship. Information may be shared only to the extent necessary to achieve the purposes of the consultation.

Principle III

Professional Competence and Integrity

Marriage and family therapists maintain high standards of professional competence and integrity.

3.1. Marriage and family therapists pursue knowledge of new developments and maintain competence in marriage and family therapy through education, training, or supervised experience.

3.2. Marriage and family therapists maintain adequate knowledge of and adhere to applicable laws, ethics, and professional standards.

3.3. Marriage and family therapists seek appropriate professional assistance for their personal problems or conflicts that may impair work performance or clinical judgment.

3.4.   Marriage and family therapists do not provide services that create a conflict of interest that may impair work performance or clinical judgment.

3.5.   Marriage and family therapists, as presenters, teachers, supervisors, consultants, and researchers, are dedicated to high standards of scholarship, present accurate information, and disclose potential conflicts of interest.

3.6.   Marriage and family therapists maintain accurate and adequate clinical and financial records.

3.7.   While developing new skills in specialty areas, marriage and family therapists take steps to ensure the competence of their work and to protect clients from possible harm. Marriage and family therapists practice in specialty areas new to them only after appropriate education, training, or supervised experience.

3.8.   Marriage and family therapists do not engage in sexual or other forms of harassment of clients, students, trainees, supervisees, employees, colleagues, or research subjects.

3.9.   Marriage and family therapists do not engage in the exploitation of clients, students, trainees, supervisees, employees, colleagues, or research subjects.

3.10.   Marriage and family therapists do not give to or receive from clients (a) gifts of substantial value or (b) gifts that impair the integrity or efficacy of the therapeutic relationship.

3.11.   Marriage and family therapists do not diagnose, treat, or advise on problems outside the recognized boundaries of their competencies.

3.12.   Marriage and family therapists make efforts to prevent the distortion or misuse of their clinical and research findings.

3.13.   Marriage and family therapists, because of their ability to influence and alter the lives of others, exercise special care when making public their professional recommendations and opinions through testimony or other public statements.

3.14.   To avoid a conflict of interests, marriage and family therapists who treat minors or adults involved in custody or visitation actions may not also perform forensic evaluations for custody, residence, or visitation of the minor. The marriage and family therapist who treats the minor may provide the court or mental health professional performing the evaluation with information about the minor from the marriage and family therapist's perspective as a treating marriage and family therapist, so long as the marriage and family therapist does not violate confidentiality.

3.15.   Marriage and family therapists are in violation of this Code and subject to termination of membership or other appropriate action if they: (a) are convicted of any felony; (b) are convicted of a misdemeanor related to their qualifications or functions; (c) engage in conduct which could lead to conviction of a felony, or a misdemeanor related to their qualifications or functions; (d) are expelled from or disciplined by other professional organizations; (e) have their licenses or certificates suspended or revoked or are otherwise disciplined by regulatory bodies; (f) continue to practice marriage and family therapy while no longer competent to do so because they are impaired by physical or mental causes or the abuse of alcohol or other substances; or (g) fail to cooperate with the Association at any point from the inception of an ethical complaint through the completion of all proceedings regarding that complaint.

Principle IV

Responsibility to Students and Supervisees

Marriage and family therapists do not exploit the trust and dependency of students and supervisees.

4.1.   Marriage and family therapists are aware of their influential positions with respect to students and supervisees, and they avoid exploiting the trust and dependency of such persons. Therapists, therefore, make every effort to avoid conditions and multiple relationships that could impair professional objectivity or increase the risk of exploitation. When the risk of impairment or exploitation exists due to conditions or multiple roles, therapists take appropriate precautions.

4.2.   Marriage and family therapists do not provide therapy to current students or supervisees.

4.3.   Marriage and family therapists do not engage in sexual intimacy with students or supervisees during the evaluative or training relationship between the therapist and student or supervisee. Should a supervisor engage in sexual activity with a former supervisee, the burden of proof shifts to the supervisor to demonstrate that there has been no exploitation or injury to the supervisee.

4.4.   Marriage and family therapists do not permit students or supervisees to perform or to hold themselves out as competent to perform professional services beyond their training, level of experience, and competence.

4.5.   Marriage and family therapists take reasonable measures to ensure that services provided by supervisees are professional.

4.6.   Marriage and family therapists avoid accepting as supervisees or students those individuals with whom a prior or existing relationship could compromise the therapist's objectivity. When such situations cannot be avoided, therapists take appropriate precautions to maintain objectivity. Examples of such relationships include, but are not limited to, those individuals with whom the therapist has a current or prior sexual, close personal, immediate familial, or therapeutic relationship.

4.7.   Marriage and family therapists do not disclose supervisee confidences except by written authorization or waiver, or when mandated or permitted by law. In educational or training settings where there are multiple supervisors, disclosures are permitted only to other professional colleagues, administrators, or employers who share responsibility for training of the supervisee. Verbal authorization will not be sufficient except in emergency situations, unless prohibited by law.

Principle V

Responsibility to Research Participants

Investigators respect the dignity and protect the welfare of research participants, and are aware of applicable laws and regulations and professional standards governing the conduct of research.

5.1.   Investigators are responsible for making careful examinations of ethical acceptability in planning studies. To the extent that services to research participants may be compromised by participation in research, investigators seek the ethical advice of qualified professionals not directly involved in the investigation and observe safeguards to protect the rights of research participants.

5.2.   Investigators requesting participant involvement in research inform participants of the aspects of the research that might reasonably be expected to influence willingness to participate. Investigators are especially sensitive to the possibility of diminished consent when participants are also receiving clinical services, or have impairments which limit understanding and/or communication, or when participants are children.

5.3.   Investigators respect each participant's freedom to decline participation in or to withdraw from a research study at any time. This obligation requires special thought and consideration when investigators or other members of the research team are in positions of authority or influence over participants. Marriage and family therapists, therefore, make every effort to avoid multiple relationships with research participants that could impair professional judgment or increase the risk of exploitation.

5.4.   Information obtained about a research participant during the course of an investigation is confidential unless there is a waiver previously obtained in writing. When the possibility exists that others, including family members, may obtain access to such information, this possibility, together with the plan for protecting confidentiality, is explained as part of the procedure for obtaining informed consent.

Principle VI

Responsibility to the Profession

Marriage and family therapists respect the rights and responsibilities of professional colleagues and participate in activities that advance the goals of the profession.

6.1.   Marriage and family therapists remain accountable to the standards of the profession when acting as members or employees of organizations. If the mandates of an organization with which a marriage and family therapist is affiliated, through employment, contract, or otherwise, conflict with the AAMFT Code of Ethics, marriage and family therapists make known to the organization their commitment to the AAMFT Code of Ethics and attempt to resolve the conflict in a way that allows the fullest adherence to the Code of Ethics.

6.2. Marriage and family therapists assign publication credit to those who have contributed to a publication in proportion to their contributions and in accordance with customary professional publication practices.

6.3. Marriage and family therapists do not accept or require authorship credit for a publication based on research from a student's program, unless the therapist made a substantial contribution beyond being a faculty adviser or research committee member. Coauthorship on a student thesis, dissertation, or project should be determined in accordance with principles of fairness and justice.

6.4. Marriage and family therapists who are the authors of books or other materials that are published or distributed do not plagiarize or fail to cite persons to whom credit for original ideas or work is due.

6.5. Marriage and family therapists who are the authors of books or other materials published or distributed by an organization take reasonable precautions to ensure that the organization promotes and advertises the materials accurately and factually.

6.6. Marriage and family therapists participate in activities that contribute to a better community and society, including devoting a portion of their professional activity to services for which there is little or no financial return.

6.7. Marriage and family therapists are concerned with developing laws and regulations pertaining to marriage and family therapy that serve the public interest, and with altering such laws and regulations that are not in the public interest.

6.8. Marriage and family therapists encourage public participation in the design and delivery of professional services and in the regulation of practitioners.

Principle VII

Financial Arrangements

Marriage and family therapists make financial arrangements with clients, third-party payors, and supervisees that are reasonably understandable and conform to accepted professional practices.

7.1. Marriage and family therapists do not offer or accept kickbacks, rebates, bonuses, or other remuneration for referrals; fee-for-service arrangements are not prohibited.

7.2. Prior to entering into the therapeutic or supervisory relationship, marriage and family therapists clearly disclose and explain to clients and supervisees: (a) all financial arrangements and fees related to professional services, including charges for canceled or missed appointments; (b) the use of collection agencies or legal measures for nonpayment; and (c) the procedure for obtaining payment from the client, to the extent allowed by law, if payment is denied by the third-party payor. Once services have begun, therapists provide reasonable notice of any changes in fees or other charges.

7.3. Marriage and family therapists give reasonable notice to clients with unpaid balances of their intent to seek collection by agency or legal recourse. When such action is taken, therapists will not disclose clinical information.

7.4. Marriage and family therapists represent facts truthfully to clients, third-party payors, and supervisees regarding services rendered.

7.5. Marriage and family therapists ordinarily refrain from accepting goods and services from clients in return for services rendered. Bartering for professional services may be conducted only if: (a) the supervisee or client requests it, (b) the relationship is not exploitative, (c) the professional relationship is not distorted, and (d) a clear written contract is established.

7.6. Marriage and family therapists may not withhold records under their immediate control that are requested and needed for a client's treatment solely because payment has not been received for past services, except as otherwise provided by law.

Principle VIII

Advertising

Marriage and family therapists engage in appropriate informational activities, including those that enable the public, referral sources, or others to choose professional services on an informed basis.

8.1. Marriage and family therapists accurately represent their competencies, education, training, and experience relevant to their practice of marriage and family therapy.

8.2. Marriage and family therapists ensure that advertisements and publications in any media (such as directories, announcements, business cards, newspapers, radio, television, Internet, and facsimiles) convey information that is necessary for the public to make an appropriate selection of professional services. Information could include: (a) office information, such as name, address, telephone number, credit card acceptability, fees, languages spoken, and office hours; (b) qualifying clinical degree (see subprinciple 8.5); (c) other earned degrees (see subprinciple 8.5) and state or provincial licensures and/or certifications; (d) AAMFT clinical member status; and (e) description of practice.

8.3. Marriage and family therapists do not use names that could mislead the public concerning the identity, responsibility, source, and status of those practicing under that name, and do not hold themselves out as being partners or associates of a firm if they are not.

8.4. Marriage and family therapists do not use any professional identification (such as a business card, office sign, letterhead, Internet, or telephone or association directory listing) if it includes a statement or claim that is false, fraudulent, misleading, or deceptive.

8.5. In representing their educational qualifications, marriage and family therapists list and claim as evidence only those earned degrees: (a) from institutions accredited by regional accreditation sources recognized by the United States Department of Education, (b) from institutions recognized by states or provinces that license or certify marriage and family therapists, or (c) from equivalent foreign institutions.

8.6. Marriage and family therapists correct, wherever possible, false, misleading, or inaccurate information and representations made by others concerning the therapist's qualifications, services, or products.

8.7. Marriage and family therapists make certain that the qualifications of their employees or supervisees are represented in a manner that is not false, misleading, or deceptive.

8.8. Marriage and family therapists do not represent themselves as providing specialized services unless they have the appropriate education, training, or supervised experience.

American Counseling Association (ACA) Code of Ethics and Standards of Practice[1]

ACA Code of Ethics Preamble

The American Counseling Association is an educational, scientific, and professional organization whose members are dedicated to the enhancement of human development throughout the life span. Association members recognize diversity in our society and embrace a cross-cultural approach in support of the worth, dignity, potential, and uniqueness of each individual.

The specification of a code of ethics enables the association to clarify to current and future members, and to those served by members, the nature of the ethical responsibilities held in common by its members. As the Code of Ethics of the association, this document establishes principles that define the ethical behavior of association members. All members of the American Counseling Association are required to adhere to the Code of Ethics and the Standards of Practice. The Code of Ethics will serve as the basis for processing ethical complaints initiated against members of the association.

B

Appendix

Section A: The Counseling Relationship

A.1. Client Welfare

a. *Primary responsibility.* The primary responsibility of counselors is to respect the dignity and to promote the welfare of clients.

b. *Positive growth and development.* Counselors encourage client growth and development in ways that foster the clients' interest and welfare; counselors avoid fostering dependent counseling relationships.

c. *Counseling plans.* Counselors and their clients work jointly in devising integrated, individual counseling plans that offer reasonable promise of success and are consistent with abilities and circumstances of clients. Counselors and clients regularly review counseling plans to ensure their continued viability and effectiveness, respecting clients' freedom of choice. (See A.3.b.)

---

[1] Reprinted from www.counciling.org/resources/codeofethics.html. © ACA. Reprinted with permission. No further reproductions authorized without written permission of the American Counseling Association.

d. *Family involvement.* Counselors recognize that families are usually important in clients' lives and strive to enlist family understanding and involvement as a positive resource, when appropriate.

e. *Career and employment needs.* Counselors work with their clients in considering employment in jobs and circumstances that are consistent with the clients' overall abilities, vocational limitations, physical restrictions, general temperament, interest and aptitude patterns, social skills, education, general qualifications, and other relevant characteristics and needs. Counselors neither place nor participate in placing clients in positions that will result in damaging the interest and the welfare of clients, employers, or the public.

A.2. Respecting Diversity

a. *Nondiscrimination.* Counselors do not condone or engage in discrimination based on age, color, culture, disability, ethnic group, gender, race, religion, sexual orientation, marital status, or socioeconomic status. (See C.5.a., C.5.b., and D.1.i.)

b. *Respecting differences.* Counselors will actively attempt to understand the diverse cultural backgrounds of the clients with whom they work. This includes, but is not limited to, learning how the counselor's own cultural/ethnic/racial identity impacts her or his values and beliefs about the counseling process. (See E.8. and F.2.i.)

A.3. Client Rights

a. *Disclosure to clients.* When counseling is initiated, and throughout the counseling process as necessary, counselors inform clients of the purposes, goals, techniques, procedures, limitations, potential risks, and benefits of services to be performed, and other pertinent information. Counselors take steps to ensure that clients understand the implications of diagnosis, the intended use of tests and reports, fees, and billing arrangements. Clients have the right to expect confidentiality and to be provided with an explanation of its limitations, including supervision and/or treatment team professionals; to obtain clear information about their case records; to participate in the ongoing counseling plans; and to refuse any recommended services and be advised of the consequences of such refusal. (See E.5.a. and G.2.)

b. *Freedom of choice.* Counselors offer clients the freedom to choose whether to enter into a counseling relationship and to determine which professional(s) will provide counseling. Restrictions that limit choices of clients are fully explained. (See A.1.c.)

c. *Inability to give consent.* When counseling minors or persons unable to give voluntary informed consent, counselors act in these clients' best interests. (See B.3.)

A.4. Clients Served by Others

If a client is receiving services from another mental health professional, counselors, with client consent, inform the professional persons already involved and develop clear agreements to avoid confusion and conflict for the client. (See C.6.c.)

A.5. Personal Needs and Values

a. *Personal needs.* In the counseling relationship, counselors are aware of the intimacy and responsibilities inherent in the counseling relationship, maintain respect for clients, and avoid actions that seek to meet their personal needs at the expense of clients.

b. *Personal values.* Counselors are aware of their own values, attitudes, beliefs, and behaviors and how these apply in a diverse society, and avoid imposing their values on clients. (See C.5.a.)

A.6. Dual Relationships

a. *Avoid when possible.* Counselors are aware of their influential positions with respect to clients, and they avoid exploiting the trust and dependency of clients. Counselors make every effort to avoid dual relationships with clients that could impair professional judgment or increase the risk of harm to clients. (Examples of such relationships include, but are not limited to, familial, social, financial, business, or close personal relationships with clients.) When a dual relationship cannot be avoided, counselors take appropriate professional precautions such as informed consent, consultation, supervision, and documentation to ensure that judgment is not impaired and no exploitation occurs. (See F.1.b.)

b. *Superior/subordinate relationships.* Counselors do not accept as clients superiors or subordinates with whom they have administrative, supervisory, or evaluative relationships.

A.7. Sexual Intimacies with Clients

a. *Current clients.* Counselors do not have any type of sexual intimacies with clients and do not counsel persons with whom they have had a sexual relationship.

b. *Former clients.* Counselors do not engage in sexual intimacies with former clients within a minimum of two years after terminating the counseling relationship. Counselors who engage in such relationship after two years following termination have the responsibility to examine and document thoroughly that such relations did not have an exploitative nature, based on factors such as duration of counseling, amount of time since counseling, termination circumstances, client's personal history and mental status, adverse impact on the client, and actions by the counselor suggesting a plan to initiate a sexual relationship with the client after termination.

A.8. Multiple Clients

When counselors agree to provide counseling services to two or more persons who have a relationship (such as husband and wife, or parents and children), counselors clarify at the outset which person or persons are clients and the nature of the relationships they will have with each involved person. If it becomes apparent that counselors may be called upon to perform potentially conflicting roles, they clarify, adjust, or withdraw from roles appropriately. (See B.2. and B.4.d.)

A.9. Group Work

a. *Screening.* Counselors screen prospective group counseling/therapy participants. To the extent possible, counselors select members whose needs and goals are compatible with goals of the group, who will not impede the group process, and whose well-being will not be jeopardized by the group experience.

b. *Protecting clients.* In a group setting, counselors take reasonable precautions to protect clients from physical or psychological trauma.

A.10. Fees and Bartering (See D.3.a. and D.3.b.)

a. *Advance understanding.* Counselors clearly explain to clients, prior to entering the counseling relationship, all financial arrangements related to professional services including the use of collection agencies or legal measures for nonpayment. (A.11.c.)

b. *Establishing fees.* In establishing fees for professional counseling services, counselors consider the financial status of clients and locality. In the event that the established fee structure is inappropriate for a client, assistance is provided in attempting to find comparable services of acceptable cost. (See A.10.d., D.3.a., and D.3.b.)

c. *Bartering discouraged.* Counselors ordinarily refrain from accepting goods or services from clients in return for counseling services because such arrangements create inherent potential for conflicts, exploitation, and distortion of the professional relationship. Counselors may participate in bartering only if the relationship is not exploitative, if the client requests it, if a clear written contract is established, and if such arrangements are an accepted practice among professionals in the community. (See A.6.a.)

d. *Pro bono service.* Counselors contribute to society by devoting a portion of their professional activity to services for which there is little or no financial return (pro bono).

A.11. Termination and Referral

a. *Abandonment prohibited.* Counselors do not abandon or neglect clients in counseling. Counselors assist in making appropriate arrangements for the continuation of treatment, when necessary, during interruptions such as vacations, and following termination.

b. *Inability to assist clients.* If counselors determine an inability to be of professional assistance to clients, they avoid entering or immediately terminate a counseling relationship. Counselors are knowledgeable about referral resources and suggest appropriate alternatives. If clients decline the suggested referral, counselors should discontinue the relationship.

c. *Appropriate termination.* Counselors terminate a counseling relationship, securing client agreement when possible, when it is reasonably clear that the client is no longer benefiting, when services are no longer required, when counseling no longer serves the client's needs or interests, when clients do not pay fees charged, or when agency or institution limits do not allow provision of further counseling services. (See A.10.b. and C.2.g.)

A.12. Computer Technology

a. *Use of computers.* When computer applications are used in counseling services, counselors ensure that (1) the client is intellectually, emotionally, and physically capable of using the computer application; (2) the computer application is appropriate for the needs of the client; (3) the client understands the purpose and operation of the computer applications; and (4) a follow-up of client use of a computer application is provided to correct possible misconceptions, discover inappropriate use, and assess subsequent needs.

b. *Explanation of limitations.* Counselors ensure that clients are provided information as a part of the counseling relationship that adequately explains the limitations of computer technology.

c. *Access to computer applications.* Counselors provide for equal access to computer applications in counseling services. (See A.2.a.)

Section B: Confidentiality

B.1. Right to Privacy

a. *Respect for privacy.* Counselors respect their client's right to privacy and avoid illegal and unwarranted disclosures of confidential information. (See A.3.a. and B.6.a.)

b. *Client waiver.* The right to privacy may be waived by the client or his or her legally recognized representative.

c. *Exceptions.* The general requirement that counselors keep information confidential does not apply when disclosure is required to prevent clear and imminent danger to the client or others or when legal requirements demand that confidential information be revealed. Counselors consult with other professionals when in doubt as to the validity of an exception.

d. *Contagious, fatal diseases.* A counselor who receives information confirming that a client has a disease commonly known to be both communicable and fatal is justified in disclosing information to an identifiable third party, who by his or her relationship with the client is at a high risk of contracting the disease. Prior to making a disclosure the counselor should ascertain that the client has not already informed the third party about his or her disease and that the client is not intending to inform the third party in the immediate future. (See B.1.c and B.1.f.)

e. *Court-ordered disclosure.* When court ordered to release confidential information without a client's permission, counselors request to the court that the disclosure not be required due to potential harm to the client or counseling relationship. (See B.1.c.)

f. *Minimal disclosure.* When circumstances require the disclosure of confidential information, only essential information is revealed. To the extent possible, clients are informed before confidential information is disclosed.

g. *Explanation of limitations.* When counseling is initiated and throughout the counseling process as necessary, counselors inform clients of the limitations of confidentiality and identify foreseeable situations in which confidentiality must be breached. (See G.2.a.)

h. *Subordinates.* Counselors make every effort to ensure that privacy and confidentiality of clients are maintained by subordinates including employees, supervisees, clerical assistants, and volunteers. (See B.1.a.)

i. *Treatment teams.* If client treatment will involve a continued review by a treatment team, the client will be informed of the team's existence and composition.

B.2. Groups and Families

a. *Group work.* In group work, counselors clearly define confidentiality and the parameters for the specific group being entered, explain its importance, and discuss the difficulties related to confidentiality involved in group work. The fact that confidentiality cannot be guaranteed is clearly communicated to group members.

b. *Family counseling.* In family counseling, information about one family member cannot be disclosed to another member without permission. Counselors protect the privacy rights of each family member. (See A.8., B.3., and B.4.d.)

B.3. Minor or Incompetent Clients

When counseling clients who are minors or individuals who are unable to give voluntary, informed consent, parents or guardians may be included in the counseling process as appropriate. Counselors act in the best interests of clients and take measures to safeguard confidentiality. (See A.3.c.)

B.4. Records

a. *Requirement of records.* Counselors maintain records necessary for rendering professional services to their clients and as required by laws, regulations, or agency or institution procedures.

b. *Confidentiality of records.* Counselors are responsible for securing the safety and confidentiality of any counseling records they create, maintain, transfer, or destroy whether the records are written, taped, computerized, or stored in any other medium. (See B.1.a.)

c. *Permission to record or observe.* Counselors obtain permission from clients prior to electronically recording or observing sessions. (See A.3.a.)

d. *Client access.* Counselors recognize that counseling records are kept for the benefit of clients, and therefore provide access to records and copies of records when requested by competent clients, unless the records contain information that may be misleading and detrimental to the client. In situations involving multiple clients, access to records is limited to those parts of records that do not include confidential information related to another client. (See A.8., B.1.a., and B.2.b.)

e. *Disclosure or transfer.* Counselors obtain written permission from clients to disclose or transfer records to legitimate third parties unless exceptions to confidentiality exist as listed in Section B.1. Steps are taken to ensure that receivers of counseling records are sensitive to their confidential nature.

B.5. Research and Training

a. *Data disguise required.* Use of data derived from counseling relationships for purposes of training, research, or publication is confined to content that is disguised to ensure the anonymity of the individuals involved. (See B.1.g. and G.3.d.)

b. *Agreement for identification.* Identification of a client in a presentation or publication is permissible only when the client has reviewed the material and has agreed to its presentation or publication. (See G.3.d.)

B.6. Consultation

a. *Respect for privacy.* Information obtained in a consulting relationship is discussed for professional purposes only with persons clearly concerned with the case. Written and oral reports present data germane to the purposes of the consultation, and every effort is made to protect client identity and avoid undue invasion of privacy.

b. *Cooperating agencies.* Before sharing information, counselors make efforts to ensure that there are defined policies in other agencies serving the counselor's clients that effectively protect the confidentiality of information.

Section C: Professional Responsibility

C.1. Standards Knowledge

Counselors have a responsibility to read, understand, and follow the Code of Ethics and the Standards of Practice.

C.2. Professional Competence

a. *Boundaries of competence.* Counselors practice only within the boundaries of their competence, based on their education, training, supervised experience, state and national professional credentials, and appropriate professional experience. Counselors will demonstrate a commitment to gain knowledge, personal awareness, sensitivity, and skills pertinent to working with a diverse client population.

b. *New specialty areas of practice.* Counselors practice in specialty areas new to them only after appropriate education, training, and supervised experience. While developing skills in new specialty areas, counselors take steps to ensure the competence of their work and to protect others from possible harm.

c. *Qualified for employment.* Counselors accept employment only for positions for which they are qualified by education, training, supervised experience, state and national professional credentials, and appropriate professional experience. Counselors hire for professional counseling positions only individuals who are qualified and competent.

d. *Monitor effectiveness.* Counselors continually monitor their effectiveness as professionals and take steps to improve when necessary. Counselors in private practice take reasonable steps to seek out peer supervision to evaluate their efficacy as counselors.

e. *Ethical issues consultation.* Counselors take reasonable steps to consult with other counselors or related professionals when they have questions regarding their ethical obligations or professional practice. (See H.1.)

f. *Continuing education.* Counselors recognize the need for continuing education to maintain a reasonable level of awareness of current scientific and professional information in their fields of activity. They take steps to maintain competence in the skills they use, are open to new procedures, and keep current with the diverse and/or special populations with whom they work.

g. *Impairment.* Counselors refrain from offering or accepting professional services when their physical, mental, or emotional problems are likely to harm a client or others. They are alert to the signs of impairment, seek assistance for problems, and, if necessary, limit, suspend, or terminate their professional responsibilities. (See A.11.c.)

C.3. Advertising and Soliciting Clients

a. *Accurate advertising.* There are no restrictions on advertising by counselors except those that can be specifically justified to protect the public from deceptive practices. Counselors advertise or represent their services to the public by identifying their credentials in an accurate manner that is not false, misleading, deceptive, or fraudulent. Counselors may only advertise the highest degree earned which is in counseling or a closely related field from a college or university that was accredited when the degree was awarded by one of the regional accrediting bodies recognized by the Council on Postsecondary Accreditation.

b. *Testimonials.* Counselors who use testimonials do not solicit them from clients or other persons who, because of their particular circumstances, may be vulnerable to undue influence.

c. *Statements by others.* Counselors make reasonable efforts to ensure that statements made by others about them or the profession of counseling are accurate.

d. *Recruiting through employment.* Counselors do not use their places of employment or institutional affiliation to recruit or gain clients, supervisees, or consultees for their private practices. (See C.5.e.)

e. *Products and training advertisements.* Counselors who develop products related to their profession or conduct workshops or training events ensure that the advertisements concerning these products or events are accurate and disclose adequate information for consumers to make informed choices.

f. *Promoting to those served.* Counselors do not use counseling, teaching, training, or supervisory relationships to promote their products or training events in a manner that is deceptive or would exert undue influence on individuals who may be vulnerable. Counselors may adopt textbooks they have authored for instructional purposes.

g. *Professional association involvement.* Counselors actively participate in local, state, and national associations that foster the development and improvement of counseling.

C.4. Credentials

a. *Credentials claimed.* Counselors claim or imply only professional credentials possessed and are responsible for correcting any known misrepresentations of their credentials by others. Professional credentials include graduate degrees in counseling or closely related mental health fields, accreditation of graduate programs, national voluntary certifications, government-issued certifications or licenses, ACA professional membership, or any other credential that might indicate to the public specialized knowledge or expertise in counseling.

b. *ACA professional membership.* ACA professional members may announce to the public their membership status. Regular members may not announce their ACA membership in a manner that might imply they are credentialed counselors.

c. *Credential guidelines.* Counselors follow the guidelines for use of credentials that have been established by the entities that issue the credentials.

d. *Misrepresentation of credentials.* Counselors do not attribute more to their credentials than the credentials represent, and do not imply that other counselors are not qualified because they do not possess certain credentials.

e. *Doctoral degrees from other fields.* Counselors who hold a master's degree in counseling or a closely related mental health field, but hold a doctoral degree from other than counseling or a closely related field, do not use the title "Dr." in their practices and do not announce to the public in relation to their practice or status as a counselor that they hold a doctorate.

C.5. Public Responsibility

a. *Nondiscrimination.* Counselors do not discriminate against clients, students, or supervisees in a manner that has a negative impact based on their age, color, culture, disability, ethnic group, gender, race, religion, sexual orientation, or socioeconomic status, or for any other reason. (See A.2.a.)

b. *Sexual harassment.* Counselors do not engage in sexual harassment. Sexual harassment is defined as sexual solicitation, physical advances, or verbal or nonverbal conduct that is sexual in nature, that occurs in connection with professional activities or roles, and that either (1) is unwelcome, is offensive, or creates a hostile workplace environment, and counselors know or are told this; or (2) is sufficiently severe or intense to be perceived as harassment to a reasonable person in the context. Sexual harassment can consist of a single intense or severe act or multiple persistent or pervasive acts.

c. *Reports to third parties.* Counselors are accurate, honest, and unbiased in reporting their professional activities and judgments to appropriate third parties including courts, health insurance companies, those who are the recipients of evaluation reports, and others. (See B.1.g.)

d. *Media presentations.* When counselors provide advice or comment by means of public lectures, demonstrations, radio or television programs, prerecorded tapes, printed articles, mailed material, or other media, they take reasonable precautions to ensure that (1) the statements are based on appropriate professional counseling literature and practice; (2) the statements are otherwise consistent with the Code of Ethics and the Standards of Practice; and (3) the recipients of the information are not encouraged to infer that a professional counseling relationship has been established. (See C.6.b.)

e. *Unjustified gains.* Counselors do not use their professional positions to seek or receive unjustified personal gains, sexual favors, unfair advantage, or unearned goods or services. (See C.3.d.)

C.6. Responsibility to Other Professionals

a. *Different approaches.* Counselors are respectful of approaches to professional counseling that differ from their own. Counselors know and take into account the traditions and practices of other professional groups with which they work.

b. *Personal public statements.* When making personal statements in a public context, counselors clarify that they are speaking from their personal perspectives and that they are not speaking on behalf of all counselors or the profession. (See C.5.d.)

c. *Clients served by others*. When counselors learn that their clients are in a professional relationship with another mental health professional, they request release from clients to inform the other professionals and strive to establish positive and collaborative professional relationships. (See A.4.)

Section D: Relationships with Other Professionals

D.1. Relationships with Employers and Employees

a. *Role definition*. Counselors define and describe for their employers and employees the parameters and levels of their professional roles.

b. *Agreements*. Counselors establish working agreements with supervisors, colleagues, and subordinates regarding counseling or clinical relationships, confidentiality, adherence to professional standards, distinction between public and private material, maintenance and dissemination of recorded information, work load, and accountability. Working agreements in each instance are specified and made known to those concerned.

c. *Negative conditions*. Counselors alert their employers to conditions that may be potentially disruptive or damaging to the counselor's professional responsibilities or that may limit their effectiveness.

d. *Evaluation*. Counselors submit regularly to professional review and evaluation by their supervisor or the appropriate representative of the employer.

e. *In-service*. Counselors are responsible for in-service development of self and staff.

f. *Goals*. Counselors inform their staff of goals and programs.

g. *Practices*. Counselors provide personnel and agency practices that respect and enhance the rights and welfare of each employee and recipient of agency services. Counselors strive to maintain the highest levels of professional services.

h. *Personnel selection and assignment*. Counselors select competent staff and assign responsibilities compatible with their skills and experiences.

i. *Discrimination*. Counselors, as either employers or employees, do not engage in or condone practices that are inhumane, illegal, or unjustifiable (such as considerations based on age, color, culture, disability, ethnic group, gender, race, religion, sexual orientation, or socioeconomic status) in hiring, promotion, or training. (See A.2.a. and C.5.b.)

j. *Professional conduct*. Counselors have a responsibility both to clients and to the agency or institution within which services are performed to maintain high standards of professional conduct.

k. *Exploitative relationships*. Counselors do not engage in exploitative relationships with individuals over whom they have supervisory, evaluative, or instructional control or authority.

l. *Employer policies*. The acceptance of employment in an agency or institution implies that counselors are in agreement with its general policies and principles. Counselors strive to reach agreement with employers as to acceptable standards of conduct that allow for changes in institutional policy conducive to the growth and development of clients.

D.2. Consultation (See B.6.)

a. *Consultation as an option.* Counselors may choose to consult with any other professionally competent persons about their clients. In choosing consultants, counselors avoid placing the consultant in a conflict of interest situation that would preclude the consultant being a proper party to the counselor's efforts to help the client. Should counselors be engaged in a work setting that compromises this consultation standard, they consult with other professionals whenever possible to consider justifiable alternatives.

b. *Consultant competency.* Counselors are reasonably certain that they have or the organization represented has the necessary competencies and resources for giving the kind of consulting services needed and that appropriate referral resources are available.

c. *Understanding with clients.* When providing consultation, counselors attempt to develop with their clients a clear understanding of problem definition, goals for change, and predicted consequences of interventions selected.

d. *Consultant goals.* The consulting relationship is one in which client adaptability and growth toward self-direction are consistently encouraged and cultivated. (See A.1.b.)

D.3. Fees for Referral

a. *Accepting fees from agency clients.* Counselors refuse a private fee or other remuneration for rendering services to persons who are entitled to such services through the counselor's employing agency or institution. The policies of a particular agency may make explicit provisions for agency clients to receive counseling services from members of its staff in private practice. In such instances, the clients must be informed of other options open to them should they seek private counseling services. (See A.10.a., A.11.b., and C.3.d.)

b. *Referral fees.* Counselors do not accept a referral fee from other professionals.

D.4. Subcontractor Arrangements

When counselors work as subcontractors for counseling services for a third party, they have a duty to inform clients of the limitations of confidentiality that the organization may place on counselors in providing counseling services to clients. The limits of such confidentiality ordinarily are discussed as part of the intake session. (See B.1.e. and B.1.f.)

Section E: Evaluation, Assessment, and Interpretation

E.1. General

a. *Appraisal techniques.* The primary purpose of educational and psychological assessment is to provide measures that are objective and interpretable in either comparative or absolute terms. Counselors recognize the need to interpret the statements in this section as applying to the whole range of appraisal techniques, including test and nontest data.

b. *Client welfare.* Counselors promote the welfare and best interests of the client in the development, publication, and utilization of educational and psychological assessment techniques. They do not misuse assessment results and interpretations and take reasonable steps to prevent others from misusing the information these techniques provide. They respect the client's right to know the results, the interpretations made, and the bases for their conclusions and recommendations.

E.2. Competence to Use and Interpret Tests

a. *Limits of competence.* Counselors recognize the limits of their competence and perform only those testing and assessment services for which they have been trained. They are familiar with reliability, validity, related standardization, error of measurement, and proper application of any technique utilized. Counselors using computer-based test interpretations are trained in the construct being measured and the specific instrument being used prior to using this type of computer application. Counselors take reasonable measures to ensure the proper use of psychological assessment techniques by persons under their supervision.

b. *Appropriate use.* Counselors are responsible for the appropriate application, scoring, interpretation, and use of assessment instruments, whether they score and interpret such tests themselves or use computerized or other services.

c. *Decisions based on results.* Counselors responsible for decisions involving individuals or policies that are based on assessment results have a thorough understanding of educational and psychological measurement, including validation criteria, test research, and guidelines for test development and use.

d. *Accurate information.* Counselors provide accurate information and avoid false claims or misconceptions when making statements about assessment instruments or techniques. Special efforts are made to avoid unwarranted connotations of such terms as IQ and grade equivalent scores. (See C.5.c.)

E.3. Informed Consent

a. *Explanation to clients.* Prior to assessment, counselors explain the nature and purposes of assessment and the specific use of results in language the client (or other legally authorized person on behalf of the client) can understand, unless an explicit exception to this right has been agreed upon in advance. Regardless of whether scoring and interpretation are completed by counselors, by assistants, or by computer or other outside services, counselors take reasonable steps to ensure that appropriate explanations are given to the client.

b. *Recipients of results.* The examinee's welfare, explicit understanding, and prior agreement determine the recipients of test results. Counselors include accurate and appropriate interpretations with any release of individual or group test results. (See B.1.a. and C.5.c.)

E.4. Release of Information to Competent Professionals

a. *Misuse of results.* Counselors do not misuse assessment results, including test results and interpretations, and take reasonable steps to prevent the misuse of such by others. (See C.5.c.)

b. *Release of raw data.* Counselors ordinarily release data (e.g., protocols, counseling or interview notes, or questionnaires) in which the client is identified only with the consent of the client or the client's legal representative. Such data are usually released only to persons recognized by counselors as competent to interpret the data. (See B.1.a.)

E.5. Proper Diagnosis of Mental Disorders

a. *Proper Diagnosis.* Counselors take special care to provide proper diagnosis of mental disorders. Assessment techniques (including personal interview) used to determine client care (e.g., locus of treatment, type of treatment, or recommended follow-up) are carefully selected and appropriately used. (See A.3.a. and C.5.c.)

b. *Cultural sensitivity.* Counselors recognize that culture affects the manner in which clients' problems are defined. Clients' socioeconomic and cultural experience is considered when diagnosing mental disorders.

E.6. Test Selection

a. *Appropriateness of instruments.* Counselors carefully consider the validity, reliability, psychometric limitations, and appropriateness of instruments when selecting tests for use in a given situation or with a particular client.

b. *Culturally diverse populations.* Counselors are cautious when selecting tests for culturally diverse populations to avoid inappropriateness of testing that may be outside of socialized behavioral or cognitive patterns.

E.7. Conditions of Test Administration

a. *Administration conditions.* Counselors administer tests under the same conditions that were established in their standardization. When tests are not administered under standard conditions or when unusual behavior or irregularities occur during the testing session, those conditions are noted in interpretation, and the results may be designated as invalid or of questionable validity.

b. *Computer administration.* Counselors are responsible for ensuring that administration programs function properly to provide clients with accurate results when a computer or other electronic methods are used for test administration. (See A.12.b.)

c. *Unsupervised test taking.* Counselors do not permit unsupervised or inadequately supervised use of tests or assessments unless the tests or assessments are designed, intended, and validated for self-administration and/or scoring.

d. *Disclosure of favorable conditions.* Prior to test administration, conditions that produce most favorable test results are made known to the examinee.

E.8. Diversity in Testing

Counselors are cautious in using assessment techniques, making evaluations, and interpreting the performance of populations not represented in the norm group on which an instrument was standardized. They recognize the effects of age, color, culture, disability, ethnic group, gender, race, religion, sexual orientation, and socioeconomic status on test administration and interpretation and place test results in proper perspective with other relevant factors. (See A.2.a.)

E.9. Test Scoring and Interpretation

a. *Reporting reservations.* In reporting assessment results, counselors indicate any reservations that exist regarding validity or reliability because of the circumstances of the assessment or the inappropriateness of the norms for the person tested.

b. *Research instruments.* Counselors exercise caution when interpreting the results of research instruments possessing insufficient technical data to support respondent results. The specific purposes for the use of such instruments are stated explicitly to the examinee.

c. *Testing services.* Counselors who provide test scoring and test interpretation services to support the assessment process confirm the validity of such interpretations. They accurately describe the purpose, norms, validity, reliability, and applications of the procedures and any special qualifications applicable to their use. The public offering of an automated test interpretations service is considered a professional-to-professional consultation. The formal responsibility of the consultant is to the consultee, but the ultimate and overriding responsibility is to the client.

E.10. Test Security

Counselors maintain the integrity and security of tests and other assessment techniques consistent with legal and contractual obligations. Counselors do not appropriate, reproduce, or modify published tests or parts thereof without acknowledgment and permission from the publisher.

E.11. Obsolete Tests and Outdated Test Results

Counselors do not use data or test results that are obsolete or outdated for the current purpose. Counselors make every effort to prevent the misuse of obsolete measures and test data by others.

E.12. Test Construction

Counselors use established scientific procedures, relevant standards, and current professional knowledge for test design in the development, publication, and utilization of educational and psychological assessment techniques.

Section F: Teaching, Training, and Supervision

F.1. Counselor Educators and Trainers

a. *Educators as teachers and practitioners.* Counselors who are responsible for developing, implementing, and supervising educational programs are skilled as teachers and practitioners. They are knowledgeable regarding the ethical, legal, and regulatory aspects of the profession, are skilled in applying that knowledge, and make students and supervisees aware of their responsibilities. Counselors conduct counselor education and training programs in an ethical manner and serve as role models for professional behavior. Counselor educators should make an effort to infuse material related to human diversity into all courses and/or workshops that are designed to promote the development of professional counselors.

b. *Relationship boundaries with students and supervisees.* Counselors clearly define and maintain ethical, professional, and social relationship boundaries with their students and supervisees. They are aware of the differential in power that exists and the student's or supervisee's possible incomprehension of that power differential. Counselors explain to students and supervisees the potential for the relationship to become exploitive.

c. *Sexual relationships.* Counselors do not engage in sexual relationships with students or supervisees and do not subject them to sexual harassment. (See A.6. and C.5.b)

d. *Contributions to research.* Counselors give credit to students or supervisees for their contributions to research and scholarly projects. Credit is given through coauthorship, acknowledgment, footnote statement, or other appropriate means, in accordance with such contributions. (See G.4.b. and G.4.c.)

e. *Close relatives.* Counselors do not accept close relatives as students or supervisees.

f. *Supervision preparation.* Counselors who offer clinical supervision services are adequately prepared in supervision methods and techniques. Counselors who are doctoral students serving as practicum or internship supervisors to master's level students are adequately prepared and supervised by the training program.

g. *Responsibility for services to clients.* Counselors who supervise the counseling services of others take reasonable measures to ensure that counseling services provided to clients are professional.

h. *Endorsement.* Counselors do not endorse students or supervisees for certification, licensure, employment, or completion of an academic or training program if they believe students or supervisees are not qualified for the endorsement. Counselors take reasonable steps to assist students or supervisees who are not qualified for endorsement to become qualified.

F.2. Counselor Education and Training Programs

a. *Orientation.* Prior to admission, counselors orient prospective students to the counselor education or training program's expectations, including but not limited to the following: (1) the type and level of skill acquisition required for successful completion of the training, (2) subject matter to be covered, (3) basis for evaluation, (4) training components that encourage self-growth or self-disclosure as part of the training process, (5) the type of supervision settings and requirements of the sites for required clinical field experiences, (6) student and supervisee evaluation and dismissal policies and procedures, and (7) up-to-date employment prospects for graduates.

b. *Integration of study and practice.* Counselors establish counselor education and training programs that integrate academic study and supervised practice.

c. *Evaluation.* Counselors clearly state to students and supervisees, in advance of training, the levels of competency expected, appraisal methods, and timing of evaluations for both didactic and experiential components. Counselors provide students and supervisees with periodic performance appraisal and evaluation feedback throughout the training program.

d. *Teaching ethics.* Counselors make students and supervisees aware of the ethical responsibilities and standards of the profession and the students' and supervisees' ethical responsibilities to the profession. (See C.1. and F.3.e.)

e. *Peer relationships.* When students or supervisees are assigned to lead counseling groups or provide clinical supervision for their peers, counselors take steps to ensure that students and supervisees placed in these roles do not have personal or adverse relationships with peers and that they understand they have the same ethical obligations as counselor educators, trainers, and supervisors. Counselors make every effort to ensure that the rights of peers are not compromised when students or supervisees are assigned to lead counseling groups or provide clinical supervision.

f. *Varied theoretical positions.* Counselors present varied theoretical positions so that students and supervisees may make comparisons and have opportunities to develop their own positions. Counselors provide information concerning the scientific bases of professional practice. (See C.6.a.)

g. *Field placements.* Counselors develop clear policies within their training program regarding field placement and other clinical experiences. Counselors provide clearly stated roles and responsibilities for the student or supervisee, the site supervisor, and the program supervisor. They confirm that site supervisors are qualified to provide supervision and are informed of their professional and ethical responsibilities in this role.

h. *Dual relationships as supervisors.* Counselors avoid dual relationships such as performing the role of site supervisor and training program supervisor in the student's or supervisee's training program. Counselors do not accept any form of professional services, fees, commissions, reimbursement, or remuneration from a site for student or supervisee placement.

i. *Diversity in programs.* Counselors are responsive to their institution's and program's recruitment and retention needs for training program administrators, faculty, and students with diverse backgrounds and special needs. (See A.2.a.)

F.3. Students and Supervisees

a. *Limitations.* Counselors, through ongoing evaluation and appraisal, are aware of the academic and personal limitations of students and supervisees that might impede performance. Counselors assist students and supervisees in securing remedial assistance when needed, and dismiss from the training program supervisees who are unable to provide competent service due to academic or personal limitations. Counselors seek professional consultation and document their decision to dismiss or refer students or supervisees for assistance. Counselors ensure that students and supervisees have recourse to address decisions made to require them to seek assistance or to dismiss them.

b. *Self-growth experiences.* Counselors use professional judgment when designing training experiences conducted by the counselors themselves that require student and supervisee self-growth or self-disclosure. Safeguards are provided so that students and supervisees are aware of the ramifications their self-disclosure may have on counselors whose primary role as teacher, trainer, or supervisor requires acting on ethical obligations to the profession. Evaluative components of experiential training experiences explicitly delineate predetermined academic standards that are separate and do not depend on the student's level of self-disclosure. (See A.6.)

c. *Counseling for students and supervisees.* If students or supervisees request counseling, supervisors or counselor educators provide them with acceptable referrals. Supervisors or counselor educators do not serve as counselor to students or supervisees over whom they hold administrative, teaching, or evaluative roles unless this is a brief role associated with a training experience. (See A.6.b.)

d. *Clients of students and supervisees.* Counselors make every effort to ensure that the clients at field placements are aware of the services rendered and the qualifications of the students and supervisees rendering those services. Clients receive professional disclosure information and are informed of the limits of confidentiality. Client permission is obtained in order for the students and supervisees to use any information concerning the counseling relationship in the training process. (See B.1.e.)

e. *Standards for students and supervisees.* Students and supervisees preparing to become counselors adhere to the Code of Ethics and the Standards of Practice. Students and supervisees have the same obligations to clients as those required of counselors. (See H.1.)

Section G: Research and Publication

G.1. Research Responsibilities

a. *Use of human subjects.* Counselors plan, design, conduct, and report research in a manner consistent with pertinent ethical principles, federal and state laws, host institutional regulations, and scientific standards governing research with human subjects. Counselors design and conduct research that reflects cultural sensitivity appropriateness.

b. *Deviation from standard practices.* Counselors seek consultation and observe stringent safeguards to protect the rights of research participants when a research problem suggests a deviation from standard acceptable practices. (See B.6.)

c. *Precautions to avoid injury.* Counselors who conduct research with human subjects are responsible for the subjects' welfare throughout the experiment and take reasonable precautions to avoid causing injurious psychological, physical, or social effects to their subjects.

d. *Principal researcher responsibility.* The ultimate responsibility for ethical research practice lies with the principal researcher. All others involved in the research activities share ethical obligations and full responsibility for their own actions.

e. *Minimal interference.* Counselors take reasonable precautions to avoid causing disruptions in subjects' lives due to participation in research.

f. *Diversity.* Counselors are sensitive to diversity and research issues with special populations. They seek consultation when appropriate. (See A.2.a. and B.6.)

G.2. Informed Consent

a. *Topics disclosed.* In obtaining informed consent for research, counselors use language that is understandable to research participants and that (1) accurately explains the purpose and procedures to be followed; (2) identifies any procedures that are experimental or relatively untried; (3) describes the attendant discomforts and risks; (4) describes the benefits or changes in individuals or organizations that might be reasonably expected; (5) discloses appropriate alternative procedures that would be advantageous for subjects; (6) offers to answer any inquiries concerning the procedures; (7) describes any limitations on confidentiality; and (8) instructs that subjects are free to withdraw their consent and to discontinue participation in the project at any time. (See B.1.f.)

b. *Deception.* Counselors do not conduct research involving deception unless alternative procedures are not feasible and the prospective value of the research justifies the deception. When the methodological requirements of a study necessitate concealment or deception, the investigator is required to explain clearly the reasons for this action as soon as possible.

c. *Voluntary participation.* Participation in research is typically voluntary and without any penalty for refusal to participate. Involuntary participation is appropriate only when it can be demonstrated that participation will have no harmful effects on subjects and is essential to the investigation.

d. *Confidentiality of information.* Information obtained about research participants during the course of an investigation is confidential. When the possibility exists that others may obtain access to such information, ethical research practice requires that the possibility, together with the plans for protecting confidentiality, be explained to participants as a part of the procedure for obtaining informed consent. (See B.1.e.)

e. *Persons incapable of giving informed consent.* When a person is incapable of giving informed consent, counselors provide an appropriate explanation, obtain agreement for participation, and obtain appropriate consent from a legally authorized person.

f. *Commitments to participants.* Counselors take reasonable measures to honor all commitments to research participants.

g. *Explanations after data collection.* After data are collected, counselors provide participants with full clarification of the nature of the study to remove any misconceptions. Where scientific or human values justify delaying or withholding information, counselors take reasonable measures to avoid causing harm.

h. *Agreements to cooperate.* Counselors who agree to cooperate with another individual in research or publication incur an obligation to cooperate as promised in terms of punctuality of performance and with regard to the completeness and accuracy of the information required.

i. *Informed consent for sponsors.* In the pursuit of research, counselors give sponsors, institutions, and publication channels the same respect and opportunity for giving informed consent that they accord to individual research participants. Counselors are aware of their obligation to future research workers and ensure that host institutions are given feedback information and proper acknowledgment.

G.3. Reporting Results

a. *Information affecting outcome.* When reporting research results, counselors explicitly mention all variables and conditions known to the investigator that may have affected the outcome of a study or the interpretation of data.

b. *Accurate results.* Counselors plan, conduct, and report research accurately and in a manner that minimizes the possibility that results will be misleading. They provide thorough discussions of the limitations of their data and alternative hypotheses. Counselors do not engage in fraudulent research, distort data, misrepresent data, or deliberately bias their results.

c. *Obligation to report unfavorable results.* Counselors communicate to other counselors the results of any research judged to be of professional value. Results that reflect unfavorably on institutions, programs, services, prevailing opinions, or vested interests are not withheld.

d. *Identity of subjects.* Counselors who supply data, aid in the research of another person, report research results, or make original data available take due care to disguise the identity of respective subjects in the absence of specific authorization from the subjects to do otherwise. (See B.1.g. and B.5.a.)

e. *Replication studies.* Counselors are obligated to make available sufficient original research data to qualified professionals who may wish to replicate the study.

G.4. Publication

a. *Recognition of others.* When conducting and reporting research, counselors are familiar with and give recognition to previous work on the topic, observe copyright laws, and give full credit to those to whom credit is due. (See F.1.d. and G.4.c.)

b. *Contributors.* Counselors give credit through joint authorship, acknowledgment, footnote statements, or other appropriate means to those who have contributed significantly to research or concept development in accordance with such contributions. The principal contributor is listed first and minor technical or professional contributions are acknowledged in notes or introductory statements.

c. *Student research.* For an article that is substantially based on a student's dissertation or thesis, the student is listed as the principal author. (See F.1.d. and G.4.a.)

d. *Duplicate submission.* Counselors submit manuscripts for consideration to only one journal at a time. Manuscripts that are published in whole or in substantial part in another journal or published work are not submitted for publication without acknowledgment and permission from the previous publication.

e. *Professional review.* Counselors who review material submitted for publication, research, or other scholarly purposes respect the confidentiality and proprietary rights of those who submitted it.

Section H: Resolving Ethical Issues

H.1. Knowledge of Standards

Counselors are familiar with the Code of Ethics and the Standards of Practice and other applicable ethics codes from other professional organizations of which they are member, or from certification and licensure bodies. Lack of knowledge or misunderstanding of an ethical responsibility is not a defense against a charge of unethical conduct. (See F.3.e.)

H.2. Suspected Violations

a. *Ethical behavior expected.* Counselors expect professional associates to adhere to the Code of Ethics. When counselors possess reasonable cause that raises doubts as to whether a counselor is acting in an ethical manner, they take appropriate action. (See H.2.d. and H.2.e.)

b. *Consultation.* When uncertain as to whether a particular situation or course of action may be in violation of the Code of Ethics, counselors consult with other counselors who are knowledgeable about ethics, with colleagues, or with appropriate authorities.

c. *Organization conflicts.* If the demands of an organization with which counselors are affiliated pose a conflict with the Code of Ethics, counselors specify the nature of such conflicts and express to their supervisors or other responsible officials their commitment to the Code of Ethics. When possible, counselors work toward change within the organization to allow full adherence to the Code of Ethics.

d. *Informal resolution.* When counselors have reasonable cause to believe that another counselor is violating an ethical standard, they attempt to first resolve the issue informally with the other counselor if feasible, providing that such action does not violate confidentiality rights that may be involved.

e. *Reporting suspected violations.* When an informal resolution is not appropriate or feasible, counselors, upon reasonable cause, take action such as reporting the suspected ethical violation to state or national ethics committees, unless this action conflicts with confidentiality rights that cannot be resolved.

f. *Unwarranted complaints.* Counselors do not initiate, participate in, or encourage the filing of ethics complaints that are unwarranted or intend to harm a counselor rather than to protect clients or the public.

H.3. Cooperation with Ethics Committees

Counselors assist in the process of enforcing the Code of Ethics. Counselors cooperate with investigations, proceedings, and requirements of the ACA Ethics Committee or ethics committees of other duly constituted associations or boards having jurisdiction over those charged with a violation. Counselors are familiar with the ACA Policies and Procedures and use it as a reference in assisting the enforcement of the Code of Ethics.

ACA Standards of Practice

All members of the American Counseling Association (ACA) are required to adhere to the Standards of Practice and the Code of Ethics. The Standards of Practice represent minimal behavioral statements of the Code of Ethics. Members should refer to the applicable section of the Code of Ethics for further interpretation and amplification of the applicable Standard of Practice.

Section A: The Counseling Relationship

Standard of practice one (SP-1): Nondiscrimination. Counselors respect diversity and must not discriminate against clients because of age, color, culture, disability, ethnic group, gender, race, religion, sexual orientation, marital status, or socioeconomic status. (See A.2.a.)

Standard of practice two (SP-2): Disclosure to clients. Counselors must adequately inform clients, preferably in writing, regarding the counseling process and counseling relationship at or before the time it begins and throughout the relationship. (See A.3.a.)

Standard of practice three (SP-3): Dual relationships. Counselors must make every effort to avoid dual relationships with clients that could impair their professional judgment or increase the risk of harm to clients. When a dual relationship cannot be avoided, counselors must take appropriate steps to ensure that judgment is not impaired and that no exploitation occurs. (See A.6.a. and A.6.b.)

Standard of practice four (SP-4): Sexual intimacies with clients. Counselors must not engage in any type of sexual intimacies with current clients and must not engage in sexual intimacies with former clients within a minimum of two years after terminating the counseling relationship. Counselors who engage in such relationship after two years following termination have the responsibility to examine and document thoroughly that such relations did not have an exploitative nature.

Standard of practice five (SP-5): Protecting clients during group work. Counselors must take steps to protect clients from physical or psychological trauma resulting from interactions during group work. (See A.9.b.)

Standard of practice six (SP-6): Advance understanding of fees. Counselors must explain to clients, prior to their entering the counseling relationship, financial arrangements related to professional services. (See A.10. a–d. and A.11.c.)

Standard of practice seven (SP-7): Termination. Counselors must assist in making appropriate arrangements for the continuation of treatment of clients, when necessary, following termination of counseling relationships. (See A.11.a.)

Standard of practice eight (SP-8): Inability to assist clients. Counselors must avoid entering or immediately terminating a counseling relationship if it is determined that they are unable to be of professional assistance to a client. The counselor may assist in making an appropriate referral for the client. (See A.11.b.)

Section B: Confidentiality

Standard of practice nine (SP-9): Confidentiality requirement. Counselors must keep information related to counseling services confidential unless disclosure is in the best interest of clients, is required for the welfare of others, or is required by law. When disclosure is required, only information that is essential is revealed and the client is informed of such disclosure. (See B.1. a–f.)

Standard of practice ten (SP-10): Confidentiality requirements for subordinates. Counselors must take measures to ensure that privacy and confidentiality of clients are maintained by subordinates. (See B.1.h.)

Standard of practice eleven (SP-11): Confidentiality in group work. Counselors must clearly communicate to group members that confidentiality cannot be guaranteed in group work. (See B.2.a.)

Standard of practice twelve (SP-12): Confidentiality in family counseling. Counselors must not disclose information about one family member in counseling to another family member without prior consent. (See B.2.b.)

Standard of practice thirteen (SP-13): Confidentiality of records. Counselors must maintain appropriate confidentiality in creating, storing, accessing, transferring, and disposing of counseling records. (See B.4.b.)

Standard of practice fourteen (SP-14): Permission to record or observe. Counselors must obtain prior consent from clients in order to record electronically or observe sessions. (See B.4.c.)

Standard of practice fifteen (SP-15): Disclosure or transfer of records. Counselors must obtain client consent to disclose or transfer records to third parties, unless exceptions listed in SP-9 exist. (See B.4.e.)

Standard of practice sixteen (SP-16): Data disguise required. Counselors must disguise the identity of the client when using data for training, research, or publication. (See B.5.a.)

Section C: Professional Responsibility

Standard of practice seventeen (SP-17): Boundaries of competence. Counselors must practice only within the boundaries of their competence. (See C.2.a.)

Standard of practice eighteen (SP-18): Continuing education. Counselors must engage in continuing education to maintain their professional competence. (See C.2.f.)

Standard of practice nineteen (SP-19): Impairment of professionals. Counselors must refrain from offering professional services when their personal problems or conflicts may cause harm to a client or others. (See C.2.g.)

Standard of practice twenty (SP-20): Accurate advertising. Counselors must accurately represent their credentials and services when advertising. (See C.3.a.)

Standard of practice twenty-one (SP-21): Recruiting through employment. Counselors must not use their place of employment or institutional affiliation to recruit clients for their private practices. (See C.3.d.)

Standard of practice twenty-two (SP-22): Credentials claimed. Counselors must claim or imply only professional credentials possessed and must correct any known misrepresentations of their credentials by others. (See C.4.a.)

Standard of practice twenty-three (SP-23): Sexual harassment. Counselors must not engage in sexual harassment. (See C.5.b.)

Standard of practice twenty-four (SP-24): Unjustified gains. Counselors must not use their professional positions to seek or receive unjustified personal gains, sexual favors, unfair advantage, or unearned goods or services. (See C.5.e.)

Standard of practice twenty-five (SP-25): Clients served by others. With the consent of the client, counselors must inform other mental health professionals serving the same client that a counseling relationship between the counselor and client exists. (See C.6.c.)

Standard of practice twenty-six (SP-26): Negative employment conditions. Counselors must alert their employers to institutional policy or conditions that may be potentially disruptive or damaging to the counselor's professional responsibilities, or that may limit their effectiveness or deny clients' rights. (See D.1.c.)

Standard of practice twenty-seven (SP-27): Personnel selection and assignment. Counselors must select competent staff and must assign responsibilities compatible with staff skills and experiences. (See D.1.h.)

Standard of practice twenty-eight (SP-28): Exploitative relationships with subordinates. Counselors must not engage in exploitative relationships with individuals over whom they have supervisory, evaluative, or instructional control or authority. (See D.1.k.)

Section D: Relationship with Other Professionals

Standard of practice twenty-nine (SP-29): Accepting fees from agency clients. Counselors must not accept fees or other remuneration for consultation with persons entitled to such services through the counselor's employing agency or institution. (See D.3.a.)

Standard of practice thirty (SP-30): Referral fees. Counselors must not accept referral fees. (See D.3.b.)

Section E: Evaluation, Assesment, and Interpretation

Standard of practice thirty-one (SP-31): Limits of competence. Counselors must perform only testing and assessment services for which they are competent. Counselors must not allow the use of psychological assessment techniques by unqualified persons under their supervision. (See E.2.a.)

Standard of practice thirty-two (SP-32): Appropriate use of assessment instruments. Counselors must use assessment instruments in the manner for which they were intended. (See E.2.b.)

Standard of practice thirty-three (SP-33): Assessment explanations to clients. Counselors must provide explanations to clients prior to assessment about the nature and purposes of assessment and the specific uses of results. (See E.3.a.)

Standard of practice thirty-four (SP-34): Recipients of test results. Counselors must ensure that accurate and appropriate interpretations accompany any release of testing and assessment information. (See E.3.b.)

Standard of practice thirty-five (SP-35): Obsolete tests and outdated test results. Counselors must not base their assessment or intervention decisions or recommendations on data or test results that are obsolete or outdated for the current purpose. (See E.11.)

Section F: Teaching, Training, and Supervision

Standard of practice thirty-six (SP-36): Sexual relationships with students or supervisees. Counselors must not engage in sexual relationships with their students and supervisees. (See F.1.c.)

Standard of practice thirty-seven (SP-37): Credit for contributions to research. Counselors must give credit to students or supervisees for their contributions to research and scholarly projects. (See F.1.d.)

Standard of practice thirty-eight (SP-38): Supervision preparation. Counselors who offer clinical supervision services must be trained and prepared in supervision methods and techniques. (See F.1.f.)

Standard of practice thirty-nine (SP-39): Evaluation information. Counselors must clearly state to students and supervisees in advance of training the levels of competency expected, appraisal methods, and timing of evaluations. Counselors must provide students and supervisees with periodic performance appraisal and evaluation feedback throughout the training program. (See F.2.c.)

Standard of practice forty (SP-40): Peer relationships in training. Counselors must make every effort to ensure that the rights of peers are not violated when students and supervisees are assigned to lead counseling groups or provide clinical supervision. (See F.2.e.)

Standard of practice forty-one (SP-41): Limitations of students and supervisees. Counselors must assist students and supervisees in securing remedial assistance, when needed, and must dismiss from the training program students and supervisees who are unable to provide competent service due to academic or personal limitations. (See F.3.a.)

Standard of practice forty-two (SP-42): Self-growth experiences. Counselors who conduct experiences for students or supervisees that include self-growth or self-disclosure must inform participants of counselors' ethical obligations to the profession and must not grade participants based on their nonacademic performance. (See F.3.b.)

Standard of practice forty-three (SP-43): Standards for students and supervisees. Students and supervisees preparing to become counselors must adhere to the Code of Ethics and the Standards of Practice of counselors. (See F.3.e.)

Section G: Research and Publication

Standard of practice forty-four (SP-44): Precautions to avoid injury in research. Counselors must avoid causing physical, social, or psychological harm or injury to subjects in research. (See G.1.c.)

Standard of practice forty-five (SP-45): Confidentiality of research information. Counselors must keep confidential information obtained about research participants. (See G.2.d.)

Standard of practice forty-six (SP-46): Information affecting research outcome. Counselors must report all variables and conditions known to the investigator that may have affected research data or outcomes. (See G.3.a.)

Standard of practice forty-seven (SP-47): Accurate research results. Counselors must not distort or misrepresent research data, nor fabricate or intentionally bias research results. (See G.3.b.)

Standard of practice forty-eight (SP-48): Publication contributors. Counselors must give appropriate credit to those who have contributed to research. (See G.4.a. and G.4.b.)

Section H: Resolving Ethical Issues

Standard of practice forty-nine (SP-49): Ethical behavior expected. Counselors must take appropriate action when they possess reasonable cause that raises doubts as to whether counselors or other mental health professionals are acting in an ethical manner. (See H.2.a.)

Standard of practice fifty (SP-50): Unwarranted complaints. Counselors must not initiate, participate in, or encourage the filing of ethics complaints that are unwarranted or intended to harm a mental health professional rather than to protect clients or the public. (See H.2.f.)

Standard of practice fifty-one (SP-51): Cooperation with ethics committees. Counselors must cooperate with investigations, proceedings, and requirements of the ACA Ethics Committee or ethics committees of other duly constituted associations or boards having jurisdiction over those charged with a violation. (See H.3.)

American Psychological Association (APA) Ethical Principles of Psychologists and Code of Conduct[1]

Appendix

Introduction

The American Psychological Association's Ethical Principles of Psychologists and Code of Conduct (hereinafter referred to as the Ethics Code) consists of an Introduction, a Preamble, six General Principles (A-F), and specific Ethical Standards. The Introduction discusses the intent, organization, procedural considerations, and scope of application of the Ethics Code. The Preamble and General Principles are aspirational goals to guide psychologists toward the highest ideals of psychology. Although the Preamble and General Principles are not themselves enforceable rules, they should be considered by psychologists in arriving at an ethical course of action and may be considered by ethics bodies in interpreting the Ethical Standards. The Ethical Standards set forth enforceable rules for conduct as psychologists. Most of the Ethical Standards are written broadly, in order to apply to psychologists in varied roles, although the application of an Ethical Standard may vary depending on the context. The Ethical Standards are not exhaustive. The fact that a given conduct is not specifically addressed by the Ethics Code does not mean that it is necessarily either ethical or unethical.

Membership in the APA commits members to adhere to the APA Ethics Code and to the rules and procedures used to implement it. Psychologists and students, whether or not they are APA members, should be aware that the Ethics Code may be applied to them by state psychology boards, courts, or other public bodies. This Ethics Code applies only to psychologists' work-related activities, that is, activities that are part of the psychologists' scientific and professional functions or that are psychological in nature. It includes the clinical or counseling practice of psychology, research, teaching, supervision of trainees, development of assessment instruments, conducting assessments, educational counseling, organizational consulting, social intervention, administration, and other activities as well. These work-related activities can be distinguished from the purely private conduct of a psychologist, which ordinarily is not within the purview of the Ethics Code.

The Ethics Code is intended to provide standards of professional conduct that can be applied by the APA and by other bodies that choose to adopt them. Whether or not a psychologist has violated the Ethics Code does not by itself determine whether he or she is legally liable in a court action, whether a contract is enforceable, or whether other legal consequences occur. These results are based on legal rather than ethical rules. However, compliance with or violation of the Ethics Code may be admissible as evidence in some legal proceedings, depending on the circumstances.

In the process of making decisions regarding their professional behavior, psychologists must consider this Ethics Code, in addition to applicable laws and psychology board regulations. If the Ethics Code establishes a higher standard of conduct than is required by law, psychologists must meet the higher ethical standard. If the Ethics Code standard appears to conflict with the requirements of law, then psychologists make known their commitment to the Ethics Code and take steps to resolve the conflict in a responsible manner. If neither law nor the Ethics Code resolves an issue, psychologists should consider other professional materials[2] and the dictates of their own conscience, as well as seek consultation with others within the field when this is practical.

The procedures for filing, investigating, and resolving complaints of unethical conduct are described in the current Rules and Procedures of the APA Ethics Committee. The actions that APA may take for violations of the Ethics Code include actions such as reprimand, censure, termination of APA membership, and referral of the matter to other bodies. Complainants who seek remedies such as monetary damages in alleging ethical violations by a psychologist must resort to private negotiation, administrative bodies, or the courts. Actions that violate the Ethics Code may lead to the imposition of sanctions on a psychologist by bodies other than APA, including state psychological associations, other professional groups, psychology boards, other state or federal agencies, and payors for health services. In addition to actions for violation of the Ethics Code, the APA bylaws provide that APA may take action against a member after his or her conviction of a felony, expulsion or suspension from an affiliated state psychological association, or suspension or loss of licensure.

---

[2] Professional materials that are most helpful in this regard are guidelines and standards that have been adopted or endorsed by professional psychological organizations. Such guidelines and standards, whether adopted by the American Psychological Association (APA) or its Divisions, are not enforceable as such by this Ethics Code, but are of educative value to psychologists, courts, and professional bodies. Such materials include, but are not limited to, the APA's General Guidelines for Providers of Psychological Services (1987), Specialty Guidelines for the Delivery of Services by Clinical Psychologists, Counseling Psychologists, Industrial/Organizational Psychologists, and School Psychologists (1981), Guidelines for Computer Based Tests and Interpretations (1987), Standards for Educational and Psychological Testing (1985), Ethical Principles in the Conduct of Research With Human Participants (1982), Guidelines for Ethical Conduct in the Care and Use of Animals (1986), Guidelines for Providers of Psychological Services to Ethnic, Linguistic, and Culturally Diverse Populations (1990), and Publication Manual of the American Psychological Association (3rd ed., 1983). Materials not adopted by APA as a whole include the APA Division 41 (Forensic Psychology)/American Psychology-Law Society's Specialty Guidelines for Forensic Psychologists (1991).

Preamble

Psychologists work to develop a valid and reliable body of scientific knowledge based on research. They may apply that knowledge to human behavior in a variety of contexts. In doing so, they perform many roles, such as researcher, educator, diagnostician, therapist, supervisor, consultant, administrator, social interventionist, and expert witness. Their goal is to broaden knowledge of behavior and, where appropriate, to apply it pragmatically to improve the condition of both the individual and society. Psychologists respect the central importance of freedom of inquiry and expression in research, teaching, and publication. They also strive to help the public in developing informed judgments and choices concerning human behavior. This Ethics Code provides a common set of values upon which psychologists build their professional and scientific work.

This Code is intended to provide both the general principles and the decision rules to cover most situations encountered by psychologists. It has as its primary goal the welfare and protection of the individuals and groups with whom psychologists work. It is the individual responsibility of each psychologist to aspire to the highest possible standards of conduct. Psychologists respect and protect human and civil rights, and do not knowingly participate in or condone unfair discriminatory practices.

The development of a dynamic set of ethical standards for a psychologist's work-related conduct requires a personal commitment to a lifelong effort to act ethically; to encourage ethical behavior by students, supervisees, employees, and colleagues, as appropriate; and to consult with others, as needed, concerning ethical problems. Each psychologist supplements, but does not violate, the Ethics Code's values and rules on the basis of guidance drawn from personal values, culture, and experience.

General Principles

Principle A: Competence

Psychologists strive to maintain high standards of competence in their work. They recognize the boundaries of their particular competencies and the limitations of their expertise. They provide only those services and use only those techniques for which they are qualified by education, training, or experience. Psychologists are cognizant of the fact that the competencies required in serving, teaching, and/or studying groups of people vary with the distinctive characteristics of those groups. In those areas in which recognized professional standards do not yet exist, psychologists exercise careful judgment and take appropriate precautions to protect the welfare of those with whom they work. They maintain knowledge of relevant scientific and professional information related to the services they render, and they recognize the need for ongoing education. Psychologists make appropriate use of scientific, professional, technical, and administrative resources.

Principle B: Integrity

Psychologists seek to promote integrity in the science, teaching, and practice of psychology. In these activities psychologists are honest, fair, and respectful of others. In describing or reporting their qualifications, services, products, fees, research, or teaching, they do not make statements that are false, misleading, or deceptive. Psychologists strive to be aware of their own belief systems, values, needs, and limitations and the effect of these on their work. To the extent feasible, they attempt to clarify for relevant parties the roles they are performing and to function appropriately in accordance with those roles. Psychologists avoid improper and potentially harmful dual relationships.

Principle C: Professional and Scientific Responsibility

Psychologists uphold professional standards of conduct, clarify their professional roles and obligations, accept appropriate responsibility for their behavior, and adapt their methods to the needs of different populations. Psychologists consult with, refer to, or cooperate with other professionals and institutions to the extent needed to serve the best interests of their patients, clients, or other recipients of their services. Psychologists' moral standards and conduct are personal matters to the same degree as is true for any other person, except as psychologists' conduct may compromise their professional responsibilities or reduce the public's trust in psychology and psychologists. Psychologists are concerned about the ethical compliance of their colleagues' scientific and professional conduct. When appropriate, they consult with colleagues in order to prevent or avoid unethical conduct.

Principle D: Respect for People's Rights and Dignity

Psychologists accord appropriate respect to the fundamental rights, dignity, and worth of all people. They respect the rights of individuals to privacy, confidentiality, self-determination, and autonomy, mindful that legal and other obligations may lead to inconsistency and conflict with the exercise of these rights. Psychologists are aware of cultural, individual, and role differences, including those due to age, gender, race, ethnicity, national origin, religion, sexual orientation, disability, language, and socioeconomic status. Psychologists try to eliminate the effect on their work of biases based on those factors, and they do not knowingly participate in or condone unfair discriminatory practices.

Principle E: Concern for Others' Welfare

Psychologists seek to contribute to the welfare of those with whom they interact professionally. In their professional actions, psychologists weigh the welfare and rights of their patients or clients, students, supervisees, human research participants, and other affected persons, and the welfare of animal subjects of research. When conflicts occur among psychologists' obligations or concerns, they attempt to resolve these conflicts and to perform their roles in a responsible fashion that avoids or minimizes harm. Psychologists are sensitive to real and ascribed differences in power between themselves and others, and they do not exploit or mislead other people during or after professional relationships.

Principle F: Social Responsibility

Psychologists are aware of their professional and scientific responsibilities to the community and the society in which they work and live. They apply and make public their knowledge of psychology in order to contribute to human welfare. Psychologists are concerned about and work to mitigate the causes of human suffering. When undertaking research, they strive to advance human welfare and the science of psychology. Psychologists try to avoid misuse of their work. Psychologists comply with the law and encourage the development of law and social policy that serve the interests of their patients and clients and the public. They are encouraged to contribute a portion of their professional time for little or no personal advantage

Ethical Standards

1. *General Standards*

    These General Standards are potentially applicable to the professional and scientific activities of all psychologists.

1.01 *Applicability of the Ethics Code.* The activity of a psychologist subject to the Ethics Code may be reviewed under these Ethical Standards only if the activity is part of his or her work-related functions or the activity is psychological in nature. Personal activities having no connection to or effect on psychological roles are not subject to the Ethics Code.

1.02 *Relationship of Ethics and Law.* If psychologists' ethical responsibilities conflict with law, psychologists make known their commitment to the Ethics Code and take steps to resolve the conflict in a responsible manner.

1.03 *Professional and Scientific Relationship.* Psychologists provide diagnostic, therapeutic, teaching, research, supervisory, consultative, or other psychological services only in the context of a defined professional or scientific relationship or role. (See also Standards 2.01, Evaluation, Diagnosis, and Interventions in Professional Context, and 7.02, Forensic Assessments.)

1.04 *Boundaries of Competence.*

    (a) Psychologists provide services, teach, and conduct research only within the boundaries of their competence, based on their education, training, supervised experience, or appropriate professional experience.

    (b) Psychologists provide services, teach, or conduct research in new areas or involving new techniques only after first undertaking appropriate study, training, supervision, and/or consultation from persons who are competent in those areas or techniques.

    (c) In those emerging areas in which generally recognized standards for preparatory training do not yet exist, psychologists nevertheless take reasonable steps to ensure the competence of their work and to protect patients, clients, students, research participants, and others from harm.

1.05 *Maintaining Expertise.* Psychologists who engage in assessment, therapy, teaching, research, organizational consulting, or other professional activities maintain a reasonable level of awareness of current scientific and professional information in their fields of activity, and undertake ongoing efforts to maintain competence in the skills they use.

1.06 *Basis for Scientific and Professional Judgments.* Psychologists rely on scientifically and professionally derived knowledge when making scientific or professional judgments or when engaging in scholarly or professional endeavors.

1.07 *Describing the Nature and Results of Psychological Services.*

(a) When psychologists provide assessment, evaluation, treatment, counseling, supervision, teaching, consultation, research, or other psychological services to an individual, a group, or an organization, they provide, using language that is reasonably understandable to the recipient of those services, appropriate information beforehand about the nature of such services and appropriate information later about results and conclusions. (See also Standard 2.09, Explaining Assessment Results.)

(b) If psychologists will be precluded by law or by organizational roles from providing such information to particular individuals or groups, they so inform those individuals or groups at the outset of the service.

1.08 *Human Differences.* Where differences of age, gender, race, ethnicity, national origin, religion, sexual orientation, disability, language, or socioeconomic status significantly affect psychologists' work concerning particular individuals or groups, psychologists obtain the training, experience, consultation, or supervision necessary to ensure the competence of their services, or they make appropriate referrals.

1.09 *Respecting Others.* In their work-related activities, psychologists respect the rights of others to hold values, attitudes, and opinions that differ from their own.

1.10 *Nondiscrimination.* In their work-related activities, psychologists do not engage in unfair discrimination based on age, gender, race, ethnicity, national origin, religion, sexual orientation, disability, socioeconomic status, or any basis proscribed by law.

1.11 *Sexual Harassment.*

(a) Psychologists do not engage in sexual harassment. Sexual harassment is sexual solicitation, physical advances, or verbal or nonverbal conduct that is sexual in nature, that occurs in connection with the psychologist's activities or roles as a psychologist, and that either: (1) is unwelcome, is offensive, or creates a hostile workplace environment, and the psychologist knows or is told this; or (2) is sufficiently severe or intense to be abusive to a reasonable person in the context. Sexual harassment can consist of a single intense or severe act or of multiple persistent or pervasive acts.

(b) Psychologists accord sexual harassment complainants and respondents dignity and respect. Psychologists do not participate in denying a person academic admittance or advancement, employment, tenure, or promotion, based solely upon their having made, or their being the subject of, sexual harassment charges. This does not preclude taking action based upon the outcome of such proceedings or consideration of other appropriate information.

1.12 *Other Harassment.* Psychologists do not knowingly engage in behavior that is harassing or demeaning to persons with whom they interact in their work based on factors such as those persons' age, gender, race, ethnicity, national origin, religion, sexual orientation, disability, language, or socioeconomic status.

1.13 *Personal Problems and Conflicts.*

(a) Psychologists recognize that their personal problems and conflicts may interfere with their effectiveness. Accordingly, they refrain from undertaking an activity when they know or should know that their personal problems are likely to lead to harm to a patient, client, colleague, student, research participant, or other person to whom they may owe a professional or scientific obligation.

(b) In addition, psychologists have an obligation to be alert to signs of, and to obtain assistance for, their personal problems at an early stage, in order to prevent significantly impaired performance.

(c) When psychologists become aware of personal problems that may interfere with their performing work-related duties adequately, they take appropriate measures, such as obtaining professional consultation or assistance, and determine whether they should limit, suspend, or terminate their work-related duties.

1.14 *Avoiding Harm.* Psychologists take reasonable steps to avoid harming their patients or clients, research participants, students, and others with whom they work, and to minimize harm where it is foreseeable and unavoidable.

1.15 *Misuse of Psychologists' Influence.* Because psychologists' scientific and professional judgments and actions may affect the lives of others, they are alert to and guard against personal, financial, social, organizational, or political factors that might lead to misuse of their influence.

1.16 *Misuse of Psychologists' Work.*

(a) Psychologists do not participate in activities in which it appears likely that their skills or data will be misused by others, unless corrective mechanisms are available. (See also Standard 7.04, Truthfulness and Candor.)

(b) If psychologists learn of misuse or misrepresentation of their work, they take reasonable steps to correct or minimize the misuse or misrepresentation.

1.17 *Multiple Relationships.*

(a) In many communities and situations, it may not be feasible or reasonable for psychologists to avoid social or other nonprofessional contacts with persons such as patients, clients, students, supervisees, or research participants. Psychologists must always be sensitive to the potential harmful effects of other contacts on their work and on those persons with whom they deal. A psychologist refrains from entering into or promising another personal, scientific, professional, financial, or other relationship with such persons if it appears likely that such a relationship reasonably might impair the psychologist's objectivity or otherwise interfere with the psychologist's effectively performing his or her functions as a psychologist, or might harm or exploit the other party.

(b) Likewise, whenever feasible, a psychologist refrains from taking on professional or scientific obligations when preexisting relationships would create a risk of such harm.

(c) If a psychologist finds that, due to unforeseen factors, a potentially harmful multiple relationship has arisen, the psychologist attempts to resolve it with due regard for the best interests of the affected person and maximal compliance with the Ethics Code.

1.18 *Barter (with Patients or Clients).* Psychologists ordinarily refrain from accepting goods, services, or other nonmonetary remuneration from patients or clients in return for psychological services because such arrangements create inherent potential for conflicts, exploitation, and distortion of the professional relationship. A psychologist may participate in bartering only if (1) it is not clinically contraindicated, and (2) the relationship is not exploitative. (See also Standards 1.17, Multiple Relationships, and 1.25, Fees and Financial Arrangements.)

1.19 *Exploitative Relationships.*

(a) Psychologists do not exploit persons over whom they have supervisory, evaluative, or other authority such as students, supervisees, employees, research participants, and clients or patients. (See also Standards 4.05–4.07 regarding sexual involvement with clients or patients.)

(b) Psychologists do not engage in sexual relationships with students or supervisees in training over whom the psychologist has evaluative or direct authority, because such relationships are so likely to impair judgment or be exploitative.

1.20 *Consultations and Referrals.*

(a) Psychologists arrange for appropriate consultations and referrals based principally on the best interests of their patients or clients, with appropriate consent, and subject to other relevant considerations, including applicable law and contractual obligations. (See also Standards 5.01, Discussing the Limits of Confidentiality, and 5.06, Consultations.)

(b) When indicated and professionally appropriate, psychologists cooperate with other professionals in order to serve their patients or clients effectively and appropriately.

(c) Psychologists' referral practices are consistent with law.

1.21 *Third-Party Requests for Services.*

(a) When a psychologist agrees to provide services to a person or entity at the request of a third party, the psychologist clarifies to the extent feasible, at the outset of the service, the nature of the relationship with each party. This clarification includes the role of the psychologist (such as therapist, organizational consultant, diagnostician, or expert witness), the probable uses of the services provided or the information obtained, and the fact that there may be limits to confidentiality.

(b) If there is a foreseeable risk of the psychologist's being called upon to perform conflicting roles because of the involvement of a third party, the psychologist clarifies the nature and direction of his or her responsibilities, keeps all parties appropriately informed as matters develop, and resolves the situation in accordance with this Ethics Code.

1.22 *Delegation to and Supervision of Subordinates.*

(a) Psychologists delegate to their employees, supervisees, and research assistants only those responsibilities that such persons can reasonably be expected to perform competently, on the basis of their education, training, or experience, either independently or with the level of supervision being provided.

(b) Psychologists provide proper training and supervision to their employees or supervisees and take reasonable steps to see that such persons perform services responsibly, competently, and ethically.

(c) If institutional policies, procedures, or practices prevent fulfillment of this obligation, psychologists attempt to modify their role or to correct the situation to the extent feasible.

1.23 *Documentation of Professional and Scientific Work.*

(a) Psychologists appropriately document their professional and scientific work in order to facilitate provision of services later by them or by other professionals, to ensure accountability, and to meet other requirements of institutions or the law.

(b) When psychologists have reason to believe that records of their professional services will be used in legal proceedings involving recipients of or participants in their work, they have a responsibility to create and maintain documentation in the kind of detail and quality that would be consistent with reasonable scrutiny in an adjudicative forum. (See also Standard 7.01, Professionalism, under Forensic Activities.)

1.24 *Records and Data.*

Psychologists create, maintain, disseminate, store, retain, and dispose of records and data relating to their research, practice, and other work in accordance with law and in a manner that permits compliance with the requirements of this Ethics Code. (See also Standard 5.04, Maintenance of Records.)

1.25 *Fees and Financial Arrangements.*

(a) As early as is feasible in a professional or scientific relationship, the psychologist and the patient, client, or other appropriate recipient of psychological services reach an agreement specifying the compensation and the billing arrangements.

(b) Psychologists do not exploit recipients of services or payors with respect to fees.

(c) Psychologists' fee practices are consistent with law.

(d) Psychologists do not misrepresent their fees.

(e) If limitations to services can be anticipated because of limitations in financing, this is discussed with the patient, client, or other appropriate recipient of services as early as is feasible. (See also Standard 4.08, Interruption of Services.)

(f) If the patient, client, or other recipient of services does not pay for services as agreed, and if the psychologist wishes to use collection agencies or legal measures to collect the fees, the psychologist first informs the person that such measures will be taken and provides that person an opportunity to make prompt payment. (See also Standard 5.11, Withholding Records for Nonpayment.)

1.26 *Accuracy in Reports to Payors and Funding Sources.* In their reports to payors for services or sources of research funding, psychologists accurately state the nature of the research or service provided, the fees or charges, and where applicable, the identity of the provider, the findings, and the diagnosis. (See also Standard 5.05, Disclosures.)

1.27 *Referrals and Fees.* When a psychologist pays, receives payment from, or divides fees with another professional other than in an employer-employee relationship, the payment to each is based on the services (clinical, consultative, administrative, or other) provided and is not based on the referral itself.

2. *Evaluation, Assessment, or Intervention*

2.01 *Evaluation, Diagnosis, and Interventions in Professional Context.*

(a) Psychologists perform evaluations, diagnostic services, or interventions only within the context of a defined professional relationship. (See also Standards 1.03, Professional and Scientific Relationship.)

(b) Psychologists' assessments, recommendations, reports, and psychological diagnostic or evaluative statements are based on information and techniques (including personal interviews of the individual when appropriate) sufficient to provide appropriate substantiation for their findings. (See also Standard 7.02, Forensic Assessments.)

2.02 *Competence and Appropriate Use of Assessments and Interventions.*

(a) Psychologists who develop, administer, score, interpret, or use psychological assessment techniques, interviews, tests, or instruments do so in a manner and for purposes that are appropriate in light of the research on or evidence of the usefulness and proper application of the techniques.

(b) Psychologists refrain from misuse of assessment techniques, interventions, results, and interpretations and take reasonable steps to prevent others from misusing the information these techniques provide. This includes refraining from releasing raw test results or raw data to persons, other than to patients or clients as appropriate, who are not qualified to use such information. (See also Standards 1.02, Relationship of Ethics and Law, and 1.04, Boundaries of Competence.)

2.03 *Test Construction.* Psychologists who develop and conduct research with tests and other assessment techniques use scientific procedures and current professional knowledge for test design, standardization, validation, reduction or elimination of bias, and recommendations for use.

2.04   *Use of Assessment in General and with Special Populations.*

(a) Psychologists who perform interventions or administer, score, interpret, or use assessment techniques are familiar with the reliability, validation, and related standardization or outcome studies of, and proper applications and uses of, the techniques they use.

(b) Psychologists recognize limits to the certainty with which diagnoses, judgments, or predictions can be made about individuals.

(c) Psychologists attempt to identify situations in which particular interventions or assessment techniques or norms may not be applicable or may require adjustment in administration or interpretation because of factors such as individuals' gender, age, race, ethnicity, national origin, religion, sexual orientation, disability, language, or socioeconomic status.

2.05   *Interpreting Assessment Results.* When interpreting assessment results, including automated interpretations, psychologists take into account the various test factors and characteristics of the person being assessed that might affect psychologists' judgments or reduce the accuracy of their interpretations. They indicate any significant reservations they have about the accuracy or limitations of their interpretations.

2.06   *Unqualified Persons.* Psychologists do not promote the use of psychological assessment techniques by unqualified persons. (See also Standard 1.22, Delegation to and Supervision of Subordinates.)

2.07   *Obsolete Tests and Outdated Test Results.*

(a) Psychologists do not base their assessment or intervention decisions or recommendations on data or test results that are outdated for the current purpose.

(b) Similarly, psychologists do not base such decisions or recommendations on tests and measures that are obsolete and not useful for the current purpose.

2.08   *Test Scoring and Interpretation Services.*

(a) Psychologists who offer assessment or scoring procedures to other professionals accurately describe the purpose, norms, validity, reliability, and applications of the procedures and any special qualifications applicable to their use.

(b) Psychologists select scoring and interpretation services (including automated services) on the basis of evidence of the validity of the program and procedures as well as on other appropriate considerations.

(c) Psychologists retain appropriate responsibility for the application, interpretation, and use of assessment instruments, whether they score and interpret such tests themselves or use automated or other services.

2.09   *Explaining Assessment Results.* Unless the nature of the relationship is clearly explained to the person being assessed in advance and precludes provision of an explanation of results (such as in some organizational consulting, preemployment or security screenings, and forensic evaluations), psychologists ensure that an explanation of the results is provided using language that is reasonably understandable to the person assessed or to another legally authorized person on behalf of the client. Regardless of whether the scoring and interpretation are done by the psychologist, by assistants, or by automated or other outside services, psychologists take reasonable steps to ensure that appropriate explanations of results are given.

2.10   *Maintaining Test Security.* Psychologists make reasonable efforts to maintain the integrity and security of tests and other assessment techniques consistent with law, contractual obligations, and in a manner that permits compliance with the requirements of this Ethics Code. (See also Standard 1.02, Relationship of Ethics and Law.)

3.   *Advertising and Other Public Statements*

3.01   *Definition of Public Statements.* Psychologists comply with this Ethics Code in public statements relating to their professional services, products, or publications or to the field of psychology. Public statements include but are not limited to paid or unpaid advertising, brochures, printed matter, directory listings, personal resumes or curriculum vitae, interviews or comments for use in media, statements in legal proceedings, lectures and public oral presentations, and published materials.

3.02   *Statements by Others.*

(a) Psychologists who engage others to create or place public statements that promote their professional practice, products, or activities retain professional responsibility for such statements.

(b) In addition, psychologists make reasonable efforts to prevent others whom they do not control (such as employers, publishers, sponsors, organizational clients, and representatives of the print or broadcast media) from making deceptive statements concerning psychologists' practice or professional or scientific activities.

(c) If psychologists learn of deceptive statements about their work made by others, psychologists make reasonable efforts to correct such statements.

(d) Psychologists do not compensate employees of press, radio, television, or other communication media in return for publicity in a news item.

(e) A paid advertisement relating to the psychologist's activities must be identified as such, unless it is already apparent from the context.

3.03   *Avoidance of False or Deceptive Statements.*

(a) Psychologists do not make public statements that are false, deceptive, misleading, or fraudulent, either because of what they state, convey, or suggest or because of what they omit, concerning their research, practice, or other work activities or those of persons or organizations with which they are affiliated. As examples (and not in limitation) of this standard, psychologists do not make false or deceptive statements concerning (1) their training, experience, or competence; (2) their academic degrees; (3) their credentials; (4) their institutional or association affiliations; (5) their services; (6) the scientific or clinical basis for, or results or degree of success of, their services; (7) their fees; or (8) their publications or research findings. (See also Standards 6.15, Deception in Research, and 6.18, Providing Participants with Information About the Study.)

(b) Psychologists claim as credentials for their psychological work, only degrees that (1) were earned from a regionally accredited educational institution or (2) were the basis for psychology licensure by the state in which they practice.

3.04 *Media Presentations.* When psychologists provide advice or comment by means of public lectures, demonstrations, radio or television programs, prerecorded tapes, printed articles, mailed material, or other media, they take reasonable precautions to ensure that (1) the statements are based on appropriate psychological literature and practice, (2) the statements are otherwise consistent with this Ethics Code, and (3) the recipients of the information are not encouraged to infer that a relationship has been established with them personally.

3.05 *Testimonials.* Psychologists do not solicit testimonials from current psychotherapy clients or patients or other persons who because of their particular circumstances are vulnerable to undue influence.

3.06 *In-Person Solicitation.* Psychologists do not engage, directly or through agents, in uninvited in-person solicitation of business from actual or potential psychotherapy patients or clients or other persons who because of their particular circumstances are vulnerable to undue influence. However, this does not preclude attempting to implement appropriate collateral contacts with significant others for the purpose of benefitting an already engaged therapy patient.

4. *Therapy*

4.01 *Structuring the Relationship.*

(a) Psychologists discuss with clients or patients as early as is feasible in the therapeutic relationship appropriate issues, such as the nature and anticipated course of therapy, fees, and confidentiality. (See also Standards 1.25, Fees and Financial Arrangements, and 5.01, Discussing the Limits of Confidentiality.)

(b) When the psychologist's work with clients or patients will be supervised, the above discussion includes that fact, and the name of the supervisor, when the supervisor has legal responsibility for the case.

(c) When the therapist is a student intern, the client or patient is informed of that fact.

(d) Psychologists make reasonable efforts to answer patients' questions and to avoid apparent misunderstandings about therapy. Whenever possible, psychologists provide oral and/or written information, using language that is reasonably understandable to the patient or client.

4.02 *Informed Consent to Therapy.*

(a) Psychologists obtain appropriate informed consent to therapy or related procedures, using language that is reasonably understandable to participants. The content of informed consent will vary depending on many circumstances; however, informed consent generally implies that the person (1) has the capacity to consent, (2) has been informed of significant information concerning the procedure, (3) has freely and without undue influence expressed consent, and (4) consent has been appropriately documented.

(b) When persons are legally incapable of giving informed consent, psychologists obtain informed permission from a legally authorized person, if such substitute consent is permitted by law.

(c) In addition, psychologists (1) inform those persons who are legally incapable of giving informed consent about the proposed interventions in a manner commensurate with the persons' psychological capacities, (2) seek their assent to those interventions, and (3) consider such persons' preferences and best interests.

4.03 *Couple and Family Relationships.*

(a) When a psychologist agrees to provide services to several persons who have a relationship (such as husband and wife or parents and children), the psychologist attempts to clarify at the outset (1) which of the individuals are patients or clients and (2) the relationship the psychologist will have with each person. This clarification includes the role of the psychologist and the probable uses of the services provided or the information obtained. (See also Standard 5.01, Discussing the Limits of Confidentiality.)

(b) As soon as it becomes apparent that the psychologist may be called on to perform potentially conflicting roles (such as marital counselor to husband and wife, and then witness for one party in a divorce proceeding), the psychologist attempts to clarify and adjust, or withdraw from, roles appropriately. (See also Standard 7.03, Clarification of Role, under Forensic Activities.)

4.04 *Providing Mental Health Services to Those Served by Others.* In deciding whether to offer or provide services to those already receiving mental health services elsewhere, psychologists carefully consider the treatment issues and the potential patient's or client's welfare. The psychologist discusses these issues with the patient or client, or another legally authorized person on behalf of the client, in order to minimize the risk of confusion and conflict, consults with the other service providers when appropriate, and proceeds with caution and sensitivity to the therapeutic issues.

4.05 *Sexual Intimacies with Current Patients or Clients.* Psychologists do not engage in sexual intimacies with current patients or clients.

4.06 *Therapy with Former Sexual Partners.* Psychologists do not accept as therapy patients or clients persons with whom they have engaged in sexual intimacies.

4.07 *Sexual Intimacies with Former Therapy Patients.*

(a) Psychologists do not engage in sexual intimacies with a former therapy patient or client for at least two years after cessation or termination of professional services.

(b) Because sexual intimacies with a former therapy patient or client are so frequently harmful to the patient or client, and because such intimacies undermine public confidence in the psychology profession and thereby deter the public's use of needed services, psychologists do not engage in sexual intimacies with former therapy patients and clients even after a two-year interval except in the most unusual circumstances. The psychologist who engages in such activity after the two years following cessation or termination of treatment bears the burden of demonstrating that there has been no exploitation, in light of all relevant factors, including (1) the amount of time that has passed since therapy terminated, (2) the nature and duration of the therapy, (3) the circumstances of termination, (4) the patient's or client's personal history, (5) the patient's or client's current mental status, (6) the likelihood of adverse impact on the patient or client and others, and (7) any statements or actions made by the therapist during the course of therapy suggesting or inviting the possibility of a posttermination sexual or romantic relationship with the patient or client. (See also Standard 1.17, Multiple Relationships.)

4.08 *Interruption of Services.*

    (a) Psychologists make reasonable efforts to plan for facilitating care in the event that psychological services are interrupted by factors such as the psychologist's illness, death, unavailability, or relocation or by the client's relocation or financial limitations. (See also Standard 5.09, Preserving Records and Data.)

    (b) When entering into employment or contractual relationships, psychologists provide for orderly and appropriate resolution of responsibility for patient or client care in the event that the employment or contractual relationship ends, with paramount consideration given to the welfare of the patient or client.

4.09 *Terminating the Professional Relationship.*

    (a) Psychologists do not abandon patients or clients. (See also Standard 1.25e, under Fees and Financial Arrangements.)

    (b) Psychologists terminate a professional relationship when it becomes reasonably clear that the patient or client no longer needs the service, is not benefitting, or is being harmed by continued service.

    (c) Prior to termination for whatever reason, except where precluded by the patient's or client's conduct, the psychologist discusses the patient's or client's views and needs, provides appropriate pretermination counseling, suggests alternative service providers as appropriate, and takes other reasonable steps to facilitate transfer of responsibility to another provider if the patient or client needs one immediately.

5. *Privacy and Confidentiality*

These Standards are potentially applicable to the professional and scientific activities of all psychologists.

5.01 *Discussing the Limits of Confidentiality.*

    (a) Psychologists discuss with persons and organizations with whom they establish a scientific or professional relationship (including, to the extent feasible, minors and their legal representatives) (1) the relevant limitations on confidentiality, including limitations where applicable in group, marital, and family therapy or in organizational consulting, and (2) the foreseeable uses of the information generated through their services.

(b) Unless it is not feasible or is contraindicated, the discussion of confidentiality occurs at the outset of the relationship and thereafter as new circumstances may warrant.

(c) Permission for electronic recording of interviews is secured from clients and patients.

5.02   *Maintaining Confidentiality.* Psychologists have a primary obligation and take reasonable precautions to respect the confidentiality rights of those with whom they work or consult, recognizing that confidentiality may be established by law, institutional rules, or professional or scientific relationships. (See also Standard 6.26, Professional Reviewers.)

5.03   *Minimizing Intrusions on Privacy.*

(a) In order to minimize intrusions on privacy, psychologists include in written and oral reports, consultations, and the like, only information germane to the purpose for which the communication is made.

(b) Psychologists discuss confidential information obtained in clinical or consulting relationships, or evaluative data concerning patients, individual or organizational clients, students, research participants, supervisees, and employees, only for appropriate scientific or professional purposes and only with persons clearly concerned with such matters.

5.04   *Maintenance of Records.* Psychologists maintain appropriate confidentiality in creating, storing, accessing, transferring, and disposing of records under their control, whether these are written, automated, or in any other medium. Psychologists maintain and dispose of records in accordance with law and in a manner that permits compliance with the requirements of this Ethics Code.

5.05   *Disclosures.*

(a) Psychologists disclose confidential information without the consent of the individual only as mandated by law, or where permitted by law for a valid purpose, such as (1) to provide needed professional services to the patient or the individual or organizational client, (2) to obtain appropriate professional consultations, (3) to protect the patient or client or others from harm, or (4) to obtain payment for services, in which instance disclosure is limited to the minimum that is necessary to achieve the purpose.

(b) Psychologists also may disclose confidential information with the appropriate consent of the patient or the individual or organizational client (or of another legally authorized person on behalf of the patient or client), unless prohibited by law.

5.06   *Consultations.* When consulting with colleagues, (1) psychologists do not share confidential information that reasonably could lead to the identification of a patient, client, research participant, or other person or organization with whom they have a confidential relationship unless they have obtained the prior consent of the person or organization or the disclosure cannot be avoided, and (2) they share information only to the extent necessary to achieve the purposes of the consultation. (See also Standard 5.02, Maintaining Confidentiality.)

5.07   *Confidential Information in Databases.*

(a) If confidential information concerning recipients of psychological services is to be entered into databases or systems of records available to persons whose access has not been consented to by the recipient, then psychologists use coding or other techniques to avoid the inclusion of personal identifiers.

(b) If a research protocol approved by an institutional review board or similar body requires the inclusion of personal identifiers, such identifiers are deleted before the information is made accessible to persons other than those of whom the subject was advised.

(c) If such deletion is not feasible, then before psychologists transfer such data to others or review such data collected by others, they take reasonable steps to determine that appropriate consent of personally identifiable individuals has been obtained.

5.08   *Use of Confidential Information for Didactic or Other Purposes.*

(a) Psychologists do not disclose in their writings, lectures, or other public media, confidential, personally identifiable information concerning their patients, individual or organizational clients, students, research participants, or other recipients of their services that they obtained during the course of their work, unless the person or organization has consented in writing or unless there is other ethical or legal authorization for doing so.

(b) Ordinarily, in such scientific and professional presentations, psychologists disguise confidential information concerning such persons or organizations so that they are not individually identifiable to others and so that discussions do not cause harm to subjects who might identify themselves.

5.09   *Preserving Records and Data.* A psychologist makes plans in advance so that confidentiality of records and data is protected in the event of the psychologist's death, incapacity, or withdrawal from the position or practice.

5.10   *Ownership of Records and Data.* Recognizing that ownership of records and data is governed by legal principles, psychologists take reasonable and lawful steps so that records and data remain available to the extent needed to serve the best interests of patients, individual or organizational clients, research participants, or appropriate others.

5.11   *Withholding Records for Nonpayment.* Psychologists may not withhold records under their control that are requested and imminently needed for a patient's or client's treatment solely because payment has not been received, except as otherwise provided by law.

6.   *Teaching, Training Supervision, Research, and Publishing*

6.01   *Design of Education and Training Programs.* Psychologists who are responsible for education and training programs seek to ensure that the programs are competently designed, provide the proper experiences, and meet the requirements for licensure, certification, or other goals for which claims are made by the program.

6.02   *Descriptions of Education and Training Programs.*

(a) Psychologists responsible for education and training programs seek to ensure that there is a current and accurate description of the program content, training goals and objectives, and requirements that must be met for satisfactory completion of the program. This information must be made readily available to all interested parties.

(b) Psychologists seek to ensure that statements concerning their course outlines are accurate and not misleading, particularly regarding the subject matter to be covered, bases for evaluating progress, and the nature of course experiences. (See also Standard 3.03, Avoidance of False or Deceptive Statements.)

(c) To the degree to which they exercise control, psychologists responsible for announcements, catalogs, brochures, or advertisements describing workshops, seminars, or other nondegree-granting educational programs ensure that they accurately describe the audience for which the program is intended, the educational objectives, the presenters, and the fees involved.

6.03   *Accuracy and Objectivity in Teaching.*

(a) When engaged in teaching or training, psychologists present psychological information accurately and with a reasonable degree of objectivity.

(b) When engaged in teaching or training, psychologists recognize the power they hold over students or supervisees and therefore make reasonable efforts to avoid engaging in conduct that is personally demeaning to students or supervisees. (See also Standards 1.09, Respecting Others, and 1.12, Other Harassment.)

6.04   *Limitation on Teaching.* Psychologists do not teach the use of techniques or procedures that require specialized training, licensure, or expertise, including but not limited to hypnosis, biofeedback, and projective techniques, to individuals who lack the prerequisite training, legal scope of practice, or expertise.

6.05   *Assessing Student and Supervisee Performance.*

(a) In academic and supervisory relationships, psychologists establish an appropriate process for providing feedback to students and supervisees.

(b) Psychologists evaluate students and supervisees on the basis of their actual performance on relevant and established program requirements.

6.06   *Planning Research.*

(a) Psychologists design, conduct, and report research in accordance with recognized standards of scientific competence and ethical research.

(b) Psychologists plan their research so as to minimize the possibility that results will be misleading.

(c) In planning research, psychologists consider its ethical acceptability under the Ethics Code. If an ethical issue is unclear, psychologists seek to resolve the issue through consultation with institutional review boards, animal care and use committees, peer consultations, or other proper mechanisms.

(d) Psychologists take reasonable steps to implement appropriate protections for the rights and welfare of human participants, other persons affected by the research, and the welfare of animal subjects.

6.07 *Responsibility.*

(a) Psychologists conduct research competently and with due concern for the dignity and welfare of the participants.

(b) Psychologists are responsible for the ethical conduct of research conducted by them or by others under their supervision or control.

(c) Researchers and assistants are permitted to perform only those tasks for which they are appropriately trained and prepared.

(d) As part of the process of development and implementation of research projects, psychologists consult those with expertise concerning any special population under investigation or most likely to be affected.

6.08 *Compliance with Law and Standards.* Psychologists plan and conduct research in a manner consistent with federal and state law and regulations, as well as professional standards governing the conduct of research, and particularly those standards governing research with human participants and animal subjects.

6.09 *Institutional Approval.* Psychologists obtain from host institutions or organizations appropriate approval prior to conducting research, and they provide accurate information about their research proposals. They conduct the research in accordance with the approved research protocol.

6.10 *Research Responsibilities.* Prior to conducting research (except research involving only anonymous surveys, naturalistic observations, or similar research), psychologists enter into an agreement with participants that clarifies the nature of the research and the responsibilities of each party.

6.11 *Informed Consent to Research.*

(a) Psychologists use language that is reasonably understandable to research participants in obtaining their appropriate informed consent (except as provided in Standard 6.12, Dispensing with Informed Consent). Such informed consent is appropriately documented.

(b) Using language that is reasonably understandable to participants, psychologists inform participants of the nature of the research; they inform participants that they are free to participate or to decline to participate or to withdraw from the research; they explain the foreseeable consequences of declining or withdrawing; they inform participants of significant factors that may be expected to influence their willingness to participate (such as risks, discomfort, adverse effects, or limitations on confidentiality, except as provided in Standard 6.15, Deception in Research); and they explain other aspects about which the prospective participants inquire.

(c) When psychologists conduct research with individuals such as students or subordinates, psychologists take special care to protect the prospective participants from adverse consequences of declining or withdrawing from participation.

(d)   When research participation is a course requirement or opportunity for extra credit, the prospective participant is given the choice of equitable alternative activities.

(e)   For persons who are legally incapable of giving informed consent, psychologists nevertheless (1) provide an appropriate explanation, (2) obtain the participant's assent, and (3) obtain appropriate permission from a legally authorized person, if such substitute consent is permitted by law.

6.12   *Dispensing with Informed Consent.* Before determining that planned research (such as research involving only anonymous questionnaires, naturalistic observations, or certain kinds of archival research) does not require the informed consent of research participants, psychologists consider applicable regulations and institutional review board requirements, and they consult with colleagues as appropriate.

6.13   *Informed Consent in Research Filming or Recording.* Psychologists obtain informed consent from research participants prior to filming or recording them in any form, unless the research involves simply naturalistic observations in public places and it is not anticipated that the recording will be used in a manner that could cause personal identification or harm.

6.14   *Offering Inducements for Research Participants.*

(a)   In offering professional services as an inducement to obtain research participants, psychologists make clear the nature of the services, as well as the risks, obligations, and limitations. (See also Standard 1.18, Barter [with Patients or Clients].)

(b)   Psychologists do not offer excessive or inappropriate financial or other inducements to obtain research participants, particularly when it might tend to coerce participation.

6.15   *Deception in Research.*

(a)   Psychologists do not conduct a study involving deception unless they have determined that the use of deceptive techniques is justified by the study's prospective scientific, educational, or applied value and that equally effective alternative procedures that do not use deception are not feasible.

(b)   Psychologists never deceive research participants about significant aspects that would affect their willingness to participate, such as physical risks, discomfort, or unpleasant emotional experiences.

(c)   Any other deception that is an integral feature of the design and conduct of an experiment must be explained to participants as early as is feasible, preferably at the conclusion of their participation, but no later than at the conclusion of the research. (See also Standard 6.18, Providing Participants with Information About the Study.)

6.16   *Sharing and Utilizing Data.* Psychologists inform research participants of their anticipated sharing or further use of personally identifiable research data and of the possibility of unanticipated future uses.

6.17   *Minimizing Invasiveness.* In conducting research, psychologists interfere with the participants or milieu from which data are collected only in a manner that is warranted by an appropriate research design and that is consistent with psychologists' roles as scientific investigators.

6.18   *Providing Participants with Information About the Study.*

   (a)   Psychologists provide a prompt opportunity for participants to obtain appropriate information about the nature, results, and conclusions of the research, and psychologists attempt to correct any misconceptions that participants may have.

   (b)   If scientific or humane values justify delaying or withholding this information, psychologists take reasonable measures to reduce the risk of harm.

6.19   *Honoring Commitments.* Psychologists take reasonable measures to honor all commitments they have made to research participants.

6.20   *Care and Use of Animals in Research.*

   (a)   Psychologists who conduct research involving animals treat them humanely.

   (b)   Psychologists acquire, care for, use, and dispose of animals in compliance with current federal, state, and local laws and regulations, and with professional standards.

   (c)   Psychologists trained in research methods and experienced in the care of laboratory animals supervise all procedures involving animals and are responsible for ensuring appropriate consideration of their comfort, health, and humane treatment.

   (d)   Psychologists ensure that all individuals using animals under their supervision have received instruction in research methods and in the care, maintenance, and handling of the species being used, to the extent appropriate to their role.

   (e)   Responsibilities and activities of individuals assisting in a research project are consistent with their respective competencies.

   (f)   Psychologists make reasonable efforts to minimize the discomfort, infection, illness, and pain of animal subjects.

   (g)   A procedure subjecting animals to pain, stress, or privation is used only when an alternative procedure is unavailable and the goal is justified by its prospective scientific, educational, or applied value.

   (h)   Surgical procedures are performed under appropriate anesthesia; techniques to avoid infection and minimize pain are followed during and after surgery.

   (i)   When it is appropriate that the animal's life be terminated, it is done rapidly, with an effort to minimize pain, and in accordance with accepted procedures.

6.21   *Reporting of Results.*

   (a)   Psychologists do not fabricate data or falsify results in their publications.

(b) If psychologists discover significant errors in their published data, they take reasonable steps to correct such errors in a correction, retraction, erratum, or other appropriate publication means.

6.22 *Plagiarism.* Psychologists do not present substantial portions or elements of another's work or data as their own, even if the other work or data source is cited occasionally.

6.23 *Publication Credit.*

(a) Psychologists take responsibility and credit, including authorship credit, only for work they have actually performed or to which they have contributed.

(b) Principal authorship and other publication credits accurately reflect the relative scientific or professional contributions of the individuals involved, regardless of their relative status. Mere possession of an institutional position, such as Department Chair, does not justify authorship credit. Minor contributions to the research or to the writing for publications are appropriately acknowledged, such as in footnotes or in an introductory statement.

(c) A student is usually listed as principal author on any multiple-authored article that is substantially based on the student's dissertation or thesis.

6.24 *Duplicate Publication of Data.* Psychologists do not publish, as original data, data that have been previously published. This does not preclude republishing data when they are accompanied by proper acknowledgment.

6.25 *Sharing Data.* After research results are published, psychologists do not withhold the data on which their conclusions are based from other competent professionals who seek to verify the substantive claims through reanalysis and who intend to use such data only for that purpose, provided that the confidentiality of the participants can be protected and unless legal rights concerning proprietary data preclude their release.

6.26 *Professional Reviewers.* Psychologists who review material submitted for publication, grant, or other research proposal review respect the confidentiality of and the proprietary rights in such information of those who submitted it.

7. *Forensic Activities*

7.01 *Professionalism.* Psychologists who perform forensic functions, such as assessments, interviews, consultations, reports, or expert testimony, must comply with all other provisions of this Ethics Code to the extent that they apply to such activities. In addition, psychologists base their forensic work on appropriate knowledge of and competence in the areas underlying such work, including specialized knowledge concerning special populations. (See also Standards 1.06, Basis for Scientific and Professional Judgments; 1.08, Human Differences; 1.15, Misuse of Psychologists' Influence; and 1.23, Documentation of Professional and Scientific Work.)

7.02 *Forensic Assessments.*

(a) Psychologists' forensic assessments, recommendations, and reports are based on information and techniques (including personal interviews of the individual, when appropriate) sufficient to provide appropriate substantiation for their findings. (See also Standards 1.03, Professional and Scientific Relationship; 1.23, Documentation of Professional and Scientific Work; 2.01, Evaluation, Diagnosis, and Interventions in Professional Context; and 2.05, Interpreting Assessment Results.)

(b) Except as noted in (c), below, psychologists provide written or oral forensic reports or testimony of the psychological characteristics of an individual only after they have conducted an examination of the individual adequate to support their statements or conclusions.

(c) When, despite reasonable efforts, such an examination is not feasible, psychologists clarify the impact of their limited information on the reliability and validity of their reports and testimony, and they appropriately limit the nature and extent of their conclusions or recommendations.

7.03 *Clarification of Role.* In most circumstances, psychologists avoid performing multiple and potentially conflicting roles in forensic matters. When psychologists may be called on to serve in more than one role in a legal proceeding-for example, as consultant or expert for one party or for the court and as a fact witness-they clarify role expectations and the extent of confidentiality in advance to the extent feasible, and thereafter as changes occur, in order to avoid compromising their professional judgment and objectivity and in order to avoid misleading others regarding their role.

7.04 *Truthfulness and Candor.*

(a) In forensic testimony and reports, psychologists testify truthfully, honestly, and candidly and, consistent with applicable legal procedures, describe fairly the bases for their testimony and conclusions.

(b) Whenever necessary to avoid misleading, psychologists acknowledge the limits of their data or conclusions.

7.05 *Prior Relationships.* A prior professional relationship with a party does not preclude psychologists from testifying as fact witnesses or from testifying to their services to the extent permitted by applicable law. Psychologists appropriately take into account ways in which the prior relationship might affect their professional objectivity or opinions and disclose the potential conflict to the relevant parties.

7.06 *Compliance with Law and Rules.* In performing forensic roles, psychologists are reasonably familiar with the rules governing their roles. Psychologists are aware of the occasionally competing demands placed upon them by these principles and the requirements of the court system, and attempt to resolve these conflicts by making known their commitment to this Ethics Code and taking steps to resolve the conflict in a responsible manner. (See also Standard 1.02, Relationship of Ethics and Law.)

8. *Resolving Ethical Issues*

8.01 *Familiarity with Ethics Code.* Psychologists have an obligation to be familiar with this Ethics Code, other applicable ethics codes, and their application to psychologists' work. Lack of awareness or misunderstanding of an ethical standard is not itself a defense to a charge of unethical conduct.

8.02   *Confronting Ethical Issues.* When a psychologist is uncertain whether a particular situation or course of action would violate this Ethics Code, the psychologist ordinarily consults with other psychologists knowledgeable about ethical issues, with state or national psychology ethics committees, or with other appropriate authorities in order to choose a proper response.

8.03   *Conflicts between Ethics and Organizational Demands.* If the demands of an organization with which psychologists are affiliated conflict with this Ethics Code, psychologists clarify the nature of the conflict, make known their commitment to the Ethics Code, and to the extent feasible, seek to resolve the conflict in a way that permits the fullest adherence to the Ethics Code.

8.04   *Informal Resolution of Ethical Violations.* When psychologists believe that there may have been an ethical violation by another psychologist, they attempt to resolve the issue by bringing it to the attention of that individual if an informal resolution appears appropriate and the intervention does not violate any confidentiality rights that may be involved.

8.05   *Reporting Ethical Violations.* If an apparent ethical violation is not appropriate for informal resolution under Standard 8.04 or is not resolved properly in that fashion, psychologists take further action appropriate to the situation, unless such action conflicts with confidentiality rights in ways that cannot be resolved. Such action might include referral to state or national committees on professional ethics or to state licensing boards.

8.06   *Cooperating with Ethics Committees.* Psychologists cooperate in ethics investigations, proceedings, and resulting requirements of the APA or any affiliated state psychological association to which they belong. In doing so, they make reasonable efforts to resolve any issues as to confidentiality. Failure to cooperate is itself an ethics violation.

8.07   *Improper Complaints.* Psychologists do not file or encourage the filing of ethics complaints that are frivolous and are intended to harm the respondent rather than to protect the public.

National Association of Social Workers (NASW) Code of Ethics[1]

Overview

The NASW *Code of Ethics* is intended to serve as a guide to the everyday professional conduct of social workers. This *Code* includes four sections. The first Section, "Preamble," summarizes the social work profession's mission and core values. The second section, "Purpose of the NASW *Code of Ethics*," provides an overview of the *Code's* main functions and a brief guide for dealing with ethical issues or dilemmas in social work practice. The third section, "Ethical Principles," presents broad ethical principles, based on social work's core values, that inform social work practice. The final section, "Ethical Standards," includes specific ethical standards to guide social workers' conduct and to provide a basis for adjudication.

The NASW *Code of Ethics* applies only to NASW members. If you believe a social work member of NASW is in violation of this *Code of Ethics*, one of your options is to file a complaint with NASW (see *NASW Procedures for Professional Review*). If you are a member of NASW and you believe your employer or agency has unfairly imposed limits on, or penalties for, professional action on behalf of clients, or has violated their own personnel standards, one of your options is to file a professional action or personnel standards complaint with NASW (see *NASW Procedures for Professional Review*).

Appendix

Preamble

The primary mission of the social work profession is to enhance human well-being and help meet the basic human needs of all people, with particular attention to the needs and empowerment of people who are vulnerable, oppressed, and living in poverty. A historic and defining feature of social work is the profession's focus on individual well-being in a social context and the well-being of society. Fundamental to social work is attention to the environmental forces that create, contribute to, and address problems in living.

Social workers promote social justice and social change with and on behalf of clients. "Clients" is used inclusively to refer to individuals, families, groups, organizations, and communities. Social workers are sensitive to cultural and ethnic

---

[1] Copyright © 1999, National Association of Social Workers, Inc., Code of Ethics.

diversity and strive to end discrimination, oppression, poverty, and other forms of social injustice. These activities may be in the form of direct practice, community organizing, supervision, consultation, administration, advocacy, social and political action, policy development and implementation, education, and research and evaluation. Social workers seek to enhance the capacity of people to address their own needs. Social workers also seek to promote the responsiveness of organizations, communities, and other social institutions to individuals' needs and social problems.

The mission of the social work profession is rooted in a set of core values. These core values, embraced by social workers throughout the profession's history, are the foundation of social work's unique purpose and perspective:

- Service.
- Social justice.
- Dignity and worth of the person.
- Importance of human relationships.
- Integrity.
- Competence.

This constellation of core values reflects what is unique to the social work profession. Core values, and the principles that flow from them, must be balanced within the context and complexity of the human experience.

Purpose of the NASW Code of Ethics

Professional ethics are at the core of social work. The profession has an obligation to articulate its basic values, ethical principles, and ethical standards. The *NASW Code of Ethics* sets forth these values, principles, and standards to guide social workers' conduct.

The *Code* is relevant to all social workers and social work students, regardless of their professional functions, the settings in which they work, or the populations they serve.

The *NASW Code of Ethics* serves six purposes:

- The *Code* identifies core values on which social work's mission is based.
- The *Code* summarizes broad ethical principles that reflect the profession's core values and establishes a set of specific ethical standards that should be used to guide social work practice.
- The *Code* is designed to help social workers identify relevant considerations when professional obligations conflict or ethical uncertainties arise.
- The *Code* provides ethical standards to which the general public can hold the social work profession accountable.
- The *Code* socializes practitioners new to the field to social work's mission, values, ethical principles, and ethical standards.

■ The *Code* articulates standards that the social work profession itself can use to assess whether social workers have engaged in unethical conduct. NASW has formal procedures to adjudicate ethics complaints filed against its members.[2] In subscribing to this *Code,* social workers are required to cooperate in its implementation, participate in NASW adjudication proceedings, and abide by any NASW disciplinary rulings or sanctions based on it.

The *Code* offers a set of values, principles, and standards to guide decision making and conduct when ethical issues arise. It does not provide a set of rules that prescribe how social workers should act in all situations. Specific applications of the *Code* must take into account the context in which it is being considered and the possibility of conflicts among the *Code's* values, principles, and standards. Ethical responsibilities flow from all human relationships, from the personal and familial to the social and professional.

Further, the *NASW Code of Ethics* does not specify which values, principles, and standards are most important and ought to outweigh others in instances when they conflict. Reasonable differences of opinion can and do exist among social workers with respect to the ways in which values, ethical principles, and ethical standards should be rank ordered when they conflict. Ethical decision making in a given situation must apply the informed judgment of the individual social worker and should also consider how the issues would be judged in a peer review process where the ethical standards of the profession would be applied.

Ethical decision making is a process. There are many instances in social work where simple answers are not available to resolve complex ethical issues. Social workers should take into consideration all the values, principles, and standards in this *Code* that are relevant to any situation in which ethical judgment is warranted. Social workers' decisions and actions should be consistent with the spirit as well as the letter of this *Code.*

In addition to this *Code,* there are many other sources of information about ethical thinking that may be useful. Social workers should consider ethical theory and principles generally, social work theory and research, laws, regulations, agency policies, and other relevant codes of ethics, recognizing that among codes of ethics social workers should consider the *NASW Code of Ethics* as their primary source. Social workers also should be aware of the impact on ethical decision making of their clients' and their own personal values and cultural and religious beliefs and practices. They should be aware of any conflicts between personal and professional values and deal with them responsibly. For additional guidance social workers should consult the relevant literature on professional ethics and ethical decision making and seek appropriate consultation when faced with ethical dilemmas. This may involve consultation with an agency-based or social work organization's ethics committee, a regulatory body, knowledgeable colleagues, supervisors, or legal counsel.

Instances may arise when social workers' ethical obligations conflict with agency policies or relevant laws or regulations. When such conflicts occur, social workers must make a responsible effort to resolve the conflict in a manner that is

---

[2] For information on NASW adjudication procedures, see *NASW Procedures for the Adjudication of Grievances.*

consistent with the values, principles, and standards expressed in this *Code*. If a reasonable resolution of the conflict does not appear possible, social workers should seek proper consultation before making a decision.

The *NASW Code of Ethics* is to be used by NASW and by individuals, agencies, organizations, and bodies (such as licensing and regulatory boards, professional liability insurance providers, courts of law, agency boards of directors, government agencies, and other professional groups) that choose to adopt it or use it as a frame of reference. Violation of standards in this Code does not automatically imply legal liability or violation of the law. Such determination can only be made in the context of legal and judicial proceedings. Alleged violations of the *Code* would be subject to a peer review process. Such processes are generally separate from legal or administrative procedures and insulated from legal review or proceedings to allow the profession to counsel and discipline its own members.

A code of ethics cannot guarantee ethical behavior. Moreover, a code of ethics cannot resolve all ethical issues or disputes or capture the richness and complexity involved in striving to make responsible choices within a moral community. Rather, a code of ethics sets forth values, ethical principles, and ethical standards to which professionals aspire and by which their actions can be judged. Social workers' ethical behavior should result from their personal commitment to engage in ethical practice. The *NASW Code of Ethics* reflects the commitment of all social workers to uphold the profession's values and to act ethically. Principles and standards must be applied by individuals of good character who discern moral questions and, in good faith, seek to make reliable ethical judgments.

Ethical Principles

The following broad ethical principles are based on social work's core values of service, social justice, dignity and worth of the person, importance of human relationships, integrity, and competence. These principles set forth ideals to which all social workers should aspire.

Value: Service

Ethical Principle: Social workers' primary goal is to help people in need and to address social problems.

Social workers elevate service to others above self-interest. Social workers draw on their knowledge, values, and skills to help people in need and to address social problems. Social workers are encouraged to volunteer some portion of their professional skills with no expectation of significant financial return (pro bono service).

Value: Social Justice

Ethical Principle: Social workers challenge social injustice.

Social workers pursue social change, particularly with and on behalf of vulnerable and oppressed individuals and groups of people. Social workers' social change efforts are focused primarily on issues of poverty, unemployment, discrimination, and other forms of social injustice. These activities seek to promote sensitivity to and knowledge about oppression and cultural and ethnic diversity. Social workers strive to ensure access to needed information, services, and resources; equality of opportunity; and meaningful participation in decision making for all people.

Value: Dignity and Worth of the Person

Ethical Principle: Social workers respect the inherent dignity and worth of the person.

Social workers treat each person in a caring and respectful fashion, mindful of individual differences and cultural and ethnic diversity. Social workers promote clients' socially responsible self-determination. Social workers seek to enhance clients' capacity and opportunity to change and to address their own needs. Social workers are cognizant of their dual responsibility to clients and to the broader society. They seek to resolve conflicts between clients' interests and the broader society's interests in a socially responsible manner consistent with the values, ethical principles, and ethical standards of the profession.

Value: Importance of Human Relationships

Ethical Principle: Social workers recognize the central importance of human relationships. Social workers understand that relationships between and among people are an important vehicle for change. Social workers engage people as partners in the helping process. Social workers seek to strengthen relationships among people in a purposeful effort to promote, restore, maintain, and enhance the well-being of individuals, families, social groups, organizations, and communities.

Value: Integrity

Ethical Principle: Social workers behave in a trustworthy manner.

Social workers are continually aware of the profession's mission, values, ethical principles, and ethical standards and practice in a manner consistent with them. Social workers act honestly and responsibly and promote ethical practices on the part of the organizations with which they are affiliated.

Value: Competence

Ethical Principle: Social workers practice within their areas of competence and develop and enhance their professional expertise.

Social workers continually strive to increase their professional knowledge and skills and to apply them in practice. Social workers should aspire to contribute to the knowledge base of the profession.

Ethical Standards

1. SOCIAL WORKERS' ETHICAL RESPONSIBILITIES TO CLIENTS

1.01 *Commitment to Clients*

Social workers' primary responsibility is to promote the well-being of clients. In general, clients' interests are primary. However, social workers' responsibility to the larger society or specific legal obligations may on limited occasions supersede the loyalty owed clients, and clients should be so advised. (Examples include when a social worker is required by law to report that a client has abused a child or has threatened to harm self or others.)

1.02   *Self-Determination*

Social workers respect and promote the right of clients to self-determination and assist clients in their efforts to identify and clarify their goals. Social workers may limit clients' right to self-determination when, in the social workers' professional judgment, clients' actions or potential actions pose a serious, foreseeable, and imminent risk to themselves or others.

1.03   *Informed Consent*

(a) Social workers should provide services to clients only in the context of a professional relationship based, when appropriate, on valid informed consent. Social workers should use clear and understandable language to inform clients of the purpose of the services, risks related to the services, limits to services because of the requirements of a third-party payer, relevant costs, reasonable alternatives, clients' right to refuse or withdraw consent, and the time frame covered by the consent. Social workers should provide clients with an opportunity to ask questions.

(b) In instances when clients are not literate or have difficulty understanding the primary language used in the practice setting, social workers should take steps to ensure clients' comprehension. This may include providing clients with a detailed verbal explanation or arranging for a qualified interpreter or translator whenever possible.

(c) In instances when clients lack the capacity to provide informed consent, social workers should protect clients' interests by seeking permission from an appropriate third party, informing clients consistent with the clients' level of understanding. In such instances social workers should seek to ensure that the third party acts in a manner consistent with clients' wishes and interests. Social workers should take reasonable steps to enhance such clients' ability to give informed consent.

(d) In instances when clients are receiving services involuntarily, social workers should provide information about the nature and extent of services and about the extent of clients' right to refuse service.

(e) Social workers who provide services via electronic media (such as computer, telephone, radio, and television) should inform recipients of the limitations and risks associated with such services.

(f) Social workers should obtain clients' informed consent before audiotaping or videotaping clients or permitting observation of services to clients by a third party.

1.04   *Competence*

(a) Social workers should provide services and represent themselves as competent only within the boundaries of their education, training, license, certification, consultation received, supervised experience, or other relevant professional experience.

(b) Social workers should provide services in substantive areas or use intervention techniques or approaches that are new to them only after engaging in appropriate study, training, consultation, and supervision from people who are competent in those interventions or techniques.

(c) When generally recognized standards do not exist with respect to an emerging area of practice, social workers should exercise careful judgment and take responsible steps (including appropriate education, research, training, consultation, and supervision) to ensure the competence of their work and to protect clients from harm.

1.05 *Cultural Competence and Social Diversity*

(a) Social workers should understand culture and its function in human behavior and society, recognizing the strengths that exist in all cultures.

(b) Social workers should have a knowledge base of their clients' cultures and be able to demonstrate competence in the provision of services that are sensitive to clients' cultures and to differences among people and cultural groups.

(c) Social workers should obtain education about and seek to understand the nature of social diversity and oppression with respect to race, ethnicity, national origin, color, sex, sexual orientation, age, marital status, political belief, religion, and mental or physical disability.

1.06 *Conflicts of Interest*

(a) Social workers should be alert to and avoid conflicts of interest that interfere with the exercise of professional discretion and impartial judgment. Social workers should inform clients when a real or potential conflict of interest arises and take reasonable steps to resolve the issue in a manner that makes the clients' interests primary and protects clients' interests to the greatest extent possible. In some cases, protecting clients' interests may require termination of the professional relationship with proper referral of the client.

(b) Social workers should not take unfair advantage of any professional relationship or exploit others to further their personal, religious, political, or business interests.

(c) Social workers should not engage in dual or multiple relationships with clients or former clients in which there is a risk of exploitation or potential harm to the client. In instances when dual or multiple relationships are unavoidable, social workers should take steps to protect clients and are responsible for setting clear, appropriate, and culturally sensitive boundaries. (Dual or multiple relationships occur when social workers relate to clients in more than one relationship, whether professional, social, or business. Dual or multiple relationships can occur simultaneously or consecutively.)

(d) When social workers provide services to two or more people who have a relationship with each other (for example, couples, family members), social workers should clarify with all parties which individuals will be considered clients and the nature of social workers' professional obligations to the various individuals who are receiving services. Social workers who anticipate a conflict of interest among the individuals receiving services or who anticipate having to perform in potentially conflicting roles (for example, when a social worker is asked to testify in a child custody dispute or divorce proceedings involving clients) should clarify their role with the parties involved and take appropriate action to minimize any conflict of interest.

1.07   *Privacy and Confidentiality*

    (a)   Social workers should respect clients' right to privacy. Social workers should not solicit private information from clients unless it is essential to providing services or conducting social work evaluation or research. Once private information is shared, standards of confidentiality apply.

    (b)   Social workers may disclose confidential information when appropriate with valid consent from a client or a person legally authorized to consent on behalf of a client.

    (c)   Social workers should protect the confidentiality of all information obtained in the course of professional service, except for compelling professional reasons. The general expectation that social workers will keep information confidential does not apply when disclosure is necessary to prevent serious, foreseeable, and imminent harm to a client or other identifiable person. In all instances, social workers should disclose the least amount of confidential information necessary to achieve the desired purpose; only information that is directly relevant to the purpose for which the disclosure is made should be revealed.

    (d)   Social workers should inform clients, to the extent possible, about the disclosure of confidential information and the potential consequences, when feasible before the disclosure is made. This applies whether social workers disclose confidential information on the basis of a legal requirement or client consent.

    (e)   Social workers should discuss with clients and other interested parties the nature of confidentiality and limitations of clients' right to confidentiality. Social workers should review with clients circumstances where confidential information may be requested and where disclosure of confidential information may be legally required. This discussion should occur as soon as possible in the social worker-client relationship and as needed throughout the course of the relationship.

    (f)   When social workers provide counseling services to families, couples, or groups, social workers should seek agreement among the parties involved concerning each individual's right to confidentiality and obligation to preserve the confidentiality of information shared by others. Social workers should inform participants in family, couples, or group counseling that social workers cannot guarantee that all participants will honor such agreements.

    (g)   Social workers should inform clients involved in family, couples, marital, or group counseling of the social worker's, employer's, and agency's policy concerning the social worker's disclosure of confidential information among the parties involved in the counseling.

    (h)   Social workers should not disclose confidential information to third-party payers unless clients have authorized such disclosure.

(i)   Social workers should not discuss confidential information in any setting unless privacy can be ensured. Social workers should not discuss confidential information in public or semipublic areas such as hallways, waiting rooms, elevators, and restaurants.

(j)   Social workers should protect the confidentiality of clients during legal proceedings to the extent permitted by law. When a court of law or other legally authorized body orders social workers to disclose confidential or privileged information without a client's consent and such disclosure could cause harm to the client, social workers should request that the court withdraw the order or limit the order as narrowly as possible or maintain the records under seal, unavailable for public inspection.

(k)   Social workers should protect the confidentiality of clients when responding to requests from members of the media.

(l)   Social workers should protect the confidentiality of clients' written and electronic records and other sensitive information. Social workers should take reasonable steps to ensure that clients' records are stored in a secure location and that clients' records are not available to others who are not authorized to have access.

(m) Social workers should take precautions to ensure and maintain the confidentiality of information transmitted to other parties through the use of computers, electronic mail, facsimile machines, telephones and telephone answering machines, and other electronic or computer technology. Disclosure of identifying information should be avoided whenever possible.

(n)   Social workers should transfer or dispose of clients' records in a manner that protects clients' confidentiality and is consistent with state statutes governing records and social work licensure.

(o)   Social workers should take reasonable precautions to protect client confidentiality in the event of the social worker's termination of practice, incapacitation, or death.

(p)   Social workers should not disclose identifying information when discussing clients for teaching or training purposes unless the client has consented to disclosure of confidential information.

(q)   Social workers should not disclose identifying information when discussing clients with consultants unless the client has consented to disclosure of confidential information or there is a compelling need for such disclosure.

(r)   Social workers should protect the confidentiality of deceased clients consistent with the preceding standards.

1.08 *Access to Records*

(a)   Social workers should provide clients with reasonable access to records concerning the clients. Social workers who are concerned that clients' access to their records could cause serious misunderstanding or harm to the client should provide assistance in interpreting the records and consultation with the client regarding the records. Social workers should limit clients' access to their records, or portions of their records, only in exceptional circumstances when there is compelling evidence that such access would cause serious harm to the client. Both clients' requests and the rationale for withholding some or all of the record should be documented in clients' files.

(b) When providing clients with access to their records, social workers should take steps to protect the confidentiality of other individuals identified or discussed in such records.

1.09 *Sexual Relationships*

(a) Social workers should under no circumstances engage in sexual activities or sexual contact with current clients, whether such contact is consensual or forced.

(b) Social workers should not engage in sexual activities or sexual contact with clients' relatives or other individuals with whom clients maintain a close personal relationship when there is a risk of exploitation or potential harm to the client. Sexual activity or sexual contact with clients' relatives or other individuals with whom clients maintain a personal relationship has the potential to be harmful to the client and may make it difficult for the social worker and client to maintain appropriate professional boundaries. Social workers—not their clients, their clients' relatives, or other individuals with whom the client maintains a personal relationship—assume the full burden for setting clear, appropriate, and culturally sensitive boundaries.

(c) Social workers should not engage in sexual activities or sexual contact with former clients because of the potential for harm to the client. If social workers engage in conduct contrary to this prohibition or claim that an exception to this prohibition is warranted because of extraordinary circumstances, it is social workers—not their clients—who assume the full burden of demonstrating that the former client has not been exploited, coerced, or manipulated, intentionally or unintentionally.

(d) Social workers should not provide clinical services to individuals with whom they have had a prior sexual relationship. Providing clinical services to a former sexual partner has the potential to be harmful to the individual and is likely to make it difficult for the social worker and individual to maintain appropriate professional boundaries.

1.10 *Physical Contact*

Social workers should not engage in physical contact with clients when there is a possibility of psychological harm to the client as a result of the contact (such as cradling or caressing clients). Social workers who engage in appropriate physical contact with clients are responsible for setting clear, appropriate, and culturally sensitive boundaries that govern such physical contact.

1.11 *Sexual Harassment*

Social workers should not sexually harass clients. Sexual harassment includes sexual advances, sexual solicitation, requests for sexual favors, and other verbal or physical conduct of a sexual nature.

1.12 *Derogatory Language*

Social workers should not use derogatory language in their written or verbal communications to or about clients. Social workers should use accurate and respectful language in all communications to and about clients.

1.13 *Payment for Services*

(a) When setting fees, social workers should ensure that the fees are fair, reasonable, and commensurate with the services performed. Consideration should be given to clients' ability to pay.

(b) Social workers should avoid accepting goods or services from clients as payment for professional services. Bartering arrangements, particularly involving services, create the potential for conflicts of interest, exploitation, and inappropriate boundaries in social workers' relationships with clients. Social workers should explore and may participate in bartering only in very limited circumstances when it can be demonstrated that such arrangements are an accepted practice among professionals in the local community, considered to be essential for the provision of services, negotiated without coercion, and entered into at the client's initiative and with the client's informed consent. Social workers who accept goods or services from clients as payment for professional services assume the full burden of demonstrating that this arrangement will not be detrimental to the client or the professional relationship.

(c) Social workers should not solicit a private fee or other remuneration for providing services to clients who are entitled to such available services through the social workers' employer or agency.

1.14 *Clients Who Lack Decision-Making Capacity*

When social workers act on behalf of clients who lack the capacity to make informed decisions, social workers should take reasonable steps to safeguard the interests and rights of those clients.

1.15 *Interruption of Services*

Social workers should make reasonable efforts to ensure continuity of services in the event that services are interrupted by factors such as unavailability, relocation, illness, disability, or death.

1.16 *Termination of Services*

(a) Social workers should terminate services to clients and professional relationships with them when such services and relationships are no longer required or no longer serve the clients' needs or interests.

(b) Social workers should take reasonable steps to avoid abandoning clients who are still in need of services. Social workers should withdraw services precipitously only under unusual circumstances, giving careful consideration to all factors in the situation and taking care to minimize possible adverse effects. Social workers should assist in making appropriate arrangements for continuation of services when necessary.

(c) Social workers in fee-for-service settings may terminate services to clients who are not paying an overdue balance if the financial contractual arrangements have been made clear to the client, if the client does not pose an imminent danger to self or others, and if the clinical and other consequences of the current nonpayment have been addressed and discussed with the client.

(d) Social workers should not terminate services to pursue a social, financial, or sexual relationship with a client.

(e) Social workers who anticipate the termination or interruption of services to clients should notify clients promptly and seek the transfer, referral, or continuation of services in relation to the clients' needs and preferences.

(f) Social workers who are leaving an employment setting should inform clients of appropriate options for the continuation of services and of the benefits and risks of the options.

2.   SOCIAL WORKERS' ETHICAL RESPONSIBILITIES TO COLLEAGUES

2.01   *Respect*

(a) Social workers should treat colleagues with respect and should represent accurately and fairly the qualifications, views, and obligations of colleagues.

(b) Social workers should avoid unwarranted negative criticism of colleagues in communications with clients or with other professionals. Unwarranted negative criticism may include demeaning comments that refer to colleagues' level of competence or to individuals' attributes such as race, ethnicity, national origin, color, sex, sexual orientation, age, marital status, political belief, religion, and mental or physical disability.

(c) Social workers should cooperate with social work colleagues and with colleagues of other professions when such cooperation serves the well-being of clients.

2.02   *Confidentiality*

Social workers should respect confidential information shared by colleagues in the course of their professional relationships and transactions. Social workers should ensure that such colleagues understand social workers' obligation to respect confidentiality and any exceptions related to it.

2.03   *Interdisciplinary Collaboration*

(a) Social workers who are members of an interdisciplinary team should participate in and contribute to decisions that affect the well-being of clients by drawing on the perspectives, values, and experiences of the social work profession. Professional and ethical obligations of the interdisciplinary team as a whole and of its individual members should be clearly established.

(b) Social workers for whom a team decision raises ethical concerns should attempt to resolve the disagreement through appropriate channels. If the disagreement cannot be resolved, social workers should pursue other avenues to address their concerns consistent with client well-being.

2.04   *Disputes Involving Colleagues*

(a)   Social workers should not take advantage of a dispute between a colleague and an employer to obtain a position or otherwise advance the social workers' own interests.

(b)   Social workers should not exploit clients in disputes with colleagues or engage clients in any inappropriate discussion of conflicts between social workers and their colleagues.

2.05   *Consultation*

(a)   Social workers should seek the advice and counsel of colleagues whenever such consultation is in the best interests of clients.

(b)   Social workers should keep themselves informed about colleagues' areas of expertise and competencies. Social workers should seek consultation only from colleagues who have demonstrated knowledge, expertise, and competence related to the subject of the consultation.

(c)   When consulting with colleagues about clients, social workers should disclose the least amount of information necessary to achieve the purposes of the consultation.

2.06   *Referral for Services*

(a)   Social workers should refer clients to other professionals when the other professionals' specialized knowledge or expertise is needed to serve clients fully or when social workers believe that they are not being effective or making reasonable progress with clients and that additional service is required.

(b)   Social workers who refer clients to other professionals should take appropriate steps to facilitate an orderly transfer of responsibility. Social workers who refer clients to other professionals should disclose, with clients' consent, all pertinent information to the new service providers.

(c)   Social workers are prohibited from giving or receiving payment for a referral when no professional service is provided by the referring social worker.

2.07   *Sexual Relationships*

(a)   Social workers who function as supervisors or educators should not engage in sexual activities or contact with supervisees, students, trainees, or other colleagues over whom they exercise professional authority.

(b)   Social workers should avoid engaging in sexual relationships with colleagues when there is potential for a conflict of interest. Social workers who become involved in, or anticipate becoming involved in, a sexual relationship with a colleague have a duty to transfer professional responsibilities, when necessary, to avoid a conflict of interest.

2.08   *Sexual Harassment*

Social workers should not sexually harass supervisees, students, trainees, or colleagues. Sexual harassment includes sexual advances, sexual solicitation, requests for sexual favors, and other verbal or physical conduct of a sexual nature.

2.09 *Impairment of Colleagues*

(a) Social workers who have direct knowledge of a social work colleague's impairment that is due to personal problems, psychosocial distress, substance abuse, or mental health difficulties and that interferes with practice effectiveness should consult with that colleague when feasible and assist the colleague in taking remedial action.

(b) Social workers who believe that a social work colleague's impairment interferes with practice effectiveness and that the colleague has not taken adequate steps to address the impairment should take action through appropriate channels established by employers, agencies, NASW, licensing and regulatory bodies, and other professional organizations.

2.10 *Incompetence of Colleagues*

(a) Social workers who have direct knowledge of a social work colleague's incompetence should consult with that colleague when feasible and assist the colleague in taking remedial action.

(b) Social workers who believe that a social work colleague is incompetent and has not taken adequate steps to address the incompetence should take action through appropriate channels established by employers, agencies, NASW, licensing and regulatory bodies, and other professional organizations.

2.11 *Unethical Conduct of Colleagues*

(a) Social workers should take adequate measures to discourage, prevent, expose, and correct the unethical conduct of colleagues.

(b) Social workers should be knowledgeable about established policies and procedures for handling concerns about colleagues' unethical behavior. Social workers should be familiar with national, state, and local procedures for handling ethics complaints. These include policies and procedures created by NASW, licensing and regulatory bodies, employers, agencies, and other professional organizations.

(c) Social workers who believe that a colleague has acted unethically should seek resolution by discussing their concerns with the colleague when feasible and when such discussion is likely to be productive.

(d) When necessary, social workers who believe that a colleague has acted unethically should take action through appropriate formal channels (such as contacting a state licensing board or regulatory body, an NASW committee on inquiry, or other professional ethics committees).

(e) Social workers should defend and assist colleagues who are unjustly charged with unethical conduct.

3. SOCIAL WORKERS' ETHICAL RESPONSIBILITIES IN PRACTICE SETTINGS

3.01 *Supervision and Consultation*

(a) Social workers who provide supervision or consultation should have the necessary knowledge and skill to supervise or consult appropriately and should do so only within their areas of knowledge and competence.

(b) Social workers who provide supervision or consultation are responsible for setting clear, appropriate, and culturally sensitive boundaries.

(c) Social workers should not engage in any dual or multiple relationships with supervisees in which there is a risk of exploitation of or potential harm to the supervisee.

(d) Social workers who provide supervision should evaluate supervisees' performance in a manner that is fair and respectful.

3.02 *Education and Training*

(a) Social workers who function as educators, field instructors for students, or trainers should provide instruction only within their areas of knowledge and competence and should provide instruction based on the most current information and knowledge available in the profession.

(b) Social workers who function as educators or field instructors for students should evaluate students' performance in a manner that is fair and respectful.

(c) Social workers who function as educators or field instructors for students should take reasonable steps to ensure that clients are routinely informed when services are being provided by students.

(d) Social workers who function as educators or field instructors for students should not engage in any dual or multiple relationships with students in which there is a risk of exploitation or potential harm to the student. Social work educators and field instructors are responsible for setting clear, appropriate, and culturally sensitive boundaries.

3.03 *Performance Evaluation*

Social workers who have responsibility for evaluating the performance of others should fulfill such responsibility in a fair and considerate manner and on the basis of clearly stated criteria.

3.04 *Client Records*

(a) Social workers should take reasonable steps to ensure that documentation in records is accurate and reflects the services provided.

(b) Social workers should include sufficient and timely documentation in records to facilitate the delivery of services and to ensure continuity of services provided to clients in the future.

(c) Social workers' documentation should protect clients' privacy to the extent that is possible and appropriate and should include only information that is directly relevant to the delivery of services.

(d) Social workers should store records following the termination of services to ensure reasonable future access. Records should be maintained for the number of years required by state statutes or relevant contracts.

3.05 *Billing*

Social workers should establish and maintain billing practices that accurately reflect the nature and extent of services provided and that identify who provided the service in the practice setting.

3.06 *Client Transfer*

    (a) When an individual who is receiving services from another agency or colleague contacts a social worker for services, the social worker should carefully consider the client's needs before agreeing to provide services. To minimize possible confusion and conflict, social workers should discuss with potential clients the nature of the clients' current relationship with other service providers and the implications, including possible benefits or risks, of entering into a relationship with a new service provider.

    (b) If a new client has been served by another agency or colleague, social workers should discuss with the client whether consultation with the previous service provider is in the client's best interest.

3.07 *Administration*

    (a) Social work administrators should advocate within and outside their agencies for adequate resources to meet clients' needs.

    (b) Social workers should advocate for resource allocation procedures that are open and fair. When not all clients' needs can be met, an allocation procedure should be developed that is nondiscriminatory and based on appropriate and consistently applied principles.

    (c) Social workers who are administrators should take reasonable steps to ensure that adequate agency or organizational resources are available to provide appropriate staff supervision.

    (d) Social work administrators should take reasonable steps to ensure that the working environment for which they are responsible is consistent with and encourages compliance with the *NASW Code of Ethics*. Social work administrators should take reasonable steps to eliminate any conditions in their organizations that violate, interfere with, or discourage compliance with the *Code*.

3.08 *Continuing Education and Staff Development*

Social work administrators and supervisors should take reasonable steps to provide or arrange for continuing education and staff development for all staff for whom they are responsible. Continuing education and staff development should address current knowledge and emerging developments related to social work practice and ethics.

3.09 *Commitments to Employers*

    (a) Social workers generally should adhere to commitments made to employers and employing organizations.

    (b) Social workers should work to improve employing agencies' policies and procedures and the efficiency and effectiveness of their services.

    (c) Social workers should take reasonable steps to ensure that employers are aware of social workers' ethical obligations as set forth in the *NASW Code of Ethics* and of the implications of those obligations for social work practice.

    (d) Social workers should not allow an employing organization's policies, procedures, regulations, or administrative orders to interfere with their ethical practice of social work. Social workers should take reasonable steps to ensure that their employing organizations' practices are consistent with the *NASW Code of Ethics.*

(e) Social workers should act to prevent and eliminate discrimination in the employing organization's work assignments and in its employment policies and practices.

(f) Social workers should accept employment or arrange student field placements only in organizations that exercise fair personnel practices.

(g) Social workers should be diligent stewards of the resources of their employing organizations, wisely conserving funds where appropriate and never misappropriating funds or using them for unintended purposes.

3.10 *Labor-Management Disputes*

(a) Social workers may engage in organized action, including the formation of and participation in labor unions, to improve services to clients and working conditions.

(b) The actions of social workers who are involved in labor-management disputes, job actions, or labor strikes should be guided by the profession's values, ethical principles, and ethical standards. Reasonable differences of opinion exist among social workers concerning their primary obligation as professionals during an actual or threatened labor strike or job action. Social workers should carefully examine relevant issues and their possible impact on clients before deciding on a course of action.

4. SOCIAL WORKERS' ETHICAL RESPONSIBILITIES AS PROFESSIONALS

4.01 *Competence*

(a) Social workers should accept responsibility or employment only on the basis of existing competence or the intention to acquire the necessary competence.

(b) Social workers should strive to become and remain proficient in professional practice and the performance of professional functions. Social workers should critically examine and keep current with emerging knowledge relevant to social work. Social workers should routinely review the professional literature and participate in continuing education relevant to social work practice and social work ethics.

(c) Social workers should base practice on recognized knowledge, including empirically based knowledge, relevant to social work and social work ethics.

4.02 *Discrimination*

Social workers should not practice, condone, facilitate, or collaborate with any form of discrimination on the basis of race, ethnicity, national origin, color, sex, sexual orientation, age, marital status, political belief, religion, or mental or physical disability.

4.03 *Private Conduct*

Social workers should not permit their private conduct to interfere with their ability to fulfill their professional responsibilities.

4.04   *Dishonesty, Fraud, and Deception*

Social workers should not participate in, condone, or be associated with dishonesty, fraud, or deception.

4.05   *Impairment*

(a)   Social workers should not allow their own personal problems, psychosocial distress, legal problems, substance abuse, or mental health difficulties to interfere with their professional judgment and performance or to jeopardize the best interests of people for whom they have a professional responsibility.

(b)   Social workers whose personal problems, psychosocial distress, legal problems, substance abuse, or mental health difficulties interfere with their professional judgment and performance should immediately seek consultation and take appropriate remedial action by seeking professional help, making adjustments in workload, terminating practice, or taking any other steps necessary to protect clients and others.

4.06   *Misrepresentation*

(a)   Social workers should make clear distinctions between statements made and actions engaged in as a private individual and as a representative of the social work profession, a professional social work organization, or the social worker's employing agency.

(b)   Social workers who speak on behalf of professional social work organizations should accurately represent the official and authorized positions of the organizations.

(c)   Social workers should ensure that their representations to clients, agencies, and the public of professional qualifications, credentials, education, competence, affiliations, services provided, or results to be achieved are accurate. Social workers should claim only those relevant professional credentials they actually possess and take steps to correct any inaccuracies or misrepresentations of their credentials by others.

4.07   *Solicitations*

(a)   Social workers should not engage in uninvited solicitation of potential clients who, because of their circumstances, are vulnerable to undue influence, manipulation, or coercion.

(b)   Social workers should not engage in solicitation of testimonial endorsements (including solicitation of consent to use a client's prior statement as a testimonial endorsement) from current clients or from other people who, because of their particular circumstances, are vulnerable to undue influence.

4.08   *Acknowledging Credit*

(a)   Social workers should take responsibility and credit, including authorship credit, only for work they have actually performed and to which they have contributed.

(b)   Social workers should honestly acknowledge the work of and the contributions made by others.

5. SOCIAL WORKERS' ETHICAL RESPONSIBILITIES TO THE SOCIAL WORK PROFESSION

5.01 *Integrity of the Profession*

(a) Social workers should work toward the maintenance and promotion of high standards of practice.

(b) Social workers should uphold and advance the values, ethics, knowledge, and mission of the profession. Social workers should protect, enhance, and improve the integrity of the profession through appropriate study and research, active discussion, and responsible criticism of the profession.

(c) Social workers should contribute time and professional expertise to activities that promote respect for the value, integrity, and competence of the social work profession. These activities may include teaching, research, consultation, service, legislative testimony, presentations in the community, and participation in their professional organizations.

(d) Social workers should contribute to the knowledge base of social work and share with colleagues their knowledge related to practice, research, and ethics. Social workers should seek to contribute to the profession's literature and to share their knowledge at professional meetings and conferences.

(e) Social workers should act to prevent the unauthorized and unqualified practice of social work.

5.02 *Evaluation and Research*

(a) Social workers should monitor and evaluate policies, the implementation of programs, and practice interventions.

(b) Social workers should promote and facilitate evaluation and research to contribute to the development of knowledge.

(c) Social workers should critically examine and keep current with emerging knowledge relevant to social work and fully use evaluation and research evidence in their professional practice.

(d) Social workers engaged in evaluation or research should carefully consider possible consequences and should follow guidelines developed for the protection of evaluation and research participants. Appropriate institutional review boards should be consulted.

(e) Social workers engaged in evaluation or research should obtain voluntary and written informed consent from participants, when appropriate, without any implied or actual deprivation or penalty for refusal to participate; without undue inducement to participate; and with due regard for participants' well-being, privacy, and dignity. Informed consent should include information about the nature, extent, and duration of the participation requested and disclosure of the risks and benefits of participation in the research.

(f) When evaluation or research participants are incapable of giving informed consent, social workers should provide an appropriate explanation to the participants, obtain the participants' assent to the extent they are able, and obtain written consent from an appropriate proxy.

(g) Social workers should never design or conduct evaluation or research that does not use consent procedures, such as certain forms of naturalistic observation and archival research, unless rigorous and responsible review of the research has found it to be justified because of its prospective scientific, educational, or applied value and unless equally effective alternative procedures that do not involve waiver of consent are not feasible.

(h) Social workers should inform participants of their right to withdraw from evaluation and research at any time without penalty.

(i) Social workers should take appropriate steps to ensure that participants in evaluation and research have access to appropriate supportive services.

(j) Social workers engaged in evaluation or research should protect participants from unwarranted physical or mental distress, harm, danger, or deprivation.

(k) Social workers engaged in the evaluation of services should discuss collected information only for professional purposes and only with people professionally concerned with this information.

(l) Social workers engaged in evaluation or research should ensure the anonymity or confidentiality of participants and of the data obtained from them. Social workers should inform participants of any limits of confidentiality, the measures that will be taken to ensure confidentiality, and when any records containing research data will be destroyed.

(m) Social workers who report evaluation and research results should protect participants' confidentiality by omitting identifying information unless proper consent has been obtained authorizing disclosure.

(n) Social workers should report evaluation and research findings accurately. They should not fabricate or falsify results and should take steps to correct any errors later found in published data using standard publication methods.

(o) Social workers engaged in evaluation or research should be alert to and avoid conflicts of interest and dual relationships with participants, should inform participants when a real or potential conflict of interest arises, and should take steps to resolve the issue in a manner that makes participants' interests primary.

(p) Social workers should educate themselves, their students, and their colleagues about responsible research practices.

6. SOCIAL WORKERS' ETHICAL RESPONSIBILITIES TO THE BROADER SOCIETY

6.01 *Social Welfare*

Social workers should promote the general welfare of society, from local to global levels, and the development of people, their communities, and their environments. Social workers should advocate for living conditions conducive to the fulfillment of basic human needs and should promote social, economic, political, and cultural values and institutions that are compatible with the realization of social justice.

6.02   *Public Participation*

Social workers should facilitate informed participation by the public in shaping social policies and institutions.

6.03   *Public Emergencies*

Social workers should provide appropriate professional services in public emergencies to the greatest extent possible.

6.04   *Social and Political Action*

(a) Social workers should engage in social and political action that seeks to ensure that all people have equal access to the resources, employment, services, and opportunities they require to meet their basic human needs and to develop fully. Social workers should be aware of the impact of the political arena on practice and should advocate for changes in policy and legislation to improve social conditions in order to meet basic human needs and promote social justice.

(b) Social workers should act to expand choice and opportunity for all people, with special regard for vulnerable, disadvantaged, oppressed, and exploited people and groups.

(c) Social workers should promote conditions that encourage respect for cultural and social diversity within the United States and globally. Social workers should promote policies and practices that demonstrate respect for difference, support the expansion of cultural knowledge and resources, advocate for programs and institutions that demonstrate cultural competence, and promote policies that safeguard the rights of and confirm equity and social justice for all people.

(d) Social workers should act to prevent and eliminate domination of, exploitation of, and discrimination against any person, group, or class on the basis of race, ethnicity, national origin, color, sex, sexual orientation, age, marital status, political belief, religion, or mental or physical disability.

References

Abernathy, A. D., & Lancia, J. J. (1998). Religion and the psychotherapeutic relationship. *Journal of Psychotherapy Practice and Research, 7,* 281–289.

Albany, A. P. (1984). Clinical implications of religious loyalties: A contextual view. *Counseling and Values, 28,* 128–133.

Albright, R. H. (2001). *A view of William James.* Retrieved November 30, 2001 from http://world .std.com/~albright/james.html.

Alcoholics Anonymous World Services. (1953). *Twelve steps and twelve traditions.* New York: Author.

Al-Krenawi, A. (1999). An overview of rituals in Western therapies and intervention: Argument for their use in cross-cultural therapy. *International Journal for the Advancement of Counseling, 21,* 3–17.

Allison, D. (1995). *Two or three things I know for sure.* New York: Penguin Books.

Allport, G. W. (1950). *The individual and his religion: A psychological interpretation.* New York: Macmillan.

Alpers, R. R. (1995). Spiritual reading as bibliotherapy. In R. J. Kus (Ed.), *Spirituality and chemical dependency* (pp. 49–63). Binghamton, NY: Haworth Press.

American Association for Marriage and Family Therapy. (2001). *Code of ethics.* Retrieved December 29, 2001, from www.aamft.org.

American Counseling Association. (2001). *Code of ethics and standards of practice.* Retrieved December 29, 2001, from http://www.counseling .org/resources/codeofethics.html.

American Psychological Association. (1998). *What practitioners should know about working with older adults.* Washington, DC: Author.

Andreas, B. (1999). *Creations, 13,* 1.

Astin, J. A. (1997). Stress reduction through mindfulness meditation. *Psychotherapy and Psychosomatics, 66,* 97–106.

Atkinson, D. R., Morten, G., & Sue, D. W. (1993). *Counseling American minorities: A cross-cultural perspective* (4th ed.). Madison, WI: Brown & Benchmark.

Baker, B. (1997, July/August). The faith factor. *Common Boundary,* 20–26.

Ballou, M. (1995). Women and spirit: Two nonfits in psychology. *Women and Therapy, 16,* 9–20.

Barna, G. (1991). *What Americans believe: An annual survey of values and religious views in the United States.* Ventura, CA: Regal Books.

Barnett, J. E., & Fiorentino, N. (2000). Spirituality and religion: Clinical and ethical issues for psychotherapists. Part II. *Psychological Bulletin, 35,* 32–35.

Batson, C. D., & Ventis, W. L. (1982). *The religious experience.* New York: Oxford University Press.

Becvar, D. S. (1997). *Soul healing: A spiritual orientation in counseling and therapy.* New York: Basic Books.

Belenky, M. F., Clinchy, B. M., Goldberger, N. R., & Tarule, J. M. (1986). *Women's ways of knowing: The development of self, voice, and mind.* New York: Basic Books.

Benson, H. (1993). The relaxation response. In D. Goleman & J. Gurin (Eds.), *Mind-body medicine: How to use your mind for better health* (pp. 233–257). Yonkers, NY: Consumer Reports Books.

Bergin, A. E. (1992). Three contributions of a spiritual perspective to counseling, psychotherapy, and behavior change. In M. T. Burke & J. G. Miranti (Eds.), *Ethical and spiritual values in counseling* (pp. 5–15). Alexandria, VA: American Counseling Association.

297

Bergin, A. E., Payne, I. R., & Richards, P. S. (1996). Values in psychotherapy. In E. P. Shafranske (Ed.), *Religion and the clinical practice of psychology* (pp. 297–325). Washington, DC: American Psychological Association.

Berthrong, J. H., & Berthrong, E. N. (2000). *Confucianism: A short introduction.* Boston: Oneworld Publications.

Bibbins, K. (2000, September). Cultural spirituality. *Counseling Today, 34,* 40.

Birdsall, B. (2001). Ethical challenges, guidelines for spirituality, counseling. *Counseling Today, 36,* 44, 48.

Birodkar, S. (n.d.). *A Hindu history: A search for our present in history.* Retrieved December 29, 2001, from http://www.hindubooks.org /sudheer_birodkar/hindu_history/sikhism .html.

Bishop, D. R. (1992). Religious values as cross-cultural issues in counseling. *Counseling and Values, 36,* 179–191.

Boeree, C. G. (1997). *Personality theories: Erich Fromm 1900–1980.* Retrieved November 30, 2001, from Shippensburg University, Psychology Department Web site, http://www.ship .edu/~cgboeree/fromm.html.

Boeree, C. G. (1998). *Personality theories: Gordon Allport 1897–1967.* Retrieved November 30, 2001, from Shippensburg University, Psychology Department Web site, http://www.ship .edu/~cgboeree/allport.html.

Bonvillain, N. (1996). *Native American religion.* New York: Chelsea House.

Bowdein, H. W. (1999). Christianity. In *The world book encyclopedia* (Vol. 3, pp. 523–524). Chicago: World Book.

Brady, J. L., Guy, J. D., Poelstra, P. L., & Brokaw, B. F. (1999). Vicarious traumatization, spirituality, and the treatment of sexual abuse survivors: A national survey of women psychotherapists. *Professional Psychology: Research and Practice, 30,* 386–393.

Breuilly, E., O'Brien, J., & Palmer, M. (1997). *Religions of the world: The illustrated guide to origins, beliefs, traditions, and festivals.* New York: Transedition Limited and Ferneigh Books.

Bristow-Braitman, A. (1995) Addiction recovery: 12 Step programs and cognitive-behavioral psychology. *Journal of Counseling and Development, 73,* 414–418.

Brown, H. P., Peterson, J. H., & Cunningham, O. (1988). Rationale and theoretical basis for a behavioral/cognitive approach to spirituality. *Alcoholism Treatment Quarterly, 5,* 47–59.

Burke, M. T., Hackney, H., Hudson, P., Miranti, J., Watts, G. A., & Epp, L. (1999). Spirituality, religion, and CACREP curriculum standards. *Journal of Counseling and Development, 77,* 251–257.

Byrd, E. K. (1997). Concepts related to inclusion of the spiritual component in services to persons with disability and chronic illness. *Journal of Applied Rehabilitation Counseling, 28,* 26–29.

Byrd, E. K. (1998). A discussion of helping theory, Christian beliefs, and persons with disabilities. *Journal of Applied Rehabilitation Counseling, 29,* 25–30.

Cadwalader, S. L. (2001). Native Americans in contemporary society. *Microsoft Encarta Online Encyclopedia.* Retrieved December 29, 2001, from http://encarta.msn.com/find/print.asp? &pg=8&ti=761570777&sc=58&pt=1&pn=9.

Canda, E. R. (1990). An holistic approach to prayer for social work practice. *Social Thoughts, 16,* 3–13.

Cantwell et al. v. State of Conneticut, 310 U.S. 296 (1940) No. 632.

Carl Gustav Jung (1875–1961). (2001). Retrieved November 29, 2001, from http://www .kirjasto.sci.fi/cjung.htm.

Carr, W. (2000). Some reflections on spirituality, religion, and mental health. *Mental Health, Religion, and Culture, 3,* 1–12.

Carrington, P. (1977). *Freedom in meditation.* Garden City, NY: Anchor Press/Doubleday.

Carrington, P. (1993). Modern forms of meditation. In P. M. Lehrer & R. Woolfolk (Eds.), *Principles and practice of stress management* (pp. 139–168). New York: Guilford Press.

Chapman, R. J. (1996). Spirituality in the treatment of alcoholism: A worldview approach. *Counseling and Values, 41,* 39–50.

Chappelle, W. (2000). A series of progressive legal and ethical decision-making steps for using Christian spiritual interventions in psychotherapy. *Journal of Psychology and Theology, 28,* 43–53.

Childress, D. (1998, March). Understanding Shinto. *Calliope: World History for Kids*, 5–7.

Chodron, P. (1996). *Awakening loving-kindness*. Boston: Shambhala.

Christ, C. P. (1995). *Diving deep and surfacing: Women writers on spiritual quest* (3rd ed.). Boston: Beacon Press.

Christian, M. (1994). In L. P. Frankel (Ed.), *Kindling the spirit: Acts of kindness and words of courage for women* (p. 162). Deerfield Beach, FL: Health Communications.

The Church of Jesus Christ of Latter-day Saints. (1981). *The Book of Mormon: Another testament of Jesus Christ.* Salt Lake City, UT: Author.

Clark, P. (1998). *Zoroastrianism*. Portland, OR: Sussex.

Clements, G., Krenner, L., & Molk, W. (1988). The use of Transcendental Meditation programme in the prevention of drug abuse and in the treatment of drug-addicted persons. *Bulletin on Narcotics, 40*, 51–56.

Cohen, L. J. (1994). Bibliotherapy: A valid treatment modality. *Journal of Psychosocial Nursing, 32*, 40–44.

Corey, G. (1996). *Theory and practice of counseling and psychotherapy* (5th ed.). Pacific Grove, CA: Brooks/Cole.

Cornett, C. (1998). *The soul of psychotherapy.* New York: Free Press.

Cort, J. E. (1997). Recent fieldwork studies of the contemporary Jains. *Religious Studies Review, 23*, 103–110.

Corveleyn, J. (2000). In defense of benevolent neutrality: Against a spiritual strategy. *Journal of Individual Psychology, 56*, 343–352.

Cowen, E. L. (1994). The enhancement of psychological wellness: Challenges and opportunities. *American Journal of Community Psychology, 22*, 149–179.

Curtis, R. C., & Davis, K. M. (1999). Spirituality and multimodal therapy: A practical approach to incorporating spirituality in counseling. *Counseling and Values, 43*, 199–210.

Das, A. K. (1989). Beyond self-actualization. *International Journal for the Advancement of Counseling, 12*, 13–27.

Dastoor, D. P. (1994). Re-focusing the vision of Zarathustra. *Ecumenism, 115*, 31–33.

Davis, J. (1914). *Moral and vocational guidance.* Boston: Ginn.

Daya, R. (2000). Buddhist psychology, a theory of change processes: Implications for counsellors. *International Journal for the Advancement of Counselling, 22*, 257–271.

DeLange, N. (2000). *An introduction to Judaism.* Cambridge, England: Cambridge University Press.

Denzin, N. K. (1974). The methodological implications of symbolic interactionsim for the study of deviance. *British Journal of Sociology, 25*, 269–282.

De Silva, P. (1993). Buddhism and counseling. *British Journal of Guidance and Counselling, 21*, 30–34.

Dhalla, H. B. (1998). The message of Lord Zarathustra. *Dialogue and Alliance, 12*, 5–19.

Dobbins, R. D. (2000). Psychotherapy with Pentecostal protestants. In P. S. Richards & A. E. Bergin (Eds.), *Handbook of psychotherapy and religious diversity* (pp. 155–184). Washington, DC: American Psychological Association.

Ehrlich, M. P. (1986). Taoism and psychotherapy. *Journal of Contemporary Psychotherapy, 16*, 23–38.

Elias, J. J. (1999). *Islam.* Upper Saddle River, NJ: Prentice-Hall.

Elkind, D., & Elkind, S. (1962). Varieties of religious experience in adolescents. *Journal for the Scientific Study of Religion, 11*, 102–112.

Encyclopedia Britannica. (2001). Table: Worldwide adherents to all religions by six continental areas, mid 1998. *Encyclopedia Britannica Online.* Retrieved December 29, 2001, from *http://www.eb.com:180/bol/topic?tbl_id=2742.*

Evans, R. I. (1981). *Introduction: Dialogue with Gordon Allport* (p. xv). New York: Praeger.

Everson v. Board of Education of Ewing TP. Et al., U.S. 1 (1947) No. 52.

Faiver, C., Ingersoll, R. E., O'Brien, E., & McNally, C. (2001). *Explorations in counseling and spirituality.* Belmont, CA: Brooks/Cole.

Farnsworth, K. E. (1996). The devil sends errors in pairs. *Journal of Psychology and Christianity, 15*, 123–132.

Fielding, R. G., & Llewelyn, S. (1996). The new religions and psychotherapy: Similarities and differences. In G. Claxton (Ed.), *Beyond therapy: The impact of Eastern religions on psychological theory and practice* (pp. 271–289). Dorset, England: Prism.

Fisher, M. P. (1994). Sikhing for truth. *Areopagus, 7,* 26–29.

Flood, G. (1996). *An introduction to Hinduism.* Cambridge, England: Cambridge University Press.

Flores, P. J. (1988). Alcoholics Anonymous: A phenomenological and existential perspective. *Alcoholism Treatment Quarterly, 5,* 73–94.

Fowler, J. (1981). *Stages of faith: The psychology of human development and the quest for meaning.* San Francisco: Harper & Row.

Fowler, J. (1991). Stages in faith consciousness. In F. K. Oser & W. G. Scarlett (Eds.), Religious development in childhood and adolescence [Special issue]. *New Directions for Child Development, 52,* 27–45.

Fowler, J. (1997). *Hinduism: Beliefs and practices.* Portland, OR: Sussex.

Freud, S. (1927). *The future of an illusion.* Garden City, NY: Doubleday.

Fromm, E. (1950). *Psychoanalysis and religion.* New Haven, CT: Yale University Press.

Fukuyama, M. A., & Sevig, T. D. (1997). Spiritual issues in counseling: A new course. *Counselor Education and Supervision, 36,* 233–244.

Fukuyama, M. A., & Sevig, T. D. (1999). *Integrating spirituality into multicultural counseling.* London: Sage.

Gandhi, S. L. (1997). The nonviolent Jain tradition: Unique features and common values. *Dialogue and Alliance, 11,* 116–124.

Garrett, M. (1998). *Walking on the wind.* Rochester, VT: Bear & Company.

Garrett, M. T. (1999). Understanding the "medicine" of Native American traditional values: An integrative review. *Counseling and Values, 43,* 84–98.

Gartner, J. (1996). Religious commitment, mental health, and prosocial behavior: A review of the empirical literature. In E. P. Shafranske (Ed.), *Religion and the clinical practice of psychology* (pp. 187–214). Washington, DC: American Psychological Association.

Gendler, J. R. (1988). *The book of qualities.* New York: Harper/Perennial.

Genia, V. (2000). Religious issues in secularly based psychotherapy. *Counseling and Values, 44,* 213–221.

Gethin, R. (1998). *The foundations of Buddhism.* New York: Oxford University Press.

Goldstein, S. V. (1990). You are what you read: The use of bibliotherapy to facilitate psychotherapy. *Journal of Psychosocial Nursing, 28,* 7–10.

Gordon, M. (1991). *Islam: World religions.* New York: Facts on File.

Granello, D. H. (2000). Using a contextual approach in counseling men. *Journal of Psychotherapy in Independent Practice, 1,* 43–52.

Green, W. S. (1994). Religion and society in America. In J. Neusner (Ed.), *World religions in America* (pp. 293–301). Louisville, KY: Westminster/John Knox Press.

Grossman, S., & Haut, R. (Eds.). (1992). *Daughters of the king: Women in the synagogue: A survey of history, halachah and contemporary reality.* Philadelphia: Jewish Publication Society of America.

Guinee, J. P. (1999). Self-disclosure of faith in secular counseling agencies. *Journal of Psychology and Christianity, 18,* 69–74.

Hall, T. W., Brokaw, B. F., Edwards, K. J., & Pike, P. L. (1998). An empirical exploration of psychoanalysis and religion: Spiritual maturity and object relations development. *Journal for the Scientific Study of Religion, 37,* 303–313.

Harris, I. M. (1997). The ten tenets of male spirituality. *Journal of Men's Studies, 6,* 29–53.

Hartz, P. (1993). *Taoism: World religions.* New York: Facts on File.

The Harvard Mental Health Letter. (2001, June). Religion and mortality: New data. *The Harvard Mental Health Letter, 17,* 7–8.

Haug, I. E. (1998). Including a spiritual dimension in family therapy: Ethical considerations. *Contemporary Family Therapy, 20,* 181–194.

Hausdorff, D. (1972). *Erich Fromm.* New York: Twayne.

Hawkins, I. L., & Bullock, S. L. (1995). Informed consent and religious values: A neglected area of diversity. *Psychotherapy, 32,* 293–300.

Hawks, S. R., Hull, M. L., Thalman, R. L., & Richins, P. M. (1995). Review of spiritual health: Definition, role, and intervention strategies in health promotion. *American Journal of Health Promotion, 9,* 371–378.

Henning, L. H., & Tirrell, F. J. (1982). Counselor resistance to spiritual exploration. *Personnel and Guidance Journal, 61,* 92–95.

Hermon, D. A., & Hazler, R. J. (1999). Adherence to a wellness model and perceptions of psychological well-being. *Journal of Counseling and Development, 77,* 339–343.

Hermsen, E. (1996). Person-centered psychology and Taoism: The reception of Lao-tzu by Carl R. Rogers. *International Journal for the Psychology of Religion, 6,* 107–125.

Hesselgrave, D. J. (1988). Beyond pragmatism: Brief therapy and Christian counseling. *Journal of Psychology and Theology, 16,* 246–253.

Hickson, J., Housley, W., & Wages, D. (2000). Counselors' perceptions of spirituality in the therapeutic process. *Counseling and Values, 45,* 58–66.

Hinduism in Transition [600 B.C.–322 B.C.]. (n.d.). Retrieved November 30, 2001, from http://www.historyofindia.com/hinduism.html.

Hindu Succession Act, 1956, Act No. 30 of year 1956, dated 17th June, 1956.

Hinterkopf, E. (1998). *Integrating spirituality in counseling: A manual for using the experiential focusing method.* Alexandria, VA: American Counseling Association.

Hogan, L. (1986). Women: Doing and being. In C. Bruchac, L. Hogan, & J. McDaniel (Eds.), *The stories we hold secret: Tales of women's spiritual development* (pp. ix–xv). Greenfield Center, NY: Greenfield Review.

Hoge, D. R. (2000). Religion in America: The demographics of belief and affiliation. In E. P. Shafranske (Ed.), *Religion and the clinical practice of psychology* (pp. 21–41). Washington, DC: American Psychological Association.

Hoobler, T., & Hoobler, D. (1993). *Confucianism: World religions.* New York: Facts on File.

Humphries, R. H. (1982). Therapeutic neutrality reconsidered. *Journal of Religion and Health, 21,* 124–131.

Jacobs, J. L. (1992). Religious ritual and mental health. In J. F. Schumaker (Ed.), *Religion and mental health* (pp. 291–299). New York: Oxford University Press.

Jaffee, M. (1997). *Early Judaism.* Upper Saddle River, NJ: Prentice-Hall.

Jain, S. J. (1995). *An introduction to Jaina Sadhana.* Jawahar Nagar, India: Vardham Printing Press.

Jain, S. K. (1997). *Glimpses of Jainism.* Delhi, India: Motilal Banarsidass.

James, W. (1985). *The varieties of religious experience: A study in human nature.* Cambridge, MA: Harvard University Press. (Original work published 1902)

Johanson, G., & Kurtz, R. (1991). *Grace unfolding: Psychotherapy in the spirit of the Tao-Te Ching.* New York: Bell Tower.

Johnson, P. N., & Phelps, G. L. (1991). Effectiveness in self-help groups: Alcoholics Anonymous as a prototype. *Family and Community Health, 14,* 22–27.

Johnson, W. B., Ridley, C. R., & Nielsen, S. L. (2000). Religiously sensitive rational emotive behavior therapy: Elegant solutions and ethical risks. *Professional Psychology: Research and Practice, 31,* 14–20.

Judge, M. G. (1994). Recovery's next step. *Common Boundary, 12,* 16–24.

Kabat-Zinn, J. (1982). An outpatient program in behavioral medicine for chronic pain patients based on the practice of mindfulness meditation: Theoretical considerations and preliminary results. *General Hospital Psychiatry, 4,* 33–47.

Kahoe, R. E., & Meadow, M. J. (1984). *Psychology of religion: Religion in individual lives.* New York: Harper & Row.

Kaiser, D. L. (1991). Religious problem-solving styles and guilt. *Journal for the Scientific Study of Religion, 30,* 94–98.

Keller, R. R. (2000). Religious diversity in North America. In P. S. Richards & A. E. Bergin (Eds.), *Handbook of psychotherapy and religious diversity* (pp. 27–55). Washington, DC: American Psychological Association.

Kelly, E. W. (1990). Counselor responsiveness to client religiousness. *Counseling and Values, 35,* 69–72.

Kelly, E. W. (1995). *Spirituality and religion in counseling and psychotherapy: Diversity in theory and practice.* Alexandria, VA: American Counseling Association.

Khantzian, E. J., & Mack, J. E. (1994). How AA works and why it's important for clinicians to understand. *Journal of Substance Abuse Treatment, 11,* 77–92.

Kochems, T. (1993). Countertransference and transference aspects of religious material in psychotherapy: The isolation or integration of religious material. In M. L. Randour (Ed.),

Exploring sacred landscapes: Religious and spiritual experiences in psychotherapy (pp. 34–54). New York: Columbia University Press.

Koenig, H. G., George, L. K., & Peterson, B. L. (1998). Religiosity and remission of depression in medically ill older patients. *American Journal of Psychiatry, 155,* 536–542.

Koenig, H. G., Larson, D. B., & Matthews, D. A. (1995, March). *Religion and psychotherapy with older adults.* Paper presented at the Boston Society for Gerontologic Psychiatry, Boston.

Koenig, H. G., & Pritchett, J. (1998). Religion and psychotherapy. In H. G. Koenig (Ed.), *Handbook of religion and mental health* (pp. 323–336). San Diego, CA: Academic Press.

Kogan, M. (2001). Where happiness lies. *Monitor on Psychology, 32,* 74–76.

Kohn, L. (1993). *The Taoist experience: An anthology.* Albany: State University of New York Press.

Krasner, L. (1962). The therapist as a social reinforcement machine. In H. H. Strupp & L. Luborsky (Eds.), *Research in psychotherapy* (Vol. 2, pp. 61–94). Washington, DC: American Psychological Association.

Kurtz, E. (1988). *A.A.: The story.* San Francisco: Harper & Row.

Kus, R. J. (1995). Prayer and meditation in addiction recovery. In R. J. Kus (Ed.), *Spirituality and chemical dependency* (pp. 101–115). Binghamton, NY: Haworth Press.

Lahav, R. (1996). Philosophical counseling and Taoism. *Journal of Chinese Philosophy, 23,* 259–276.

Lal, V., & Lal, A. (1999). Jainism. In *The world book encyclopedia* (Vol. 10, p. 117). Chicago: World Book.

Lannert, J. L. (1991). Resistance and countertransference issues with spiritual and religious clients. *Journal of Humanistic Psychology, 31,* 68–76.

Larson, D. B., Swyers, J. P., & McCullough, M. E. (Eds.). (1997). *Scientific research on spirituality and health: A consensus report.* Rockville, MD: National Institute for Healthcare Research.

Le, C., Ingvarson, E. P., & Page, R. C. (1995). Alcoholics Anonymous and the counseling profession: Philosophies in conflict. *Journal of Counseling and Development, 73,* 603–609.

Leahey, T. H. (1987). *A history of psychology* (2nd ed.). Englewood Cliffs, NJ: Prentice-Hall.

LeShan, L. (1974). *How to meditate.* Boston: Little, Brown.

Lester, R. C. (1987). *Buddhism.* San Francisco: Harper & Row.

Lincoln, C. E., & Mamiya, L. H. (1990). *The Black church in the African American experience.* Durham, NC: Duke University Press.

Lincoln, L. N. (1999). Introduction. In A. Billingsley (Ed.), *Mighty like a river: The Black church and social reform* (pp. xix–xxiv). New York: Oxford University Press.

Linder, S., Miller, G., & Johnson, P. (2000). Counseling and spirituality: The use of emptiness and the importance of timing. *Resources in Education,* CG029855.

Lovinger, R. J. (1984). *Working with religious issues in therapy.* New York: Aronson.

Lovinger, R. J. (1996). Considering the religious dimension in assessment and treatment. In E. P. Shafranske (Ed.), *Religion and the clinical practice of psychology* (pp. 327–364). Washington, DC: American Psychological Association.

Lovinger, S. L., Miller, L., & Lovinger, R. J. (1999). Some clinical applications of religious development in adolescence. *Journal of Adolescence, 22,* 269–277.

Lukoff, D., Lu, F. G., & Turner, R. (1995). Cultural considerations in the assessment and treatment of religious and spiritual problems. *Cultural Psychiatry, 18,* 467–485.

Marlatt, G. A., & Kristeller, J. L. (1999). Mindfulness and meditation. In W. R. Miller (Ed.), *Integrating spirituality into treatment* (pp. 67–84). Washington, DC: American Psychological Association.

Masters, R., & Houston, J. (1972). *Mind games.* New York: Dell.

Mattson, D. L. (1994). Religious counseling: To be used, not feared. *Counseling and Values, 38,* 187–192.

McBride, J. (1996). *The color of water.* New York: Riverhead Books.

McClelland, D. (1979). *Power: The inner experience.* New York: Irvington.

McCloud, A. B. (1995). *African American Islam.* New York: Routledge.

McCullough, M. E., & Larson, D. B. (1999). Prayer. In W. R. Miller (Ed.), *Integrating spirituality into treatment* (pp. 85–110). Washington, DC: American Psychological Association.

McCullough, M. E., Weaver, A. J., Larson, D. B., & Aay, K. R. (2000). Psychotherapy with mainline protestants: Lutheran, Presbyterian, Espiscopal/Anglican, and Methodist. In P. S. Richards & A. E. Bergin (Eds.), *Handbook of psychotherapy and religious diversity* (pp. 105–129). Washington, DC: American Psychological Association.

McFadden, J. (1999). *Transcultural counseling.* Alexandria, VA: American Counseling Association.

McGrath, A. E. (1997). *An introduction to Christianity.* Cambridge, MA: Blackwell.

McLeod, H. (1997). *Sikhism.* New York: Penguin.

Miller, G. (1992). Integrating religion and psychology in therapy: Issues and recommendations. *Counseling and Values, 36,* 112–122.

Miller, G. (1999a). The development of the spiritual focus in counseling and counselor education. *Journal of Counseling and Development, 77,* 498–501.

Miller, G. (1999b). *Learning the language of addiction counseling.* Boston: Allyn & Bacon.

Miller, G. (2000). Sharon's journey. *Counseling and Values, 44,* 124–128.

Miller, G. (2001). Finding happiness for ourselves and our clients. *Journal of Counseling and Development, 79,* 382–384.

Miller, G., Arena, P., Johnson, P., Lewin, N., Smelzer, R., & Valentine, M. (1999, February). *Infusing spirituality into counselor educator curriculum.* Paper presented at the North Carolina Counseling Association Conference, Greensboro, NC.

Miller, G., Eller, M., Evans, R., Fleming, W., Glasgow, S., Johnson, P., et al. (2001, February). *Collaborations across spiritual perspectives in counseling.* Paper presented at the North Carolina Counseling Association Conference, Greensboro, NC.

Miller, G., Evans, R., & Youngblood, C. (1998, March). *Breathing under water: The use of spirituality by women to cope with oppression.* Paper presented at the Appalachian Humanities Program, Boone, NC.

Miller, G., Fleming, W., Brown-Anderson, F., Henderson, L., Gregory, K., Hogwood, W., et al. (1998, April). *Professor/student reflections on spiritual views impacting counselor development.* Paper presented at the meeting of the American Counseling Association World Conference, Indianapolis, IN.

Miller, G., Lassiter, P., Gardner, P., & Hamilton, K. (1999, February). *Integrating spirituality in counseling and counselor education.* Paper presented at the North Carolina Counseling Association, Greensboro, NC.

Miller, G., Yang, J., & Chen, M. (1997). Counseling Taiwan Chinese in America: Training issues for counselors. *Counselor Education and Supervision, 37,* 22–34.

Miller, G. D., & Baldwin, D. C. (1987). Implications of the wounded-healer paradigm for the use of the self in therapy. In M. Baldwin & V. Satir (Eds.), *The use of self in therapy* (pp. 130–151). New York: Haworth Press.

Miller, J. B. (1976). *Toward a new psychology of women.* Boston: Beacon Press.

Miller, L., & Lovinger, R. J. (2000). Psychotherapy with conservative and reform Jews. In P. S. Richards & A. E. Bergin (Eds.), *Handbook of psychotherapy and religious diversity* (pp. 259–286). Washington, DC: American Psychological Association.

Miller, W. R., & Kurtz, E. (1994). Models of alcoholism used in treatment: Contrasting AA and other perspectives with which it is often confused. *Journal of Studies on Alcohol, 55,* 159–166.

Miller, W. R., & Thoresen, C. E. (1999). Spirituality and health. In W. R. Miller (Ed.), *Integrating spirituality into treatment: Resources for practitioners* (pp. 3–18). Washington, DC: American Psychological Association.

Ming-Dao. (1992). *365 TAO: Daily meditations.* San Francisco: Harper.

Morgan, R. (1991). The pedestrian woman. In M. Sewell (Ed.), *Cries of the spirit* (pp. 194–195). Boston: Beacon Press.

Morris, J. R., & Robinson, D. T. (1996). Community and Christianity in the Black church. *Counseling and Values, 41,* 59–69.

Mountain, D. A., & Muir, W. J. (2000). Spiritual well-being in psychiatric patients. *Irish Journal of Psychological Medicine, 17,* 123–127.

Myers, B. K. (1997). *Young children and spirituality.* New York: Routledge.

Myers, D. G. (2000). The funds, friends, and faith of happy people. *American Psychologist, 55,* 56–67.

National Association of Social Workers. (1999). *National Association of Social Workers code of ethics.* Retrieved December 29, 2001, from http://www.naswdc.org/code/ethics.html

Neusner, J. (1994). Introduction. In J. Neusner (Ed.), *World religions in America* (pp. 1–10). Louisville, KY: Westminster/John Knox Press.

Nigosian, S. A. (1996). Tradition and modernity in contemporary Zoroastrian communities. *Journal of Asian and African Studies, 31,* 206–216.

Northrup, M. (1998, March). The basic tenets of Shinto. *Calliope: World History for Kids,* 8–9.

Nyanaponika, T. (1996). *The heart of Buddhist meditation.* York Beach, ME: Samuel Weiser.

O'Dwyer, P. (1993). Alcoholism treatment facilities. In S. L. A. Straussner (Ed.), *Clinical work with substance-abusing clients* (pp. 119–134). New York: Guilford Press.

Ogden, J. (1996). *Health psychology.* Philadelphia: Open University Press.

Pargament, K. I. (1996). Religious methods of coping: Resources for the conservation and transformation of significance. In E. P. Shafranske (Ed.), *Religion and the clinical practice of psychology* (pp. 215–239). Washington, DC: American Psychological Association.

Pargament, K. I., Kennell, J., Hathaway, W., Grevengoed, N., Newman, J., & Jones, W. (1988). Religion and the problem-solving process: Three styles of coping. *Journal for the Scientific Study of Religion, 27,* 90–104.

Pargament, K. I., Smith, B. W., Koenig, H. G., & Perez, L. (1998). Patterns of positive and negative religious coping with major life stressors. *Journal for the Scientific Study of Religion, 37,* 711–725.

Parrinder, G. (1971). *World religions: From ancient history to the present.* New York: Hamlyn.

Parsons, F. (1909). *Choosing a vocation.* Boston: Houghton Mifflin.

Parsons, F. (1911). *Legal doctrine and social progress.* New York: B. W. Huebsch.

Pate, R. H., & High, H. J. (1995). The importance of client religious beliefs and practices in the education of counselors in CACREP-accredited programs. *Counseling and Values, 40,* 2–5.

Pattison, E. M. (1965). Transference and countertransference in pastoral care. *Journal of Pastoral Care, 21,* 193–202.

Picken, S. D. B. (1994). *Essentials of Shinto: An analytical guide to principal teachings.* Westport, CT: Greenwood Press.

Pitts, M. (1998). An introduction to health psychology. In M. Pitts & K. Phillips (Eds.), *The psychology of health: An introduction* (pp. 3–23). New York: Routledge.

Poloma, M. M., & Pendleton, B. F. (1989). Exploring types of prayer and quality of life: A research note. *Review of Religious Research, 31,* 46–53.

Poloma, M. M., & Pendleton, B. F. (1991). The effects of prayer and prayer experiences on measures of general well-being. *Journal of Psychology and Theology, 19,* 71–83.

A position paper of the Association for Spiritual, Ethical, and Religious Values in Counseling. (n.d.). Retrieved November 30, 2001, from http://www.counseling.org/aservic/Spirituality.html.

Princeton Religion Research Center. (1994). *Religion in America* (Suppl.). Princeton, NJ: Gallop Poll.

Propst, L. R. (1980). The comparative efficacy of religious and nonreligious imagery for the treatment of mild depression in religious individuals. *Cognitive Therapy and Research, 4,* 167–178.

Rabinor, J. R. (1998). The therapist's voice. *Eating Disorders, 6,* 253–266.

Rabinowitz, A. (2000). Psychotherapy with orthodox Jews. In P. S. Richards & A. E. Bergin (Eds.), *Handbook of psychotherapy and religious diversity* (pp. 237–258). Washington, DC: American Psychological Association.

Rabinowitz, F. E., & Cochran, S. V. (2002). *Deepening psychotherapy with men.* Washington, DC: American Psychological Association.

Raboteau, A. J. (1999). *African-American religion.* New York: Oxford University Press.

Rainer, T. (1978). *The new diary.* Los Angeles: J. P. Tarcher.

Rando, T. A. (1985). Creating therapeutic rituals in the psychotherapy of the bereaved. *Psychotherapy, 22,* 236–240.

Reader, I. (1998). *The simple guide to Shinto.* Kent, England: Global Books.

Remen, N., May, R., Young, D., & Bertand, W. (1985). The wounded healer. *Saybrook Review, 5,* 84–93.

Reynolds, F. E. (1999). Buddhism. In *The world book encyclopedia* (Vol. 2, p. 668). Chicago: World Book.

Richards, P. S., & Bergin, A. E. (1997). *A spiritual strategy for counseling and psychotherapy.* Washington, DC: American Psychological Association.

Richards, P. S., & Bergin, A. E. (Eds.). (2000). *Handbook of psychotherapy and religious diversity.* Washington, DC: American Psychological Association.

Richards, P. S., Rector, J. M., & Tjeltveit, A. C. (1999). Values, spirituality, and psychotherapy. In W. R. Miller (Ed.), *Integrating spirituality into treatment* (pp. 133–160). Washington, DC: American Psychological Association.

Rigal-Cellard, B. (1995). The Peyote Way Church of God: Native Americans v. new religions v. the law. *Native American Studies, 9,* 35–44.

Rinbochay, L. (1986). *Mind in Tibetan Buddhism.* Ithaca, NY: Snow Lion.

Riordan, R. J., & Walsh, L. (1994). Guidelines for professional referral to Alcoholics Anonymous and other twelve step groups. *Journal of Counseling and Development, 72,* 351–355.

Rizzuto, A. M. (1979). *The birth of the living God.* Chicago: University of Chicago Press.

Robinson, B. A. (1995). *Taoism (a.k.a. Daoism).* Retrieved December 29, 2001, from http://www.religioustolerance.org/taoism.htm.

Rogers, C. R. (1987). The underlying theory: Drawn from experiences with individuals and groups. *Counseling and Values, 32,* 38–45.

Ross, N. (1990). Exploring ecofeminism. *Journal of Experiential Education, 13,* 23–28.

Schank, J. A., & Skovholt, T. M. (1999). Dual-relationship dilemmas of rural and small-community psychologists. In D. N. Bersoff (Ed.), *Ethical conflicts in psychology* (pp. 377–382). Washington, DC: American Psychological Association.

Schiffman, L. H. (1999). Judaism. In *The world book encyclopedia* (Vol. 11, pp. 179–182). Chicago: World Book.

Seligman, M. E. P., & Csikszentmihalyi, M. (2000). Positive psychology: An introduction. *American Psychologist, 55,* 5–14.

Shafii, M. (1985). *Freedom from the self: Sufism, meditation and psychotherapy.* New York: Human Sciences.

Shafranske, E. P. (1996). Religious beliefs, affiliations, and practices of clinical psychologists. In E. P. Shafranske (Ed.), *Religion and the clinical practice of psychology* (pp. 149–162). Washington, DC: American Psychological Association.

Shafranske, E. P. (2000). Psychotherapy with Roman Catholics. In P. S. Richards & A. E. Bergin (Eds.), *Handbook of psychotherapy and religious diversity* (pp. 59–88). Washington, DC: American Psychological Association.

Sharma, A. R. (2000). Psychotherapy with Hindus. In P. S. Richards & A. E. Bergin (Eds.), *Handbook of psychotherapy and religious diversity* (pp. 341–365). Washington, DC: American Psychological Association.

Shattuck, C. (1999). *Hinduism.* Upper Saddle River, NJ: Prentice-Hall.

Shrodes, C. (1950). *Bibliotherapy: A theoretical and clinical-experimental study.* Unpublished doctoral dissertation, University of California, Berkeley.

Siegel, R. J., Choldin, S., & Orost, J. H. (1995). Impact of three patriarchal religions on women. In J. C. Chrisler & A. H. Hemstreet (Eds.), *Variations on a theme: Diversity and the psychology of women* (pp. 107–144). Albany: State University of New York Press.

Simmons, J. (2001). Headlines: Study: Lack of spirit may shorten life. *Counseling Today, 44,* 3.

Singh, K. (1998). Sikhism. In *The new encyclopedia Britannica* (Vol. 27, p. 284). Chicago: Encyclopedia Britannica.

Singh, N.-G. K. (1993). *Sikhism: World religions.* New York: Facts on File.

Skinner, B. F. (1953). *Science and human behavior.* New York: Macmillan.

Sloat, D. (1990). *Growing up holy and wholly: Understanding and hope for adult children of Evangelicals.* Brentwood, NJ: Wolgemugh & Hyatt.

Sollod, R. N. (1993). Integrating spiritual healing approaches and techniques into psychotherapy. In G. Stricker & J. R. Gold (Eds.), *Comprehensive handbook of psychotherapy integration* (pp. 237–248). New York: Plenum Press.

Solomon, N. (1996). *Judaism: A very short introduction.* New York: Oxford University Press.

Sonne, J. L. (1999). Multiple relationships: Does the new ethics code answer the right questions. In

D. N. Bersoff (Ed.), *Ethical conflicts in psychology* (2nd ed., pp. 227–230). Washington, DC: American Psychological Association.

Sopa, G. L. (1985). *The special theory of pratityasamutpada: The cycle of dependent origination.* Oregon, WI: Deer Park.

Sparks, E. E., & Park, A. H. (2000). The integration of feminism and multiculturalism: Ethical dilemmas at the border. In M. M. Brabeck (Ed.), *Practicing feminist ethics in psychology* (pp. 203–224). Washington, DC: American Psychological Association.

Spelman, E. V. (1988). *Inessential woman: Problems of exclusion in feminist thought.* Boston: Beacon Press.

Spero, M. H. (1981). Countertransference in religious therapists of religious patients. *American Journal of Psychotherapy, 35,* 565–576.

Spero, M. H. (1985). Transference as a religious phenomenon in psychotherapy. *Journal of Religion and Health, 24,* 8–25.

Sperry, L., & Giblin, P. (1996). Marital and family therapy with religious persons. In E. P. Shafranske (Ed.), *Religion and the clinical practice of psychology* (pp. 511–532). Washington, DC: American Psychological Association.

Spilka, B. (1986). Spiritual issues: Do they belong in psychological practice? Yes-But! *Psychotherapy in Private Practice, 4,* 93–100.

Spiritual compentencies. (2000, Winter). *Interaction, 4,* 6.

Sprunger, M. (n.d.). *An introduction to Shinto.* Retrieved November 30, 2001, from http://www.fefadmin.org/archive/readers/601_shinto.htm.

Stem, E. M. (1985). Psychotheology of religious commitment. In E. M. Stem (Ed.), *Psychotherapy and the religiously committed patient* (pp. 1–11). New York: Haworth.

Stotland, N. L. (1999). When religion collides with medicine. *American Journal of Psychiatry, 156,* 304–308.

Suler, J. R. (1993). *Contemporary psychoanalysis and Eastern thought.* Albany: State University of New York Press.

Surry, J. (1985). The "self-in-relation": A theory of women's development. *Work in progress* (No. 13). Wellesley, MA: Stone Center Working Papers Series.

Swearingen, C. J. (1994). Women's ways of writing, or, images, self-images, and graven images. *College Composition and Communication, 45,* 251–263.

Talbot, G. D. (1990). Commentary on "divine intervention and the treatment of chemical dependency." *Journal of Substance Abuse, 2,* 460–471.

Tan, S.-Y. (1996). Religion in clinical practice: Implicit and explicit integration. In E. P. Shafranske (Ed.), *Religion and the clinical practice of psychology* (pp. 365–387). Washington, DC: American Psychological Association.

Tan, S.-Y. (2000). Religion and psychotherapy. In A. E. Kazdin (Ed.), *Encyclopedia of psychology.* Washington, DC: American Psychological Association/Oxford University Press.

Tan, S.-Y., & Dong, N. J. (2000). Psychotherapy with members of Asian American churches and spiritual traditions. In E. P. Shafranske (Ed.), *Religion and the clinical practice of psychology* (pp. 421–444). Washington, DC: American Psychological Association.

Theodore, R. M. (1992). Utilization of spiritual values in counseling: An ignored dimension. In M. T. Burke & J. G. Miranti (Eds.), *Ethical and spiritual values in counseling* (pp. 17–22). Alexandria, VA: American Counseling Association.

Thompson, L. G. (1993). What is Taoism? *Taoist Resources, 4,* 9–22.

Thurrell, R. J. (2000). Religion and spirituality in the lives of psychiatrists and their patients. *Psychiatric Annals, 30,* 556–559.

Thurston, N. (2000). Psychotherapy with evangelical and fundamentalist protestants. In P. S. Richards & A. E. Bergin (Eds.), *Handbook of psychotherapy and religious diversity* (pp. 131–153). Washington, DC: American Psychological Association.

Tick, E. (1992). Attending the soul. *Voices, 28,* 7–8.

Ulrich, W. L., Richards, P. S., & Bergin, A. E. (2000). Psychotherapy with Latter-Day Saints. In P. S. Richards & A. E. Bergin (Eds.), *Handbook of psychotherapy and religious diversity* (pp. 185–209). Washington, DC: American Psychological Association.

Vande Kemp, H. (1996). Historical perspective: Religion and clinical psychology in America. In

E. P. Shafranske (Ed.), *Religion and the clinical practice of psychology* (pp. 71–112). Washington, DC: American Psychological Association.

Vedanthan, P. K., Lakshmyya, N. K., Murthy, K. C., Duvall, K., Hall, M. J., Baker, S., et al. (1998). Clinical study of yoga techniques in university students with asthma: A controlled study. *Allergy and Asthma Procedures, 19*, 3–9.

Wallis, C. (1996, June 24). Faith and healing. *Time*, 58–64.

Wangu, M. B. (1991). *Hinduism*. New York: Facts on File.

Wangu, M. B. (1993). *Buddhism: World religions*. New York: Facts on File.

West, W. (2000). *Psychotherapy & spirituality*. Thousand Oaks, CA: Sage.

Westgate, C. E. (1996). Spiritual wellness and depression. *Journal of Counseling and Development, 75*, 26–35.

Williams, R. C., & Myer, R. A. (1992). The men's movement: An adjunct to traditional counseling approaches. *Journal of Mental Health Counseling, 14*, 393–404.

Wilson, J. (1980). *Chandrakirti's sevenfold reasoning: Meditation on the selflessness of persons*. Dharmsala, H. P. India: Library of Tibetan Works and Archives.

Wolgien, C. S., & Coady, N. F. (1997). Good therapists' beliefs about the development of their helping ability: The wounded healer paradigm revisited. *Clinical Supervisor, 15*, 19–35.

Wright, E. (1999). Lucia Rijker. *Rolling Stone, 814*, 101–103.

Wulff, D. M. (1996). The psychology of religion: An overview. In E. P. Shafranske (Ed.), *Religion and the clinical practice of psychology* (pp. 43–70). Washington, DC: American Psychological Association.

Wulff, D. M. (1997). *Psychology of religion: Classic and contemporary*. New York: Wiley.

Yao, X. (2000). *An introduction to Confucianism*. New York: Cambridge University Press.

Yarhouse, M. A., & VanOrman, B. T. (1999). When psychologists work with religious clients: Application of the general principles of ethical conduct. *Professional Psychology: Research and Practice, 30*, 557–562.

Young, K. K. (1994). Introduction. In A. Sharma (Ed.), *Religion and women* (pp. 1–38). New York: State University of New York Press.

Young, T. R. (2000). Psychotherapy with Eastern Orthodox Christians. In P. S. Richards & A. E. Bergin (Eds.), *Handbook of psychotherapy and religious diversity* (pp. 89–104). Washington, DC: American Psychological Association.

Youniss, J., McLellan, J. A., & Yates, M. (1999). Religion, community service, and identity in American youth. *Journal of Adolescence, 22*, 243–253.

Zeiger, M., & Lewis, J. E. (1998). The spiritually responsible therapist: Religious material in the psychotherapeutic setting. *Psychotherapy, 35*, 415–424.

Zinnbauer, B. J., & Pargament, K. I. (2000). Working with the sacred: Four approaches to religious and spiritual issues in counseling. *Journal of Counseling and Development, 78*, 162–171.

Zydenbos, R. J. (1993). *The concept of divinity in Jainism*. Toronto, Ontario, Canada: University of Toronto, Centre for South Asian Studies.

Author Index

Aay, K. R., 66, 302
Abernathy, A. D., 27, 28, 34, 122, 127, 128, 297
Albany, A. P., 150, 297
Albright, R. H., 31, 297
Al-Krenawi, A., 207, 297
Allison, D., 35, 297
Allport, G. W., 22, 31, 32, 297, 298, 299
Alpers, R. R., 156, 297
Andreas, B., 11, 297
Arena, P., 5, 303
Astin, J. A., 204, 205, 297
Atkinson, D. R., 56, 297

Baker, B., 1, 297
Baker, S., 307
Baldwin, D. C., 158, 303
Ballou, M., 49, 297
Barna, G., 53, 297
Barnett, J. E., 164, 166, 176, 177, 182, 297
Batson, C. D., 143, 160, 297
Becvar, D. S., 191, 205, 214, 297
Belenky, M. F., 202, 297
Benson, H., 204, 206, 297
Bergin, A. E., 3, 6, 11, 13, 14, 19, 23, 30, 32, 33, 70, 89, 117, 131, 145, 164, 172, 173, 174, 176, 178, 181, 182, 188, 195, 196, 197, 211, 214, 297, 298, 299, 301, 303, 304, 305, 306, 307
Bertand, W., 158, 304
Berthrong, E. N., 109, 110, 298
Berthrong, J. H., 109, 110, 298
Bibbins, K., 157, 298

Birdsall, B., 164, 179, 298
Birodkar, S., 81, 298
Bishop, D. R., 23, 56, 133, 135, 298
Boeree, C. G., 31, 298
Bonvillain, N., 84, 89, 298
Bowdein, H. W., 62, 298
Brady, J. L., 29, 298
Breuilly, E., 81, 82, 95, 100, 102, 103, 104, 112, 298
Brokaw, B. F., 29, 36, 298, 300
Brown, H. P., 153, 298
Brown-Anderson, F., 303
Bullock, S. L., 164, 180, 300
Burke, M. T., 129, 297, 298, 306
Byrd, E. K., 54, 157, 298

Cadwalader, S. L., 83, 298
Canda, E. R., 192, 298
Cantwell, 45, 298
Carr, W., 36, 298
Carrington, P., 204, 298
Chapman, R. J., 156, 298
Chappelle, W., 166, 177, 178, 181, 182, 298
Chen, M., 110, 303
Childress, D., 100, 298
Chodron, P., 22, 298
Choldin, S., 46, 305
Christ, C. P., 50, 299
Christian, M., 23, 299
Clark, P., 77, 80, 89, 299
Clements, G., 205, 299
Clinchy, B. M., 202, 297
Coady, N. F., 158, 307
Cochran, S. V., 52, 304
Cohen, L. J., 199, 201, 299
Corey, G., 36, 299

Cornett, C., 6, 126, 127, 128, 129, 130, 140, 299
Cort, J. E., 102, 117, 299
Corveleyn, J., 25, 299
Cowen, E. L., 156, 299
Csikszentmihalyi, M., 157, 162, 305
Cunningham, O., 153, 298
Curtis, R. C., 157, 173, 299

Das, A. K., 37, 299
Dastoor, D. P., 77, 299
Davis, J., 32, 299
Davis, K. M., 157, 173, 299
Daya, R., 38, 204, 205, 299
DeLange, N., 58, 60, 89, 299
Denzin, N. K., 207, 299
De Silva, P., 38, 299
Dhalla, H. B., 77, 78, 89, 299
Dobbins, R. D., 69, 195, 299
Dong, N. J., 110, 112, 114, 306
Duvall, K., 307

Edwards, K. J., 36, 300
Ehrlich, M. P., 38, 55, 299
Elias, J. J., 74, 75, 76, 89, 299
Elkind, D., 52, 299
Elkind, S., 52, 299
Eller, M., 303
Epp, L., 298
Evans, R., 31, 50, 299, 303
Everson, 45, 299

Faiver, C., 204, 207, 214, 299
Farnsworth, K. E., 39, 299
Fielding, R. G., 123, 299
Fiorentino, N., 164, 166, 176, 177, 182, 297
Fisher, M. P., 81, 89, 299

Fleming, W., 4, 73, 303
Flood, G., 94, 95, 117, 300
Flores, P. J., 4, 155, 300
Fowler, J., 95, 97, 117, 141, 300
Freud, S., 22, 24, 25, 31, 133, 300
Fromm, E., 22, 31, 32, 298, 300
Fukuyama, M. A., 50, 55, 84, 89, 190, 191, 207, 210, 300

Gandhi, S. L., 94, 104, 300
Gardner, P., 143, 303
Garrett, M., 83, 84, 86, 89, 197, 300
Gartner, J., 3, 300
Gendler, J. R., 121, 300
Genia, V., 129, 146, 171, 190, 300
George, L. K., 54, 302
Gethin, R., 107, 300
Giblin, P., 196, 306
Glasgow, S., 303
Goldberger, N. R., 202, 297
Goldstein, S. V., 199, 300
Gordon, M., 74, 94, 300
Granello, D. H., 51, 300
Green, W. S., 45, 300
Gregory, K., 303
Grevengoed, N., 304
Grossman, S., 60, 300
Guinee, J. P., 29, 181, 300
Guy, J. D., 29, 298

Hackney, H., 298
Hall, M. J., 307
Hall, T. W., 36, 300
Hamilton, K., 143, 303
Harris, I. M., 51, 300
Hartz, P., 112, 117, 300
Hathaway, W., 304
Haug, I. E., 178, 190, 300
Hausdorff, D., 31, 300
Haut, R., 60, 300
Hawkins, I. L., 164, 180, 300
Hawks, S. R., 204, 300
Hazler, R. J., 156, 301
Henderson, L., 303
Henning, L. H., 35, 300

Hermon, D. A., 156, 301
Hermsen, E., 37, 301
Hesselgrave, D. J., 39, 301
Hickson, J., 24, 301
High, H. J., 4, 304
Hinterkopf, E., 201, 301
Hogan, L., 50, 301
Hoge, D. R., 123, 301
Hogwood, W., 303
Hoobler, D., 109, 117, 301
Hoobler, T., 109, 117, 301
Housley, W., 24, 301
Houston, J., 210, 302
Hudson, P., 298
Hull, M. L., 204, 300
Humphries, R. H., 29, 301

Ingersoll, R. E., 204, 214, 299
Ingvarson, E. P., 4, 155, 302

Jacobs, J. L., 210, 301
Jaffee, M., 59, 301
Jain, S. J., 104, 301
Jain, S. K., 103, 104, 117, 301
James, W., 22, 31, 32, 127, 297, 301
Johanson, G., 113, 117, 301
Johnson, P., 4, 182, 301, 303
Johnson, W. B., 182, 202, 302
Jones, W., 304
Judge, M. G., 4, 153, 301
Jung, C. G., 22, 31, 32, 298

Kabat-Zinn, J., 205, 301
Kahoe, R. E., 28, 301
Kaiser, D. L., 161, 301
Keller, R. R., 66, 69, 72, 82, 83, 301
Kelly, E. W., 4, 6, 19, 25, 129, 130, 142, 146, 150, 161, 189, 193, 194, 204, 210, 301
Kennell, J., 304
Khantzian, E. J., 4, 155, 301
Kochems, T., 122, 126, 128, 301
Koenig, H. G., 2, 53, 54, 147, 193, 194, 214, 302, 304
Kogan, M., 157, 302

Kohn, L., 112, 302
Krasner, L., 26, 302
Krenner, L., 205, 299
Kristeller, J. L., 205, 302
Kurtz, E., 153, 302, 303
Kurtz, R., 113, 117, 301
Kus, R. J., 156, 297, 302

Lahav, R., 113, 302
Lakshmyya, N. K., 307
Lal, A., 103, 302
Lal, V., 103, 302
Lancia, J. J., 27, 28, 34, 122, 127, 128, 297
Lannert, J. L., 28, 180, 183, 302
Larson, D. B., 2, 53, 66, 191, 192, 193, 302
Lassiter, P., 143, 303
Le, C., 4, 155, 302
LeShan, L., 204, 302
Lester, R. C., 105, 106, 107, 108, 117, 302
Lewin, N., 303
Lewis, J. E., 22, 24, 35, 129, 140, 307
Lincoln, C. E., 72, 73, 302
Lincoln, L. N., 72, 302
Linder, S., 202, 203, 302
Llewelyn, S., 123, 299
Lovinger, R. J., 29, 53, 59, 61, 72, 129, 142, 147, 148, 159, 162, 302, 303
Lovinger, S. L., 53, 302
Lu, F. G., 145, 302
Lukoff, D., 145, 146, 302

Mack, J. E., 4, 155, 301
Mamiya, L. H., 72, 73, 302
Marlatt, G. A., 205, 302
Masters, R., 33, 86, 107, 111, 112, 210, 302
Matthews, D. A., 53, 302
Mattson, D. L., 34, 302
May, R., 158, 304
McBride, J., 133, 302
McClelland, D., 49, 302
McCloud, A. B., 76, 77, 89, 302

McCullough, M. E., 2, 66, 191, 192, 193, 302
McFadden, J., 73, 83, 84, 303
McGrath, A. E., 62, 63, 89, 303
McLellan, J. A., 52, 307
McLeod, H., 81, 89, 303
McNally, C., 204, 214, 299
Meadow, M. J., 28, 209, 301
Miller, G., 4, 5, 14, 50, 55, 57, 73, 110, 122, 127, 141, 143, 144, 146, 153, 154, 156, 157, 158, 162, 175, 202, 302, 303
Miller, J. B., 49, 303
Miller, L., 53, 59, 61, 302, 303
Ming-Dao, 7, 303
Miranti, J., 297, 298, 306
Molk, W., 205, 299
Morgan, R., 13, 303
Morris, J. R., 74, 303
Morten, G., 56, 297
Mountain, D. A., 24, 303
Muir, W. J., 24, 303
Murthy, K. C., 307
Myer, R. A., 52, 307
Myers, B. K., 207, 303
Myers, D. G., 15, 157, 303

Neusner, J., 45, 179, 300, 304
Newman, J., 304
Nielsen, S. L., 182, 301
Nigosian, S. A., 79, 304
Northrup, M., 100, 304
Nyanaponika, T., 11, 304

O'Brien, E., 204, 214, 299
O'Brien, J., 95, 298
O'Dwyer, P., 153, 304
Ogden, J., 157, 304
Orost, J. H., 46, 305

Page, R. C., 4, 155, 302
Palmer, M., 95, 298
Pargament, K. I., 2, 11, 133, 135, 140, 147, 159, 210, 304, 307
Park, A. H., 106, 179, 306
Parrinder, G., 76, 95, 304

Parsons, F., 32, 304
Pate, R. H., 4, 304
Pattison, E. M., 126, 304
Payne, I. R., 164, 188, 298
Pendleton, B. F., 191, 304
Perez, L., 147, 304
Peterson, B. L., 54, 302
Peterson, J. H., 153, 298
Picken, S. D. B., 100, 101, 117, 304
Pike, P. L., 36, 300
Pitts, M., 156, 304
Poelstra, P. L., 29, 298
Poloma, M. M., 191, 304
Pritchett, J., 193, 194, 302
Propst, L. R., 2, 304

Rabinor, J. R., 202, 204, 304
Rabinowitz, A., 196, 304
Rabinowitz, F. E., 52, 304
Raboteau, A. J., 72, 73, 89, 304
Rainer, T., 202, 304
Rando, T. A., 207, 304
Reader, I., 100, 117, 304
Rector, J. M., 127, 305
Remen, N., 158, 304
Reynolds, F. E., 105, 305
Richards, P. S., 3, 6, 11, 13, 14, 19, 23, 30, 43, 70, 89, 117, 127, 131, 145, 164, 172, 173, 174, 176, 178, 181, 182, 188, 195, 196, 197, 211, 214, 298, 299, 301, 303, 304, 305, 306, 307
Richins, P. M., 204, 300
Ridley, C. R., 182, 301
Rigal-Cellard, B., 85, 305
Rinbochay, L., 11, 305
Riordan, R. J., 4, 305
Rizzuto, A. M., 36, 305
Robinson, B. A., 111, 305
Robinson, D. T., 74, 303
Rogers, C. R., 37, 57, 301, 305
Ross, N., 12, 305

Schank, J. A., 176, 305
Schiffman, L. H., 58, 305
Seligman, M. E. P., 157, 162, 305

Sevig, T. D., 50, 55, 84, 89, 190, 191, 207, 210, 300
Shafii, M., 204, 305
Shafranske, E. P., 14, 16, 19, 24, 43, 62, 65, 127, 162, 188, 214, 298, 300, 301, 302, 304, 305, 306, 307
Sharma, A. R., 97, 98, 99, 117, 305, 307
Shattuck, C., 94, 95, 96, 98, 99, 305
Shrodes, C., 199, 305
Siegel, R. J., 46, 49, 50, 60, 61, 62, 63, 64, 67, 68, 95, 96, 98, 305
Simmons, J., 2, 305
Singh, K., 81, 82, 83, 89, 118, 305
Skinner, B. F., 22, 26, 305
Skovholt, T. M., 176, 305
Sloat, D., 68, 305
Smelzer, R., 303
Smith, B. W., 70, 147, 304
Sollod, R. N., 189, 305
Solomon, N., 59, 60, 89, 305
Sonne, J. L., 175, 305
Sopa, G. L., 11, 306
Sparks, E. E., 179, 306
Spelman, E. V., 49, 306
Spero, M. H., 126, 129, 130, 306
Sperry, L., 196, 306
Spilka, B., 146, 147, 159, 160, 306
Sprunger, M., 100, 306
Stem, E. M., 26, 36, 106, 128, 145, 150, 306
Stotland, N. L., 29, 306
Sue, D. W., 56, 297
Suler, J. R., 36, 37, 46, 306
Surry, J., 49, 306
Swearingen, C. J., 203, 306
Swyers, J. P., 2, 302

Talbot, G. D., 306
Tan, S.-Y., 110, 112, 114, 131, 140, 149, 192, 194, 196, 197, 306

Tarule, J. M., 202, 297
Thalman, R. L., 204, 300
Theodore, R. M., 24, 306
Thompson, L. G., 111, 306
Thoresen, C. E., 2, 3, 6, 303
Thurrell, R. J., 24, 28, 306
Thurston, N., 67, 68, 197, 199, 306
Tick, E., 12, 22, 306
Tirrell, F. J., 35, 300
Tjeltveit, A. C., 127, 305
Turner, R., 145, 302

Ulrich, W. L., 70, 71, 306

Valentine, M., 303
Vande Kemp, H., 30, 32, 33, 43, 306
VanOrman, B. T., 166, 173, 177, 178, 182, 307

Vedanthan, P. K., 204, 307
Ventis, W. L., 143, 160, 297

Wages, D., 24, 301
Wallis, C., 1, 307
Walsh, L., 4, 305
Wangu, M. B., 95, 106, 107, 108, 118, 307
Watts, G. A., 298
Weaver, A. J., 66, 143, 302
West, W., 2, 6, 7, 12, 19, 22, 25, 80, 81, 95, 98, 106, 129, 130, 140, 192, 195, 196, 197, 307
Westgate, C. E., 157, 307
Williams, R. C., 52, 307
Wilson, J., 11, 307
Wolgien, C. S., 158, 307
Wright, E., 11, 307

Wulff, D. M., 22, 23, 25, 26, 31, 191, 307

Yang, J., 37, 110, 112, 303
Yao, X., 109, 110, 307
Yarhouse, M. A., 166, 173, 177, 178, 182, 307
Yates, M., 52, 307
Young, D., 158, 304
Young, K. K., 50, 71, 78, 81, 83, 307
Young, T. R., 64, 307
Youngblood, C., 50, 303
Youniss, J., 52, 307

Zeiger, M., 22, 24, 35, 129, 140, 307
Zinnbauer, B. J., 133, 135, 140, 307
Zydenbos, R. J., 102, 104, 307

Subject Index

Abortion, 65–66, 67
Academy of Religion and Mental Health, 33
Accreditation. *See* Council for Accreditation of
    Counseling and Related Educational
    Programs (CACREP) standards/accreditation
Actualizing tendency, 37
Addiction recovery, 153–156
Adolescents, 181–182
African Americans:
  Islam, 91
  religion in United States, 72–74
    model, six-pair dialectical, 73–74
    overview of beliefs, 72–73
    possible impact of belief on counseling,
      73–74
  Web sites, 91
Age, spirituality and, 52–54, 99, 151, 191
Al-Anon, 155, 156
Alcoholics Anonymous, 4, 154, 155
Alcoholism, prayer and, 147
Allport, Gordon (historical figure in developing
    link between spirituality and psychology), 31,
    32
AMCAP (Association of Mormon Counselors and
    Psychotherapists), 71
American Academy of Religion, 33
American-based denominations, 67, 69–72
American Counseling Association (ACA), 3, 33
American culture, growing interest in spirituality,
    1, 45
American Foundation of Religion and Psychiatry,
    33
American Psychiatric Association (APA), 24
American Psychological Association (APA), 3,
    156
Amnesty International United States (AIUSA)
    Interfaith Network for Human Rights, 2
Asian Americans, and Eastern religions, 113–114
Assemblies of God, 69

Assessment:
  biopsychosocial, 28–29
  of client's religious and spiritual views, 48,
    145–149
  determining religious/secular counseling,
    171–172, 190
    amount of client disturbance and, 171, 172,
      190
    client comfort with secular counseling and,
      171, 172, 190
    type of religious issues, 171, 190
  of a religious/spiritual community's health, 198
  religious readings and, 196
  sexual behavior or orientation and, 146
Association for Spiritual, Ethical, and Religious
    Values in Counseling (ASERVIC), 3, 6
Association for Spiritual, Ethical, and Religious
    Values in Counseling (in American
    Counseling Association), 33
Atomism, 25
Attunement, 34

Baptists, 47, 67, 72
Barriers between spirituality/religion and therapy,
    23–30
BASIC ID Sp, 173
Behavior, explanatory approach to, 24
Behaviorism, 26
Bible:
  African Americans and, 72
  religious adjustment/pathology and, 148, 149
  types of religious counselor and:
    BGG type counselor (Bible-grounded and
      Bible-guided), 39
    CBS type counselor (Christ-centered, Bible-
      based, and Spirit-inspired), 39
Bibliotherapy, 199–200
  changes in ways of feeling and ways of
    knowing, 201

313

Bibliotherapy *(Continued)*
  interactive use of, 199
  psychosocial support, 199
  questions for counselor/for client (before/after assignment), 200
  self-help, 199
Biopsychosocial assessment, 28–29
Black religion in United States. *See* African Americans
Boundaries of counselor's work settings, 181–182
"Breathing under water," 51
Buddhism:
  forms of, 37, 106
  Four Noble Truths, 107–108
  mind (defined; Tibetan), 11
  overview of beliefs, 106–108
  perspective applied to counseling, 38
  possible impact of beliefs on counseling, 108
  statistics, 105–106
  Web sites, 118–119
Buffers (mental health and illness), 157

Catholics, 62, 63, 65–66
Christian Association for Psychological Studies, 33
Christian counselors:
  in secular counseling agency (disclosure), 181
  types:
    BGG (Bible-grounded and Bible-guided), 39
    CBS (Christ-centered, Bible-based, and Spirit-inspired), 39
    CNO: Christians in Name Only, 39
Christianity, 62–74. *See also specific denomination/ group*
  classification/groups, 62, 63
    American-based denominations, 69–72
    Black churches, 72–73
    Catholic, 65–66
    Eastern Orthodox, 64–65
    Protestant, 66–69
  dominance of, 46
  overview of beliefs, 62–63
  possible impact of beliefs on counseling, 63–64
  statistics, 62
  twelve-step programs and, 4, 153
  variance in denominations of, 46
  Web sites, 90
"Christian privilege," 46

Christian Science, 72, 142
Church and state, separation of, 45, 124, 181
Church of Jesus Christ of Latter-Day Saints. *See* Latter Day Saints (Mormons)
Client(s):
  amount of disturbance and secular *vs.* religious counseling, 171, 172, 190
  assessment of religious and spiritual views of, 48, 145–149
  comfort with secular counseling and, 171, 172, 190
  dual/multiple relationships with, 175–177
  issues (religious/nonreligious), 150
  relationship dynamics, 175
  story as metaphor, 7, 89
  taxonomy of responsiveness:
    hostile to religion, 151, 189
    nonreligious, 151, 189
    religiously and spiritually open, 150, 189
    religiously committed, 150, 189
    religiously loyal, 150, 189
    religiously tolerant and indifferent, 151, 189
    spiritually committed, 150, 189
    superficially religious, 150–151, 189
  testing counselor, 8
  transference (*see* Transference)
  type of religious issues, 171, 190
Client-Centered therapy, 37
Cognitive psychology, 31, 32–33
Collaborative style, 147
Colloquial prayer, 191
Community(ies):
  assessment of a religious community's spiritual health, 198
  referral to religious professional in, 135–136, 197
  religious community (as treatment technique), 197–199
  small (and dual/multiple relationships with clients), 175–177
  supportive spiritual, 15–17
Competence, counselor, 132, 182–184
Confession (as ritual), 14
Confucianism:
  overview of beliefs, 109–110
  possible impact of beliefs on counseling, 110–111

statistics, 108–109
Web sites, 119
Conjunctive (stage in faith development model), 142
Conservational coping, 11
Constructivist (counselor orientation), 133, 134, 135
Consultation, 34
Conversion, attempts at, 5, 29
Coping:
    collaborative, 147
    conservational, 11
    deferring, 147
    older adults, 53
    pleading, 147
    self-directing, 147
    spiritual realm as resource for, 23, 53, 54
    transformational, 11
Council for Accreditation of Counseling and Related Educational Programs (CACREP) standards/accreditation, 3, 4
Counseling, incorporating spirituality in, 1–19. *See also* Integration
    avenues, 153–158
        addiction recovery, 153–156
        wellness/positive psychology, 156–157
        wounded healer framework of counseling, 158
    case application, 151–153
    creation of a sacred place, 6–9
    encouragement of self-care, 9–11
    encouragement of spiritual practice, 11–17
        refuge, 12–13
        ritual, 13–14
        safe places, 14–15
        sense of community, 15–17
    ethical issues (*see* Ethical issues)
    exercises/case studies, 158–162
    helping clients develop a spiritual identity, 141–151
        assessment, 145–149
        supervision, 142–145
        treatment, 149–153
    historical perspective on (*see* Psychology and religion, historical development)
    honoring client's story, 8–9
    impact of specific religions (*see* Eastern religions; Western religions)

interventions (*see* Interventions, religious/spiritual)
    questions (three) to be addressed, 5, 141
    safety, 7–8
    suggested readings, 162
    treatment (*see* Interventions, religious/spiritual; Techniques, specific)
Counselor(s):
    boundaries of work settings, 181–182
    competence, 132, 182–184
    constructivist orientation, 133, 134, 135
    disclosure, inappropriate, 29
    empathetic-interest-in-other-people view, 179
    exclusivist orientation, 133, 134, 179
    focus, 9
    inclusivist orientation, 179
    nonverbal messages (office/attire), 8
    orientations, 133
    pluralist orientation, 133, 134–135, 179
    reactions/biases (*see* Countertransference)
    rejectionist orientation, 133–134
    self awareness, 180
    self disclosure when using prayer with clients, 195
    training, counselor, 4, 189–190 (*see also* Supervision)
Countertransference, 26–30, 128–131. *See also* Transference
    behaviors (six) that may indicate, 129–130
    in case application, 152–153
    extremes on a continuum, 129
    interreligious/intrareligious, 28
    negative (occurring in two main ways), 129
    recommendations, 130, 142, 163–164
    suggestions for working with, 56, 94
    supervision and, 130–131, 142–143, 152–153
    trauma survivors and, 29–30
Crisis, and religious faith, 15
Cults, 123–124
Cultural issues:
    clients, 5, 191
    cultural isolation, 124
    ethical issues, and counselor understanding of context of culture, 180
    multicultural counseling, 46, 55–62, 133–136

Decision-making tree, ethical, 165
Deferring style, 147

Determinism, 25
Disability, 54–55
Diversity. *See* Cultural issues
Dual/multiple relationships, 175–177

Eastern Orthodox, 62, 63, 64–65
Eastern religions, 93–119
   Buddhism, 105–108
   case studies/exercises, 114–117
   chronology/timeline, 93
   Confucianism, 108–111
   Hinduism, 94–99
   integrating Eastern/Western ideas, 37
   Jainism, 102–105
   overview, 93
   Shintoism, 99–102
   suggested readings, 117–118
   Taoism, 110–114
   Web sites, 118–119
Elderly, 53, 99
Empathetic-interest-in-other-people view, 179
Ends (spiritual continuum), 143, 144–145
Ethical decision-making tree, 165, 190
Ethical issues, 163–188
   boundaries of counselor's work settings,
      181–182
   case studies and exercises, 184–188
   codes/guidelines, 164
   collaboration with clients' religious leaders,
      177–178
   counselor's area of competence, 182–184, 190
   determination of secular or religious
      counseling, 171–172
   development of a spiritual identity, 172–175
   dual/multiple relationships, 175–177
   informed consent, 164–170
      sample form, professional disclosure
         statement, 167–168
      sample form, stating spiritual/religious
         perspective, 169–170
   overview, 163–164
   respect for clients' religious or spiritual values,
      178–181
   suggested readings, 188
Ethical relativism, 24
European perspectives *vs.* North American,
   incorporating spirituality, 25

Evangelicals, 67, 197
Exclusivist (counselor orientation), 133, 134,
   179
Exercises/case studies:
   counseling focus integration, 158–162
   Eastern religions, 114–117
   ethical issues, 184–188
   historical development, 39–43
   introduction, 17–19
   theoretical integration, 136–140
   treatment techniques, 211–214
   Western religions, 86–89
Existence, making sense of our, 34–39
   psychological perspectives, 36–38
   religious perspectives, 38–39
Existence of Higher Power (*vs.* scientific view of
   psychology), 26
Existential(ism):
   humanistic-existential psychology, 31
   questions (misinterpretation of), 28, 128
   rituals, 207
Explicit integration, 131, 149–150, 193

Faith development model (stages listed),
   141–142
Feminist perspective. *See* Women
First Amendment, 45–46
Focusing technique (six steps), 201–202
Fromm, Erich (historical figure in developing link
   between spirituality and psychology), 31, 32
Fundamentalists, 67–68, 197
Funerals, 14

Gender, 49–52, 191
Guided imagery, 205–210

Healer, wounded (framework of counseling), 158
Healing, using self-care for, 10–11
Healing prayer, inner (technique), 194
Health:
   defined, 2
   psychology, 156–157
   spirituality and, 2–3
Higher Power:
   existence of (*vs.* scientific view of psychology),
      26
   "of your choosing" (twelve step programs), 156

use of term instead of "God," 147
Higher Power box (prayer technique), 192–193
Hinduism, 94–99
    humanistic perspective, and similarity of
        Maslow and Rogers to Vendandic, 37
    overview of beliefs, 95–96
    possible impact of beliefs on counseling, 97–99
    statistics, 94–95
    Web sites, 118
Hostile to religion (client taxonomy), 151
Humanistic-existential psychology, 31
Humanistic psychology, 37–38

Idealizing transference, 126
Identity, spiritual. *See* Spiritual identity, helping
    clients develop
Illusory (religious control), 146
Imagery. *See* Guided imagery
Implicit integration, 131, 149, 192
Inclusivist counselor view, 179
Individuative-reflective (stage in faith
    development model), 142
Informed consent, 164–170, 190–191
    sample form, professional disclosure statement,
        167–168
    sample form, stating spiritual/religious
        perspective, 169–170
Inner healing prayer, 194
Integration, 121–140
    bridges between spirituality/religion and
        therapy, 30–39
    continuum of, 132–133, 149
    countertransference issues, 128–131
    cultural implications, 133–136
    evidence of, in professional journals, 33
    exercises/case studies, 136–140
    explicit, 131, 149–150
    implicit, 131, 149
    intentional, 131–132, 149, 150
    professional societies emphasizing, 33
    suggested readings, 140
    therapy integration, 121–126
    three-Rs approach (refuge, rituals, and
        resources), 122–123, 149
    transference issues, 126–128
    types of, 131–133, 149
Intentional integration, 131–132, 150

Intercessory prayer, 191
Interpretation, 34
Interpretive (religious control), 146
Interreligious countertransference/transference,
    28, 128
Interventions, religious/spiritual:
    documenting, 181–182
    general process suggestions (list) for using, 174
    meditation/relaxation/imagery, 204–207
    prayer, 191–195
    rituals, 207–211
    sacred writings (religious bibliotherapy),
        195–197
    techniques, 191–199, 204–211
    use of religious community, 197–199
Intrareligious countertransference/transference,
    28, 128
Introject, 36
Intuitive-projective (stage in faith development
    model), 141–142
Islam:
    African American, 91
    overview of beliefs, 74–76
    possible impact of beliefs on counseling, 76–77
    statistics, 74
    Web sites, 91
Isolation:
    attitudes, 122
    cultural isolation, 124
    interpersonal, 122

Jainism:
    overview of beliefs, 103–104
    possible impact of beliefs on counseling,
        104–105
    statistics, 102–103
    Web sites, 118
James, William (historical figure in developing
    link between spirituality and psychology), 31
Jehovah's Witnesses:
    beliefs of, 70, 71–72
    classification within Protestants, 67, 69
    medical situation, 29
    Web sites, 90–91
Job interviews, 125–126
Journal(s), professional (evidence of integration
    in), 33

Journal writing (technique), 202–204
Judaism:
    overview of beliefs, 58–60
    possible impact of beliefs on counseling, 60–62
    statistics, 58
    Web sites, 89–90
Jung, Carl (historical figure in developing link between spirituality and psychology), 31, 32

Latter Day Saints (Mormons):
    beliefs, 69–71
    classification, 67, 69
    Family Services, 71
    history, 70–71
    possible issues, 71
    Web sites, 90
Limit setting, 196–197
Literacy level, 151
Lutherans, 47, 66

Male socialization/spirituality, 51–52
    mythopoetic approach of men's movement, 52
    ten tenets of male spirituality, 51–52
Marriage, 65, 66, 98
Meaninglessness, issues related to experiencing, 7
Means (spiritual continuum), 143, 144–145
Mechanism (definition), 25
Meditation, 204–207
    male spirituality and, 52
    meditative prayer, 191
    mindfulness, 205
    stress reduction program using, 205
    transcendental (TM), 205
Mental health and illness buffers, 157
Metaphor:
    client's story as, 7, 8–9
    use of, 52
Mind (Buddhist definition), 11
Mindfulness, 205
Minnesota Model, 153
Mirroring/witnessing, 10
Mormons. *See* Latter Day Saints (Mormons)
Multicultural counseling. *See* Cultural issues
Multimodal Therapy (BASIC ID), 173

Multiple relationships with clients, 175–177
Mythic-literal (stage in faith development model), 142

Native American:
    folk tale, 163
    religions (described), 83–86
    Web sites, 92
New age spirituality, 127
Nonreligious (client taxonomy), 151
Nonverbal messages of, 8

Object relations theory, 36
OK human being approach, 149, 152
Older adults, 53, 99
Openness, 34
Oppression, history (awareness of), 180
"Other" (in definition of spirituality), 6

P(s), three (place/person/philosophy), 34
Pathology, ten markers of religious, 147–148
Peer supervision, 190
Pentecostal, 69
Person (three Ps), 34
Personality development, theories of, 26
Petitionary prayer, 191
Philosophy (three Ps), 34
Place (three Ps), 34
Pleading style, 147
Pluralist (counselor orientation), 133, 134–135, 179
Positive psychology, 156–157
Prayer, 191–195
    client belief in and struggle with failure of, 147
    colloquial, 191
    concerns about use of, 194
    as explicit integration, 193
    guidelines for using in counseling, 193
    impact on therapeutic relationship, 193–194
    as implicit integration, 192
    inner healing prayer (seven steps), 194
    intercessory, 191
    meditative, 191
    petitionary, 191
    "praying through," 195
    ritualistic, 191

technique: praying through, 195
types of, 191–192
Predictive (religious control), 146
Problem solving, flexibility in, 180
Professional organizations, 3, 6, 24, 33, 71, 156
Protestants, 62, 63, 66–69
  American-based denominations, 67
  Church of Jesus Christ of Latter-Day Saints (Mormon), 67
  common beliefs, 66–67
  Episcopal, 66
  Evangelicals, 67, 197
  Fundamentalists, 67, 197
  Jehovah's Witnesses, 67
  Lutherans, 47, 66
  Mainline, 66
  Methodists, 66
  Pentecostals, 67
  Presbyterians, 66
  Seventh-Day Adventists, 67
  Upstart, 66, 67
Psychoanalysis/psychoanalytic counseling approaches, 25, 26, 36
Psychological Interpretations in Theology within the American Academy of Religion, 33
Psychology:
  cognitive, 31
  health/wellness/positive, 156–157
  humanistic-existential, 31
Psychology and religion, historical development, 3–4, 21–43. *See also* Counseling, incorporating spirituality in
  barriers, 23–30
  bridges, 30–39
  descriptive approach, 22–23
  explanatory approach, 22
  historical figures in developing link between spirituality and psychology, 31
    Allport, Gordon, 31, 32
    Fromm, Erich, 31, 32
    James, William, 31
    Jung, Carl, 31, 32
  making sense of our existence, 34–39
  movements contrasting scientific perspective, 31
  scientific emphasis, 26, 31

separateness and integration, 21–23
Psychology of Religion (division within American Psychological Association), 33
Psychosocial support, 199
Psychotherapist (defined), 12, 22
Public/secular settings, 29, 181
Purification rituals, 14, 101

Quest (spiritual continuum), 143, 144–145

R(s), three (refuge/rituals/resources), 122–123, 149
Readings, religious:
  assessment process and, 196
  bibliotherapy, 199–200
Readings, suggested:
  counseling focus integration, 162
  Eastern religions, 117–118
  ethical issues, 188
  historical development, 43
  introduction, 19
  theoretical integration, 140
  treatment techniques, 214
  Western religions, 89
Reassurance, using self-care for, 10
Reconciliation ritual, 14
Reductionism, 25
Referral/collaboration with religious leaders, 135–136, 177–178, 192–193, 197
Refuge, spiritual, 12–13, 23, 122–123, 149
Rejectionist (counselor orientation), 133–134
Relationship dynamics (counselor/client), 175
Relaxation techniques, 56–57, 205–207
Religion(s). *See also* Spirituality:
  in counseling (*see* Counseling, incorporating spirituality in)
  monotheistic (*see* Western religions)
  negative views of (historical perspective), 24
  psychology and (*see* Psychology and religion, historical development)
  specific (*see* Eastern religions; Western religions)
  spirituality *vs.* (distinguishing between), 122
Religious adjustment:
  health, five indicators of, 148–149
  pathology, ten markers of, 147–148

Religious community:
    supportive, 15–17, 175–177
    as treatment technique, 197–199
Religious control (four types), 146
Religious "fingers," 47
Religious interventions. *See* Interventions,
    religious/spiritual
Religious leaders, collaboration/referral, 135–136,
    177–178, 192–193, 197
Religious perspective (making sense of our
    existence), 38–39
Ritual(s), 13–14, 101, 151, 207–211
Ritualistic prayer, 191
Roman Catholics, 62, 63, 65–66

Sacred place, creating, 6–9, 16–17
Sacred writings (religious bibliotherapy),
    195–197
Safety/safe places, 7–8, 14–15
Science, psychology as (*vs.* spirituality), 26, 31
Secular agencies, religious counselors working in,
    29, 181
Secular counseling (*vs.* religious), determination
    of, 171–172, 190
    amount of client disturbance and, 171, 172,
      190
    client comfort with secular counseling and,
      171, 172, 190
    type of religious issues, 171, 190
Self awareness, counselor's, 180
Self-care:
    encouragement of, 9–11, 16–17
    using for healing, 10–11
    using for reassurance, 10
    women and, 49–50
Self-directing style, 147
Self-empowerment (women), 49
Self-exploration, 9–10
    bibliotherapy, 201
    journal writing, 202
Self-help bibliotherapy, 199
Separation of church and state, 45, 124, 181
Seventh-Day Adventist Church, 67, 69, 70
Sexual abuse, 99
Sexuality, and religion, 65, 66–67, 69, 71, 146
Shintoism:
    overview of beliefs, 100–102
    possible impact of beliefs on counseling, 102

    statistics, 99–100
    Web sites, 118
Sikhism:
    overview of beliefs, 81–82
    possible impact of beliefs on counseling, 83
    statistics, 81
    Web sites, 92
Sixteen Steps, 155
Southern Baptist Convention. *See* Baptists
Spiritual continua (three: quest/ends/means),
    143, 144–145
Spiritual identity, helping clients develop, 5,
    141–151
    assessment, 145–149
    case application, 151–153
    definition, 172
    ethical issues, 172–175
    overview, 141–142
    supervision, 142–145
    treatment, 149–153
Spiritual interventions. *See* Interventions,
    religious/spiritual
Spirituality:
    age and, 52–54
    in context of counseling, 1–6 (*see also*
      Counseling, incorporating spirituality in)
    definition, 6
    disability and, 54–55
    gender and, 49–52
    religion *vs.*, 122 (*see also* Religion(s))
Spiritually committed client (taxonomy), 150
Stereotyping, 145
Stimulus-response exchange/reactions, 26
Stress, coping with (and spiritual realm), 11, 23
Stress Reduction and Relaxation Program (SRRP),
    205
Suffering, views of, 9, 121–122
Suicide, 66, 146
Superficially religious (client taxonomy),
    150–151
Supervision. *See also* Training:
    case application, 151–153
    contract, 182
    and countertransference, 130–131, 142–143,
      152–153
    using continua (quest/means/ends), 144–145
Supportive religious community, 15–17, 175–177,
    197–199

Synthetic-conventional (stage in faith development model), 142

Taoism:
    example: psychological/religious perspectives, 36–37, 38–39
    overview of beliefs, 111–113
    possible impact of beliefs on counseling, 113–114
    statistics, 111
    Web sites, 119
Taxonomy of responsiveness:
    hostile to religion, 151, 189
    nonreligious, 151, 189
    religiously and spiritually open, 150, 189
    religiously committed, 150, 189
    religiously loyal, 150, 189
    religiously tolerant and indifferent, 151, 189
    spiritually committed, 150, 189
    superficially religious, 150–151, 189
Techniques, specific, 189–214
    case studies and exercises, 211–214
    general practices, 199–204
        bibliotherapy, 199–200
        focusing technique (six steps), 201–202
        journal writing, 202–204
    overview, 189–191
    religious and general practices, 204–211
        meditation/relaxation/imagery, 204–207
        rituals, 207–211
    religious practices, 191–199
        prayer, 191–195
        religious community (use of), 197–199
        sacred writings (religious bibliotherapy), 195–197
    shaping to client's needs, 5
    suggested readings, 214
Theoretical biases, 26
Therapy integration, 121–126. *See also* Integration
Timelines:
    Eastern religions, 93
    Western religions, 58
Training, counselor, 4, 189–190. *See also* Supervision
Transcendental meditation (TM), 205
Transference, 126–128. *See also* Countertransference
    defined, 126–127

    idealizing, 126
    interreligious/intrareligious, 128
    recommendations, 142, 163–164
    resolution of issues, 149
Transformational coping, 11
Transitional object, 36
Trauma, and spirituality, 29–30
Treatment techniques. *See* Techniques, specific
Twelve-step programs, 153–155
Typecasting clients (avoiding), 151

Universalizing (stage in faith development model), 142
Upstart Protestants, 67

Values, respect for client's (*vs.* imposition of counselor's values), 178–181
Vicarious (religious control), 146

Web sites:
    Eastern religions, 118–119
    use of, 48–49
    Western religions, 89–93
Wellness/positive psychology, 156–157
Western religions, 45–92. *See also specific religion*
    age and, 52–54
    case studies and exercises, 86–89
    Christianity, 62–74
    chronology/timeline, 58
    disability and, 54–55
    gender and, 49–52
    integrating Eastern/Western ideas, 37
    Islam, 74–77
    Judaism, 58–62
    Native American religions, 83–86
    overview, 45–55
    Sikhism, 81–83
    suggested readings, 89
    Web sites, 89–93
    Zoroastrianism, 77–81
Witnessing/mirroring, 10
Women:
    feminist perspective, general counseling conflict, 179–180
    feminist spirituality, 49–51
    fundamentalism and, 67
    Hinduism and, 98–99
    Judaism and, 61–62

Women for Sobriety (WFS), 155, 156
Workplace culture, 124–125
Work settings, boundaries of counselor's, 181–182
World Conference of Friends at Swarthmore (Friends Conference on Religion and Psychology), 33
World religions practiced in United States, 45. *See also* Eastern religions; Western religions

Wounded healer framework of counseling, 158

Yin/yang, 37
Yoga, 56

Zoroastrianism, 77–81, 92